Women and Gender
in Southern Africa to 1945

S0-BHY-590

Women and Gender in Southern Africa to 1945

edited by
CHERRYL WALKER

DAVID PHILIP
Cape Town

JAMES CURREY
London

Barnard
HQ
1800
.W65
1990g
c.3

First published 1990 in southern Africa by David Philip Publishers (Pty) Ltd,
208 Werdmuller Centre, Claremont 7700, South Africa

Published 1990 in the United Kingdom by James Currey Ltd, 54b Thornhill
Square, Islington, London N1 1BE

ISBN 0-86486-090-0 (David Philip)
ISBN 0-85255-205-X (James Currey)

© David Philip Publishers 1990

All rights reserved

British Library Cataloguing in Publication Data:
Women and gender in Southern Africa to 1945–.
    1. Africa. Southern Africa. Black women. Social conditions, history
    I. Walker, Cherryl 1951–
    305.488968

    ISBN 0-85255-205-X

Printed by Clyson Printers (Pty) Ltd, 11th Avenue, Maitland, Cape

Contents

Contributors

Jo Beall has lectured in the Department of African Studies at the University of Natal, Durban.

P. L. Bonner is Associate Professor in the Department of History at the University of the Witwatersrand.

Elsabe Brink is currently lecturing in the Department of History at the Rand Afrikaans University.

Sandra Burman is a Research Fellow at Queen Elizabeth House, Oxford University, and a Visiting Research Fellow at the Socio-Legal Unit, University of Cape Town.

Linda Chisholm is a lecturer in the Department of Education at the University of the Witwatersrand.

Jacklyn Cock is a senior lecturer in the Sociology Department at the University of the Witwatersrand.

Deborah Gaitskell teaches history at London University's Extra-Mural Centre and for the Workers' Education Association.

Jeff Guy teaches African history at the University of Trondheim, Norway.

Heather Hughes is a lecturer in the Department of African Studies at the University of Natal, Durban.

Anne McClintock is an Assistant Professor in English and Comparative Literature at Columbia University, New York.

Sheila Meintjes is a lecturer in the Department of Political Studies at the University of the Witwatersrand.

Cherryl Walker is a lecturer in the Sociology Department at the University of Natal, Durban.

To Zac,
whose arrival in my life during the work on this book
has led me to look at 'woman' and 'gender' with fresh eyes.

Preface

Many people have helped in different ways with the process of producing this book, not least, of course, the contributors. I would like to single out the following individuals for particular thanks for their contributions: Jacklyn Cock, for her encouragement and input at the early stage of conceptualising and planning; the director and fellow academics at the Center for Research on Women (now the Institute for Research on Women and Gender) at Stanford University, California, for welcoming me to the Affiliated Scholar programme between 1984 and 1986; Russell Martin at David Philip, for his patience and faith in the project; and Judith Shier, for executing the large project of indexing with care and good humour. Finally I should like to express my special gratitude to John Crumley for his multi-layered support.

Women and gender in southern Africa to 1945: An overview

CHERRYL WALKER

The years spanned by this book – from the early nineteenth century to the Second World War – saw profound changes in the economic, political and social life of southern Africa: from precapitalist to capitalist relations of production, from African political independence to subjugation, from rural to urban forms of social and spatial organisation, and from white co-existence with indigenous societies to white supremacy within a new, racially structured state, the Union of South Africa. These developments impinged directly and indirectly on the position of women; in the new society so violently brought into being the organisation of gender underwent far-reaching changes as well. This period saw the transition, in African society, from a system in which gender relations, specifically the exploitation of female reproductive and productive capacity by men, held structural primacy to one in which these relations were filtered through the net of racially informed class relations.

In an important article entitled 'Marxism, Feminism and South African Studies', Bozzoli (1983) puts forward the idea of a 'patchwork quilt of patriarchies' in nineteenth-century southern Africa: everywhere women were subordinate to men but there were important contrasts in the operation of gender between different social systems in the region. While the patchwork analogy brings out the variety in the female experience, it seems useful to reduce the various forms of patriarchy[1] in operation to two dominant systems, the one broadly characteristic of the precapitalist Bantu-speaking societies of the region, the other of the colonial states established by the European settlers. For convenience these are described here as the indigenous and the settler sex–gender systems;[2] it is with their interaction that much of this book is concerned.

In the chapters that follow one can observe the collision of these two systems and the domination, under the unifying forces of colonialism and capitalism, of the settler over the indigenous. It was, however, never an undisputed dominance, nor was it a pure form of the settler system that prevailed. The incorporation of the indigenous people into the new social order involved their active engagement with the invasive forces of domination, as women and men struggled to defend their own interests and wrest what they could from the new opportunities and constraints. Ideological currents from the indigenous sex–gender system continued to flow through African society in complex ways, even as relations between the sexes in colonial society were being restructured by the economic imperatives and values of a market-oriented, increasingly industrialised and urbanised society. In the political and economic transformation of the region the organisation of gender constituted a critical battleground: here not only men and women confronted each other, but also the colonisers and the colonised.

This is the frame in which the chapters that follow are set. Each of them looks at selected aspects of the canvas, not always from exactly the same perspective. The task of this introductory overview is to place the chapters in their frame and link them, both chronologically and thematically, to the overall concern of the book – developments in the organisation of gender relations before the Second World War, as this affected women. The discussion is divided into three main parts: women's studies and the scope of this book; chapter overview; major themes.

WOMEN'S STUDIES: HISTORY AND THEORY
That black women in South Africa suffer a triple oppression, of gender, race and class, has become a rhetorical commonplace. White women, too, it is generally recognised, are discriminated against as women, although their membership of a privileged racial group softens the impact of gender discrimination and works against their identification with black women as women, with shared problems. While this much is widely accepted, there is considerable disagreement, not to say confusion, about how to explain women's oppression in contemporary South Africa, as well as how to analyse the intricate interrelationship of gender, race and class and their differential impact on women. We are still a long way simply from mapping women's position, both historically and in the present, while much must be done to integrate these findings into our conceptualisation of society.

One major difficulty, noted in many of the chapters, is the absence from the historical record of women's voices, most pronounced in the case of black women. This weights research towards organisations, events and individual lives that are documented, and creates a bias towards institutions with records (mission stations, schools, organisations of the literate), major eruptions or disturbances, and the experience of middle-class and literate women. In the case of the great mass of women, documentary silence may be erroneously equated with historical passivity or, even worse, with historical insignificance, so that women simply disappear from our view of the past. Where women's presence is acknowledged, it is often to subsume them within the family or hide them behind abstractions such as 'reproduction' and 'oppression' – even 'gender' – so that the full complexity of their lives, as well as their historical agency, becomes obscured. Gender has recently become a more respectable concept in southern African studies, but exactly how and where it fits into social analysis have not been comfortably resolved. Furthermore, despite a welcome recognition of the need to probe gender relations, there is a tendency to confine the analysis to women's studies only, or, once the formal acknowledgement of gender has been made, to proceed without further reference to it.

This book is intended to add a much-needed historical dimension to our understanding of the workings of gender and women's place in society.[3] In the preface to her study, *Women's Oppression Today*, Barrett argues for an analysis of 'the how and why of women's oppression' that is based on an historical rather than a purely theoretical approach:

Can we see women's oppression in capitalism as independent of the general operation of the capitalist mode of production? Do we see women's oppression as taking place exclusively at the level of ideology? Neither of these questions is likely to be resolved by some 'correct' formulation that encapsulates the problem and specifies its answer by juggling with the terms 'capitalism', 'patriarchy' and 'articulation'.... The questions that concern me are the how and why of women's oppression today, but I am sure that the answers to these questions cannot be deduced in strictly theoretical terms. Accordingly, I argue for an historical approach ... (1980: 5).

An over-concern with the correctness of one's theoretical position vis-à-vis the compelling debates on race and class – with theoretical pedigree – has, perhaps, been one of the more insidious constraints on the development of women's studies in southern Africa. At least partly responsible, it seems, is the concern for legitimacy in an extremely exacting political environment, where relevance requires so much more than fashionable rhetorical embellishments to one's academic work. It is, however, a concern which can lead to a restrictive reluctance to question the authority of respected texts, even where these have little or nothing to say about gender; it can degenerate into the unilluminating repetition of formulae, such as that of the 'triple oppression' already mentioned.

This is not to discount the crucial importance of theoretical models for ordering the mass of empirical data that the world throws up in its daily round – nor the pertinence of an analysis of race and class to women's studies. But, as feminist researchers have stressed, the construction of an adequate theory of gender requires not simply rigour but critical imagination and a willingness to rethink many of the basic assumptions of social theory as well. One cannot bend gender to fit the mould created by existing theories of class and race; issues like sexuality, the ordering and control of female fertility, patriarchal relations within the family, and sexual violence cannot be adequately accommodated in gender-blind theories.

However, before one can construct a more sophisticated theory of gender, one needs to have a far better understanding of the dynamics of men and women's experience in society and cross-culturally – one's theory needs to be empirically grounded. It is here that this book makes a contribution. While not engaging directly with contemporary debates, its historical approach provides a useful corrective to overly simplistic formulations about women and their place in society in the past – and, by extension, the present.

A number of overlapping questions have helped shape the scope of the enquiry:

— What was the position of women and how were indigenous sex–gender systems organised in the independent African chiefdoms of southern Africa[4] in the early nineteenth century?

— What was the impact of colonialism and the spread of capitalist relations of production on the position of women and the organisation of gender relations in African societies?

— What part did gender relations play in determining the manner in which the various African chiefdoms were incorporated into modern South Africa?

— How did indigenous and settler sex–gender systems interact? To what extent were indigenous gender relations transformed as African societies were conquered, Christianised, proletarianised and urbanised? To what extent did indigenous family forms and ideologies of gender retain some autonomy into the twentieth century? To what extent could a common, overarching sex–gender system be said to have been established in southern Africa by the mid-twentieth century?

— What kinds of struggle or accommodation have taken place in the course of this interaction, between men and women, elders and youth, black and white? How did women respond to the new forces at work in the subcontinent – to Christianity, the growth of towns, industrialisation?

— What was the role of the settler state in directing, constructing or maintaining the position of women, and how did this role differ with regard to black and white women?

— Has gender become less important a principle of social organisation over time? What has its relationship been to race and class in determining the position different groups of women have occupied in southern African society at different historical junctures? How have women interacted across the divisions of race and class?

Not all these questions are treated equally in the chapters that follow. This book is the product of that unavoidable process of trying to match work that was offered with the overall aims of the book; it did not grow out of a conference or set of specially commissioned pieces but, rather, drew on work already in progress. Inevitably there is a certain amount of overlap between some of the chapters, while several important issues are dealt with only in passing or not at all. There is also a noticeable unevenness in the geographical range of these chapters. Developments in Natal and Basutoland are covered in some detail, while the Western Cape, Orange Free State and even the Transvaal receive far less attention.

Issues warranting more in-depth treatment than they receive here include developments in female labour-force participation; the position of 'coloured' women (the intention however was never to treat the various ethnic categories of apartheid 'separately but equally'); changing patterns of child-care, including the role of the state, hired domestic workers, private agencies and informal networks; female health, as well as attitudes towards fertility, child-bearing and female sexuality, including the commoditisation of sex and the development of a market for prostitution.

Developments in non-mission African communities during the colonial period are neglected, while gender relations within the white community in the nineteenth century require further study – for one thing, the blunt notion of Victorian gender ideology needs sharpening, to apply it more effectively to the local situation. The precolonial period is also under-represented, with just one chapter providing a very broad overview of precolonial African society in general and another looking at the legal position of women in precolonial Lesotho as background to a discussion on the impact of colonial rule on the legal and social standing of Basotho women. Further case-studies, as well as an analysis of the mechanisms by which male rights to the forces of production were maintained within precolonial southern Africa – initiation ceremonies, taboos, ritual, language, etc. – would have highlighted the precolonial period as an area of study in its own right, rather than simply the backdrop to the colonial and contemporary eras.[5]

Imperialist research?

A gap of a different sort that needs to be addressed concerns the identity of the researchers who have contributed to this book, all of whom are white. That this should be so is an unfortunate but nonetheless explicit reflection of race and gender oppression in this country generally and their manifestation in the academic discipline of history more particularly. The dearth of black historians, which is especially pronounced in the area of women's studies, is not something about which any of us, least of all those committed to the new social history, can afford to be complacent.

Clearly, too, the racial (and class and sex) identity of the authors affects their choice and treatment of their subjects. However, this is not to say it predetermines their work, nor does it automatically invalidate their conclusions, as would seem to be the contention of Nkululeko (a black South African woman), in a recent article entitled 'The Right to Self-Determination in Research: Azanian Women' (1987: 88). 'Can an oppressed nation or segment of it, engaged in a struggle for liberation from its oppressors, rely on knowledge produced, researched and theorized by others, no matter how progressive, who are members of the oppressor nation?' Her argument is that the 'subjects of historical knowledge' are the ones who should be carrying out research and writing about themselves, since they have the most intimate knowledge of their experience. Outsiders, even the most 'progressive', will always be hampered by 'the trappings of their own history, values, culture and ideology' (ibid.: 89); their work will, therefore, always be fatally flawed. More seriously, going beyond the charge of subjectivity and bias, Nkululeko condemns the academic work of 'outsiders' as part of the larger forces of oppression and exploitation whereby oppressed people are denied access to the resources that will empower them.

That researchers – all researchers – approach their subject with the trappings of their own 'history, values', etc. is not denied. That this means that only blacks can write about black experience, or women about women's experience – or French people about French history – does not follow. For one thing, the subjective experience of a condition or situation does not guarantee the ability to reflect critically and analytically upon it, nor does it preclude the problem of bias. For another, which social attributes one chooses to privilege in order to define the boundaries of who is or is not the legitimate 'subject-researcher', the insider, is itself a matter of political and intellectual choice: for instance, the assumption that race should be privileged above class or gender, thereby allowing black women to write about both middle-class and working-class black women, and, perhaps, black men to write about both male and female blacks, but debarring all whites, male and female, from writing about blacks, whether of the same class and/or sex or not. One of the advantages of using gender as an organising principle is precisely that it moves the analysis beyond the preoccupation with particular categories of women, and abstracts the notion of womanhood/woman-ness (as well as manhood/man-ness) as it operates in society – in particular societies. In any case, an important conclusion to emerge from this book is that just as 'woman' has not meant the same thing over time and across cultures, so the broad category 'black woman' does not deal adequately with the significant variables of class, age and social system that have affected the worlds of black women differentially in southern Africa. If one were to follow Nkululeko's point to its logical conclusion, one would end up in a solipsistic cage where the historian would have to abandon her or his work in favour of autobiography and the specifics of personal experience only.

Clearly the authors of these chapters believe they have a useful contribution to make to our understanding of women's position in southern Africa historically. This is not to claim that they have a monopoly on either the material or the analysis, nor to deny the need for and the importance of the academic work of those who, in the words of Guy in chapter 1, are 'closer in terms of culture, language, class, race and gender' to the 'lived experience' of black women in this region.

THE CHAPTERS: AN OVERVIEW

The transition from the precolonial era

The discussion begins with a review by Guy of the position of African women in the precolonial era. His is a theoretical piece, sketching in broad outline the features of women's oppression in the precapitalist, farming societies of southern Africa. This oppression, Guy argues, was not merely an aspect of these societies. Rather, it constituted their central dynamic – the appropriation and control of women's productive and reproductive capacity by men was the axis on which these societies turned. In the context of a relatively simple technology, the accumulation of people, rather than of things, became of paramount importance – hence the importance of control over women, the bearers of children. The institution in which male control over women and over female fertility specifically found expression was marriage, and the social practice which legitimated marriage and the male transfer of rights over women (and their unborn children) was that of bridewealth,[6] which most characteristically took the form of cattle. Although Guy does not develop the comparison, his analysis thus establishes a critical difference between the organisation of gender relations in precolonial society, where the oppression of women was pivotal to its total functioning, and that in settler society, where the sex–gender system was not structurally definitive to the same degree.

Guy's account goes beyond the familiar description of husband, wives and cattle, to argue that the productive and reproductive cycle

encompassed within the homestead unit constituted the most important economic relationship within even the largest of the precolonial
chiefdoms and kingdoms. While recognising that there were differences in the way in which the various farming peoples gave expression
to these social principles, Guy argues that such differences were not
structurally significant – in other words, one broadly similar sex–
gender system can be discerned within all the precapitalist 'farming
peoples' south of the Limpopo.

However, while Guy applies the terms oppression and exploitation
to the position of women in precapitalist southern Africa, he makes it
clear that the condition he describes cannot be understood in terms
of our contemporary notion of oppression. Women exercised control
over the agricultural process and, by virtue of the central importance
of their fertility to society, enjoyed considerable status and a degree
of autonomy not appreciated – or replicated – within colonial society.
The very centrality of women's productive and reproductive labour
to society ensured their social prestige and a limited but nevertheless
clearly recognised authority.

This chapter thus sets out a conceptual framework for analysing
not only gender relations within precapitalist society but also the
transition to capitalist relations of production and the accompanying
reorganisation of the relations of gender. Once male control over
female labour power no longer remained central to the reproduction
of African society – once wages or cash income earned in external
markets became more important – then the precapitalist era could be
said to have passed, and with that the structural centrality of gender
in the organisation of society. It is an analytical benchmark that Guy
is proposing, not a date: as subsequent chapters make clear, the actual
process of incorporation experienced by the different polities of
southern Africa within the ambit of the new economic and political
order was not uniform in its timing or its geographical reach.

From Guy the focus shifts to this incorporative process, first to the
clash of the indigenous and settler sex–gender systems, and then to
the uneven process whereby new definitions of what it meant to be a
woman were grafted onto the stump of the indigenous formulation.
It was, it becomes clear, a highly complex process, full of contradictory
elements which are difficult to order. At the level of gender, African
women found themselves enmeshed in new forms of oppression, as
the colonial state intervened to restructure the homestead economy
in the service of a male migrant labour system, and as missionaries,
employers and officials applied their own culture-bound concepts of
gender to the situation – often in the name of women's emancipation.
The assumption of male authority over women that was central to
both the indigenous and settler sex–gender systems was, in many
respects, reinforced by the encounter between the two. Western norms

and gender definitions, especially as espoused in church and school, did not recognise women as productive members of society. They circumscribed the position of black women and undermined a precolonial ideology that emphasised female initiative, activity and self-reliance.

There were, however, many ambiguities in this process, which the subsequent discussion makes clear. As the migrant labour system began to bite, the institution of the African family came under pressure. While the old patriarchal controls were undermined, the price women had to pay for their new independence was a devastating increase in economic and emotional insecurity. At the same time, despite the limitations on women's position in colonial society, some African women, at least, saw prospects for emancipation from the constraints of their society in the new dispensation; women's responses to Christianity and the growth of towns and a market economy spanned the spectrum from active appropriation of elements of the new order to a spirited defence of the old. The dialectic between women's resistance to and exploration of the new dispensation forms a recurring theme in the book and is discussed further in the third part of the present overview. In this context, age and marital status were important factors in shaping the way different women responded: generally older women, whose status and security were invested in the perpetuation of the homestead system through the marriage of their sons, were most active in its defence.

Burman's chapter straddles one aspect of the precolonial–colonial shift, the clash between settler and indigenous systems of family and personal law in Cape-ruled Basutoland[7] and its complex reverberations for women. By the very nature of the differences between the two societies, she argues, Basotho women bore the brunt of this collision (as did indigenous women in similar encounters elsewhere in southern Africa). While many of the legal changes introduced by the colonial administration were intended to give women greater freedom of action, particularly in marriage and the custody of their children, in practice the individual rights promoted by colonial magistrates and missionaries – rights which were embedded in the essential individualism of a profit-seeking economy – tore holes in the tightly woven fabric of Basotho society. This stressed communal responsibilities and kin, rather than individual, rights. The missionaries and colonial authorities failed to understand the social significance of many precolonial practices – for instance that the institution of bridewealth was not a sale of women and had social, political and economic ramifications that went far beyond the married couple – and their intervention to curb or halt practices which they, in their arrogance and ignorance, found abhorrent, weakened the precolonial family and its support systems, often to the detriment of women.

Burman argues that the colonial magistrates and missionaries were not insensitive to the stress and confusion created by the legal changes they introduced. Nevertheless, as both she and other contributors point out, despite the dedication and sensitivity of many missionaries, overall their role as defenders of their flocks against settler avarice and prejudice was limited by their own deep commitment to the superiority of Western culture and the 'civilising' power of wage labour.

Burman's chapter looks at a small slice of time in Basutoland when, for a variety of reasons, the authorities favoured a dualistic approach to the problem of reconciling indigenous legal systems with the norms of colonial society. A similar approach is noted by both Meintjes (chapter 5) and Hughes (chapter 8) in colonial Natal. However, by the early twentieth century the colonial authorities generally had begun to favour a far more conservative policy, involving the restructuring and entrenchment of customary law in a manner that greatly exacerbated the disabilities of African women, preserving the outer form of the indigenous sex–gender system as its inner logic was inexorably destroyed. This was a development of central importance in the elaboration of a racially stratified sex–gender system in modern South Africa, in which African women were discriminated against not simply as women but as black women – the racial and sexual elements being inextricably fused in the definition of their social inferiority. My own chapter on the migrant labour system links this process to the evolution of a settler 'native policy' in the context of the voracious demand for cheap black labour emanating from mining and manufacturing industry; this looked to the preservation of the 'traditional' system of homestead production, within native reserves, to underwrite the male migrant labour system.

There were, in any case, clear limits to the degree of individual freedom that women – all women – were allowed in terms of the settler sex–gender system. Both the settler and the indigenous ideologies of gender were in agreement that ultimately men must order the lives of women: the 'emancipation' African women were offered in Cape-ruled Basutoland was firmly circumscribed by the patriarchal ideology of their colonial rulers. This convergence of indigenous and settler ideologies of male authority is a theme that is picked up and developed further in my chapter on the migrant labour system and, in a somewhat different context, in the chapter by Beall on Indian indentured labour.

Colonial patriarchy

The settler ideology of gender was thus a significant factor in marking the permissible boundaries of the new female world. Regrettably, Guy's chapter is not matched by a similar, systematic account of the fashioning of the settler sex–gender system in the nineteenth century. The interaction of the values imported mainly (but not exclusively) from Victorian England with those of already established Dutch-speaking communities, in a backward, racially stratified society, remains an under-researched subject. However, some of the major features of this system do emerge in the chapters by Cock, McClintock and Meintjes at the beginning of the book, and by Brink and myself (on the suffrage movement) at the end.

In settler society women's proper place centred on the domestic sphere of children and kitchen, which was set apart from the world of money and power, the domain of men. This does not mean that women were not involved in economic activity beyond the home, but that such work was not recognised as intrinsically 'female', certainly not as properly 'feminine'. Within the household, settler women played an active role in the domestic economy but the dominant ideology stressed their role as reproducers rather than producers. Women's domestic labour was, in any case, not the central productive force in colonial society that it was in precapitalist African society.

In South Africa the sexual division of labour imported from Europe was played out within the bounds of a market-oriented economy that was being built on the appropriation of the land and labour of the indigenous people. Following Guy, one could argue that since women's reproductive and productive labour in the home was not a direct source of value, it did not confer on them the social prestige enjoyed by African women either.

In South Africa the operation of the colonial ideology of gender was further refracted through the prism of race. Cock's chapter looks at the settler household as an important foundry of both racial and gender attitudes on the Cape eastern frontier in the nineteenth century. Here the incorporation of African (in this case Xhosa) women into colonial society started earlier and involved a far more direct assimilation, through the institution of domestic service, than in other parts of southern Africa, where widespread employment of black women in white households only became the norm in the twentieth century. Nevertheless, Cock's analysis is pertinent to this later situation as well. In her study she notes how, on the frontier, the settlers' class-based attitudes towards domestic workers assumed a racial form: many of the attributes of inferiority associated with domestic servants in Britain were transferred to blacks. Thus although a situational intimacy existed between white and black women in the white household, the dense intermeshing of racial, cultural and class differences blocked their recognition of each other as sisters or allies. This is an important theme that emerges again in my concluding chapter, on the women's suffrage movement of the early twentieth century.

The chapter by McClintock is also concerned with the intermeshing of the ideologies of gender and race in Victorian culture and their particular application in colonial southern Africa. She examines their manifestation in Rider Haggard's hugely popular novel, *King Solomon's Mines*, a Victorian adventure story about treasure, degeneration and white male redemption in Kukuanaland (a thinly disguised Zululand). Writing from within the discipline of literary rather than historical studies, McClintock analyses this novel as an attempt to resolve 'the economic and psychosexual anxieties swirling in Victorian culture around female labour and sexuality', both within the metropolis and within the colonies. A particularly striking illustration of the interlocking of economic and sexual themes in the book is the explicitly sexualised map that leads the adventurers to the treasure. McClintock thus introduces the issue of sexuality and its social power into the discussion, pointing beyond the purely functionalist reduction of sexuality to biological reproduction, to its densely layered psychosocial dimensions.

The colonies, McClintock argues, provided men of Haggard's class – the declining rural squirearchy – with the possibility of regeneration, with the reassertion of a 'phallic authority' that was threatened in the metropolis not only by the rise of a new, manufacturing class but also by working-class and female insurgency. Patriarchy was 'reinvented' in the colonies and applied not simply to relations between men and women but to the relations between coloniser and colonised as well. Nineteenth-century Social Darwinist thought had a significant impact on the metropolitan, and colonial, ideology of both gender and race. Haggard's intensely eurocentric and androcentric story is contextualised within the linked discourses of degeneration – in which the races and the sexes were ranked according to their alleged distance from the mental, physical and moral superiority of the adult British male – and that of the family of man – which proposed an evolution of human society from the black child-races to the mature civilisation of the white male. In *King Solomon's Mines* the intertwined themes of black female degeneration, fertility and socio-sexual power come together in the figure of Gagool, the black she-witch, guardian of the hidden treasure. (The idea of degeneration found fertile ground in southern Africa; it surfaces again as a sub-theme in the chapters by Brink and Chisholm, in the context of the emergence of 'the poor-white problem' and the blurring of racial boundaries in the urban areas of South Africa in the early twentieth century.)

McClintock argues further that *King Solomon's Mines* can be analysed as an attempt to resolve in fiction the conflicts then beginning to manifest themselves in Natal around settler determination to harness black male labour to their needs: a project which, as already noted, necessitated settler control over the labour process within the homestead, and thus over black women. The climax of the story is reached when, Gagool destroyed, the adventurers claim the treasure for themselves, thus asserting symbolically that the path to white male control over the mineral wealth of the continent lay through the control of black women.

Christianity and education for domesticity

In the reorganisation of gender relations under colonial rule, Christianity played a very active part. The chapters by Cock, Meintjes and Hughes examine the specific role of the missionaries, men and women, in promoting European concepts of gender through the socialising institutions of mission household, church and school.[8] Black women's own often enthusiastic appropriation of Christianity is looked at in Gaitskell's chapter on the *manyanos*, or women's prayer unions, that developed from the late nineteenth century.

The missionaries who flocked to southern Africa in the nineteenth century have long been recognised as operating, whether consciously or not, in the vanguard of colonialism and capitalism. The mission stations and reserves that they established provided the base on which a new class of petty commodity-producing peasants developed in African society; in time this group came to form the nucleus of a national African petty bourgeoisie. It has been argued (Stamp, 1986) that elsewhere in Africa the process of peasantisation that took place under colonial rule was based on the exploitation of female labour and the appropriation of women's surplus product by their husbands and male guardians. In southern Africa, however, where there was a large, labour-hungry settler population, the process of peasantisation followed a different course. It was most advanced on the mission stations, where the missionaries' vision of what constituted appropriate female behaviour set severe limits to African women's continued involvement in agriculture. The missionaries were strenuously opposed to what they perceived as male indolence and female slave-labour in African society: a perception which, though not always intentionally, served to support the settler clamour for measures that would force black men into their employ. In her chapter on the mission community at Edendale, in Natal, Meintjes shows how the stress on female domesticity marginalised Christian women from agricultural work. This process was not complete – in Edendale women continued to labour in the fields and even produce a small surplus for sale – but it marked a significant shift for Christian women, away from their former productive role to one approximating more closely to the settler ideal of restricted female domesticity.

As described in these chapters, the missionaries elaborated an ideology of female domesticity that laid stress on women's reproductive and nurturing roles above their autonomy and productivity. The attributes of the good Christian woman were obedience to the authority of husband and father, piety, decorum, thrift, and service to others. The missionaries also promoted a profoundly different vision of marital and sexual relationships. Marriage was to be a monogamous partnership, based on the mutual affection of the couple within an essentially nuclear conception of the family, while in sexual matters the missionaries emphasised delicacy, discretion, and privacy. The Victorian prudery of the missionaries stood in profound contrast to the far greater sexual openness of precolonial African society. Here, as previously noted by Guy, the dominant concern was with the control of female fertility rather than sexuality as such. While women in precolonial society did not enjoy the same degree of sexual freedom as men – the distinction between sexuality and fertility being in any case difficult to maintain in practice in a society without an efficient method of contraception – female sexuality was given a social recognition that was unthinkable in settler society (where the distinction between fertility and sexuality did not have the same productive significance and female sexuality *per se* was strictly policed).

However, the ideology of domesticity which the missionaries elaborated was not concerned simply with the ordering of sex roles within the family. Their vision of African women's proper position in society was also influenced by their position as female members of a subjected race. African women's place within the domestic realm had two not wholly compatible aspects. The one involved the 'proper' management of their own households as wives and mothers, the other service in other (almost invariably white) households as domestic workers. While the former served to incorporate African women within an inclusive vision of Christian womanhood, the latter grew out of and reinforced the hierarchical ranking of women as 'us' and 'them', in which racial and class differences took precedence. In the educational institutions which the missionaries developed, the distinction between these two dimensions of domesticity was not necessarily clearly demarcated; many girls in fact combined both in their careers, finding in the one, perhaps, the social legitimation denied them in the other. Overall, however, mission education for African women supported rather than challenged the structures of racial and class discrimination.

That said, it would be misleading to characterise mission education as concerned only with turning African girls into good servants. For one thing it is important to remember that, beyond the Eastern Cape, the virtually blanket identification of domestic service and black women in the modern period was by no means established at this stage. Not only were black men domestic servants. As the chapter by Chisholm on female industrial schools and reformatories shows, domestic service was also considered a suitable option for white working-class girls into the twentieth century. Furthermore, not all education for girls was aimed at preparing them for positions of unmediated subservience within the race–class hierarchy, as Hughes establishes in her chapter on the Inanda Seminary. The missionaries looked to their African converts, male and female, to spread their evangelical message, and thus from the start trained African teachers, lay preachers and clergy.

Hughes's chapter traces the growth of the Inanda Seminary from local school with a pronounced emphasis on 'industrial', or practical, training, into an institution offering an academic education for the daughters (and future wives) of an emergent African petty bourgeoisie. In a way the history of the seminary can be seen as a barometer of change in the emergence and self-definition of this class. As it grew, it, in turn, began to make certain demands of the church and to influence the education on offer. By the mid-twentieth century the Inanda curriculum was gender-specific, particularly at the higher levels where women were trained in housewifery or for the female professions of teaching and nursing, but it was not vocational. Although the number of African girls who were educated in this way was minute, yet the Seminary (and similar institutions) was extremely influential in consolidating an ideology of gender among the African elite that was anchored in Christian values. And from here there was a slow, uneven dissipation of these new ideas into the wider society.

There were thus many ambiguities in the extension of Christianity to African women, as Meintjes, Hughes and Gaitskell are at pains to point out. The culture that emerged on the mission stations was, Meintjes notes, a syncretic one in which elements of precolonial ideology and social practice engaged with settler norms with sometimes disconcerting results for the mission establishment. Examples of this could be found in women's involvement in agriculture at Edendale, despite missionary disapproval, as well as in the more difficult-to-objectify exuberance and eloquence of African women's style of Christianity that Gaitskell describes – qualities that drew on precolonial rather than settler notions of womanhood and cultural traditions.

Christianity also offered women the possibility of escape from oppressive relationships in African society, an issue touched upon by Burman, Cock and Gaitskell, and developed further in the chapters by myself, Hughes and Bonner. Gaitskell suggests that in the early stages of mission development, female and male adherents perceived these new establishments in distinctly different ways – the former, by and large, as places of refuge from 'gender-specific tribulations', such as unwanted marriages and witchcraft accusations, the latter as a means to material advantage in the form of land, training and employment. In addition, the Christian message to African women was, to borrow a term from Comaroff (1985: 2), 'polysemic'. Threaded through the dominant ideology of female subservience was a message of personal autonomy, rooted in Western individualism, which could and did speak persuasively to the disadvantaged of African society, especially women. There were other attractions as well. The women's prayer unions that proliferated in the early twentieth century met compelling social and psychological needs. In church structures, both mainstream and separatist, women found an outlet for organisational talents and energies that were otherwise frustrated by racial, patriarchal and class mechanisms of suppression and control. Immersion in Christian ritual and doctrine provided adherents with spiritual comfort and sustenance, a psycho-spiritual shield against the onslaughts of rapid and disturbing social change. Equally important, at a time when familial structures of emotional and material support were coming under pressure, church membership placed women within a network or structure of peer support – one that could be seen to draw on, yet transform, an older legacy of female-centred sociability.

Indentured labour

The chapter by Beall on the position of indentured Indian women in colonial Natal provides a useful counterpoint to the historically more prominent clash between the indigenous and the settler sex–gender systems. Imported unwillingly by the settlers, indentured Indian women, Beall suggests, found themselves at the very bottom of the class–race–gender hierarchy in the colony. As seasonal workers they served as a reserve army of labour for the planters while performing the proverbial 'double shift' in the workers' barracks, where the appalling living conditions made it extremely difficult for men and women to maintain stable sexual and familial relationships. Yet despite the extreme cheapness of their labour, towards the end of the nineteenth century Indian women began to be replaced by African male workers on the sugar estates – a relatively early example of the way in which both gender and race could be manipulated to divide the workforce. Although on average African men were paid more than Indian women, these new recruits came with their wives and children who, by law, could also be made to work for the landowner; they were thus a more profitable proposition for the planters than the dispensable Indian women.

The powerlessness of indentured women had important consequences for the relationships between Indian men and women. Beall cautions against the assumption that their relative scarcity increased the women's bargaining power vis-à-vis men. Their underlying economic and social vulnerability limited the extent to which they could exploit their scarcity value, and channelled resistance to oppression along individualistic and spontaneous, rather than collective and organised, paths. One of the more far-reaching consequences of the Indian community's experience of the miseries of indenture, Beall argues, was to invest the institution of the family with an enhanced value as 'haven in a heartless world' in the twentieth century – a process that, in the context of race and class discrimination, bore ambiguous consequences. Even though women were oppressed within it, the Indian family provided a strong rallying point for both men and women in their struggle to win rights and an identity for themselves as a community in a harshly exploitative and discriminatory society. The private space of the home thus acquired a public political significance, domestic conservatism grounding community radicalism in relation to the state. In part what this demonstrates is the degree to which Indian women themselves upheld patriarchal gender relations. At the same time, Beall's material confirms an insight already suggested by studies of the resistance by African women to the pass laws in the twentieth century (Wells, 1983; Walker, 1982): that for dominated communities, the struggle for a form of 'family life' in which women were subordinated could yet provide a focus for strong resistance to racial oppression.

Beall's chapter also highlights that congruence of male patriarchal attitudes already noted by Burman. The relationship of male employers and indentured workers with regard to the control of Indian women's sexuality was, she argues, one of 'battle and collusion'. For the male settlers, the extreme submissiveness expected of Indian women was doubly confirmed by their assumption of both sexual and racial superiority. Here Beall draws attention to the double standard of colonial sexual morality, which discriminated not simply between men and women but between white women and black women. While white women as a category were seen as in need of protection from the illegitimate advances of men (white and, even more urgently, black), black women were regarded as ready prey by their masters – here there are suggestive echoes of that fearful fascination of white Victorian men with black women's sexuality that McClintock describes.

Migrant labour and female migration to the towns

From the latter part of the nineteenth century the tempo of change within both the indigenous and the settler sex–gender systems began to quicken markedly in the wake of the mining revolution and the industrial transformation of the region that followed. As women were drawn into the maelstrom of proletarianisation and urbanisation, so pressure on both the indigenous and the settler sex–gender systems mounted. The far-reaching reverberations of this economic restructuring provide the context for the remaining chapters by myself, Bonner, Brink and Chisholm. Concern with social control on the part of the ruling class at a time of rapid social change now becomes a major theme.

My chapter on the migrant labour system spans the critical years of transition to a fully fledged industrial capitalism. It highlights the formative force of gender relations in the history of the region. The organisation of gender in African society was, I argue, of central importance in shaping the migrant labour system, by determining that it was young, unmarried men who were the first recruits to the mines, and women who shouldered more and more of the burden of agricultural production in the homestead. Initially much of the impetus behind the characteristically male and migrant nature of the early phase of African proletarianisation came from within African society itself. However, as mineowners and bosses began to appreciate the value of the migrant labour system in keeping labour costs down, so they themselves came to see the value of a restructured 'traditionalism' within the African rural areas.

As a result, from the late nineteenth century the state moved in an increasingly decisive way to shore up the patriarchal authority of chiefs and homestead heads and tie African women to homestead production – retreating from earlier suggestions of an assimilationist legal policy and consolidating a racially specific form of gender relations within the African community. Major mechanisms of control institutionalised in the first decades of the twentieth century included a national system of customary law that intensified African women's subordination to men, and various restrictions on female mobility and residence rights within the urban areas. In this process the productive significance of the precapitalist homestead was transformed. Many of its outer forms continued – women still laboured in the fields, bridewealth continued to be transferred – but their economic and social significance had been fundamentally altered.

However, the durability of precapitalist institutions cannot be explained simply in terms of the intervention of the colonial state on the side of a subjugated 'traditionalism'. The colonised were also involved in defending indigenous social relationships and practices and elaborating the concept of 'the traditional' that replaced them. Several chapters note the particularly active role of chiefs and homestead heads – those who stood to lose most by changes to the precolonial system of family law and the position of women – in their defence. Both the indigenous ruling class and the colonisers agreed, although for very different reasons, on the need to restrict the mobility and autonomy of African women. As already pointed out, many women themselves also played a part in defending indigenous marriage and kinship practices.

But, as many commentators have noted, at the centre of the migrant labour system lay a powerful contradiction. By drawing off the able-bodied men, the system put more and more strain on the rural homestead as a productive unit. This heightened tensions between the sexes and between the generations, which in turn brought further pressure to bear on the homestead as a social and economic unit. The institution of bridewealth, so pivotal to the organisation of precapitalist society, became increasingly commercialised. At the same time, as is well brought out in Bonner's chapter, state controls on female mobility proved largely ineffective in the first half of the twentieth century – largely because of women's determined resistance.

The effects of rural decline could be seen in the growing numbers of African women moving out of the African rural areas from the late nineteenth century, in defiance of both law and custom – a process dealt with directly in the chapters by myself and Bonner and indirectly in Hughes's examination of the Inanda Seminary in the post-Union years. The impact of the migrant labour system was not, however, evenly felt in the African rural areas in the period before 1930. I suggest that part of the explanation for the varied response should be sought in the specific operation of gender relations within the different African societies. Bonner, in his detailed look at the migration of Basotho women to the Rand, brings out the economic forces at work, linking the particularly high level of female migration from Basutoland – and consequent domination of the illicit liquor trade on the Reef by Basotho women – to the relatively advanced degree of rural pauperisation and social breakdown in Basotho society.

The implications of these developments for the position of women were highly complex. While rural women were able to assert themselves as *de facto* heads of households and gain a new autonomy in the absence of their husbands, they were also forced to assume more and more of the burden of an increasingly attenuated homestead production. African marriage became less and less stable an institution, with women gaining personal independence at the expense of the economic and emotional security within the precolonial family network described by Guy and Burman. At the same time, the individualism promoted by these changes did not sit easily with the ideal of female behaviour of either the reconstructed 'traditional' or the settler ideology of gender.

In the urban areas at this time the position of women was also in a complicated state of flux, as the chapters by Bonner, Brink and Chisholm reveal. The growth of a new proletarian culture and its profound consequences for the organisation of gender in African society is a focus of Bonner's chapter. Women, Bonner makes clear, were active participants in the struggle by blacks to establish themselves in town in the face of official hostility and economic hardship. In the new proletarian culture the illicit brewing of beer by women played a major role; for the local state, efforts to control the African townships in the first half of the twentieth century revolved around attempts to smash this informal liquor trade. In this they were only partially successful, the women fighting back strongly. Beer-brewing provided female migrants to town with the material means to assert a new though circumscribed independence in relation both to the state and to African men. In the volatile, often violent conditions of the African locations and shantytowns, they were far removed from the ideal of domestic cosiness glorified in the settler–mission ideology of gender and aspired to by the African churchwomen described by Gaitskell. Here women applied the qualities of initiative, self-reliance and communality fostered by their role in the homestead to very new and daunting circumstances.

Bonner criticises interpretations of women's involvement in beer-brewing as a defence of their families. Far from engaging in brewing in order to sustain their families, Bonner sees these women as 'refugees' from the consequences of rural family breakdown: the women most likely to migrate were those most marginalised in Basotho society. He also suggests that women's involvement in informal sector activity should be seen not simply as an outcome of their marginal position within the urban areas – unwanted by the urban authorities, very newly proletarianised – but as involving at least some element of choice. Many women preferred it to other, admittedly very limited, alternatives such as domestic service.

Although Bonner does not pursue this himself, his analysis points to the emergence of new family forms in the urban area, centred on women and their children, in which men were largely transitory figures. It could thus be argued that women were not rejecting their commitment to family responsibilities but, rather, redefining its scope, with the maternal role taking precedence over the conjugal. In this there is a further divergence from the norms promoted and aspired to by the 'respectable' churchwomen of the *manyanos*. While Gaitskell's and Bonner's chapters have similar backdrops (the immense dislocation of social life as a result of rapid urbanisation and industrialisation), and informal sector activity and church membership were no doubt sometimes combined, nevertheless the different worlds these chapters describe point to a growing cleavage between 'respectable' and 'unrespectable' African women, with a further suggestion, not explored here, of class differentiation.

The response of African men to the beer-brewers and the female culture that went with it was complicated, often ambivalent: they were, after all, both patrons and rejected patriarchs. Bonner's chapter points to the degree to which sexual relations were being transformed by market relations and (with the development of female prostitution) commoditised. This discussion raises questions of how to interpret the new sexual morality of the shantytowns and migrant quarters, in which a flamboyant assertion of female independence went hand in hand with an often violent insistence on male power over women. Echoes of precapitalist attitudes to sexuality can be discerned in the *famo* dances Bonner describes, but the near-hysterical mood of abandonment that characterised these dances must surely also be seen as a symptom of stress and dislocation at a time of social flux.

The reverberations of change were felt not only by the marginalised and newly proletarianised. Hughes's discussion on the Inanda Seminary in the early twentieth century brings out the concern felt by the Christian elite at the speed and direction of social change and the disintegration of older norms – a concern they shared with the seminary staff as well as with government officials. This expressed itself very clearly in the growing concern among parents, male and female, about the control of their children's and especially their adolescent daughters' sexual behaviour. Gaitskell documents this as a nation-wide concern, which sought to shift onto Christian mothers a novel and onerous responsibility for enforcing moral standards among the youth. African Christians now looked to school and church to fill the gap created by the decline of traditional agencies of socialisation, and this period saw the proliferation of youth organisations concerned with promoting a conception of 'purity' embedded in Christian ideology. Suspicion about town life and the threat it posed to social order also led to a move to promote the countryside and rural values by the Seminary, a development which, notes Hughes, complemented the official policy of segregation. As Hughes points out, segregation at this stage was not seen as necessarily incompatible with the interests of the African petty bourgeoisie.

Heroines, deviants and suffragists

The final set of chapters focuses on developments within the settler sex–gender system in the first part of the twentieth century, when the pre-industrial institutions of the nineteenth century were coming under increased pressure. The labour demands of industrial expansion in the first half of the twentieth century drew increasing numbers of women – initially mainly white, Afrikaner women – into wage labour and encouraged some loosening in the settler ideology of female domesticity. As the chapters by Brink, on the ideology of the *volksmoeder* within Afrikanerdom, and myself, on the suffrage campaign, make clear, the identification of women with home and hearth proved extremely resilient, but these developments did broaden the conception of 'women's sphere', especially for middle-class women dissatisfied with the disabilities they suffered in terms of the law, education and, most prominently, the vote. At the same time, the growth of an urban working-class culture, that also undermined racial barriers between poor blacks and poor whites, threw the issue of social control into sharp relief. During this time gender struggles became embroiled in state strategies to control the underclasses, and their thrust was significantly blunted as a result. One of the noticeable features of the emerging sex–gender system during this time was, in fact, the increased involvement of the state in defining its parameters. In addition to efforts to tighten control over African women, the state also became more involved in modernising the settler sex–gender system and regulating white family and sexual relationships.

Brink's chapter looks at the evolution of the ideology of *volksmoeder* or 'mother of the nation' as a role model for Afrikaner women and its significance in mobilising women to the cause of Afrikaner nationalism, in the context of political defeat (the Anglo–Boer War), growing rural impoverishment and proletarianisation. The concept of *volksmoeder* harnessed many of the elements of the nineteenth-century settler ideology of gender – female domesticity and nurturing, virtue and race purity – to a strong emphasis on patriotism and loyal conformity by women to the demands of a male-dominated nationalism. The very real class divisions within Afrikanerdom were effectively blurred by the ethnic consciousness promoted by the *volksmoeder* ideal, while the ideology of white superiority, together with women's role in its preservation, was consolidated. In the process an earlier strand of non-sectarianism, derived from a feminist rather than a nationalist honouring of Afrikaner women's strength and endurance during the Anglo–Boer War, was resolutely rejected.

At first sight the ideology of the *volksmoeder*, which glorified the roles of housewife and mother, had little to say to or about the large numbers of Afrikaner women flooding the labour market and struggling to survive in poorly paid factory and service jobs. However, contemporary writers who attempted to publicise the circumstances of these working women made little impression on the popular image of Afrikaner women. Brink traces how both middle-class women, organised within the *Vroue Federasie*, and working-class women, organised within the Garment Workers' Union, attempted to harness the *volksmoeder* ideal to their own situation. This was not, she suggests, simply the result of the machinations of ruthlessly patriarchal and nationalistic male ideologues. Many elements of the ideal, particularly the sub-themes of resistance and courage, reverberated with meaning for working women. At a time of immense social flux, women found comfort and a sense of identity in both the homemaker ideal and their membership in a strongly defined ethnic group striving to seize control over its future.

While women who upheld the *volksmoeder* ideal were thus rewarded by society, those who violated the standards of white womanhood had to be punished or, at least, prevented from contaminating others. Chisholm's chapter is concerned with the development of a national system of reformatories and industrial schools that was organised by race, age and sex, and the way in which female deviance was conceptualised and controlled in the years after Union. Both the theory and the practice of rehabilitation were riddled with racist, sexist and classist assumptions that drew their legitimacy from the type of Social Darwinist thinking already described by McClintock. Thus while black juvenile delinquency was largely to be expected within this schema, given the perceived inferiority of blacks to whites, white juvenile delinquency was conceived mainly in terms of racial degeneration and mental defectiveness, qualities that were most commonly attributed to poor whites. The growth of the poor-white population and concern at the inadequate socialisation of poor-white youth into their appropriate race and gender roles provided the immediate context for the development of the reformatory system.

Chisholm describes how deviance among white girls was linked most often to transgressions of the sexual code – which included flouting the taboo on miscegenation – while black girls and boys generally were most likely to be institutionalised on account of offences against property. (It is interesting that black females (usually at the bottom) and white males (usually at the top) should be linked in common perspective here – one of the insights flowing from Chisholm's chapter is the way in which social attitudes are subverted for the marginalised.) She links the increased policing of the sexuality of white women to concern at the growth of a poor-white problem and the threat to white hegemony posed by miscegenation. In the early twentieth century control over the sexuality of white women became increasingly important as a means of policing the boundaries of the white race: white male control over female sexuality thus operated to define men's relationships to other men as well as to women, and constituted a key element in the programme of more general social control.

Chisholm's chapter also shows the relative lack of colour consciousness among marginalised girls at work in one institution, the Eshowe reformatory, which, interestingly, catered for both black and white girls until the mid-1930s. While the reformatory staff distinguished between the girls in terms of the facilities and the tasks black and white girls were assigned, there is evidence that the inmates themselves did not share this concern with the racial hierarchy. The lack of colour consciousness among these social outcasts could be seen as both a reason for their being labelled as social outcasts and an outcome of it. It also points to the way in which the ruling class needs constantly to guard the social barriers that keep the underclasses divided.

In this respect Chisholm's chapter provides an interesting contrast to the final chapter, on the suffrage campaign, which looks at those barriers in operation in a white, middle-class and predominantly English-speaking organisation. Although indisputably a women's rights issue, women's suffrage in South Africa was involved from the start with the battle to uphold white privilege and power. As the arguments against the enfranchisement of women began to lose their persuasiveness in the light of the socio-economic changes affecting women's position, so ruling-class concern to ensure that black women were excluded from the vote came increasingly to the fore. In the end the enfranchisement of women became a weapon for Hertzog's National Party against the limited black male franchise prevailing in the Cape – the enfranchisement of white women only, in 1930, substantially weakened the electoral significance of black voters in that province and in the process tied white women securely to the white power bloc. While there was some debate about the morality (rarely the politics) of this within the organised suffrage movement, most suffragists saw little or no contradiction between their own enfranchisement and the votelessness of black men and women. Their conception of 'women' was shaped by an overriding identification with their own race and, in a somewhat more covert manner, their own class.

Robertson and Berger (1986) have argued that in Africa gender-specific consciousness – by which they mean women-centred – is more prevalent among 'lower-class' than middle-class women, and certainly the history of the suffrage campaign and the experience in the Eshowe reformatory would seem to bear this out for South Africa. This, the authors suggest, 'may be partly due to increased individualism and increased dependence on men' among middle-class women, 'but is also certainly linked to reduced interest in change among the privileged' (ibid.: 20). They refer to Ghana where

poor women systematically share resources and demonstrate a high level of female solidarity, while the socially ambitious or well-off are more likely to manipulate men in order to obtain superior access to resources, dropping their loyalty to women in the process. It seems, then, that there is a relationship between gender consciousness and class consciousness. Women who have the education, leisure, and organisational skills to promote gender-specific class consciousness actively, do not generally do so because it would threaten their male-dependent access to resources as well as their class position (ibid.).

In southern Africa such divisions are further exacerbated by the overlapping of class and race.

Women-centred solidarity and sharing of resources should not, however, be equated with feminist consciousness. Because it may be strong among working-class women, it does not necessarily follow that criticism of existing gender roles and consciousness of gender oppression are strong among working-class women as well. The history of Western feminism in both the late nineteenth–early twentieth century and the contemporary period suggests that gender-consciousness, in the sense of awareness of and opposition to women's oppression as women, is, in fact, more often a middle-class rather than a working-class phenomenon, at least in its explicitly organised forms. The history of the South African suffrage movement would support this general proposition. Within the major limitations already outlined, here middle-class women took the lead in challenging sexist discrimination and promoting the concept of women's rights, particularly in the legal and political arenas. Although there was no serious challenge to the ideological separation of the domestic world of women from the public world of men – a separation with which most suffragists concurred – yet organised women did succeed in building some bridges between the two domains and softening prejudices against 'respectable' women's wage employment. These developments, it is argued, had more of an impact on the organisation of gender relations in the society as a whole than the suffragists' own narrow preoccupations and prejudices would suggest.

By the Second World War a dominant ideology of gender could be discerned at work in southern Africa. Rooted in the Western and Christian model, the concept of 'woman' was organised around domesticity, subordination to male authority, childbearing and child-care. The 'traditional' position of African women which state policy sought to uphold had more in common with this model than that of the indigenous sex–gender system. But while a modified settler ideology could be seen as hegemonic, its authority was certainly not unchallenged. Older ideological constructs deriving from the indigenous sex–gender system were still at work within African society, particularly outside the Christianised elite. At the same time, the incorporation of growing numbers of women into wage labour in the early twentieth century was itself forcing some ideological adjustments within the settler sex–gender system, to allow for and contain the pressure this exerted on power relations between men and women.

MAJOR THEMES: DIFFERENCES AND DURABILITIES
While the material presented here does not add up to a comprehensive overview of the position of women in southern Africa before 1945, nevertheless certain important themes do emerge. Firstly, whether one is talking about the legal status of African women in precolonial Basutoland, or the institutionalisation of female 'delinquents', black and white, in South Africa one hundred years later, it is clear that the worlds of women and of men were differentially structured throughout the period covered by this book. Both indigen-

ous and settler societies distinguished between the sexes, assigning not only different tasks to men and women but different social values to those tasks as well.

Secondly, and an important qualifier to the above, it should also be clear that a static and culture-bound understanding of gender is inadequate for the task of delineating so complex a subject as the position of women in southern Africa during this period. Both the nature and the relative importance of the sexual division of labour underwent many changes in the 150 years covered by this book, as formerly small-scale pastoral and agricultural societies were brought into the orbit of a powerful industrial capitalism. The meaning of 'woman' was not the same in precolonial as it was in twentieth-century southern Africa; it was not the same in precolonial as it was in settler society. The differences went beyond obvious ones in the type of work and responsibilities assigned to women, to encompass the structural significance of the sexual division of labour within these societies, as well as the social meaning assigned to women's roles. While both indigenous and settler women bore and raised children, this act took place in a web of socially specific relationships that were embedded in two profoundly different sets of productive relation-ships. Wife, mother, lover, daughter, sister, mother-in-law – these terms did not have the same range of reference or resonance in the two systems and were not readily translatable, even though officials, missionaries, philanthropists, employers and ordinary members of society regularly presumed to do just that.

It is an easier point to make in the abstract than to apply in practice. Trying to pin down the meaning of 'woman' at different historical junctures becomes harder the further one moves back in time and away from one's own linguistic and cultural base. The difficulties become exacerbated if one also stops assuming that the social meaning assigned to 'man' and 'woman' would have been exactly the same for both sexes within a particular society – and recognises that, given the social power of men in the societies under consideration, it was the male meaning that dominated and was most likely to survive in the historical record.

Even within a single period the boundaries of the category 'woman' are rendered extremely elusive by the operation of other significant markers of social power. The chapters in this book highlight the sharp cleavages dividing women of diverse cultures, races and classes. While it is the racial divisions among black and white women that have usually warranted the most attention – deservedly so, as the recurring theme of racial separation in these chapters makes clear – it would be wrong to limit the analysis of female disunity to just this. In precolonial society women's social standing varied according to age, marital status and husband's rank. In the colonial period and after, the intersection of race, class and gender involved not only the politically prominent separation of black women from white, but also of white women from white and black women from black. White women have been divided along lines of both ethnicity and class. There have also been significant class cleavages among black women, as a comparison of the world of the students at the Inanda Seminary and that of the beer-brewers on the Reef makes clear, although popular articulation of these has tended to be masked by black women's common experience of racial oppression.

But thirdly, giving coherence to what might otherwise seem a bewildering range of variables is the pervasiveness of female subordination to men. Their separate realms have not involved equal access to resources and power for women and for men. The history of African women in southern Africa, Guy argues, is the history of their oppression. While the oppression suffered by women in precapitalist society cannot be understood in the same terms as the oppression of women under capitalism, in both systems the sexual division of labour has involved the social subordination of women and a gender-specific exploitation of women's labour power. The assumption of male authority over women that was intrinsic to the indigenous sex–gender systems became distorted, in many respects reinforced, by the impact of colonialism, but it was not invented by the colonists; the imperatives of capital flowed along contours already suggested by the precapitalist structuring of gender relations.

In the analysis of women's oppression the domestic has been assigned a central importance as a site where, in the words of Harris, 'gender subordination is produced and reproduced' (1981: 50). The material presented here confirms the absolute centrality of the domestic for an understanding of women's position in southern Africa, in both the precolonial and colonial periods. While the subordination of women under capitalist relations of production is often presented as a female retreat into domesticity, it is clear that women's role in precapitalist society in southern Africa was essentially domestic, focussed on the house and homestead and on reproduction and production within that, rather than on wider, societal or trans-societal structures of power and production.[9] Thus the extension of capitalist relations of production to African society did not shift African women into the domestic sphere. It did, however, fundamentally restructure the operations of this sphere and, in the process, transform the significance of 'the domestic' within African society. In the case of women drawn directly into the new relations of production, as wage workers or housewives or even traders in the informal sector, the domestic was largely divorced from production and operated more particularly as a site of reproduction and consumption. In the case of the women who remained locked into the system of homestead production within the 'native reserves', the productive cycle within the homestead was itself subordinated to the needs of capital and, at least in the period covered by this book, performed an essentially reproductive function, servicing the migrant labour system. In all cases the domestic, rather than the public world of the market and of politics, continued to be of primary importance in defining women's position and shaping both their social identity and their self-awareness. It is this, we would suggest, that has historically provided the potential to unite women as women across the cleavages of race and class already described.

The chapters in this book also point to women's childbearing capacity as the critical element to consider in analysing their position. Guy's argument about the centrality of women's oppression in pre-capitalist southern Africa hinges on the significance of female fertility in a technologically unsophisticated society. Although female fertility no longer enjoyed the same structural primacy under capitalist relations of production, yet women were still the reproducers of society, biologically and, by extension, socially. In the particular conditions of nineteenth- and twentieth-century southern Africa women's ability to bear children also made them a key group for delineating and defending ethnic boundaries, whether of the dominant or dominated classes, as the diverse material on white racial purity and the Indian family brings out. While the connection between biological and social reproduction is not, as some feminists have argued, a logical one, it appears here as an historically fashioned one of enormous authority and weight.

To suggest that women were oppressed in precolonial society takes one into that highly emotional debate on political priorities and research credentials already referred to. Some writers have construed this as a betrayal of the contemporary struggle against racial oppression, because it diverts attention from the struggle for national liberation or, more seriously, because it undermines the sustaining faith in an egalitarian African past. Thus Christine Qunta has argued that in the precolonial era, 'Contrary to the more popularly held view, African women on a continent-wide scale enjoyed great freedom and had both a legal and social equality which, among other things, enabled them to become effective heads of state and military strategists' (1987: 23–4). She attributes their contemporary position at 'the bottom of the scale of humanity' to external forces: 'the imposition of foreign religions such as Islam and Christianity coupled with the European onslaught on African values, institutions and morality' (ibid.: 12, 24).

A more nuanced interpretation within this vein is put forward by Robertson and Berger (1986). They argue that the advent of capitalism and colonialism exacerbated gender differences in Africa, by the addition of European sexism to the patriarchal elements already present within precolonial society. However, they downplay these indigenous patriarchal elements by positing a 'separate but equal' model, marked by 'separate gender hierarchies, with interlocking rights and responsibilities in production and reproduction'. According to them, 'in these settings age was often more significant than gender in determining status' (ibid.: 11).

However, neither viewpoint is borne out, for southern Africa at least, by the material presented here by Guy and Burman. While the Robertson–Berger position contains some useful insights, neither their nor Qunta's analysis addresses the critical issue of male appropriation of female reproductive and productive capacity as argued by Guy. The undoubted economic and social autonomy enjoyed by women in precolonial southern Africa operated within the clearly defined parameters of the male-dominated homestead system. The qualities of female initiative and self-reliance that it nurtured were not incompatible with – indeed, they were intimately linked to – women's structural dependence on men. In the case of the independently powerful women extolled by Qunta, these were exceptional rather than representative figures, often honorary males in effect, whose personal achievements did not subvert the association of economic and political power with social maleness. Furthermore, as the previous discussion makes clear, the impact of foreign religions and capitalist relations of production on the position of women was far more complex than Qunta suggests. It created a space in which previously contained tensions could erupt and highly qualified but nonetheless novel notions of individual autonomy take root, ideas that could, in turn, inspire and legitimate resistance to both racial and sexual oppression.

Female resistance to and acquiesence in their position

This leads into a further important issue – women's active engagement with their situation. The chapters in this book confirm the increasingly respectable view that women have not been merely passive victims of externally imposed codes of behaviour, swept along by the inexorable forces of history. Women as agents – both in defence of and in rebellion against their position – is another major theme to emerge from these chapters.

Dissatisfaction with the emphasis on women as victims of oppression has led to attempts to recast accounts of how power operates in gender relations, for instance that described by Newton and colleagues:

... women have characteristically entered into sexual struggles as something more than the passive recipients of sexual codes. Indeed, it was in coming to terms with women's resistance to oppression that historians of women began to abandon their earlier focus on victimization in order to reconceptualize the very nature and locus of power. While continuing to maintain that power is exercised by specific historical agents with access to different levels and different sources of power, they have also come to see power less as one group's 'consolidated and homogeneous domination over others' than as something 'which circulates' or functions 'in the form of a chain' (1983: 7, quoting Michel Foucault).

It has also led to the exploration of the idea of a definite women's culture, an issue touched upon by Meintjes and Gaitskell and also suggested in the chapters by Bonner and Chisholm.

While these developments have been enormously liberating for women's studies, 'agency' can become a problematic concept if treated unhistorically. What needs to be avoided is an uncritical fusing of the notion of women's agency with that of women's resistance to oppression, and to gender oppression in particular. Undoubtedly women in southern Africa have been active in rejecting their gender-allotted roles and carving out alternatives for themselves: the theme of resistance, of 'escape', crops up in virtually every chapter. Female acquiesence in their subordination could never be entirely taken for granted in any of the societies discussed here. But, as Guy points out with specific regard to the precolonial period but with more general applicability, such escape did not constitute a wholesale rejection of the dominant notion of gender relations: the broad parameters of the sexual division of labour were rarely challenged by women rebels. At any one time it was likely to be a minority of women who resisted their position, and then what was involved amounted, overall, to rebellion against particular manifestations of oppression, rather than revolution against gender relations in their entirety.

What this material establishes is that the analysis of women's agency needs to come to terms with the pervasiveness of women's conservatism – with their resistance to change. Without belittling the historical significance of women's rebelliousness, one needs to take note of how women have also acted as agents of gender socialisation on behalf of the prevailing norms of their society, as mothers of course, but also as teachers, missionaries, social workers, peers and employers. On both sides of the racial divide, female energy, initiative and solidarity have been directed at resisting but also at upholding women's subordinate position.

Various reasons for women's acceptance of their position are suggested here: socialisation[10] and the enormous power of ideology (the chapter on the suffrage movement notes how gender was not part of the language of politics, making it difficult for women even to conceptualise their oppression), the limited alternatives available to them, as well as the dangers of rebellion and the rewards of conformity. The penalties and the rewards should not be lightly dismissed. As these chapters document, women who rebelled against their prescribed roles faced isolation, economic hardship, sexual violence and imprisonment. On the other side of the coin, Guy links the strong defence by African women of the domestic community to the social harmony and cohesion it offered, in addition to relative economic well-being. Gaitskell's chapter suggests that Christian familial ideology was able to build on the value that precolonial society assigned to motherhood, and underscores the centrality of the ideology of motherhood in the self-definition and self-esteem of African church-women. Although under vastly different circumstances, something similar can be discerned in Brink's discussion of the appeal of the *volksmoeder* concept for Afrikaner women at a time of social flux and insecurity. Women's ascribed roles within the domestic sphere gave them an identity and social prestige. There was also, as the suffrage campaigners were constantly averring, an undeniable satisfaction in the role of successful homemaker and mother. The bland assertion of female subordination and male control does not adequately describe the complexity of the sexual and the emotional in the relationships between men and women and within the family network more generally (at least not as these were constructed in the settler sex–gender system and, arguably, in the indigenous). It was, indeed, often precisely their endorsement of their domestic roles that underlay black women's militant resistance to the intrusions of the colonial and South African state.

The dialectic between female resistance to and acquiesence in their subordination is a theme running throughout the book. The demarcation between the two processes was not necessarily distinct, and elements of both could mingle in individual women's lives. As Marks and Trapido (1987) point out, social actors do not require consistency of themselves – their actions are not necessarily consciously reflective. Thus white women workers who saw themselves as both workers and housewives, socialists and nationalists, white supremacists and internationalists, 'saw little reason to grapple with the contradictions' (ibid.: 26). (However, the emotional and psychological stress referred to by, amongst others, Meintjes and Hughes could, perhaps, be seen as these contradictions manifesting themselves at an unconscious level.)

It is apparent that gender relations underwent a major refashioning in southern Africa in the nineteenth and early twentieth centuries – but female subordination to men persisted, and not simply because of overt male coercion. The remarkable durability of male power over women in the face of far-reaching social, political and economic change is a sobering reminder of how deeply rooted it is, not simply in South African society in the abstract, but in the way in which men and women have been and are constituted as social actors. One of the lessons from the past is that male and female perceptions and material interests are shaped in gender-specific ways. For women to be mobilised effectively against oppression and exploitation, whether of a racial, gender or class nature, the ways in which this gender-specificity operates need to be taken very seriously.

1

Gender oppression in southern Africa's precapitalist societies

JEFF GUY

Cow god of the home, god with the moist nose; cow that makes
nations fight, you have killed many men. (Adapted from Shaw,
1974: 95)

This chapter analyses the oppression of women amongst southern
African farming peoples south of the Limpopo, in the era before
colonial subjugation – that is, amongst what are often called 'traditional' societies but which I will refer to here as southern Africa's
precapitalist societies.[1] The chapter does not try to present an overview of the vast body of scholarly literature which has attempted to
describe the role of women in these societies. Instead it delineates
certain social features which were common to all precapitalist societies in southern Africa – at least for the time for which there are
written records and possibly much earlier (Huffman, 1986) – and
argues that these features suggest that these societies were based
upon the appropriation of women's labour by men. It then points to
how these features can assist in distinguishing between areas of
change and of continuity in the history of southern African women,
as well as in assessing the impact of the precapitalist past on their
present situation.

By limiting the chapter's scope and objectives in this way, it does
become vulnerable to criticism not only from the specialist, always
ready with an ethnographic morsel served with the remark 'but
among the ...', but also, and with more justification, from those who
wish to see examined the social, cultural, lived experience of women
in these societies. However, this is something not attempted here; that
experience awaits recovery by those closer to it – closer in terms of
culture, language, class, race and gender. Nonetheless, without the
structural features provided by such abstract theoretical concepts as
those presented in this chapter, the more concrete and richer aspects
of human experience in southern Africa lie heaped in such confusion

that it is difficult to identify their shape and form with any clarity.

The chapter assumes the following: that the history of African women in southern Africa is the history of their oppression;[2] and that although this oppression gives women's history a surface continuity, the nature of this oppression and the nature of the exploitation upon which it is based, are dynamic and have undergone qualitative changes over time.

It argues that an understanding of the oppression of women in these societies is best developed from an analysis of the way in which production took place, who participated in production, and how their participation was controlled,[3] together with an examination of the form in which surplus was produced and how it was appropriated from those who created it. The chapter also argues that in southern Africa's precapitalist African societies this surplus took the form of female labour power, and, therefore, the capacity to create more labour power through reproduction placed central importance on fertility and the control of fertility.

In addressing these issues one confronts central questions about the nature of the exploitation of women, necessitating the development of analytical foundations which, in time, could be used to reach a clearer understanding of the social and cultural manifestations of the particular form of gender oppression that operated in these societies.

PRODUCTION IN SOUTHERN AFRICA'S PRECAPITALIST SOCIETIES

In the societies under discussion, production took place in the homestead. The homestead was made up of a man, his cattle and small stock, his wife or wives and their children, grouped in their different houses, each with its own arable land. Materially these homesteads were largely self-sufficient, subsisting on the cereals produced by the agricultural labour of the women as well as the milk products of the homestead's herd. Animal husbandry was the domain of men, most of the labour time being expended by boys in herding. There was a clear sexual division of labour under the control of the husband/father, who allocated arable land for the use of the various houses to which his wives belonged, on which they worked with their children for their own support and for that of the homestead.

Cattle played a pivotal role in production because, before a new homestead could be established (i.e. before a man could marry) or an existing one be extended (a new house established or wife acquired), cattle had to be passed or pledged by the husband to the father of the woman he was to marry. The organisation and control of cattle remained in the hands of males, and the homestead's stock of cattle was central to its well-being, productive capacity, and status. Above all, the cattle holding was directly related to the wealth of the homestead. Cattle provided the measure of value in exchange transactions; the passage of cattle marked all important social events and movements; and the acquisition of cattle was a dominant social goal, the number of cattle accumulated within a homestead reflecting its social standing and strength.

Aggregations of homesteads like these made up political units which are usually referred to as chiefdoms but which were occasionally of such demographic dimensions and political strength that European observers characterised them as kingdoms. While the basic features of these political units remained the same, their spatial organisation differed, and homesteads could be concentrated to make up towns, as among the Tswana, or they could be dispersed, as among the Nguni.

The chief had to allow married men access to land upon which to establish their homesteads and farm. In return he demanded acceptance of his authority and the chiefdom's laws, military service, fines, tribute, and a certain amount of labour in his fields. However, despite the importance of these exactions, together with the considerable amount of time and energy spent in the organisation and pursuit of such male activities as trade, barter, the manufacture of handicrafts, weapons and implements, I would argue that these were nevertheless activities subsidiary to female agricultural labour. In my opinion it was the labour of women in agriculture, supported by their domestic labour in the homestead, be that chiefly or commoner, which provided the subsistence base upon which the society depended and the surplus upon which it was structured.[4]

But the above account of homestead organisation is a static one, and it must be remembered that homesteads were part of a dynamic social process of termination and regeneration. Homesteads were continually passing out of existence, with the death of the men who had established them, and being created as young men left their mothers' houses to establish homesteads of their own, when they married young women who had left their fathers' homesteads to establish houses in their husbands' homesteads. This process involved the vertical transfer of property and status from father to son, through family links, and the creation of horizontal social connections between the husband's and his wife's families, through the transfer of bridewealth. These movements left their social marks in a web of lineage connections and kinship links.

Connected with kinship links, and yet having their own autonomy, were the political ties between chief and subject. Political authority was delegated by the chief to homestead heads, although there was a tendency for it to follow certain lines within a descent group. Thus political office within the chiefdom could pass from one generation to another by laws of descent.

We therefore have to try to picture societies made up of producing homesteads (in the charge of married men) that were founded upon the agricultural labour of women, largely self-sufficient materially, and connected through kinship links and grouped politically in their allegiance to a chief who was supported by the labour in his as well as his subjects' homesteads. These homesteads were continually being recreated with each generation and all major social transactions were marked by the passage of cattle and women between men.

Women, cattle and wealth

Central to this model – the one essential element – was the union between a man and a woman, that established the homestead – the unit of production which, in aggregate, made up the society. The word commonly used for this union is an inadequate one – 'marriage'. Working backwards in the search for analytical priorities, we have to note that marriage presupposed the pledge or the passing of cattle from husband's father's homestead to wife's father. It is by examining this process that we can get closer to an understanding of the role of women in these precapitalist societies.

Marriage set up the productive unit upon which the society was based. Before it could take place, there had to be an agreement on the transfer of property between two previously existing homesteads – ideally and usually in the form of cattle. It is this social institution – variously described as '*lobolo*', '*lobola*', '*bohali*', 'bridewealth', 'brideprice' – which has rightly attracted so much attention and is clearly crucial to any analysis of southern Africa's precapitalist societies and the role of women within them.

In one sense there is nothing new in this perception. The importance of bridewealth caught the attention of the first European travellers, missionaries and administrators. It has remained a central concern for all sorts of commentators on African societies, both from within and from without. But while these observers have been correct in identifying the importance of bridewealth, they have failed in so far as they have been unable to see it as the social transaction which united two great male concerns – the control of women and of cattle – in a dynamic totality. As a result, they have been unable to show *why* bridewealth was so important, or to understand its role in appropriation and the exploitation of women.

The reason for this failure is ultimately a commonplace one: the enormous difficulty one has in escaping from one's own time and the concepts which define one's own existence. It applies to the culturally arrogant and ignorant of a previous age, like the missionaries who railed against 'brideprice' as the selling of women into female slavery, or the settlers who asserted that it allowed men to live off the labour of their wives and denied them the opportunity of becoming civilised through wage labour (Simons, 1968: 15). But it also applies to the contemporary historians and anthropologists who believe they belong to a culturally more tolerant age and yet assume that the accumulation of wealth by men is a general human goal which requires no explanation and is as 'natural' as the accumulation of commodities is today. Thus the section on 'Traditional Economic Systems' in the most recent edition of *The Bantu-speaking Peoples of Southern Africa* goes so far as to use such terms as investment and corporate economic groups, and to treat 'Cattle as Capital' (Sansom, 1974: 149). There is also the related circular argument that cattle are accumulated because they confer status and wealth and are therefore the object of accumulation. In one typical statement we are told that cattle are not only a source of food, leather and transport, but are also a medium of exchange and sacrifice, and 'the means of obtaining sexual satisfaction ... [and] securing many wives and adherents, and of dispensing hospitality and generosity, on which virtues status largely depends' (Shaw, 1974: 94).

There have been attempts to contextualise wealth, power and status, and thereby to escape from such culturally blinkered interpretations and reach an explanation which has some social independence. One widely held view is that the drive to accumulate cattle was the result of an irrational, psycho-social 'cattle complex'. Then there have been attempts to counter the idea that cattle accumulation was irrational, with arguments asserting the economic and ecological rationality of cattle accumulation. While such ideas are an advance on the 'cattle are capital' approach, they still leave much unanswered, for example such fundamental questions as: what is 'wealth' in these societies, what is 'accumulation', and why should it be males who accumulate wealth? This approach still tends to assume the universality of a social drive towards the accumulation of products, and to link this unthinkingly with status, power and masculinity. This leads inevitably to a circularity of argument – cattle are accumulated because they transmit status and authority, and cattle are therefore the object of accumulation – which is based on invalid cross-cultural assumptions about a universal drive towards accumulation and male power.

A further argument – but one which contains an important insight in that it attempts to posit an independent social dynamic – asserts that these are societies in which the accumulation of people, rather than the accumulation of things, was a dominant goal. Gluckman has been the leading proposer of this view. He believed that this need to accumulate people was related to economic factors in so far as these were societies which did not have the technology to create products of sufficient variety and durability to form a basis for marked social divisions (1967: 13–14).

Meillassoux developed this approach further when he characterised 'agricultural self-sustaining formations' as those in which the
accumulation of people takes precedence over the accumulation of
things. Or, in his words, they 'rely less on the control of the *means of
material production* than on the *means of human reproduction*: subsistence and women. Their end is the reproduction of life as a precondition of production. Their primary concern is to "grow and multiply"
in the biblical sense' (1972: 101–2).

While the manner in which the word 'reproduction' is used here
has been criticised for its imprecision (Harris and Young, 1981),
Meillassoux has made a significant contribution with this emphasis
on the relative importance of reproduction – in the sense of the
creation and control of people – over production.

Exploring this idea further takes one nearer both to the nature of
gender oppression in southern Africa's precapitalist societies and the
crucial place it held in the social structure, as well as to the analytical
criteria which allow one to escape from the non-specific concepts of
accumulation and wealth found in many academic studies. But in
order to achieve a better understanding of gender oppression in these
societies, we can make use of an analytical concept with a long and
intellectually respectable, if controversial, pedigree – that of labour
power.

Labour power
'Labour power' is a concept devised by Marx and used to refer to
the productive and creative potential of people (1976: 270). The concept is crucial to Marx's analysis of capitalism. A number of scholars,
including Meillassoux, argue that the concept of labour power cannot
be applied to precapitalist societies (1981: 50; see also Harris and
Young, 1981) but, for the reasons given below, I would argue that,
while labour power's social role is very different, it is an applicable,
indeed an essential, analytical concept for understanding these societies.

Labour power is productive potential – human beings' creative
capacity. The form that it takes is socially specific and it has to be
realised through socially creative activity. Its realisation lies in the
future, and an awareness of the productive potential of labour power
depends upon an ability to project human creative potentiality into
the future. This realisation comes about through social process, as part
of a social project. It depends upon social control, planning and skills.
Labour power is realised in productive activity and in the products
of labour, as material objects, goods, articles, items of consumption
and exchange.

In capitalist societies, Marx argued, it is labour power which the
worker exchanges for the wage. Under capitalism it is, therefore, a

commodity – a commodity, moreover, which has the unique capacity to create surplus value. Although serving a different function, the concept can, I would argue, be applied to the precapitalist societies being discussed here and is particularly useful in understanding the institution of marriage – that is, in understanding the organisation of production and of gender relations.

As described above, in these societies cattle were necessary for marriage and women were denied the possession of cattle. Men exchanged cattle for women, the most important occasion being on marriage, when cattle were given by the husband to the bride's father. This exchange was, however, conditional on the bride remaining obedient to her husband and proving fertile in the marriage. These conditions were crucial. Disobedience or infertility on the part of the wife were grounds for the husband's family demanding the return of their cattle. If we place this in its wider social context, 'obedience' meant that the wife had to fulfil her function as an agricultural producer within her husband's homestead; 'fertility' meant that she had to produce children whose labour would, in time, be used for the benefit of the homestead: the labour of the sons in animal husbandry for the support and perpetuation of the homestead until they in turn created homesteads of their own; and the labour of the daughters in domestic and agricultural tasks within their father's homestead until they, in turn, were married and assumed the reproductive and productive responsibilities which would bring cattle from their husbands' homesteads to their father's homestead.

It is this cycle of production and reproduction which lies at the heart of southern Africa's precapitalist societies: the productive capacity of women in the domestic and agricultural sphere, together with their reproductive potential, being exchanged by their fathers for cattle, which allowed this value-creating cycle of production and reproduction to continue into the next generation.

The term 'productive cycle' is, however, misleading in so far as it implies repetition and reciprocity. Each cycle of exchange was asymmetrical: the number and productive capacity of women/children/cattle – that is, the amount of labour power – at a man's disposal fluctuated according to the vagaries and specifics of social existence. The point, however, is that in optimal conditions it was possible for the amount of labour power at a man's disposal to increase – women's labour, productive and reproductive, had that potential. In its simplest terms, it was possible for a woman's labour to create more labour power than the amount originally expended for her own labour power. In this way women created not only value but surplus in southern Africa's precapitalist societies.

It is the obsessive search for a *material* surplus *product*, or for objectified surplus labour, that has been the prime reason for the failure of even materialist analyses to perceive the significance of this productive cycle. The emphasis on reproduction in precapitalist societies, as in Meillassoux's work, gets closer to an understanding of this, in that it begins to acknowledge the significance of the production of producers. But reproduction is usually considered in too concrete a fashion, and those who make use of the concept are therefore unable to abstract from the process of reproduction and see that what is being reproduced is labour power – the labour power embodied in the women and the cattle which move between men.

Cattle

Productive, value-creating cycles of this kind were probably features of many societies where a low level of technological development restricted the diversity and durability of the items produced. The agricultural implements and other manufactured goods of these societies were simple. The amount of labour applied to a productive process was directly related to the amount produced. At the same time, the relative productivity of labour was low while agricultural surpluses were difficult to store for lengthy periods or to transport – conditions which did not allow for the development of substantial social differentiation between individuals or groups, based on the monopolisation of the products of labour. In southern Africa, however, there was one feature of the economy which could sustain large surpluses – surpluses which were not only durable and transportable, but could, in favoured regions, be increased at a considerable rate: surpluses in cattle.

Surplus cattle, in the possession of men, could be exchanged for a woman's productive capacity in agriculture and her reproductive capacity to create future labourers, cattle, labour power. Thus cattle not only provided crucial products for the use of those who owned them but, once they had become part of the productive cycle by realising the labour power of women, they made increased productive capacity and therefore social power available to their male owners. The object of accumulation in southern Africa's precapitalist societies was indeed cattle, but cattle as the means by which men acquired and accumulated the labour power of women.

WOMEN AND SOCIAL CATEGORIES

This control and appropriation of the productive and reproductive capacity of women was central to the structure of southern Africa's precapitalist societies. It was *the* social feature upon which society was based. Thus the importance of understanding the 'role of women' in these societies necessarily goes beyond this specific task: without an effective analysis of women's position, we lack the means to analyse these societies effectively and in their totality.

Furthermore, a clearer idea of the productive process, and of the role of women within it, enables one to begin to see 'women' in these societies as the living examples not of an eternal, biologically defined category, but of a structured social category. It also suggests ways in which to begin the essential process of 'deconstruction' – because to view women in precapitalist southern Africa in this way, to place them at the centre of analysis, must force us to reconsider all the major aspects of social life in these societies. Even if we take only the most immediately related and obvious aspects – for example, marriage, bridewealth, sexuality, age and authority, in addition to productive capacity and fertility – we can see that the deconstruction of 'women' necessarily implies the deconstruction of these concepts as well.

Thus marriage was so much more than a physical union of men and women, the social institution which allowed the onset of sexual relations, the propagation of children, the transfer of status, property and rights. Marriage, in terms of the above, initiated the productive processes upon which the society was based. These were processes that were predicated upon male control of female productive and reproductive capacity. They were productive processes which had the potential to create and increase value. Women's capacity to create value in marriage was linked with cattle, through the institution of bridewealth. These cattle were in the control of men, and the accumulation of cattle by men was a major social objective. This accumulation was based in the end on fertility – and marriage and infertility were incompatible concepts.

Writers on African society have failed to distinguish between fertility and sexuality. (See, for example, the quotation from Shaw at the head of this chapter.) In many precapitalist societies sexual relations took place before marriage, but fertile sexual relations were expected to await marriage and the establishment or expansion of a homestead. And even here, the fertility of the homestead – that is, the fertility of its women – was in many cases more important than the potency of its men. The progenitor of the child was often of little social significance. An absent or impotent or even a dead man could still become a father. In the last case a man could 'raise seed' for his dead brother, and it was the dead man, the mother and her offspring who were the important social actors. An infertile woman could be joined by her fertile sister, who would bear the children of her sister's house. One also reads in the anthropological literature of marriage between women, in which the biological father of the children is socially irrelevant (Preston-Whyte, 1974: 187–92). It was fertility that was important, because it was fertility that could create value, through its link with labour power, by means of cattle. And fertility is the preserve of women.

Similarly, we read much about the social importance of age and the respect and obedience demanded by the old of the young in these societies, but this is another concept that we have to deconstruct. What gave age much of its significance is that fertility and potency are functions of age – and in societies where fertility created value, and therefore social power, the control of fertility and sexuality by the fathers was essential for their continued dominance. The control of the fertility of the unmarried was intense and was given social prominence in initiation ceremonies as well as in the ideology of deference and obedience imposed by the old on the young.

In the larger states during the nineteenth century, the chief or king extended these demands based on age even further. In the case of the Zulu political system, and the societies related to it, the king exercised direct control over the fertility of his subjects. This manifested itself through the system, inadequately described as 'military', in which men and women were organised into age-sets or 'regiments' and were not allowed to marry until the king gave permission. By that time the men could be well into their thirties. The general tendency among commentators has been to concentrate on the martial and supposedly sexual implications of this, by suggesting that heightened military aggression sprang from sexual frustration. But again, even in the Zulu kingdom it was not so much sexual activity but fertility that was controlled. The restrictions on marriage by the king was certainly an aspect of the organisation of the Zulu military system – but it was also massive intervention in the basic productive processes of the kingdom on the part of the state, achieved by gaining a degree of control over female fertility and productivity and thereby the social and economic power which this possessed in such a system.

This control over the productive process, by means of the control over marriage, was a particular feature of the Zulu and related states. In other cases, for instance among the Sotho, the origins of political power were more direct – the appropriation, by the chiefs, of tribute labour, the accumulation of women and cattle as tribute or of tribute goods which had value in terms of cattle (Kimble, 1985). As already noted, too much has been made of the division between chiefs and commoners in these societies. It is more useful to see chiefs as the richest and most powerful of males. The limited productive capacity of available technology ensured that the chiefs were unable to build a foundation for social dominance that was independent of the cattle–labour power cycle already described. They were, therefore, also dependent, ultimately, on the reproductive and productive capacity of women. In the end it was the accumulation of women and of cattle, which gave access to women's labour power, that marked the source and indicated the direction in which political power flowed.

A better understanding of the way in which women created value also enables one to reach a better understanding of wealth in these societies. Women, their offspring and cattle did indeed indicate wealth, as we have so often been told. But except in the broadest terms – as something defined as a desirable social objective – the concept of wealth in these precapitalist societies is not comparable to that of wealth in capitalist societies. Wealth in precapitalist southern Africa was wealth created by the value of women's labour power against cattle in the possession of men. These were, therefore, societies based in the last instance on the accumulation of fertile and productive women. In this sense they were indeed societies based on the accumulation of people – and, as such, can be sharply distinguished from societies in which wealth is based upon the accumulation of things.

PRECAPITALIST AND CAPITALIST FORMS OF EXPLOITATION

The passing of this feature – the creation and control of labour power – and the introduction of social structures based on the accumulation of commodities therefore mark the passing of precapitalist society. In terms of the argument advanced in this chapter, precapitalist societies can be seen as having come to an end when they were no longer organised around the control of the labour power of women; then their reproduction was no longer premised on the value created by women's agricultural labour and their reproductive capacity.

This is an important point to establish, because without such an analytical benchmark, an understanding of subsequent developments must be confused. The retention and adaptation of older social elements in the service of the new colonial state, following the defeat of the independent African chiefdoms during the course of the nineteenth century, make social analysis difficult, especially when one is required to separate the 'traditional' from the novel. Surface social continuity so often hides fundamental change. This means that one has to be extremely wary of arguments which speak, for instance, of the continuity of 'traditional' respect demanded by the old of the young or by men of women, or of the 'traditional' role of the fathers, or of female domestic conservatism.

Thus female agricultural labour continued to be extremely important within colonial systems – but the scope of its operation was fundamentally altered. The ubiquitous hut tax, which colonial governments imposed on the various African chiefdoms during the latter half of the nineteenth century, which forced men into wage labour – and upon which the colonial state depended financially – was also a tax on the male for the productivity of his wives and their offspring – each wife being the occupant of one hut. In this sense colonialism added another layer to the already existing system of gender exploitation – the surplus created by wives and children was now appropriated not only by their husbands and fathers, but by the colonial state as well.

The system of labour migrancy that developed under capitalism in South Africa represented a welding of capitalist exploitation upon precapitalist forms. It has depended upon the exploitation of both the labourer (through the wage) and of the women who have supported him in the rural area he sees as his home. At first it was the young men who were sent out for the commodities and cash required to meet new needs created by the availability of manufactured domestic articles, agricultural implements and firearms, and to pay the taxes demanded by the colonial state. The migrant's mother and sisters provided the economic base he required until he was able to secure a wife of his own – as they had always done. But as land in the possession of Africans deteriorated or was appropriated, and as the migrant labour system bit more deeply into African societies, so the African rural areas steadily lost their already inadequate capacity to support their populations. After the young men, their fathers were obliged to follow them into wage labour. The migrant labour system, however, required that as far as possible, by social sanction and law, women and children be kept on the land, responsible for rural production under increasingly severe conditions. (For further discussion on women and the development of the migrant labour system, as well as resistance by women to efforts to tie them to the land, see chapter 7.)

Although the timing and extent differed in specific situations, the general tendency was for women to be the last to leave the rural areas; when this occurred, it was indicative of a severe crisis in rural production. By this stage the value-creating cycle at the centre of southern Africa's precapitalist societies had been largely destroyed. Its social marks – bridewealth, the extreme importance of fertility, female deference to men, the expectation that women should labour outside as well as inside the home – might all continue to exist, but now they operated in a changed situation, in which cash and commodities provided a source of value independent of the women–cattle–labour power cycle. The economic and social dynamic was, therefore, different, drawing on changed, external productive forces.

The institution of bridewealth provides a good example of this. It is still widespread in southern Africa, but it no longer fulfils the same function as it did in precapitalist societies; it is only at the most superficial level that it can be seen as the perpetuation of a traditional social feature. However, one can escape conflating the social features of different eras if, through empirical analysis, one establishes the context within which bridewealth operates: whether it is predicated on productive female labour, as it was in precapitalist societies, or whether it has been effectively commoditised and become a domestic transaction which forms part of a wider system of accumulation based on wage labour.

GENDER OPPRESSION AND CONTRADICTION

I am aware that this chapter does not provide anything like a comprehensive analysis of the role of women in precapitalist African society. It does, however, try to point to certain key concepts, structures and social practices which, I would argue, provide a way of controlling not only the mass of information about African society at our disposal, but also, by providing historically specific categories, our tendency to read aspects of our own social existence into that of the past. The analysis in this chapter points to the fundamental role of the appropriation of female labour power, the means by which this appropriation operated, and how this was linked by male control into the structure of power in these societies.

A more comprehensive account would have to move from here to examine social manifestations of these concepts: how they worked in practice, in the customs, traditions, language and attitudes of different southern African societies. Some of this work has begun. Wright (1981), for example, has written about the mechanisms by which women were subordinated socially in the Zulu kingdom, while the wearying and brutal nature of women's oppression in one Tswana society has been documented by Kinsman (1983).

At the same time, however, an awareness of the existence of structures of subordination and the nature of exploitation in these societies constitutes only a partial view. It provides a framework for analysis and a certain insight into the nature of exploitation, but it cannot convey the texture of the lived experience of the participants in the social process.

We have still to understand, for example, how women both participated in and resisted their exploitation. We catch glimpses of their resistance in the historical record – in the struggles described within the homestead, in the many accounts of daughters escaping from dominating fathers and unwanted husbands, and of mothers pursued by their sons or fleeing from their husbands. These struggles were exploited time and again by the representatives of the colonial systems to force a way into African society – for example, in the missionary concern to 'rescue' girls and women from unsatisfactory marriages (Etherington, 1978: 97–8), or in the notorious case when a woman's attempted escape from her husband was used as a pretext for the British invasion of Zululand (Fuze, 1979: 110–11). In the late 1870s in the Zulu kingdom there was a countrywide refusal by young women to marry older men – a refusal which, in view of its threat to the social order, was of such significance that it can be characterised as a women's uprising (ibid.: 106). The representatives of the Zulu state were well aware of the seriousness of such action – the refusal of the women to choose their husbands from those men selected by the authorities threatened the essential features of state power – and their response was correspondingly harsh. They ordered that the women be killed and their bodies exposed as an example to others. It was, however, an uprising, not a revolution. The women were not resisting marriage as such, but marriage to certain men, and in the background were their favoured male lovers.

Resistance to instances of gender oppression, however, in no way denies the fact that women also participated in the process as a whole – and, in fact, supported it as fervently as any other member of these precapitalist societies. Indeed, it is difficult to imagine anything but a qualified resistance in a system where a quality so inalienable as reproductive capacity was of such social importance. On the other hand, exploitation through the control of reproductive capacity must of necessity be a qualified form of subordination since it leaves a crucial autonomy and integrity with the possessor of fertility.

It is probably here that we have to locate the most significant social difference between these precapitalist societies and the capitalist one that succeeded it. This chapter began with the premise that the history of women in southern Africa was the history of their oppression and then went on to offer some ideas on the economic and social origins of this oppression as it occurred in precapitalist societies, arguing that this approach provided a means of escaping the ever-present influence of contemporary ideology on our views of the past. However, this argument applies equally to our *idea* of oppression. We cannot impose our contemporary image of oppression on the life of women in precapitalist societies. The fact that value was created by fertility gave women a significant role in society, not only as the objects of exploitation, but as the bearers of value in the technical as well as the wider, non-technical sense.

Women did have a significant degree of economic independence. On marriage they were given access to productive land, which they worked themselves. They were in control of the process of agricultural production and retained for their own use a substantial proportion of the product of that land and of their labour. Work was heavy but it took place within a community which provided substantial security. The value attached to fertility gave the possessors of that fertility social standing and social integrity. Oppression in these precapitalist societies was certainly very different from the isolation and alienation which forms of exploitation through the wage create and which provide the impressions we have today of the concept of oppression. And we have to keep such differences in mind when we attempt to understand the nature of female subordination in precapitalist society.

It seems useful to consider gender relationships in the precapitalist societies of southern Africa as exhibiting two major opposing aspects. The social manifestations of this relationship still await sensitive analysis, based not only on the documentary sources but also on language, idiom, oral history and personal testimony. However, even a superficial knowledge of the sources reveals its double-sided nature. The one side has formed the subject of this chapter. It is exploitative – objectively so – and can be analysed in terms of the creation of value by women and the appropriation of this by men. But there is the other side as well – the socially harmonious and cohesive aspect, founded on the dominant social significance of a physical capacity inherent in women – fertility – and the security provided to all members of society by the way in which production was organised in the domestic sphere. It is this latter aspect which forms the background to the tenacious defence women made of the precapitalist system. For Theophilus Shepstone was surely right when he wrote of the traditional system of marriage, 'both men and women would equally oppose any violent attempt to destroy it ...' (quoted in Welsh, 1971: 71).

Both of these aspects – participation in and the defence of the system – reach out of the precapitalist past and into the capitalist present. Thus, as has been pointed out by Bozzoli (1983: 166–7), the brave and radical protest of South African women has had a profoundly conservative, patriarchal aspect. The tenacity and courage displayed by African women in the face of enormous hardships is celebrated in popular tradition and political history. But it includes as a major theme a determination to defend the domestic community, be it in the face of military conquest in the nineteenth century, of economic and social disintegration with the onset of migrant labour and then urbanisation, or of the harsh economic exploitation and political oppression of modern times.

It is, therefore, a contradictory story. It has to include not only an acceptance by women of the need for deference to men (Walker, 1987: 436), but also ringing challenges to authority epitomised by the saying which has become identified with women's resistance in South Africa: 'When you have struck a woman you have struck a rock.' Although the connections in this history of participation and resistance to dominance have still to be fully explored, I would argue that their foundations will be found in southern Africa's precapitalist societies, where women's labour and women's fertility, though appropriated by men, still provided the bedrock upon which these societies were built.

2

Fighting a two-pronged attack: The changing legal status of women in Cape-ruled Basutoland, 1872–1884[1]

SANDRA BURMAN

On 13 July 1874, in the Thaba Bosiu district of Basutoland,[2] a woman named Maseboko was found guilty of the crime of concealment of birth. It was a crime, the chief magistrate reported, 'to which, indeed, she *pleaded* guilty on being charged with "Infanticide," which latter charge however was not fully substantiated against her' (LA, CO 3232: Chief Magistrate to Colonial Secretary, 25.8.1874).[3] The case was considered too unimportant to warrant a mention in the magistrate's annual report (CPP, G21–75) but it illustrates a number of points of interest for our topic.

The evidence of Mantahani, Maseboko's husband, was that he had for some time suspected that she was pregnant and had recommended that she therefore wean the child she was still breastfeeding, but she had steadfastly denied her pregnancy. One night when he was sleeping in her hut, she had 'begun complaining of much pain in the lower part of her stomach and of purging'. She left the hut three times during the night. The third time her husband went out to look for her but, seeing her getting up from the ground, he went inside again. After she returned to the hut he heard his dog eating something outside. The next morning he saw marks of blood where she had been sitting in the night and asked her what it was, but she claimed it was her normal monthly period. Her husband told her to go and call his first wife, but she refused, asking why she should for such a cause, and similarly refused to call the headman's wife.

Then I desired her to show me her stomach that I might see if it was in the same state as before. At first she hesitated. After some time, however, she did show me her stomach and I said to her "You are not in the same state as you were. Where is the child that has been born?" She still denied that there had been any child born at all.

He examined the place where he had seen her the night before, but could find nothing.

After sleeping on the problem for a few days, he told the headman 'all that I had observed and what I thought about my wife Maseboko; how it seemed to me that she had been hiding from me her being pregnant and the birth of a child; which child I could only conclude had been eaten by the dog (my dog).' He was sorry he had not earlier pursued the question of his wife's pregnancy more insistently with her, but 'for the present I did not see what could be done. So for a short time the matter dropped between us.' Not long afterwards, 'Tlalele sent for me to the mountain where I had been cutting grass, and said I had better go to Maseru, as my wife had already been apprehended by the police. I told Tlalele I thought it was a great pity he had not let me know before. As I had no idea the police were going to take my wife, and he ought to have informed me of their intention to do so before.' A policeman, Maseboko, and Mantahani then travelled to Maseru. Mantahani's evidence ends with the statement: 'I am not the man that brings this case before the Court; Tlalele is the man that does so.' There is no direct evidence as to Tlalele's identity, but it seems likely that he was the local chief, to whom the headman had duly reported the matter.

Maseboko's statement, which constituted the only other evidence, is given here in full:

My husband accuses me of having concealed the birth of a child, which was born about a month ago, at the close of the last moon. I shall not deny that. I had been in the family way about 7 or 8 months and Mantahani (my husband) had often said to me 'Are you not pregnant?' and I had always denied it to him. The reason I did so was that I was still suckling my eldest child, now about 2 years old, and it is a shame for a woman to become pregnant whilst suckling her last born child. Gradually after denying many times that I was pregnant, I became so much afraid to confess, that I had deceived my husband in this matter, that when the time came for the birth of the child (about 3 weeks or a month ago) I went out of the hut the night I felt the pains of childbirth coming on and was confined in the open air, just outside (a few yards outside) the 'skerrem' [reed screen] of my hut. My husband Mantahani was sleeping inside this hut that night. The child was born dead; it had no life in it at all; and I left it lying on the ground where it was born. As I left it to return to the hut, my dog, the dog that always goes about with me (a big dog, one of the breed of 'boer' dogs), ran up to the place where I had just left the body of the still-born child; what the dog did there I don't know for I entered the hut. Next morning when I and Mantahani looked for the body of the child it was gone. There were no traces of it and no remains. I think it was eaten by the dog.

My only reason for concealing the birth of the child and for concealing my pregnancy, was that stated above, namely that I was too much ashamed to do so, as I was still suckling the child now with me here before the Court. My husband never accused me of adultery and has always been a good and kind husband to me.

It seems probable that Maseboko was telling the truth about her motivation for concealment. Not only was it a disgrace to become pregnant while still suckling an earlier child (which was considered 'spoilt' by the now 'infected' milk), but Sesotho law also viewed it as a crime (LA, B, *Mokhethi* v. *Panyane*, 26.4.1876). Maseboko's husband could face a fine for her pregnancy in those circumstances, a fine which he could avoid by pointing to his wife's lover as the culprit, if there were one. Moreover, Sesotho law gave the husband of an adulterous wife a right – frequently exercised – to claim damages from her lover. Yet neither financial considerations nor natural indignation caused Mantahani to accuse Maseboko of adultery. Rather, it does indeed appear that it was the strength of the society's taboo on conception in her circumstances that had made Maseboko deny her pregnancy. Initially she probably believed that pregnancy was impossible or very unlikely while she was still breastfeeding; by the time she realised that she was indeed pregnant, she was trapped in the web of her own denials.

What she would have done had the baby cried on birth, we cannot know, but it is possible that she might have resorted to infanticide, or even did so. In Sesotho law neither infanticide nor abortion was a crime (CPP, 1873, Appendix III: 44, 47) and there is evidence in the court records of lovers suggesting to their mistresses that they kill their babies to save the lovers from fines – and, presumably, from the social and possibly violent physical consequences of their actions (LA, E, *Jonas* v. *Khaowa*, 26.8.1879; F, *Sishemane* v. *Moqalane*, 4.2.1880). In certain cases, indeed, infanticide might be considered the necessary solution to the problem of an 'embarrassing' child, such as where the child was the result of an incestuous union and the anger of the ancestors had to be allayed. Given a choice, then, between on the one hand concealing the birth of her baby, and on the other admitting to a crime which would disgrace her husband and herself, as well as 'spoil' the first child and lay her husband open to a fine, Maseboko's course of action was, if anything, that of a dutiful wife and mother faced with unpleasant alternatives. No doubt her husband's realisation of all this accounts for his hesitant behaviour in seeking to discuss the problem with his headman, and the bemused tone of his evidence in what followed.

The factor without which both he and Maseboko had reckoned, however, was the introduction of colonial rule some five years earlier, under which system infanticide was declared a crime. Until then, in so far as they would have thought of it at all, they had probably regarded the alien government as generally benevolent, embodied in a distant white man whom, indeed, they may never have seen. Now they were suddenly confronted both with its power to intervene in their lives and with the totally foreign way in which it interpreted and responded to what had happened.

Maseboko's case was an extreme example of a woman caught in the clash of two normative systems, but was far from unique. In practice, from the very nature of the differences between the two societies, women bore the brunt of the collision. This chapter explores this collision and the impact on women of the changes to the Sesotho legal system introduced in the period of Cape rule. After a brief discussion on the dearth of sources that present a female point of view, it looks at the conflict of values in the colonial and Sesotho legal systems and then discusses the position of women under Sesotho law in some detail. The chapter goes on to analyse the changes to the legal status of women introduced by Cape rule and concludes by considering whether these were ultimately of benefit to women or not.

WOMEN'S VOICES

What is particularly valuable about Maseboko's case is that even though the evidence is limited, it provides a clearer than usual glimpse into the world of a Basotho woman of that period. As is so frequently the case in southern Africa, what information exists on the way Basotho women viewed their lives tends to be filtered through the pens of Europeans, often missionary and almost always male. However, Lesotho is fortunate in having received, at Moshoeshoe's invitation, young and sympathetic missionaries as early as 1833 – men who greatly admired the exceptionally able and impressive ruler of the country, and who subsequently devoted their lives to understanding the society in which they worked. Their children grew up there, mingling almost exclusively with the Basotho in their early years (as no settler society was allowed to develop in Basutoland), speaking the language fluently, and subsequently adding their numbers to the list of the first magistrates and clerks of the administration. Moreover, several wrote about their views and experiences articulately and at length. But only one of those writers was a woman, Adèle Mabille (née Casalis), the daughter of a missionary, who married another Basutoland missionary and subscribed to the missionaries' values where they clashed with those of the Basotho. Other writers dealt at least briefly with the country during the period of Cape rule – notably soldiers, missionaries, even a doctor. Yet in this category, again only one was a woman – Fanny Barkly, the upper-class English wife of the nephew of the former British Governor. She spent some time in Basutoland while her husband served as a magistrate, but although her descriptions are fascinating, she did not have the advantage either of understanding the language or of a southern African childhood. The overwhelming impression conveyed by her description of a meeting between herself and the wives of a chief is how strange she and the Basotho women found each other, even while they were exchanging gifts and communicating through an interpreter. Their one point of contact was provided by her children; she reported that the women 'were much delighted with Harry and Nancy [the Barkly toddlers] and played with them a great deal' (Barkly, 1894: 31).

Thus the viewpoints of Basotho women remain shrouded in obscurity. There are almost no descriptions of how women behaved, apart from those who were, by definition, exceptions: prophetesses or, occasionally, women on mission stations. Women did not attend the big public gatherings, reported *verbatim* by government interpreters, at which the nation's future was discussed and decided; they did not fight in battle; they did not negotiate with the enemy; they did not usually receive and talk to visiting officials or other European strangers to the country. Their voices emerge largely from snippets of reported conversation, or from the few court records that survived the ravages of the Gun War which ended Cape rule. And there they frequently come to us through the stilted words of interpreters and official verbiage.

CONFLICTING VALUES

Unlike colonial rule in most of southern Africa, British administration arrived in Basutoland at the earnest and oft-repeated invitation of Moshoeshoe, the paramount chief, who had rightly seen that in British protection lay his last hope of saving his people from the depredations of the land-hungry Boers of the adjacent Orange Free State. Britain eventually stepped in reluctantly in 1868 with a minimal administration of three magistrates, who were fully occupied in trying to enforce the tenuous peace agreement reached with the Orange Free State; the Boers had been winning the most recent war against the Basotho and bitterly resented Britain's involvement. In 1871, as soon as it was settled that the British colony at the Cape would obtain responsible government the following year, Britain handed over direct administration of Basutoland to Colonel Charles Griffith. With his tiny team of four magistrates and a handful of police, he became responsible to the Cape government.[4]

However, by then the chiefs had largely regained their former position over their people. Towards the end of the war with the Orange Free State, traditional organisation had begun to break down as defeat forced people to disperse and eroded their confidence in their chiefs to such an extent that in many cases they refused to obey or even acknowledge them. But when the British government intervened, and fear of a major Boer attack receded, most Basotho discovered that the only authorities able to settle cases were the chiefs, who took the opportunity to recover their control. Thus Griffith and his magistrates found themselves dealing with a people for whom the memory of past obligations was fading, led by chiefs very wary of incursions into their newly regained power.

Moreover, the Cape government had accepted responsibility for Basutoland with great reluctance and on the understanding that the territory would pay for its own administration and policing. Griffith was therefore well aware that hut-tax collection and the enforcement of Cape-made laws could only be achieved with the cooperation of the chiefs. What followed, then, was a very careful and – until the policy of disarmament focussed discontent – successful encroachment on the chiefs' powers, achieved by a delicate process of compromise and negotiation in constructing a network of trust and mutual interest. In the area of law enforcement, for example, the chiefs' courts continued to operate but were forbidden to use force to ensure that a judgment was obeyed. Certain criminal cases were always to be sent to the magistrates' courts, to which civil cases could also be appealed or taken in the first instance. There the magistrates sought to amend or limit those aspects of Sesotho law most repugnant to the colonial authorities without overthrowing the system of customary law in its entirety.

In seeking to change a colonised society's legal system, colonial powers are likely to have least success with personal and family law. These both shape and result from the fabric of the society itself, embodying its values, structure and status system. Unless the society is radically restructured, changes in one or two aspects of family law are frequently either ignored or, if enforced, set off social dislocations which arouse deeply felt emotions and beliefs. Unfortunately for both British and Basotho, the prevailing belief in Britain and the Cape Colony was that it was their Christian duty to 'civilise' the African. The 'civilisation' to be introduced was that of Victorian England, with its firm belief in the superior virtues of a way of life rooted in Christianity, a profit-seeking economy, and a consequently necessary high degree of protection for the individual from the demands of the group. Basotho society, on the other hand, had developed to meet different economic and strategic requirements and as a result was based on different values.

The administration could not, therefore, hope to enforce government laws which challenged those values without the cooperation of the chiefs. Some changes were less likely than others to gain such cooperation. For instance chiefs, who were more likely than commoners to have more than one wife and also benefited in various indirect ways from the institution of polygyny (see Burman, 1981: 10, 193), were generally unwilling to assist with measures that obviously attacked polygyny. On the other hand, the criminalisation of the concealment of birth and of infanticide – the latter made an offence at the suggestion of Griffith and his magistrates (CA, CO 3193, Governor's Agent to Governor, 22.8.1871) – would have seemed far less repugnant, especially where linked, as in Maseboko's case, to a violation of the taboo against becoming pregnant while still breastfeeding an earlier child. The Basotho placed high value on children and although the society did not punish infanticide, it seems that such behaviour was generally viewed with disfavour and was rare.[5] In a situation where chiefs and administrators were engaged in a constant manoeuvring for position and where proof of cooperation by a chief was likely to gain a reciprocally helpful attitude from the magistrate next time some administrative favour was required, a chief was likely to seize upon cases which could be referred to the magistrate without endangering his (the chief's) own interests. This may well have been the reason that Maseboko's case reached the court of the Assistant Magistrate of Mafeteng, at least a day's journey from her village; and so she found herself caught between two conflicting sets of values, punished by one society for behaving according to the norms of the other as best she could in a difficult situation.

THE POSITION OF WOMEN IN SESOTHO LAW

To understand the implications of the rights given to women by the British administration in several sets of regulations during the 1870s, as well as the opposition they aroused, a brief outline of the operation of the relevant parts of the Sesotho legal system is necessary.

As in the other African societies of southern Africa, the Basotho had an essentially subsistence economy, with the homestead the main unit of production in an economy dependent principally on both agriculture and pastoralism. The sexual division of labour conformed to the pattern already sketched by Guy in chapter 1. Women and girls did most of the labour-intensive agricultural work, as well as the preparation of food, while men and boys were responsible for the pastoral activities and the defence of the cattle. (They were also the hunters, although hunting was usually a relatively minor source of food.) If the homestead head had more than one wife, each wife and her children would usually have a separate household and constitute a separate legal entity or 'house'. Each house had its own cattle and fields, formed a semi-independent unit of production, and supplied the homestead head and its own members with food and other requirements.

This system gave women a form of power neatly illustrated by the following dilemma faced by Moshoeshoe, the paramount chief, who made a large number of marriages for diplomatic reasons:

No doubt Moshoeshoe treated his wives with the tact and discretion that were habitual to him, but even so it was impossible for him to smooth out all their rivalries and jealousies. Indeed he once confessed to Casalis [one of the first missionaries in Lesotho] that there were times when, in spite of his immense wealth, he was almost starved because no one would feed him: he would wander pathetically from hut to hut, being told by each offended and sulking wife to go to his favourite, whoever she might be, since no doubt she would have some tasty morsel for him (Sanders, 1975: 140–1).

It was, nevertheless, a male-dominated structure in which the control of women was central. Women provided labour themselves, in the fields and in producing and rearing children, as well as for the future, in the form of their children, whose labour was also important for the homestead. Women were exchanged for bridewealth (termed *bohali*) which was given mainly in the form of cattle supplied by their husband's families. If the majority of their offspring were girls, these daughters would subsequently bring in a surplus of cattle to the homestead when they married, while male offspring constituted essential heirs.

Men's control of this system was based on their control of the cattle, the source of their wives as well as of dairy products and skins, and on control of the allocation of land, which provided the bulk of the food. The legal system had developed to preserve this system. It stressed the priority of the homestead, if necessary at the expense of what the British viewed as individual freedom, particularly that of the women, on whom the continuance of the family depended. Family law was thus the most highly developed aspect of Sesotho law and the one that would most affect Basotho society if changed. It was also the branch of local law containing most of the concepts that Victorians found offensive in Basotho society, such as polygyny, bridewealth and the levirate. The changes introduced by the missionaries and colonial administration were usually incompatible with it, leading to angry reactions from the men, who realised that their authority was being eroded. The result was that often, even when women were not caught between conflicting norms of the two different societies, as in Maseboko's case, they had to fight their own society if they were to avail themselves of the rights extended to them by the new order. Nor is it clear that these rights, derived from an alien society, were necessarily of good service to them.

The family head

Under Sesotho law legal authority over all the members of the extended family (which could spread over several homesteads) vested in its head. This was normally a man, since inheritance operated on a system of male primogeniture. Women were regarded as perpetual minors and only in exceptional circumstances did a woman become the head of a family. Changes by the colonial administration to this basic legal concept were to meet with strong opposition from the men of Basutoland. Sesotho marriage was at least potentially polygynous, although in practice many commoners had only one wife. Chiefs, particularly the higher chiefs, had several. Under the authority of the family head would be not only his wife or wives and their children, but any of his own younger brothers as well as those of his father who had not set up their own establishments on marriage, along with all their wives and descendants. There might also be some more distant relatives or non-kin who had voluntarily placed themselves under the head's power as clients, having lost or abandoned their own natural family heads; in effect they became part of the family.

The family head represented everyone in his establishment, making all binding contracts and, theoretically, holding all property (except such personal items as clothing and weapons) in trust for it. He had the power to sue and be sued on behalf of all the homestead's members and to dispose of the younger men and women in marriage. His authority was reinforced by the belief that he was the direct representative of the ancestors and the mediator between the living and departed members of the family. In practice, however, the arbitrary exercise of power by the head of the family was limited by custom requiring consultation with the senior men of the family, his natural affection for its members, and the fear of both public opinion and punishment by the spirits. This meant that in fact, if not in theory, there was a large degree of collective responsibility which made the whole family liable for, among other debts, those incurred if the marriage of one of its members broke up. The introduction of the concept of an age of majority by the colonial administration, as well as changes to the marriage law to provide for Christian and civil marriages, thus had economic effects on people other than only the married couple.

Marriage

Marriages were arranged by the elders of the two families involved and generally were contracts of convenience; romance seldom entered into it, although frequently a very real affection would later develop between the couple. Casalis, for example, describing his first visit to Moshoeshoe, drew a picture of the paramount's contented domesticity with his principal wife, 'MaMohato:

Mamohato was a tall and strong woman, already of somewhat ripe age, but not wanting in attractions…. Moshesh seated himself by her side, and took the youngest son Ntalimi, a little boy between four and five, between his knees. The apparently perfect union between these two, and the perfect cordiality mingled with respect with which they addressed and offered little services to each other, greatly struck me (1889: 179–80).

But the interests of the family did not necessarily coincide with the wishes of its marriageable members, and girls were sometimes forced into marriages they did not want. The colonial administration's divorce court records contain a number of cases testifying to this, such as the following evidence given by one Ramosala:

Ever since my girlhood I refused to have Modise. He courted me and I refused. He went to Mofuoa [Ramosala's father] and asked his permission. Mofuoa went and fetched me against my will – he told Mofuoa that I was willing. I always told him I wouldn't have him. He gave 16 cattle and 22 sheep....I have never loved him or had anything to do with him. My father said I must go – and I cried & said I did not love me [*sic*]. I went by force – and remained a month or two – I came away because I didn't love him.... Afterwards, Modiko, the man whom I loved with a love strong as death came and fetched me. I had one child by Modiko and I now live with his brother & I have now one by him. Jani [presumably for Modise] gave me strong medicines to make me love him & I have a weak head ever since. He got the medicine from two mahowas [whites]. I was very sick after I took the medicines and feel the effects of it to this day. He has also been very unkind to me and beat me (LA, A, *Modise* v. *Mofuoa*, 26.9.1874).

Moreover, given the *bohali* system, even a compliant woman could suffer the consequences of her husband being forced into an unwelcome marriage, as the following testimony by one Tebela indicates:

I was married to Hlweyane. He hated me from the first and beat me saying I was black & my mother was a witch. He was always hitting me to go away. He used to rouse me at night & drive me away – he said he wanted his cattle back to marry a light coloured woman – I was too black for him. This kept on, my father taking me back – I persevered – I thought that it was the way all men behaved to their wives.... I never had a child to him – he never loved me. He had already got disgusted at his marriage before I went to him. He said I was a flirt and that I was disobedient – and that I was too black (LA, A, *Hlweyane* v. *Masakale*, 7.7.1875).

Marriage by elopement was used to some extent to overcome the opposition of elders to a particular match, but whether such elopements were on the increase in the period under consideration is unclear. One witness in an 1876 case reported that his sister was married off by the cousins with whom she had been living, without his (senior) branch of the family being consulted. His protests were met by the words: 'The child is yours but she was growing up and might have run away & then you would have fallen on us – for the modern girl if she loves a young man either elopes with him or else gets in the family way among the pots' (LA, C, *Ra-Lesola* v. *MaMaloi & Thlale*, 22.11.1876). Where the girl was unmarried, the elders generally acquiesced in the elopement but exacted a fine as well as the customary marriage payment for the bride. Where, however, the marriage was not allowed, the man would be liable to pay damages for seduction to the girl's family. In contrast to European law, this was because an unmarried woman represented the potential value of her marriage cattle, which would be lessened by her seduction, and Sesotho law afforded the head of the family redress for the violation of any right representing material value. This differed from the European (and therefore missionary) way of viewing seduction as an offence against the girl herself, for affront to her dignity.

Cases involving elopement were brought before the colonial magistrates on occasion, usually when the couple could not be found, as in the case of one Moshiane. The irate father was given permission by the chief magistrate to take charge of all Moshiane's cattle and other property in the village 'until such time as he can bring an action against him in one of the Basutoland Courts of Law' (LA, S9/2/2/3, Chief Magistrate to George Moshoeshoe, 7.12.1878). But the administration intervened where possible to protect the girl in such situations, on the basis of the right granted by its regulations to all adults, women as well as men, of majority status on attaining a given age. Thus the Assistant Resident Magistrate of Thaba Bosiu District could write to a Catholic missionary at Roma in 1880:

With reference to your letter of the 6th instant, on the subject of the elopement, to Matatiele, of Sathlana of Mohkokhong with Mathias's daughter, I have the honour to inform you that if the girl is of age – viz. 21 years old, she is a free agent, & nothing can be done, except that the Father can claim a dowry, if both he & the girl are heathens, or if, had the girl got married in the ordinary course of events, a dowry would have been paid.

But if the girl is a *minor* the Father can sue Sathlana for damages.

And lastly, if *force* on the part of Sathlana can be proved a criminal action can be brought (LA, S9/2/3/1, Asst. Res. Magistrate, Thaba Bosiu, to Father Le Bihan, 27.4.1880).

If the girl was a minor, the magistrates would assist the father in pursuing the eloping pair, writing to magistrates in neighbouring territories to detain the couple (e.g. L2/1/1, Res. Magistrate, Leribe, to Res. Magistrate, Herschel, 1.10.1878). The criminal case registers also contain a few cases where men convicted of seduction (probably of Christian girls) were sentenced to imprisonment with hard labour.

Bridewealth

In customary law there were few essential requirements for a marriage to be valid: simply the consent of the contracting parties (though not necessarily of the couple involved), and usually payment or arrangements for payment of an agreed number of marriage cattle for the bride. These were distributed in set ways within the bride's family circle, with her *malome* (maternal uncle) having a claim to a large share, in return for which he also had special responsibility to the girl and her subsequent offspring. There is also evidence that formal acceptance of the marriage by the husband was required at the *tlhabiso* ceremony. This was described by Moshoeshoe's son Sofonia to the 1872 commission on Sesotho law as follows:

A marriage is said to be completed when the father of the bride has slaughtered an animal or animals as 'mafura', with the fat of which the bride and
bridegroom are anointed, and the bridegroom has the gall bladders put round
his wrist. If the bridegroom refuses to have the gall bladders put on his wrist
it is a sign that he does not like the bride, and the marriage is dissolved, the
cattle are returned, and the animals slaughtered by the bride's father are paid
for by the bridegroom or his friends (CPP, 1873, Appendix III: 49).

All other customs associated with marriage could be omitted without affecting the validity of the marriage, but these three elements
were usually considered essential, for reasons readily understandable
in the light of the role of women and cattle in the society.[6] Attacks by
the missionaries and government officials on the giving of marriage
cattle were, therefore, seen as attacks on customary marriage.

It is important to note that the payment of marriage cattle was not
regarded as payment for a purchase. The Basotho used a specific word
to denote the handing over of the marriage cattle, distinct from that
used for the payment for goods. Neither were women regarded as
objects: they could not be bought, sold, exchanged or destroyed at
will, nor given away. These points were not, however, always understood by the colonial authorities.

There were practical arguments for and against the system. Marriage payment was regarded as security given by the husband for his
own good conduct towards his wife, for if she left him because of
ill-treatment, he lost his claim for the return of the cattle; these were
then meant to provide for the woman's needs if she returned to her
parental home. Attacks on bridewealth were, therefore, attacks on the
society's insurance system for ill-treated wives. *Bohali* was also partially a payment to the father for his consent to the marriage, whereby
he lost the services of his daughter and her future children; unless the
marriage cattle were paid, the children generally remained under the
authority of the woman's family. Finally, it also guaranteed the good
behaviour of the wife to some extent because, if she left her husband
without just cause, he could claim back the marriage payment. Rather
than surrender it, her family would do everything possible to effect a
reconciliation. However, in practice, where it was unclear who was at
fault, the threat of a claim for a *bohali* refund might lead to wives being
forced to return to their husbands against their will. As a result, there
were no doubt pressures on an unhappy wife to find an alternative
man, either to pay her aggrieved family fresh *bohali* or, at least, to
protect her from their wrath. Moreover, since the giving of *bohali*
transferred the children of the marriage into the husband's family, a
wife would not normally be allowed to take her children with her if
she forsook her husband, even where she was the innocent party,

driven away by him.

In Basotho society many court cases arose from the network of debts created by the marriage payment obligations. Payment of the cattle did not always take place before the marriage. A man's family would usually provide the cattle for his first wife at least, but these cattle might become available only when his sister married and marriage cattle were received for her. If the cattle were not forthcoming from his family, a man might marry on long-term credit, promising to pay all or the balance of the cattle when the first daughter of the marriage was herself married, the marriage cattle received for her thus in effect paying for her mother. As debts were not wiped out by death, it was not considered an insuperable obstacle if there was a delay of many years before payment, even if, for example, a daughter was not born of the marriage. If all else failed, the chief's patronage might supply the essential cattle, sometimes in return for a form of clientage.[7]

Women and property

Marriage had the result of transferring to the husband the guardianship over not only the children that resulted from the union but the wife as well, although the woman's own family did retain an ultimate guardianship over her all her life. However, since each wife's house was allotted livestock and land for cultivation, she was given the right to protect these. She could appeal to the head of the village against her husband's (or his heir's) misuse of this property and, if not satisfied, to the chief himself, despite the normal rule that she could not act for herself in court. No house could be enriched at the expense of another and, by custom, any dealings with the property that attached to a house were usually undertaken by the husband in consultation with the wife in question, as well as with her eldest son when he became old enough. The head of the homestead was also expected to provide marriage cattle for his sons, wedding outfits for his daughters, and maintenance for his wives and dependants, who in turn provided for his daily needs from their allocation of land and livestock.

This system resulted in some women acquiring considerable property in practice and even, it would seem, in theory, with their ownership acknowledged by their families and communities, if the language of subsequent magistrate's court cases is not misleading. For example, the records exude the energy, acquisitiveness and determination of one such woman, Makubutu, as she and her lover argued before the magistrate over property she had acquired under Sesotho law and practice before the arrival of the colonial administration. She had been widowed, then divorced, and had then, at her suggestion, lived with one Makolometse, a rich man, as his mistress for some seventeen or eighteen years. She had, however, refused to marry him, thereby causing her three daughters by him – and their *bohali* – to remain under the guardianship of her son Adriaan, the representative of her deceased husband. An aggrieved Makolometse, taken to court by her for refusing to surrender certain property to her on their proposed separation as a result of a quarrel, expostulated:

She makes me angry when she says I drive her away. I wanted to pay for her & legitimize the children I had by her. She refused, saying she wouldn't have cattle given for her to her brother Motseko who is her enemy. She refused. She is still in my charge – she is not at Adriaan's – I pay her tax. She has 7 children & grandchildren all supported by me. She has been very wicked to me – and I have been very generous & careful of her all these years…. She came to me poor and she is now one of the richest women in Basutoland all through the care which I have taken of her and her interests (LA, A, *Makubutu* alias *Ma-Adriaan* v. *Makolometse*, 23.9.1874).

Makubutu's enumeration of the various types of property which she claimed provides an interesting insight into some of the avenues open to women for property acquisition in precolonial days, as well as attitudes towards these:

The property I claim is as follows:– Makolometse asked me to bring up a little girl of a wife of his who had died. The child was a suckling and Makolometse lent me a cow to milk for it – and said that if I brought up the child I should receive the cow called 'letsuele' (given for bringing up to the child's mother). I brought up the child her mother having died in childbirth of her. The girl grew up – she was taken from my charge some months after on acct. of my being in the family way. She is now married. After the marriage he refused to give me the 'Khomo ea letsuele' saying it would be his for his dead wife, and he gave me a young cow calf instead to which I agreed. Now he draws back from his promise and will not give it me saying that it is dead. I tell him this is unfair for they were going to bury the child with its mother if I hadn't saved its life. I carried the matter before Nkau who decided in my favour. Def[endan]t. says he will give me the cow – but that is only a verbal promise, and in a Colonial court of law I am sure I should get at least 5 head of cattle – and that is why I have come before this court.

In the second place I claim a share of the corn because my son Adrian's [*sic*] cattle helped to plough. This Def[endan]t. refused.

The goats I claim is on acct. of wheat Motseko my brother in 1866 sent for me to help him to reap – and gave me a sack. I kept 2 buckets of seed and we ate the rest. The two buckets were sown. Rasekhala bought some of the produce with a sheep. Subsequently he asked me for the sheep and gave me a goat instead. Makolometse took the lamb of the sheep however and paid it away for one of his young wives.

The next was a pig was given me by Mongote which we slaughtered – and for the fat bought a goat which had two goats – but was used by Makolometse – and he gave me one instead of it which is however lost. I don't quarrel with him about that – the he-goat he slaughtered at his daughter's wedding the same girl I brought up – and there is one she-goat left of that lot. That is all I claim. I want my hands to be washed clean of the stigma of being a Bushwo-man without property which is what Makolometse calls me (ibid.).

In the evidence it emerged that Makolometse had also given Adriaan, in addition to the *bohali* of his and Makubutu's only married daughter, five head of cattle and five goats acquired from corn grown by Makubutu; this Adriaan presumably held in trust for her. Mako-lometse's son, giving evidence that his father was not refusing the calf that Makubutu claimed but merely delaying until it had been weaned, ended his evidence with a revealing remark: 'I do not know why she says that my father refuses to give it to her. There are plenty of witnesses & my father would never dare to refuse' (ibid.).

Other cases also show how women could acquire livestock or corn on their own account, without the aid of the colonial magistrates. In one case the single daughter of a divorced woman was selling maize on her own account to a trader after being paid for harvesting (LA, A, *Senqu* v. *Mamathiso* and *Mphulanyane*, 2.6.1875); in another a woman was given a cow voluntarily by her husband as compensation for a beating he had administered when she had tried to intervene to prevent him from making her much-abused daughter return yet again to a vindictive husband (LA, A, *Hlweyane* v. *Masakale*, 7.7.1875). In a third case a widow paid all her dead husband's debts by selling her crop and giving over the five sheep she had earned from the sale of needlework in the Orange Free State (LA, B, *Moramafaru* v. *Khaba-nyane*, 2.2.1876). The records also contain various instances of women who earned money or livestock in service in the Cape Colony or the Orange Free State. Thus even before magisterial intervention, it seems that women's position in customary law in relation to the ownership of property was changing. The unwritten nature of customary law made considerable flexibility possible as circumstances altered.

The increased acceptance of women acquiring property opened avenues for an able woman to use her property to obtain rank, service and an increase in her sons' wealth – a development which the magistrates encouraged. In giving judgment in a dispute over succes-sion, for example, a magistrate summed up the story which had emerged from the lengthy evidence:

the deceased Serobanyane had two mistresses, the first arrival being Ma-Mo-sukulane (Def[endant]'s mother) and the second Ma-Mathetsa, Romoroke's mother. Neither were married & therefore until a marriage took place there could be no question of priority between them. Ma-Mathetsa receives a present of beads from her brother. With these beads medicines are purchased from Khamoaditlane and then Serobanyane and Ma-Mathetsa go to the Colony leaving Ma-Mosukulane with her friends. In the Colony they work and prosper – the man amassing cattle and Ma-Mathetsa also earning a cow, the produce of mats which she made. On their return Ma-Mathetsa induces her husband to pay for Ma-Mosukulane in order to possess herself of Mosukulane & the other children she has had by diverse fathers in his absence. He does so with the cattle earned by their joint industry, most of which were the produce of the medicines bought with her beads. Now it is evident no woman would willingly give up the first place in order with the sweat of her brow to purchase that place for an unworthy rival. No, she knew that the fact of the cows being partly hers would place Ma-Mosukulane in the lower position. Then she warns her husband that her own position must be regularized, or her friends may claim her, her children, her earnings and her 'wife' Ma-Mosukulane at any moment. Her husband takes her advice and sends cattle to her friends. She is now a wife, and in Sesotho law she is the husband, i.e. the proprietor more so than the man. Then she wants a maid & induces her husband to purchase Ma-Kapane alias Ma-Ditlane, a woman of her own tribe and who was an ugly old maid supposed to be barren. This Ma-Ditlane, being such a despicable object, is purchased cheaply with 3 head of cattle, the cow Ma-Mathetsa got for mats and its two calves. The woman turns out a good bargain and bears 3 daughters and two sons....

Ma-Mathetsa is thus in the position of having by her cleverness and good luck enabled her husband to pay for all three wives and cannot in justice be denied the place of chief wife... (LA, B, *Kapane* v. *Mosukulane*, 17.12.1875).

Dissolution of marriage

As with 'her' property, a wife's person was in practice, if not in law, quite well protected under customary law. Although in theory the power of the husband over his wife was considered absolute in everything except the actual taking of her life, in reality his family had an incentive to prevent consistently brutal treatment since, should she run home to her family because of ill-treatment, the latter had a legal right to demand additional cattle to those already given for her and to keep her until their demands were met. If she utterly refused to return to her husband, she could not be compelled to do so, and the records abound with cases of women who did indeed refuse.

Some, however, endured considerable ill-treatment before their families would accept their refusal. The evidence in the case of *'Majoro' of the Leribe District* v. *'Ramolawa', widow of Ramothapeke, now living at Lebelo's village in A. Matete's ward in the District of Thaba Bosigo*, for example, contains a long record of attempts by the woman to return to her family but each time being forced by them to return to her husband – on at least one occasion being thrashed by her brother to force her to do so. Eventually she flatly refused to return to her husband, 'saying she would rather be killed. She had scars all over her body from a thrashing he had given her.' Her father refused to accept the beast her husband brought to try to induce her family to force her to return, for fear she might commit suicide (LA, D, No. 38 of 1877, 15.11.1877).

A woman might take refuge with her *malome*, some other relative, or a lover if her guardian was unsympathetic. Her husband could demand the refund of her marriage cattle but if there had been children born of the marriage, who, as usually happened, were retained as members of his family, the refund would often be only partial, even if the husband was not at fault. However, where no refund took place, separation from her husband might not end the woman's troubles; in the *Majoro* case above, for example, the woman's eldest son, on succeeding his father, brought a case to force his mother, along with her subsequent children, to return to live at his place. In all cases of dissolution of marriage, whether any or part or all of the marriage cattle were forfeited would depend on the circumstances, including whether there were children of the marriage.

The Sesotho laws governing the dissolution of marriage differed from European legal systems, which caused problems with the colonial magistrates and missionaries. A husband, for example, might obtain a divorce unilaterally by expelling his wife from his homestead with the intention of permanently discarding her (in which case he forfeited the marriage cattle). In contrast to contemporary Roman-Dutch law, which applied in the Cape Colony, adultery on the part of the wife was not necessarily a sufficient cause for divorce, unless it was incestuous or otherwise grossly offended Sesotho morality – although the husband could claim damages from the man involved, and any child born as a result of the adultery was regarded as the child of the husband. Where a chief had a great many wives, adultery by a minor wife might, indeed, be sanctioned by him. Moshoeshoe's wives, for example, as with the wives of other major chiefs, were divided into three broad categories:

... namely, 'the great wife', in his case 'MaMohato; 'important wives', who were 'women of position', and became 'the mothers of important men'; and *lingoetsi*, who were junior wives who were attached as servants 'to the houses of the more important wives, two or three or even more to each house, according to its importance'. [Ellenberger, 1912: 279] The distinction between the second and third categories was blurred in some cases, but generally, while he jealously guarded his rights over 'MaMohato and his 'important wives', he allowed visitors and retainers to form illicit relationships with the *lingoetsi*, although their children were regarded as his (Sanders, 1975: 140).

Such arrangements were not confined to chiefs. A man might 'give' one of his wives to a younger brother, for example, or even, it appears, attempt to 'give' his wife to his own lover's husband (LA, AA, *The Queen* v. *Taoane*, 18.4.1874). It would seem, however, that even much-married men did not necessarily take a liberal view of their minor wives' adultery where they had not sanctioned it. The files, for example, contain a letter from the magistrate of Leribe notifying the Governor's Agent that one Private Motsibi, of the Basutoland Police, had been sent back to Maseru, as he has twice been found by the Chief Molapo [Moshoeshoe's son, who ranked second only to the paramount chief after the death of his father] in the huts of his wives – the first time he was fined by me £6 for criminal conv[er-sation]; the second time he was beaten out of the premises by Molapo himself and his watchman.

After the first case I gave orders that no policeman was to go to Molapo's village after dark, but this man as well as others have disobeyed these orders.

The men who came from Maseru, Chief Constable included, having no wives here are much given to visit Molapo's village to beg food, and the policemen give much annoyance to the Chief by their nocturnal prowling among the huts of his wives (LA, L2/1/1, Res. Magistrate to Governor's Agent, 4.9.1874).

It would seem that either affront to dignity or indignation that non-retainers should enjoy favours free, rather than jealousy, played a major part in Molapo's anger, since it could not have been more than five years later that he is recorded as complaining to the Leribe doctor of his seventy wives: 'What do I want with these girls? I am an old man now, and yet I have to go on marrying fresh wives to keep up my position in the eyes of my people, though they are a terrible nuisance to me' (Hadley, 1972: 43). Quite possibly much the same motivation caused Masopha, the chief next in importance to Molapo, to go so far as to charge a man in the court of his district magistrate for the crime of adultery with one of his wives (though it is not clear how senior she was). The magistrate sentenced the adulterer 'to be imprisoned and kept at hard labour for three years' – a sentence which the Governor's Agent allowed to stand despite the practice of no longer prosecuting adultery in the Cape Colony, since Masopha was 'much enraged' and it was feared he might take the law into his own hands (LA, S9/1/2/1, Governor's Agent to Sec. for Native Affairs, 20.9.1876; 20.10.1876). On occasion minor chiefs – and probably com-moners – did precisely that when an adulterer was caught in the act (e.g. LA, MF2/1/1, Res. Magistrate to Acting Governor's Agent, 29.7.1878). Nonetheless, particularly for young wives of elderly hus-bands with large establishments, there were no doubt strong reasons to encourage outsiders' advances, even at the risk of a severe beating on the orders of an enraged spouse.

When a marriage was dissolved the husband usually remained the guardian of the children, provided he had paid marriage cattle, although if they were too young to be taken from the mother's care, she might be allowed to keep them until they were older. They then had to be returned to the father, an arrangement the missionaries opposed. The woman was entitled to take from the joint property only her personal belongings. In contrast to Roman–Dutch law, marriages under Sesotho law were usually dissolved extra-judicially, by agree-ment between the families of the couple concerned. Outside intervention would be required only if they failed to agree, in which case the chief or headman would be called in to arbitrate. Thereafter, a woman's family had a duty to support her unless she remarried. The legal necessity, introduced by the colonial administration, of judicial intervention to dissolve a Christian or civil marriage, was to cause many problems when people failed to understand that family agreement had not dissolved their marriages in the eyes of the colonial law.

The sororate and the levirate

In customary law the death of the husband did not dissolve the marriage – his widow continued to be a 'wife' of his family. Although the death of the wife dissolved the union, it did not necessarily end the existence of the house created by the marriage. When a wife died (and even while she was alive in certain circumstances) a husband could marry another woman and place her in the house of his former wife to 'raise up seed' for that house. Where a wife died after a short time without having borne children, her husband might be offered another girl from his deceased wife's family (usually for half the original number of marriage cattle); usually the woman's younger sister went to take her place. Her children were counted as the children of the original wife of the house.

This institution of the sororate influenced the thinking of all sections of the community as regards marriage. Confusion as to such women's status no doubt resulted when the Governor's Agent refused to sanction such marriages among Christians, on the grounds that marriage to a deceased wife's sister was illegal under Cape Colonial law in that period (LA, S9/1/3/3, Acting Governor's Agent to Res. Magistrate, Cornet Spruit, 17.7.1878). The attitudes which generated the sororate reverberate through the pages of the extant record book of civil law divorces for the period, for instance in the testimony of Anna Khetla, a defendant in such a case:

the Pl[ainti]ff has told the truth. I left him because he has committed adultery with other women. I was barren and did not bear any children to him – I was laughed at by his concubines and treated with great disrespect by both Pl[ainti]ff & his concubines – he neglected me also – and I then made up my mind to leave him, which I did, and have remained away from him ever since (LA, Civil Divorce Book, *Antoni Khetla* v. *Anna Khetla*, No. 2 of 1873, 13.8.1873).

The centrality of childbearing in the Sesotho conceptualisation of marriage is further exemplified by the levirate provisions in Sesotho law, which ensured that a man had heirs even when his own death or failure to produce a male heir intervened. In Sesotho law anything that could be done by a man by way of 'raising seed' for himself during his lifetime could be done for him after his death. Marriage cattle could be paid out of his estate for a 'seed-raiser', and a man, usually a male relative, selected to take his place in the marriage.[8] Even if a son died unmarried, a marriage could be created for him in this way. Further, a man who had never had a son at all could pay *bohali* for a wife for an imagined son. Yet another type of marriage was occasionally arranged when a widow who had no children would act as a man by paying *bohali* for another woman. The widow would then appoint a male relative to cohabit with her 'wife' and the children would belong to her, since she had paid the *bohali*. The *Kapane* case above shows a variation of such arrangements.

The motive behind all these arrangements, which the missionaries regarded as immoral, was to obtain a male heir at all costs. Z. K. Matthews described the beliefs that gave rise to this practice and reduced the ultimate value of a daughter:

the man who has no male heir cannot have his name perpetuated in the group to which he belongs; he leaves no one to sacrifice to the ancestral spirits; no one to settle the disputes that will arise out of the distribution of his estate and to act as guardian over his children (1934: 163).

He might have added that for a woman, a son of her household to safeguard her interests in widowhood was also highly desirable.

Since the death of her husband did not dissolve her marriage, a widow was expected to remain with her husband's family, to bring up her children, assist with the work and – although she could not be forced to do so – to have further children by a relative of her husband, chosen by his family. These children would be regarded as the children of her dead husband. If she chose to return to her own homestead instead (or, if she were a Christian, to live on a mission station), her guardian was liable to refund at least part of her *bohali*. Alternatively she might be allowed to return to live with her own family without a demand for a refund of her marriage cattle, but in that case she was still regarded as part of her husband's family. If she married again, whether the marriage cattle paid by her new husband went to her father or to the heir of her deceased husband would probably depend in practice on whether she had borne children to her first husband. Intervention by the colonial administration on behalf of widows caused considerable bitterness.

CHANGING WOMEN'S RIGHTS

As can be seen, the marriage relationship was the linchpin of the system, dictating a person's status, rights, duties, and future expectations. If this relationship were altered substantially, the entire system would fail to function as an integrated whole and unexpected – and often undesirable – consequences would follow, as well as vociferous objections from large sections of the population. For these reasons, the colonial administration's interventions to improve the status of women proved to be something of a mixed blessing even for those women who benefited from the changes.

Initially the colonial administration introduced regulations recognising Christian marriages (valid without *bohali*) to be as binding as customary ones. Subsequently civil marriages by a magistrate were made legal to meet the situation of many people who were unable 'to get married by a Christian minister, either because they [were] heathens or under church discipline' (CPP, 1873, Appendix III: 6). Again, these marriages were valid without marriage cattle which the missionaries, in any case, refused to allow to be paid. The opposition this roused was considerable, since few families converted to Christianity *in toto*. Most commonly only an individual or some of the family converted. Since the institution of *bohali* was embedded in a network of kinship relations, the ramifications of this provision affected far more people than just the family head. A woman desiring to have a Christian marriage faced major opposition from her non-Christian relatives (e.g. LA, A, *Thope (a young woman)* v. *Thlou (her grandfather, paternal)*, 2.6.1875). Even where she won her struggle, it was no doubt frequently at a price, as was the case for one of the daughters of Letsie, Moshoeshoe's successor as paramount chief, who was finally permitted to marry without *bohali* after her father had given her a severe thrashing (Smith, 1939: 190–3).

Eventually the administration had to provide that a customary law marriage contracted during the subsistence of a Christian or civil one would be punished as bigamy: Mabille, a leading missionary, had shown that many men regarded a Christian marriage as 'something like a joke' (CA, UBR, vi: 281–6), a way of acquiring a wife without having to pay *bohali*, until a more valued woman could be afforded. Despite promises not to marry any additional wives by Sesotho law, many men did just that, and the second wife was then regarded as the principal one. Until the bigamy provision was passed in 1877, magistrates could use only bluff and appeals to morality to try to prevent such second marriages (e.g. LA, A, *Bereng Molomo* v. *Nthlakala (his wife)*, 7.1.1875).

Nor were the administration's initial attempts to control what they regarded as the undesirable features of customary law marriages more successful. To ensure that the woman consented to her marriage, and to assist the magistrate in judging future cases arising out of *bohali* claims, it was provided that in future *all* marriages were to be registered before a magistrate, to whom the parties had to declare their consent and pay a registration fee of two shillings and sixpence. In addition, all *bohali* paid had to be registered – otherwise no action regarding the marriage or the *bohali* could be brought before a magistrate. Since this acted as an unprecedented charge for legal recognition of a marriage, as well as a tax on polygyny, and complicated matters in the eyes of a woman's family when she did not want the marriage, it is hardly surprising that very few customary law marriages were in fact registered. The administration eventually had to bow to public opinion and abolish compulsory registration, since otherwise people were obliged to go to the chiefs' courts with disputed *bohali* cases. As a result, unless a woman was prepared to run away from her family and throw herself on the mercy of some strange magistrate or missionary or her lover, if she had one, she remained unable in practice to withstand being forced into an unwanted marriage.

However, despite the unexpected problems produced by the administration's interventions, there is evidence of women seeking to use the new protections offered them by the law. The administration provided that both boys and girls should become majors on attaining given ages, initially 15 for girls and 18 for boys, but subsequently 21 for both sexes. This gave women legal control over their own fate in situations where, before, their wishes could legally have been over-ridden by their fathers' or husbands' claims. Moreover, the magistrates upheld women's rights in a variety of situations and in various ways. Even the legal jargon of the criminal record books cannot dull such vivid vignettes as that on the charge sheet in the case of *The Queen* v. *Ra-Mokebe*:

Charged with assault and contempt of court in that on the 15th Instant having presented himself at the court to lodge a complaint against his son-in-law Seleke for not paying up cattle for his wife Mokebe – and the said Seleke having no cattle at hand the prisoner attempted by force to carry off his daughter from her husband and on *her* [emphasis added] refusal did then and there strike her and her husband – and did moreover create a disturbance of the place in front of the court room – thereby rendering himself guilty of the crime of contempt (LA, BB, *The Queen* v. *Ra-Mokebe*, 16.9.1876).

The court fined the prisoner ten shillings and 'cautioned against any breach of the peace' (ibid.).

On the same principle that women should be treated as majors, women whose marriages were not registered or who were widowed were given the right to custody of their minor children until they reached the age of majority. Widows were also given the right to remarry, although at first the regulations provided that custody of her children would then pass to the family of her deceased husband or to other relatives. Subsequently this was changed to allow the woman to retain custody of her children (but not guardianship) even in such cases. Indeed, in at least one case the magistrate gave an unmarried woman custody and even guardianship of her child, although it is not clear from the case record on what legal grounds, if any, he did so (LA, B, *Moela* v. *Matsedisa*, 27.8.1875). In mid-1877 provision was also made for magistrates to grant a divorce in *any* of the three forms of marriage, and where the marriage had been by civil law, the children were frequently awarded to the woman, even, on occasion, where she was the guilty party.

However, given the level of opposition these regulations engendered – since they greatly emasculated the power of the family head – women had to be very determined or desperate to withstand family pressure not to invoke their new-found rights. One such category consisted of women, usually brought up on mission stations, whose husbands had promised to remain monogamous but subsequently decided to take a second wife by customary law.[9] The cases in the files indicate that those women who did resort to the magistrates for protection of various newly acquired rights frequently lived on mission stations or had support from other relatives who also had claims on the women and their children. Those without alternative sources of support may well have found the arm of the distant magistrate too short to save them from beatings or other forms of intimidation by irate relatives living on the spot.

Moreover, magisterial protection may on occasion have been something of a mixed blessing. In most of the cases of widows seeking to retain custody of their children which came before the court, the magistrates appear to have given custody to them – especially, it seems, where the woman was trying to prevent her daughters being circumcised or married with *bohali* payments.[10] However, the magistrates usually awarded to the male customary-law heir any livestock the widow had retained from her husband's estate or obtained as *bohali* for her daughters, thereby leaving her without that source of food or any reward for raising her daughters on her own.

It is difficult to assess how far these limited changes introduced by the administration penetrated to the remote areas, beyond the immediate ambit of the magistrates, but it does seem that their effects were surprisingly far-reaching. Given the scarcity of court records and the random nature of their survival, there is no way of gauging what proportion of various types of cases came before the magistrates or how frequently (except in the case of the district of Thaba Bosiu, which was not typical in that it contained the main mission station of the longest-established missionaries). Certainly a considerable number of family law cases did reach the administration's courts. For example, Austen (the magistrate in the remote district of Cornet Spruit) reported for 1878, the year after the amended regulations came into force, that apart from criminal cases he had also heard 64 civil and divorce cases, 'the bulk of which have been for the restoration of dowry cattle, and custody of children, who had become separated during the late war' (CPP, G17–78: 16). The surviving records from other districts – by their nature likely to have more cases brought before the magistrates than in Cornet Spruit – contain many indications of similar cases. By 1878 the Acting Governor's Agent was able to note in his report (which covered the whole of Basutoland) that the Basotho brought most or all of their cases to the magistrates (CA, NA 275: Acting Governor's Agent to Sec. for Native Affairs, 18.3.1878), and there is reason to believe that this was an accurate assessment (Burman, 1981: 88–90).

Such spread of magisterial influence was the result of many factors, most of which would also have had effects on the status of women. Even before the arrival of the missionaries and the colonial administration, economic changes brought by the settler society to the south were already affecting the indigenous legal system. This continued at an accelerated pace after the development of the nearby diamond fields, which generated a high demand for grain and labour from Basutoland. Wages obtained there and on the Cape railway works and farms threatened the chiefs' power as men found an alternative source to their patronage in their quest for marriage cattle. By 1877 the Acting Governor's Agent estimated that of the able-bodied adult male population of 25 000, at least 15 000 went out to service each year (CA, NA 274: Acting Governor's Agent to Sec. for Native Affairs, 28.12.1877). This must have greatly affected women's role within the family and village. Alien concepts of sale began to pervade the *bohali* exchange, with an increasing tendency to see it as the sale price for a woman rather than as a binding force between two families for the preservation of the marriage. (See, for instance, CPP, 1873, Appendix III: 64.) Increasingly, too, marriage cattle were given by an individual, not a family. Traditional responsibility to one's kinship group began to break down. Although theoretically the earnings of family members came under the control of the head of the family, for common use, the growing economic independence of its members and new attitudes of individualism acquired through contact with the money economy increasingly undermined the sharing ethic.

With the arrival of Christianity, the emphasis on individual rights intensified. The missionaries brought with them the European view of marriage as a contract between individuals rather than families, a relationship that was essentially monogamous and automatically terminated on the death of the individuals concerned. Polygyny, the sororate and levirate, a woman's inability to refuse to marry a man she disliked, Sesotho attitudes towards adultery and seduction, as well as the giving of marriage cattle, all met with their extreme disfavour. They propagated their views widely, including through their newspaper and at their schools. After a brief and failed attempt by the administration to set up its own schools, it did all it could to encourage mission education, especially for girls, and by 1877 there were approximately 3 000 pupils at some 70 flourishing schools in the country (CPP, A23–73: 3; CA, NA 274, Rolland to Brownlee,

28.12.1877). By 1874 approximately one-tenth of the Basotho were Christianised (CA, NA 273, Rolland to Griffith, 30.5.1874) and by 1877 it was authoritatively estimated that 'the number of natives brought directly and indirectly under the influence of Christianity is very considerable amounting to about one half of the tribe' (CA, NA 274, Acting Governor's Agent to Sec. for Native Affairs, 28.12.1877). It can therefore be seen that attitudes towards gender roles must have been undergoing major changes in a very stressful context, no doubt generating considerable emotion and confusion among the people.

RECONCILING THE IRRECONCILABLE

These sentiments were not confined only to the Basotho in this period. There are indications that magistrates and missionaries were also painfully aware of the injustices that inevitably resulted from the conflicting claims arising from their interventions to improve the status of women and their marriages. The files, for example, contain various enquiries from missionaries and magistrates as to how to handle cases where a woman had been allowed to marry by Christian rites but the subsequent property consequences led to suits for cattle by the man who would have been her guardian in customary law. A representative example is a case brought by Molapo who 'lent' one of his wives, for whom he had paid cattle, to one Nathanaele Makotoko. The woman had a daughter by Makotoko but at some stage Makotoko converted to Christianity and married another woman in church. However, he continued to support both his daughter and her mother, who also became Christians. When the daughter was about to marry another Christian (and therefore without the payment of *bohali*), Molapo claimed that Makotoko owed him the cattle which he, Molapo, had paid for the mother, since the daughter was his, by customary law, and he had not been consulted about her Christian marriage (LA, Res. Magistrate, Leribe, to Rev. F. Coillard, 7.11.1874). The magistrate told Molapo he could not claim the *bohali*, but was obviously sufficiently unsure of his ground to refer the case to the Governor's Agent, who apparently also received correspondence on it from the local missionary (LA, Res. Magistrate, Leribe, to Governor's Agent, 18.11.1874).

Magisterial discomfort at having to apply regulations with which they were definitely not in sympathy is also evident. Griffith, for example, in directing a magistrate that the property held by a widow be restored to the male heir according to customary law, indicated where his sympathies lay with the sentence: 'But with regard to the custody or guardianship of the children until they are of age, there Section 6 of the Marriage Regulations comes to our assistance' (LA, S9/2/2/1, Governor's Agent to Res. Magistrate, Cornet Spruit, 19.7.1874). And the page still splutters with Magistrate Bell's indignation in his official description to Griffith of another such case:

Nkobokaz had reared two daughters from their birth, no notice had been taken of them by the Plaintiff, no assistance of any kind has been given to the widow and children by the Plaintiff – he had not even paid her (the widow's) Hut-Tax, but when the daughters had grown to woman-hood, and the woman began to receive cattle for them, the Plaintiff starts up and makes a claim for the cattle (LA, L2/1/1, Res. Magistrate, Leribe, to Governor's Agent, 9.1.1879).

Nonetheless, the law dictated that customary law must be followed unless some reason could be found to discredit the plaintiff's claim. Other examples occur throughout the surviving documents, and it is evident that, for those responsible for implementing the legal changes, the tangles created by the interaction of the two systems caused far more concern than could possibly have been foreseen when it was first decided to intervene on women's behalf.

Similarly, the magistrates were distressed by cases such as that of Maseboko, where they realised that the woman was the victim of the clash of two sets of values. To represent all colonial administrations as staffed by bigoted, unfeeling men is a caricature that bears as little resemblance to the truth as the contemporary view of them as bringers of light to the wretched savage. The Governor's Agent and most of the officials and missionaries in Basutoland in this period had a deep interest in and sympathy for the country's people. But they were products of their own societies, which were convinced that they had a clearer view of religious and ethical truths, and – a conviction they shared with Basotho men at least – that men must order the lives of women. On this point it may be argued that the two societies differed not so much on principle as on the extent to which women's freedom of action was to be sacrificed to the family and wider social unit; the difference between them merely appeared far greater because of the different organisation of the two societies. If the men of Basutoland were afraid of the consequences for their lifestyle of the new regulations and religion, the colonial administrators were also deeply afraid of the consequences if they bowed to rejection of the values, law, and way of life for which they stood. To them there was no choice whether or not to uphold the principle of the law, but they sought to implement its decrees with due allowance for humanitarian and pragmatic considerations where possible.

The outcome of Maseboko's case, with which we began this chapter, illustrates the point. Her sentence was four months' imprisonment because the law demanded that she be imprisoned for concealing the birth of her baby, even if infanticide could not be proved. But there was nowhere suitable to imprison women in Basutoland – an interesting indication of how few women came before the administration's courts on criminal charges in the six years it had been in the country by then. Moreover, imprisonment – especially outside Basutoland – was still regarded by the Basotho in this period as a particularly terrible punishment. Maseboko was therefore released on bail while the administration referred the case to the Colonial Secretary in Cape Town, who hastily passed it on to Charles Brownlee, the Secretary for Native Affairs. Brownlee, the son of a missionary, had grown up among the Africans of the Eastern Cape, where he had spent most of his life as an administrator, so his comment on Maseboko's offence is of particular interest:

With reference to the decision and Judgement of Mr Rolland in the case of Maseboko charged with concealment of Birth, I would recommend that the sentence be approved of but that the prisoner be pardoned. The reasons of my recommendation are, 1st the singularity of the offence, it being the first of the kind I have ever heard of & there is no probability of one of the same nature ever again coming before us; 2nd the woman was convicted on the evidence of her own husband; and 3rdly we have not the means in Basutoland of carrying out the judgement of the court (CA, CO 3232, Brownlee's minute dated 19.9.1874 on Chief Magistrate Basutoland to Colonial Secretary, 25.8 1874).

And so Maseboko escaped imprisonment, though not the publication of her conduct nor the ordeal of her arrest and trial as well as the weeks of dread as she awaited information on her deportation to the Colony and incarceration there.

BOON OR BURDEN?

Was the advent of Cape Colonial rule therefore to the benefit or detriment of Basotho women in the long run? There is no easy answer to this question. Certainly some women suffered from it, but many of the changes that took place in that period which were not to women's advantage were in fact already under way, as a result of missionary influences and economic change. The slow disintegration of communal responsibility threatened the system which, when it worked, at least ensured protection for women and their children, even if at the price of their individual free choice. As this process became more advanced women – and their children – would have become extremely vulnerable. Although this was not the reason for the administration's introduction of individual rights for women, those rights were a logical alternative protection, which were beginning to be utilised by some women. The difficulty for the administration was to allow – as political necessity demanded – the operation of two very different and, in this respect, irreconcilable systems, without allowing gross injustices to occur. Whether in practice, if not in principle, this could eventually have been achieved by a knowledgeable and sympathetic administration collaborating with a rapidly changing Basotho nation is purely speculative, for the Gun War intervened in 1880. As a result Britain resumed control of Basutoland in 1884 under a system of rule mainly by the chiefs. In the period that followed, the new administration adopted a policy of far less legal intervention in the rights of chiefs and husbands under customary law.

But the problems were not unique to Basutoland or the nineteenth century. Throughout South Africa the same set of problems, stemming from the clash between two fundamentally different socio-legal systems, occurred with the advent of colonial rule, though usually in harsher confrontations. In a more complex form they are still being teased out today.

3

Domestic service and education for domesticity: The incorporation of Xhosa women into colonial society

JACKLYN COCK

> ... in Xhosa country, *as nowhere else in black Africa*, women as well as men took employment with whites. Sometimes this was under duress, but often it was of choice. From the early nineteenth century domestic work was done on the frontier by Xhosa women rather than Xhosa men (Wilson and Thompson; 1969: 262; my emphasis).

This chapter examines how domestic service constituted a point of incorporation into colonial society for Xhosa women on the Cape eastern frontier in the nineteenth century.[1] It will be argued that a pattern of coercion and oppressive control marked these early relationships between white and black women, which has continued until the present. In elaborating an ideology of black female domesticity grounded in Western definitions of gender roles, missionary institutions played a crucial part. The two components of their policy of educating Xhosa girls for domesticity – service in white households as domestic workers and management of the girls' own future households as Christian wives – are also examined.

THE INCORPORATION OF XHOSA WOMEN INTO DOMESTIC SERVICE

As Monica Wilson notes above, the Eastern Cape was unusual in that it was black women, rather than black men, who dominated domestic service from the first days of white settlement in the region. Elsewhere in southern Africa domestic service was predominantly a male occupation until into the twentieth century.

In some instances direct coercion propelled Xhosa women into domestic as well as agricultural service with the colonists. Although until at least 1823 (the year a trading fair was instituted at Fort Willshire) segregation was the official solution to frontier conflict, Cape officials attempted fitfully to enforce their segregationist policy and at the same time secure a cheap labour force, as the following extract describing Thomas Pringle's visit to the Khoikhoi settlement of Bethelsdorp, in 1820, illustrates:

While tea was preparing and before twilight had yet closed in, my host was called out to speak to another stranger. This was a Caffer woman, accompanied by a little girl of 8 or 10 years of age and having an infant strapped on her back, above her mantle of tanned bullock's hide. She had come from the drostdy, or district town of Uitenhage, under the custody of a black constable, who stated that she was one of a number of Caffer females who had been made prisoner by order of the Commandant on the frontier for crossing the line or prescribed demarcation without permission, and that they were to be given out in servitude among the white inhabitants of this district. The woman before us, he added, was to be forwarded by the missionary, under the charge of one of his people, to the residence of a certain colonist, about 20 miles to the westward (Pringle, 1834: 15).

The appeals of this woman moved Pringle to write: 'For my own part I was not a little struck by the scene, and could not help beginning to suspect that my European countrymen, who thus made captives of harmless women and children, were in reality greater barbarians than the savage natives of Caffraria' (ibid.: 16).

There is further evidence of the direct coercion of Xhosa women into the service of the 1820 British settlers in the Eastern Cape. Thomas Stubbs, a settler who was located near the Xhosa clay pits on the Kap River,[2] relates the following incident that took place in 1822:

One morning, at about 10 o' clock, my mother saw about a dozen Kaffirs coming towards our tent, apparently all well armed. (I may mention that we had not seen any Kaffirs before.) My mother told me to call my brother and cousin, who were working in the garden, about 500 yards from the tents, and sent my younger brother to our neighbour's to ask assistance…. My mother told my cousin to go and meet them, and said 'I have loaded the guns, but we will not let them see them until we find out whether they are enemies or not.' My cousin, not liking the look of them, hesitated, when my mother told him that if he was afraid to go he should say so, and she would go herself. Feeling rather ashamed, he went to meet them when they called 'morrow, morrow'. He brought them to the tents, when my mother motioned them to sit down, and then we saw they were all women, with long stocks in their hands. We gave them a lot of Settler's bread, i.e. hard biscuit. It was not long before a lot of men arrived from our neighbours, and made all the women prisoners. They then searched the clay pits and found a lot more. They were all taken to Grahamstown, and we were given to understand, were hired out to farmers. This we learned some time afterwards from one of them who had run away and got safe back to Kaffirland. This woman came with about 500 others who brought a pass from the officer at Fort Willshire to get clay (Maxwell and McGeogh, 1978: 42).

This incident illustrates at one level the mutual incomprehension of both settlers like the Stubbs family and the indigenous people. It has a particular pathos as their different gestures of goodwill ended so tragically for the Xhosa women. Stubbs writes: 'This was the first piece of injustice done to the natives by the Government, and this we had to suffer for afterwards' (ibid.).

Apart from direct coercion, the most important factors which operated to propel Xhosa men and women into wage employment were increasing pressure upon land, as the colonists appropriated more and more, and displacement and dispersal because of war. The *Mfecane*, the scattering of African people through southern Africa as a result of the wars initiated by the rising Zulu state after 1818, indirectly provided the Cape colonists with significant numbers of agricultural and domestic servants. In this process of disintegration and dispersal, remnants of the shattered Zizi, Hlubi and Bhele clans settled among the Xhosa in the Eastern Cape. They were later known collectively as the Mfengu (Fingoes): 'We are wanderers seeking service.' After the frontier war of 1835 the Cape government settled approximately 17 000 Mfengu between the Fish and Keiskamma rivers, in the neighbourhood of Fort Peddie. The area was insufficiently large or fertile to support them so, deprived of access to the means of subsistence, they were forced to take work with colonists as agricultural and domestic wage labourers. The government permitted Mfengu children to be indentured, and contracts similar to the apprenticeships instituted in 1812 for Khoi and 'coloured' people during the Caledon governorship were approved for them.

The cattle-killing of 1857, which followed the Xhosa defeat in the 1850–3 frontier war, provided a further impetus to Xhosa proletarianisation. It has been suggested that something of the order of 20 000 Xhosa died of starvation and 30 000 survivors sought sustenance as labourers in white employment (Bundy, 1972: 374). According to Jeff Peires, 29 142 Xhosa were registered for service in the colony by the end of 1857 (1984: 164). This number included girls as well as boys, and wives as well as husbands. At the time Governor Sir George Grey was vigorously promoting a dual policy of land expropriation and 'civilisation' among the Xhosa, by which he intended the rapid creation of a distinct smallholding class side by side with a much larger wage-earning class, which would provide 'useful servants, consumers of our goods, contributors to our revenue, in short, a source of wealth and strength to this colony' (cited in Majeke, 1952: 66). The impetus given by the cattle-killing to this policy has raised the cynical question of whether Grey's agents were responsible for the tragedy (ibid.: 72–6).

The hardship that followed in the wake of the cattle-killing was appalling: 'with the trees stripped of bark and gum and the earth pitted with holes from which every conceivable root had been extracted, the starving headed for the villages of British Kaffraria and the Cape Colony to throw themselves on the mercy of the white man'

(Peires, 1984: 147). A domestic servant employed by the daughter of the 1820 settler Jeremy Goldswain described the deprivation created by the cattle-killing, which propelled Xhosa women into domestic service:

During the famine her master's home 'became crowded from morning until night with starving Kaffirs begging for food.... I was afraid the Kaffirs would kill me for refusing them food as I had not food to give them. They said I was in the white man's house and could not refuse them food.' Eventually she left her job 'but was afraid to stay in Kaffirland for fear they would eat me: so I got a Pass to come here for work.' (quoted in Long, 1947: 193–4)

A pass system had been operating since 1828, when Lieutenant-Governor Bourke gave authority for the issue of passes to African migrants who wished to enter the service of colonial farmers. The incorporation of African women into colonial society was first regularised by this Ordinance 49, a key piece of labour legislation which in many ways has a decidedly modern ring. Ordinance 49 was 'an attempt to regulate the flow of labour' (Macmillan, 1963: 88). Its stated objective was to 'augment the amount of disposable labour, by affording the greatest facility compatible with the public safety, to the admission of Foreigners from the Tribes beyond the borders of the Settlement, who may be desirous of migrating to and sojourning in the colony as Herdsmen, Field Labourers, House Servants, or in whatever capacity may be most suitable to their several inclinations and abilities' (quoted in Donaldson, 1974: 370). Ordinance 49 not only provided for the admission of Africans into the colony in a form that imposed tight constraints on their mobility, but attempted to regulate the terms of admission and of employment through contract regulations and a pass system. The contracts obliged the employer 'to provide the Foreigner ... and such of his or her family as may be present with him or her, sufficient food and decent clothing' during the contract (ibid.). Wages could be paid in cash or cattle. Most women entered the colony in terms of this Ordinance as dependants but some came as independent workers. Thus between July and December 1828, altogether 84 passes were issued in the Albany district for 137 persons, of whom 28 were wives and 25 children. During this time a further 7 passes were issued to women in their independent capacities (CA, CO 51/15.A.5).

Wages for Xhosa women were at this time extremely low. For example, in 1828 a woman called Catryn, aged 40, entered into a service contract with a Mr J. Prinsloo in Albany for a monthly cash wage of 1s 3d, plus five goats on completion of her contract (ibid.). Low cash wages were justified then, as now, on two grounds: firstly, that the value of the board and lodging given to domestic servants was considerable, and secondly, that domestic service was an un-

skilled occupation. As regards the level of skill involved, domestic
service in nineteenth-century Eastern Cape encompassed a good deal
of variation, but many workers were clearly skilled. The range
stretched from that of Archdeacon Merriman's servant at Cradock,
who was described as 'a hulking Fingo woman, the extent of whose
abilities were to light the kitchen fire, boil the kettle and milk the goats'
(Merriman, 1952: 196), to that of Mary Taylor's Mfengu servant Annie
in Healdtown, who 'now does many things I used to do. She makes
excellent sponge cakes as light as any pastry' (Mary Taylor's Journal).
The wife of the 1820 settler John Ross stated in a letter to her mother
in September 1825 that she had two servants:

The older one has been with me since I came to this country except for seven
months. She is a tall fine young woman.... I have taught her to do everything
for me. She makes candles, salts meat, churns, bakes bread, cooks, washes
and dresses, sews, knits stockings and darns them well. When I was confined
she did everything without any oversight.... Strangers have taken notice how
well they set and serve the table.... I had most trouble in teaching them to
stand when washing clothes in a tub (quoted in Long, 1947: 220).

Nevertheless, after this impressive recital Ross complains of her
servants' laziness and ends, 'still a Scotch girl will work more than
the two' (ibid.).

Ross's relationship with her domestic servants illustrates certain
more general themes. She seems to have felt somewhat ambivalent
about them. From her letters she appears to have been a warm,
compassionate and responsive person. She went to great pains to
teach her servants sewing and literacy. Yet she perceived Africans
generally and servants specifically as lazy, often stupid, lacking in
initiative, grasping, careless and ungrateful. The one quality missing
from her otherwise very modern stereotype of the domestic servant
is dishonesty: 'The Doctor's lady was astonished that I could entrust
them with everything. There is nothing locked up and I have missed
nothing (ibid.: 220).

Similarly, the Philipps family, located at Glendower, found their
servants scrupulously honest (Keppel-Jones, 1960). However, then as
now, complaining about the dishonesty of servants was a constant
theme. Thus Mary Moffat, writing in 1820, complained of servants
stealing: Africans 'seem to count all Europeans stingy' (Mary Moffat's
Journal, 11 August 1820). No doubt they often appeared so because,
as Mary Taylor expressed it, 'self denial is very remarkable in a Fingo
or Kafir as they usually think there is no end to the riches of the white
people' (ibid.). Settler women were constantly warned to be on guard
against their servants.

The Philipps family already referred to are a prime example of
benevolent employers. Mrs Philipps writes very affectionately of their

'Bechuana' family, for whom they made clothes and generally treated as 'part of the family'. 'They appear quite happy and contented,' she noted, although she found it 'astonishing they should immediately place such confidence in us, from the first moment they did not seem to have the least fear, but to think everything we did was right and for their good' (Keppel-Jones, 1960: 253). Her husband described their new servants as 'exceedingly attached': 'When I come home after a few days absence they all rush to see me and express their pleasure. What a noble race of People all the neighbouring blacks are' (ibid.: 257). He brought them presents – 'a little snuff box each' – and remarked on how the two youngest girls 'are daily improving in English and make themselves extremely useful':

Our little Sabina is everything to us, she waits at Table and her remarks and cleverness in repartee is a source of amusement to all. She is a most uncommon child, talks English perfectly, and neither in word nor action has ever betrayed conduct unworthy of a British subject. She is genteel in her appearance and was everything from the first. Her mother is a very superior person and now that we can understand her, we find her possessing extraordinary sentiments of right with an abhorrence of wrong (ibid.: 335).

Yet while there is a simple affection in these letters that is appealing, the key qualities the Philippses admired in their servants were faithfulness, trust, obedience and loyalty. These are, *par excellence*, the qualities of subordinates.

The key structural characteristics of the position of African women who entered into domestic service with the colonists were their powerlessness and their vulnerability. Relationships with their employers were consequently marked by an extreme inequality. Their content was coloured by both the racism of the frontier and, as we discuss below, settler notions of female inferiority.

The *Graham's Town Journal* of the 1830s, 1840s and 1850s provides an accurate barometer of settler attitudes towards African people. It is steeped in racist sentiments. Thus the Mfengu are described as 'a poor, spiritless, weakminded race of people', 'completely devoid of intelligence', while the Xhosa character has 'all the baser qualities ... without anything either noble or generous or possessing of one spark of honour or integrity'. Such racist remarks reach extreme expression in the writings of Harriet Ward, the wife of an army officer stationed at Grahamstown, who described 'the Kaffir' as having 'neither generosity nor gratitude', 'a liar, a thief and a beggar' (1851: 158, 165). Although less than human, 'the Kaffir, at the first onset, is perhaps less ferocious than cunning, and more intent on serving his own interests by theft than on taking life from the mere spirit of cruelty; but once roused, he is like a wild beast after the taste of blood and loses all the best attributes of humanity' (ibid.: 98).

Harriet Ward's racial attitudes were coloured by her experience of war. Yet even when the Xhosa were servants of long standing, rather than dangerous and hostile neighbours, the theme of racial degeneracy prevailed. Thus Jeremiah Goldswain maintained:

There is a few wich you may trust (of the Kaffer) but few.... I have had them more or less for the last 25 years and the more you give them the more they want: in fact they are never sitified and all the most of thous Kaffers – wether men or women – that has been in my service would gladly return into my service and wil acnolige than I ham a good master.... But if thear was another war they would be the firs to rob me and if possible to murder me and all my family. This is thear carreter (quoted in Long, 1947: 127).

In similar vein, Frederick Rex noted that Chief Pato's people, from whom his two servants were drawn, 'make most excellent servants.' However, a Mfengu servant who had been in his employ for about a month and behaved very well 'appears to be in want of a flogging now that his belly is full'. Later he wrote to his father: 'You are right about the Fingoes they are a good for nothing sort' (Long, 1947: 197). In 1835 he described twenty Mfengu (ten men and ten women) whom he intended sending from Fort Willshire to his father at Knysna as 'an ugly, dirty looking set of people more specially the women who are too filthy to look at. However I have not a doubt that having them driven to the Island and back again once a day may have a good effect on their scabby old legs' (ibid.: 177).

Even good relations with individual servants who were regarded as loyal and faithful did not necessarily undermine negative racial attitudes. The missionary Henry Calderwood declared that 'among Caffres and Hottentots, there are many excellent servants. We have had of both these classes in our house as good and faithful servants as could possibly be expected.' Despite his positive encounters with African people, he continued: 'But I fear this cannot with truth be represented as the general experience' (1858: 61). Stereotypes were entrenched and often not shifted or redefined by contradictory personal experience.

Even in the best servant–employer relationships – those containing most concern and kindness, as in the Philipps family – the African servant was implicitly viewed as a child. The child analogy involves a fundamental denial of equality, and is often a component of racist, sexist and classist ideologies. There is a clear analogy between settler attitudes towards Africans on the Eastern Cape frontier and upper- and middle-class attitudes towards the lower classes in contemporary Britain: qualities of irresponsibility, immaturity, excitability and emotionalism were attributed to both subordinate groups. Cairns has pointed to the tendency in colonial situations 'for race relations to be patterned after class relations' (1965: 92). The institution of domestic service in nineteenth-century Eastern Cape society thus represented a vehicle through which class-bound attitudes assumed racial form.

One outcome of Xhosa women's special involvement in domestic service was the creation of a social space in which Xhosa and colonial women interacted. Because on the frontier colonial women did a good deal of domestic work themselves, there developed a situational intimacy between them and their servants. A typical situation was that of Mrs Trollope and her mother at Daggaboer near Cookhouse, who employed several servants in the house but had their time fully occupied: 'For candles and soap, both had to be made and needed personal supervision. Often during the evening they would roll and knot wicks in preparation for candlemaking next day or cut the "Boerseep" into handy household squares for washing purposes' (Ralls, n.d. : 82). The ironing of the white starched collars and boiled shirt fronts of the men also took a good deal of the settler women's time 'for such particular work could not be entrusted to the Native servants who did the plain ironing' (ibid.).

Monica Wilson has stressed that 'one of the characteristics of the frontier was the interaction of women' (1972: 12). She also emphasised that the importance of this insight has often been overlooked since. The structural inequality which shaped this interaction imbued it with opposing qualities, of both intimacy and distance. The intimacy of the relationship did sometimes yield insights into a common humanity which the colonial employer had not previously recognised. Wilson points, for example, to the close relationship between Mrs Ross and her Xhosa domestic servant. But it is debatable how far this intimacy went in breaking down racist stereotypes. Thus Mary Taylor, writing from Healdtown in 1872, learned from her domestic servant Annie that Africans are capable of deep feelings. The young man to whom Annie was engaged had hanged himself, prompting Taylor to comment: 'Poor Annie was in quiet trouble which contradicted what I have heard many say, and even Fanny saying, that the natives know little of what we call love.' But she went on to note that Annie, perhaps, was the exception: 'Annie is rather a singular girl for a Fingoe, so reserved that it is difficult to approach her in order to comfort. She is a clean servant and I value her very much' (Mary Taylor's Journal).

Wilson admits that 'interacting with people is no guarantee that you will regard them as equal', but argues that it may help (1972: 15). However, the quality of interaction between African and European women which took place on the eastern frontier in the nineteenth century within the context of domestic service, was structured in terms of an extreme inequality that blocked any recognition of a common womanhood on the part of the employers. While there was a physical proximity between housewife and servant in the home, there was also considerable social distance between them. In a similar situation in West Africa, Mrs Donald Fraser highlighted her feeling of isolation among the local African women: 'My mode of life was outwardly so different from theirs that *common womanhood failed to make a point of contact*' (1932: 3; emphasis added). She pointed to a similar feeling of difference among the African women, some of whom persisted in calling her *Baba* ('Father'), which was surely expressive of this sense of difference. 'Even those who realised my sex noted the difference between us rather than our common woman-hood…' (ibid.).

One of the difficulties in coming to any other than the most tentative conclusions about nineteenth-century domestic servant–employer relations on the eastern frontier stems from the paucity of direct accounts. As Butler points out with reference to settler women, 'remi-niscences by women of this period are much rarer than reminiscences by men' (1974: 115). How do we account for this? Perhaps these women were too caught up in domestic chores. Perhaps they were too self-deprecatory – feeling their world and experiences to be trivial, insignificant and not worth recording. Because the organisation of domestic life was defined as the preserve of women, some of the most vivid settler diaries do not mention domestic details at all. Settlers such as Charles Bell and Joseph Stirk give fascinating details of busy, productive lives, but the domestic aspect lies in the shadows.[3]

Overall, as Macrone perceived, 'the frontier woman … remains a vague but substantial figure' (1937: 109). The problem involved in trying to clothe this vague figure is one germane to women's history: 'Women's history is in essence the history of the inarticulate' (Branca, 1978: 14). This difficulty becomes even more acute with regard to the Xhosa women employed as domestic servants, whose inarticulate-ness was compounded by their subordinate position within the col-onial hierarchy of class and race.

Attempts to give voice to the silent can lead to an over-correction, in terms of which all women are treated as members of a homogene-ous social category. Clearly women share certain experiences, but these experiences are shaped and coloured by different cultural and class relations. Such differences were intense in the interaction of Xhosa women and their European employers in the Eastern Cape in the nineteenth century.

THE IMPACT OF THE MISSIONARIES

On the eastern frontier where domestic work was performed by Xhosa women, rather than men, servant–employer relations were also structured by settler notions of female inferiority. Missionaries were important cultural carriers of such views. Their role in general terms is significant because the missionary effort in this region was carried out on a larger scale than had been seen hitherto anywhere else in Africa, involving a greater number of missionary societies and personnel, while their presence here was also accompanied by a sizeable settler community (Moyer, 1976: 498). The significance of this as regards women was twofold: during the nineteenth century Xhosa women became involved in Western-style education, offered by mission institutions, to a far greater degree than African women did elsewhere in southern Africa, while the presence of the settler community offered many of them the possibility, at least, of employment (Wilson and Mafeje, 1963: 71).

For these reasons missionary institutions were crucial agents in the incorporation of Xhosa women into colonial society. They passed on new occupational skills and elaborated an occupational ideology which found expression in the employment of Xhosa women as domestic workers. Their influence was not confined to those with whom they came into direct contact. What is more, they helped link an ideology of domesticity that was rooted in European gender roles to an ideology of domestication generated by the problems of controlling a colonised people.

The missionaries' concern in the field was primarily religious: education was seen as indispensable to evangelisation. However, schools were also instruments of European civilisation, and by coupling Christianity and 'civilisation' the missionary and his educational institutions became agents of Western culture.

Toward African culture, and the position of women in African society in particular, missionaries adopted on the whole a hostile and culturally aggressive response. Women were perceived to occupy a position of subordination that bordered on slavery. In the words of the missionary Young: 'The conditions of the female Kaffirs in their heathen state is one of peculiar hardship. Working in the fields, carrying home the crops, doing whatever requires to be done of a laborious nature, they are practically slaves to the other sex, and in very many cases are subjected to persecution' (1902: 123). Shepherd, the last missionary principal of Lovedale College, wrote of African women: 'They were subordinate. They were beasts of burden. They were exposed even at a tender age to customs that brutalised. And after maturity they were disposed of in marriage often without their consent and frequently as minor wives to polygamous husbands' (1940: 570).

The missionaries found a number of African customs involving women particularly offensive. Polygyny was high on the list of undesirable practices. The missionary William Shaw classed polygyny as one of several 'vicious practices' while Dr John Philip regarded it as 'one of the greatest obstacles to the success of the missionaries' (cited in Williams, 1959: 306). Govan argued that 'the evils of polygyny ...

are so great and varied, and it is in such manifest opposition to the whole spirit of the Bible that we could not see our way to any middle course' (cited by Shepherd, 1940: 471). Change was essential: 'One of the works of Christian missions is to change, root and branch, Kaffir ideas about marriage, and to introduce an order of things in which polygyny with its attendant evils shall have no place, and women's sphere as the helpmeet and no longer the slave of man, shall be universally acknowledged' (Young, 1902: 127).

The custom of bridewealth, or *lobola*, was perceived to be equally abhorrent. The missionaries were blind to the social and economic functions which this institution performed in precolonial society. In their view, besides expressing women's subjection, it had the effect of subverting the Christian ideal of marriage as a personal relationship between two individuals. Mission condemnations of *lobola* abound. This 'truly barbarous custom of buying and selling wives' represented 'one of the greatest barriers in the way of the gospel and consequently of civilisation', it 'induces to theft and must consequently demoralise society. It degrades the position and character of all females' (Calderwood, 1858: 198). James Laing argued that 'this custom of buying wives' brought females into a state of 'most revolting slavery' (cited in Williams, 1959: 306).

Other Xhosa customs involving women that the missionaries found offensive were the marriage ceremony, the levirate and *intonjane* (the initiation ceremony for young girls). The social significance of these customs was lost upon the missionaries. Clearly this blindness was linked to the cultural insensitivity and oversimplification that marked colonial contact with indigenous people. As Williams remarks: 'polygyny, bride-price, marriage ceremonies, *intonjane* and circumcision were condemned and attacked by the missionaries with a patent dogmatism rooted in the early Victorian morality of the Evangelical Revival as well as from the standpoint of the superiority of Western European civilisation' (1959: 311). Theirs was a confidence deriving from a sense of being adherents of a cause commanded by God and backed by divine assurance of success.

From this highly coloured viewpoint, the missionaries' solution to the problem of women's subordinate status in African society was evangelism. By their conversion to Christianity these 'poor degraded females' could escape from 'tribal customs' and be restored to human dignity. Through evangelism and Christian civilisation the missionaries hoped 'to raise the female character above mere animal propensities and brute labour and make them acquainted with their high destinies in another world and so give them a sense of self-respect' (Shepherd, 1940: 472).

This commitment to evangelism as the way to the liberation of African women was reinforced by the women's greater receptivity to

Christian education. 'Though generally speaking, the females are more degraded than the males, there is on the other hand more immediate prospect of improvement, because of their greater readiness to receive instruction. They show, too, on the whole, more docility and proficiency than the male scholars. No small encouragement this for those who seek their elevation' (Young, 1902: 128).

The missionaries not only hoped to liberate African women, but trusted that such women would have a civilising influence on their menfolk. Calderwood saw 'the improvement of the females' as 'a most urgent necessity' because 'the female influence' was the means to Christian civilisation. Every day he saw male converts 'being dragged backwards and downwards by their heathen wives' (1858: 206). Such wives must be converted for 'Who is so likely as a pious, judicious, educated and good-tempered woman to create and foster those very amenities which are at once the fruits and the means of civilisation?' (ibid.: 209).

Yet there was disagreement on how much the education of women could achieve. The missionary Whiteside argued that education was relatively unimportant, for 'the little learning gained is overborne by the habits and superstitions of generations' (1906: 281). He referred to an instance where the daughter of a Gcaleka chief was educated in England but returned to her original 'barbarous surroundings'. 'A few years later she greeted a Wesleyan minister in the purest English, but she wore a Kafir blanket, had bead bangles on wrists and ankles and was the wife of a polygamist. Until natives can create improved social conditions, by their own labour, school education will fail largely of its purpose' (ibid.).

Thus the missionaries' opposition to what they saw as the subordination of women in precolonial society was a complex response shaped by a number of different cultural dynamics. Overall it led to an emphasis on the gender-specific education of African women, which was valued both as a good in itself as well as a means to an end. Not only was it the means to liberating women and indirectly 'civilising' all Africans, but it was also seen as a means to transforming African people into productive workers.

Education for domesticity

The missionaries' understanding of education as a civilising process involved imparting both general and role-specific knowledge. The latter included the knowledge, skills and attitudes appropriate to the different gender roles; for African women this meant their socialisation into Western definitions of domestic roles. Western gender role definitions were paramount in the formulation of educational policy. Their cultural source was Victorian Britain from which the white settlers, missionaries and colonial administrators on the Cape eastern frontier originated. As described by McClintock in chapter 4, an aggressive, masculine tone saturated Victorian culture and was imported into the colonies. Hammond and Jablow describe this process thus: 'Most colonial officials had been reared in a patriarchal system where the segregation of the sexes began early in public school, was extended to men's clubs and generally persisted throughout life.' This exclusiveness of male society was 'inevitably accompanied by a sense of masculine superiority to which women gave assent…. The generally masculine tone of the English ethos tends to devalue women and to set them apart' (1970: 191). As Kitson Clark points out, 'there were a good many people in nineteenth-century England who thought that women did not need much education and that it was not good for them' (1967: 89). The education viewed as appropriate for women centred on the home.

Missionaries and settlers in southern Africa ignored the contrasting gender role definitions prevalent in precolonial African society. These did not stress dependence and passivity in women. African women's role in economic production demanded high levels of competence. Qualities of energy, self-reliance, stoicism, courage and endurance are demanded from peasant women everywhere. But in the mission education to which African girls were given access, Western gender role definitions predominated while indigenous female responsibilities were ignored.

For the missionaries women's core role was a domestic one – it was their influence as wives and mothers that was important. The different cultural meanings attached to this domestic role in African society were overridden. Adequate role performance required Christian education: 'A Caffre or Fingoe woman brought to a knowledge of the truth, yet uninstructed in the management of a household and the training of children, is utterly incapable of making her home comfortable' (Calderwood, 1858: 206).

These views were often rooted in a class bias; there is an important parallel in the education of working-class girls in nineteenth-century Britain. James Booth, writing in 1835 about the education of the British working-class girl, asked: 'Why should she not be taught to light a fire, sweep a room, wash crockery and glass without breaking them, wash clothes and bake bread?' (quoted in Marks, 1976: 190). The philanthropic members of the British middle and lower-middle class (from which many of South Africa's missionaries were drawn) wanted to educate working-class women to run their own homes as well. 'As a result there were many schemes to include the domestic arts in the curricula of elementary schools. Those who provided a vocational education for working-class girls worked on the assumption that girls would first become servants and then housewives' (ibid.).

This assumption was imported into a colonial context on the Cape eastern frontier. In the same way that the education of working-class girls in nineteenth-century Britain became increasingly vocational and directed to their domestic roles as servants and housewives, so the education of Xhosa girls was linked to their subordinate class position. Their education was aimed largely at socialising the girls into domestic roles both in the girls' own homes and, as servants, in those of other people. This education for domesticity fitted in with the ideology of subordination which the colonists saw as appropriate to all blacks, males as well as females.

In this ideology the inculcation of the work ethic assumed a special importance. Stewart repeatedly stressed that the objects of Lovedale College were 'Godliness, cleanliness, industry and discipline'. He maintained that 'Christianity and idleness are not compatible' (Wilson, 1972: 5). In the words of another missionary, Africans needed 'to be taught to work, for as a rule, the barbarous natives have no higher ambition than to live at the side of their huts and cattle-folds, basking in the sun and enjoying the savage luxury of utter laziness' (Young, 1902: 82).

The connection between mission education and the settler demand for domestic labour is illustrated by Mrs Philipps, writing from Glendower on 4 July 1825. She records that she was better pleased with the missionary establishment at Theopolis than she had anticipated: 'The school for the children must eventually be of advantage to us, as they teach them to speak, read and write in English. They will, if taught industrious habits, be useful as servants.... It was altogether an interesting sight, so many little black creatures brought into a state of civilisation and improvement (quoted in Keppel-Jones, 1960: 250). Writing somewhat later, Harriet Ward regretted that the connection between education and domestic labour was not more explicit. She found the idleness of the Mfengu 'almost incredible'. 'The missionaries are indefatigable in teaching them their catechism; but no attempt is made to fit the women for service. Idle they are, and idle they will be' (1851: 66).

The role the missionaries were allocated in the colonial authorities' strategy for the domestication of the African population was indicated as early as 1815 by Colonel Cuyler, when he expressed the hope to the Colonial Secretary that 'by good management on the part of the missionaries, the Kaffirs may be in time brought to that station to be quiet and *useful* neighbours' (Williams, 1967: 18). Missionary acquiesence in that role is exemplified by the missionary Thomson's admission that his task was not only to Christianise but also 'to introduce among the natives, a knowledge of the useful arts of civilised life, and to train them to habits of industry' (quoted in Williams, 1959: 238).

This linking of the civilising role of the missionaries to the government's programme of social control was most apparent in Grey's project of industrial education. He drew on rich, if brutal, experience in the pacification of native populations in Australia and New Zealand. The purpose of his proposed industrial education policy in the Eastern Cape was to 'civilise races emerging from barbarism' by turning them into a 'settled and industrious peasantry' (Majeke, 1952: 64).

Lovedale College, established in 1841, became the model *par excellence* of industrial education. In 1856 departments of masonry, carpentry, wagon-making and blacksmithing were established and in 1861 printing and bookbinding were added. Through a system of indenturing apprentices, Lovedale began producing relatively skilled workers for the labour market. Government support led to the establishment of similar industrial departments at the missions of Healdtown and Lesseyton after 1855.

At Lovedale the imported European definitions of appropriate gender roles were institutionalised. Industrial education for women focused on domestic skills. An Industrial Department opened at the Lovedale Girls' School in 1871. 'In this department women and girls were trained as domestic servants or seamstresses' (Shepherd, 1940: 475). This course continued until 1922 and tried to straddle the two aspects of 'education for domesticity' already described. As Shepherd put it, 'it tried to keep in view a two-fold aim': preparing the girls for domestic life in their own community and preparing them for domestic service in white homes:

The course referred to has tried to keep both possibilities in view. Reconciliation of the two, however, presents difficulties. Whereas a training for domestic service requires instruction in European methods employed under European conditions, the essence of a preparation for Native home life consists in acquiring a knowledge of how to make effective use of the very meagre resources available (1940: 475–6).

Under Jane Waterston, Lady Superintendent of the Girls' School until 1873, 'many Native girls came to be housed at Lovedale and trained for all kinds of domestic work' (ibid.: 474). The chief subjects of instruction during that time were 'housekeeping, cooking, sewing and laundry work' (ibid.: 425). Shepherd tells us that 'the same subjects have had a large place in the curricula for girls down to the present day' (ibid.).

Waterston's explicit intention was domestic rather than academic. She declared that her aim was not to turn out schoolgirls but women: 'I have tried to give the Institution not so much the air of a school, as of a pleasant home. I reasoned after this manner that homes are what are wanted in Kaffirland, and that the young women will never be able to make homes unless they understand and see what a home is' (ibid.). This fitted neatly with Stewart's intention, which was largely evangelical:

We have not taken these young women from their smoky hovels to spoil them with over-indulgence, or nurse them into fastidious dislike of their future fates.... We may fairly believe that great good will come out of the establishment of this training school for young women. Cleanliness, industry and application are some of the lower ends of the Institution, and the more common virtues which the inmates must practise while they remain there; the training of their hearts and the conversion of their souls to God are the higher and real aims of the place (cited by Young, 1902: 132).

Industry and application were to be expressed largely in domestic roles. As Ross wrote of Lovedale in 1883: 'the girls receive the most suitable kind of instruction that those of their class and race will receive' (Shepherd, 1940: 200). In other words, the education objectives were defined and evaluated in terms of their appropriateness to a colonised race, subordinate class and female sex. The products were often aesthetically pleasing to the producers: 'The clean, coloured print dresses of the pupils of the Girls' Institution, their upright bearing, graceful carriage, and general look of intelligence, seldom fail to impress the casual observer as in striking contrast to the condition of the native females in their heathen state' (Young, 1902: 14). The juxtaposition of two photographs in Whiteside's *History of the Wesleyan Methodist Church of South Africa* makes the same point. The one, entitled 'Raw Material', shows three young black girls scantily clad in animal skins. Facing it is a photograph entitled 'Civilisation', which shows three young black girls posing with self-conscious dignity, wearing long dresses and turbans (1906: 296).

At its nineteenth-century peak, between 600 and 800 students attended Lovedale. It was the most prominent mission school in southern Africa and served as a model for numerous other missionary institutions. At Lesseyton, Blythswood, Healdtown, Salem and St Matthews (all in the Eastern Cape and Transkei), education for girls followed much the same pattern, focusing on education for domesticity. At St Matthews, for example, domestic training was important even in the girls' academic courses. This reflects the notion that domesticity was the core component of women's role in society: 'Even for the relatively small proportion of girls whose "profession" or "trade" will lie in activities outside the home, participation in some of the major activities of the home is inevitable, and the contingency is high that sooner or later every woman will be the central figure controlling the destinies of the home and family' (Ingles, cited by Fihla, 1962: 159). 'For the girls, therefore, the secondary school found a place for domestic economy in the teaching of domestic science, laundry-work, needlework, cookery and home nursing' (ibid.).

At Healdtown there was a similar pattern of sex-specific vocational training, which restricted the access of women to all but domestic roles. Begun as a mission station for Mfengu refugees in 1853, Heald-town was transformed by John Ayliff into an industrial institution in terms of Grey's policy. While the boys studied building, carpentry, quarrying, brickmaking, agriculture, blacksmithing, wagon-making, boot- and shoemaking, tailoring and wheelwright's work, the girls were trained in 'various domestic duties' (Hewson, 1959: 169). In 1856 they 'produced 600 pieces of needlework during the year, consisting mostly of clothes and bed linen' (ibid.).

While boys were taught a variety of industrial skills, which opened up all kinds of employment opportunities, girls were restricted to education specifically for domestic roles, or to occupations such as teaching and nursing, which were extensions of these roles. Education for girls institutionalised European gender ideology, which equated femininity with domesticity. The effect was to locate black women mainly in domestic roles, either in their own or in the colonisers' households.

An analysis of the Lovedale register and biographical details of pupils at the Girls' School, drawn up by Stewart in 1887, shows that there were three main occupational alternatives open to women: as domestic servants, teachers or housewives. Lovedale female students were frequently employed in domestic service in missionary and other white homes. Those listed as having been in service at some stage of their lives numbered 85 out of a total of 838 girls or 15,8 per cent (Stewart, 1906: 188). In general women were restricted to occupations low in pay, power and prestige, with domestic service, by all three criteria, at the bottom of the occupational hierarchy. By contrast, the men who graduated from Lovedale entered a variety of occupations, becoming ministers, teachers, interpreters, magistrate's clerks, store clerks, carpenters, wagon-makers, blacksmiths, masons, policemen, printers, bookbinders, law agents, transport riders and so on.

For a small minority of women, however, mission education was the route to membership of the small black elite in southern African society. Wilson points out that Skota's *African Yearly Register*, an African 'Who's Who' published in 1931, included 19 women in a total of 325 entries. Several of them were Lovedale products, such as Mrs M. Majombozi, Martha Ngano, Mrs F. Skota, Frieda Bokwe, Sarah Poho and Cecilia Makiwane. These were exceptional women by any standard but they were few, and therefore provided fewer role models for those lower down the educational hierarchy.

The role of female missionaries
In the inculcation of a Western ideology of female domesticity, the

role of missionary wives and a few exceptional 'lady missionaries' was significant. All too often their role is subsumed in a discussion of their husbands. For instance, Maxwell and McGeogh refer to 'the missionaries drawn from many lands who dedicated their lives and their wives to what they believed to be the cause of Africa and its peoples' (1978: 19). Missionary wives were, however, the crucial female element in the colonial encounter with Africa in the early stages of colonialism. Writing of this period, Williams maintains that 'generally the evidence is too scanty for an assessment of the role of the missionary wives' at least during the period 1799–1853 (1967: 56). Many of them must, however, have had some influence on young, Christianised African women's perceptions of themselves, though how far they served as role models is difficult to say.

Some were forceful personalities. Thus Isabella Smith came out from Scotland at the age of 21 and after two years married the Rev. W. R. Thompson of the Glasgow Missionary Society but 'made it a condition of her marriage that she should continue teaching at Balfour at her school for missionaries' daughters afterwards, and she did' (Williams, 1967: 15). Williams tells us that she was 'someone of considerable courage as well as a resolute personality', but mentions very little of her in his biography of her husband. According to her obituary: 'for full sixty years she was a spiritual force and a power working for righteousness, goodness and truth in the land where her lot was cast' (*Christian Express*, 1.10.1905).

Other exceptional missionary women were Miss MacRitchie, who presided over the Lovedale Girls' School from 1874 to 1880, Mary Dodds, who came out to Lovedale in 1892, Miss Harding, Miss Thomson and Miss Ogilvie. The last-mentioned came out in 1846 and started a sewing school at a mission station in the Transkei, where she laboured with a hundred 'heathen girls' whose 'ochre-smeared skin karosses had daily to be exchanged during the hours of instruction for one or two articles of European clothing' (*Christian Express*, 1.6.1881). From 1861 she taught at Mgwali with the remarkable Rev. Tiyo Soga. During her eighteen years there 'hundreds of girls passed … into domestic life and various kinds of service' (ibid.).

By far the most impressive figure is the redoubtable Jane Waterston, founder and principal of the Lovedale Girls' School for seven years from 1866 and a pioneer in several respects. She was a woman of 'rare determination, courage and intelligence who was a unique figure in nineteenth-century South Africa' (Bean and Van Heyningen, 1983: 11). Her vivacity, energy and force earned her the Xhosa name *Noqakata*, 'the mother of activity', and the Lovedale girls were known as *Amaqakata* for some time. Certainly her ideas on education were class-bound – an 'educated woman' was to have qualities of 'refinement and delicacy' – but much about her was original, especially in terms of her middle-class origins.

These were all remarkable women, especially in the context of the limited role assigned women in Western society at the time. But while in their own lives they may have challenged some of the stereotypes of female passivity and reticence, they did not question prevailing assumptions about the kind of education suitable for black girls in a colony. Some of the missionary women had themselves been domestic servants in Britain. According to contemporary missionary wisdom, their main impact was thought to derive from their 'natural', intuitive, feminine qualities. Calderwood, who stressed the education of African women as the key to the 'civilisation' of the native races, saw European females as the best instruments, pointing to 'the affectionate influence of the pious, enlightened European females, whether these be the wives of missionaries and colonists or female teachers' (1858: 199). Missionary wives 'must recognise that this great work is their special sphere'.

No-one could fail to admire the courage of these women, just as 'no person not hopelessly prejudiced would deny the great value of the work done by Christian missionaries' (Kitson Clarke, 1967: 75). It is undeniable, however, that the effects of their work were not uniformly beneficial for the colonised. In the words of Cairns, 'they made fundamental contributions to the undermining of ideas that African societies had any right to a continuing existence…. The missionary strengthened the attitude that cultural differences were to be eliminated rather than cherished or respected' (1965: 239). They were bearers of a form of cultural imperialism which bore down upon the position of women in indigenous African society in complex ways.

CONCLUSION

Van Allen has summarised the conventional view, that the impact of Christianity on the position of African women was positive: 'Western influence has "emancipated" African women through the weakening of kinship bonds and the provision of "free choice" in Christian monogamous marriage, the suppression of "barbarous" practice, the opening of schools, the introduction of modern medicine and hygiene, and sometimes of female suffrage' (1972: 170).

Christianity did provide access to new roles for women. John Zwelibani, a Mfengu teacher and missionary, suggested in 1866 that the missionaries should devote themselves to winning women adherents as they had more to gain from Christianity than men. Moyer suggests that from a sociological perspective Zwelibani may have been correct (1976: 540). Both Williams and Moyer make much of the missionaries' liberatory role and of the mission stations as places of refuge for young Xhosa girls fleeing from 'unacceptable' African rituals, as well as unwanted marriages.

Obviously the missionaries introduced new values and attitudes in terms of which certain rituals were defined as unacceptable. But how deep did this reorientation go? How far did the missionaries' teaching involve a redefinition of self that could generate new qualities of assertiveness and independence? Monica Wilson has suggested that Christianity did imply a new independence for women:

Christianity ... tends to make women more independent because, when, as most frequently happens, the wife of a pagan man is converted, she is taught by the missionaries and forced by her convictions to assert herself against her husband in certain questions. For instance a man may wish beer brewed for a sacrifice to ancestral spirits, and a Christian wife refuses to do it. The backing of her religion and often of her teachers (though some of the missionaries consider that their women converts are in danger of becoming unduly self-assertive towards their pagan husbands) gives her courage to demand an independence of judgement and freedom of action which under the old conditions she would never have dreamed of claiming (Hunter, 1933: 274).

Against this it can be argued that Western influence weakened or destroyed women's role within precolonial society without providing alternative roles of power or autonomy in exchange.

Overall it seems that missionary education operated in complex and contradictory ways: while it may have worked to liberate a few individual African women who were provided with marketable skills, it operated in the main coercively, as an agency of socialisation, tying women to subordinate roles in colonial society. The ideology behind the educational policy as regards African women was shaped by the convergence of different definitions of the education appropriate to Africans, to women and to subordinate classes. The dominant stress in each was vocational, domestic and subservient. Thus education operated largely as the crucial agency of social control and cultural reproduction, defining and reinforcing certain social roles and initiating people into those skills and values which were essential for effective role performance. For many African women this involved a new role as domestic workers in the service of the colonisers. This is not however to exaggerate the importance of the missionaries. A complex pattern of coercion propelled Xhosa women into domestic service. These coercive factors ranged from direct, physical force to the more subtle ideological coercion exerted by the missionaries.

It is thus possible to view the missionaries as a link between two unique features of the Eastern Cape frontier: the relatively extensive involvement of African women in education and their unusually early employment in the settler community. However, to point to a connection is not the same as establishing a direct causal relation. What does seem clear is that missionary education entrenched domestic roles for black women – roles both as wives and mothers in their own homes, and as domestic servants in white households.

Nevertheless, however exploitative and onerous an occupation, domestic service must be appreciated in terms of various cultural meanings and alternatives. For African women on the Cape eastern frontier it was not only an entry point to the colonial economy but also a potential route of escape from social practices they found oppressive. It promised the possibility of earning a living, however meagre, and, therefore, offered at least the potential for economic independence to unmarried Xhosa girls. Sometimes it could also offer an escape from the forms of coercion to which women were subject in Xhosa society, as when Hena, daughter of the chief Ngqika, refused to marry a heathen and polygamist and fled into the colony to work first for a London Missionary Society family and then at Lovedale as a domestic servant (Young, 1902: 125). Similarly in eighteenth- and nineteenth-century Britain domestic service could provide girls with a route of escape from rural poverty.

Clearly there are characteristics of the institution of domestic service that were common to both the metropolitan and the colonial society – the extreme inequality of the participants; its meaning as an occupational role that allowed for movement into an urban or colonial setting; the stereotyped attitudes of employers, class-based in the one context, race-based in the other; the oppression of the domestic servant, whether measured in terms of wages, hours, dignity of treatment, extreme control or lack of fundamental securities and rights. However, there were also important differences. In the last analysis, in South Africa labour was controlled by force, whether through the legal apparatus of enslavement, apprenticeship and indenture, or through the existence of ties of dependence binding workers without property to the owners of such property.

Whatever the points of comparison between nineteenth-century domestic service in Britain and the Eastern Cape, in the two societies the institution followed an entirely different pattern of development. While the waning of the institution of domestic service in Britain by the middle of the twentieth century reflected the increased power of the working class, in South Africa the transformation of the institution into one dominated by the end of the nineteenth century by black women (rather than men) reflected the extension and elaboration of white domination. The fact that today domestic service remains a major source of employment for black women is an important indicator of the oppressive controls to which blacks generally and women in particular remain subject in contemporary South Africa.

4

Maidens, maps and mines: King Solomon's Mines *and the reinvention of patriarchy in colonial South Africa*[1]

ANNE McCLINTOCK

There are many maps of one place, and many histories of one time. (Fredriekse, 1982)
Like all proper ideologies, the family too was more than a mere lie. (Frankfurt Institute of Social Research, 1972: 138)

Until the 1860s South Africa was, from the imperial point of view, a far-flung outpost of scant allure. In 1867, however, an Afrikaner child chanced upon the first South African diamond. The discovery of the diamond fields at once drew 'this most stagnant of colonial regions' into the eddies of modern imperial capitalism, and 'a land that had seen boat-load after boat-load of emigrants for New Zealand and Australia pass it unheeding by now saw men tumbling on to its wharves and hurrying up country to the mines' (De Kiewet, 1941: 119).

Among these new arrivals was Henry Rider Haggard, a nondescript youth of 19, who, after a few years of unremarkable service in the colonial administration, returned to Britain to become the most spectacularly successful novelist of his time.[2] In 1885, a few months after the carving up of Africa among the 'lords of humankind' at Berlin, Haggard published *King Solomon's Mines*, instantly and easily outselling all his contemporary fellow authors. *She* appeared soon after, in 1887, to a riotous fanfare of applause. Almost overnight this obscure youth had become an author of unparalleled commercial success and renown.[3]

In what follows I shall argue that *King Solomon's Mines* was intimately concerned with events in South Africa following the discovery of diamonds and later gold: specifically, the reordering of black female labour within the homestead, and the struggle over black male labour on the white farms and mines. The story illuminates not simply questions about the historical force of ideology but also, in particular, the role ideology played in refashioning gender relations in South

Africa, as a nascent capitalism penetrated the region and disrupted already contested power relations within the African homestead. Despite belated recognition that some of the most crucial conflicts in the nineteenth century took place around the homestead economy, between women and men, between women and the colonists, and between white and black men over who would control the labour of the homestead's women, for the most part the story of women's work and resistance has been shunted to the sidings of history. Since, as Guy argues in chapter 1, women were the main producers and reproducers of life and labour in precapitalist southern Africa, their work was the single most valuable resource in the precolonial era, apart from the land itself. Yet we know very little about how precolonial societies were able to subordinate women's work and as little about the changes wrought on these societies by colonial conquest and the penetration of merchant and mining capital.

In this chapter I argue that Haggard's *King Solomon's Mines* can be seen to offer an unusual glimpse into some of the fundamental dynamics of that contest. I suggest that the novel was in large part a contorted attempt to resolve two overdetermined contradictions: first, the economic and psychosexual anxieties swirling around the riddles of female labour, sexuality and male generative power in the Victorian metropolis; and second, anxieties about female labour and sexuality in the colonies. The contradiction between male and female generative capacity was not only one of the obsessive themes of Haggard's work, but also a dominant paradox of his time. Much of Haggard's fascination as a writer for male Victorians was that he played out his phantasms of patriarchal power in the arena of empire, and thus evoked the unbidden relation between male (upper middle-class) power in the metropolis and the control of black female labour in the colonies. In this way *King Solomon's Mines* becomes more than a pathological Victorian curiosity and instead brings to light some of the fundamental contradictions of the colonial state and the attempts made to resolve them.

In what follows I explore how Haggard sought to resolve these contradictions within a narrative which takes the form of a journey, beginning with a mythology of racial and gender 'degeneracy', re-inventing the 'family of man' in the cradle of empire, and culminating in the regeneration of authority of the white father – in the specific historical form of the British landed squire. In other words, I shall be exploring the reorganisation of black labour and the black family, and shall argue that this reorganisation was legitimised by two primary discourses of the time: the discourse on 'degeneration' and the discourse on the reinvented 'father' of the 'family of man'. It is crucial that these discourses not be seen as monolithic impositions on a hapless people. Even less should they be seen as mere functional reflexes of the needs of the colonial state. Rather, the discourses themselves were at every moment contests for social power, as much a response to African resistance to the encroaching state as they were a product of colonial power.

This chapter is thus an attempt to explore the role of ideological practices in history. Ideological practices are dynamic social events in themselves, not the mere epiphenomenal reflection of events. As social events, they are intricately involved with other events and exert an important shaping force on history. At the same time, the story I tell has many sources, and does not promise the unearthing of a pristine past, in any event a utopian task. Rather it is an *engagement* (motivated, selective and oppositional) with historical narratives in South Africa, and the stories they tell of fathering and male authority, of female labour and resistance – stories which exclude, yet have everything to do with women.

THE FALL OF THE FAMILY OF MAN

Degeneration: a social narrative

From the outset, the idea of progress which illuminated the nineteenth century was shadowed by its dark side (see Gilman, 1985). After the 1850s Victorian social planners began to draw deeply on the medical image of 'degeneration' to figure the social crises erupting with relentless periodicity in the cities. By the end of the 1870s Britain was foundering in a severe depression, and throughout the 1880s class insurgency, feminist upheavals, the 'socialist revival', the problems of poverty and the dearth of housing and jobs fed deepening middle-class fears. Poverty was rediscovered at the same time as Britain began to feel the pinch of its imperial rivals, Germany and the United States.

The atmosphere of impending catastrophe that marked the 1880s gave rise to profound changes in social theory, which drew deeply on the poetics of degeneracy for legitimation. Biological images of disease and contagion served what Gilman has called 'the institutionalisation of fear' and came to form a cluster of social metaphors with unrivalled authority, reaching into almost every nook and cranny of Victorian social life and providing the Victorian elite with the ideology it needed to discipline and contain the 'dangerous classes' (ibid., xiv; see also Gilman, 1985a; Walter, 1956). In *Outcast London* Gareth Stedman Jones shows how London became the focus of wealthy Victorians' growing anxieties about the unregenerate poor, variously described as the 'dangerous' or 'ragged' classes, the 'casual' poor, or the 'residuum'. The slums and rookeries of the East End were figured as the hotbeds and breeding haunts of 'cholera, crime and chartism' (1971: 167; see also Mayhew, 1968; Himmelfarb, 1984). Festering in dark and filthy dens, the scavenging and vagrant poor came to be represented by images of putrefaction and debility.

The sanitation syndromes of the late nineteenth century were in part genuine attempts to combat the diseases of poverty, but they also served to rationalise the *cordon sanitaire* thrown up between the Victorian ruling elite and the 'contagious' classes – the prostitutes, the Irish, the criminals, the poor and the insane, who were as necessary to the emergent self-definition of the Victorian middle class as was the idea of degeneration to the notion of progress.

The poetics of bad blood is a poetics of social crisis. The image of bad blood is drawn from biology, but degeneration is less a biological fact than it is a social figure. The social power of the image of degeneration in Victorian Britain was twofold. Firstly, classes were described with telling frequency as 'races', 'foreign groups' or 'non-indigenous bodies' and could thus be cordoned off as biological rather than social groups. Secondly, the image provided a new ideology for justifying state intervention. Poverty and social distress were figured as biological flaws, a pathology in the body politic that posed a chronic threat to the riches, health and power of the 'imperial race'. 'For unfitness or degeneration was the condition, not of isolated individuals, but of swelling and threatening aggregates. In such circumstances, the problem of degeneration and its concomitant, chronic poverty, would ultimately have to be resolved by the state' (Jones, 1971: 313).

Thus the usefulness of the quasi-biological metaphors of 'type', 'species', 'genus' and 'race' lay in the fact that they gave full expression to anxieties about class and gender, as well as inventing a mode of containing those anxieties, without betraying the social and political nature of these distinctions. As Condorcet put it, they made 'nature herself an accomplice in the crime of political inequality' (quoted in Gould, 1981: 21).

Degeneration: race, gender and the family of man

In the poetics of degeneracy we find two opposed, dialectical narratives of human development, both elaborated within the metaphor of 'the family.' One narrative tells the story of the familial progress of humanity from degenerate native child to adult white man. The other narrative presents the converse: the historical possibility of racial decline from white fatherhood to a primordial black degeneracy incarnated in the black mother. Both these notions were very much debated at the time Haggard began to write in the 1880s (Stepan, 1982, 1985). The scientists, medical men and biologists of the day were tirelessly pondering the evidence for both, marshalling the scientific facts and elaborating the multifarious taxonomies of racial and sexual difference.

Before the 1850s two narratives of the origins of the races were in play. The first, monogenesis, described the genesis of all races from a single creative source in Adam. Simply by dwelling in different climates, races had fallen away unequally from the perfect edenic form, creating an intricately shaded hierarchy of decline. By mid-century a second, competing narrative had begun to gain ground – polygenesis, according to which different races had sprung up simultaneously in different 'centres of creation'. In this view, certain races in certain places were originally, naturally and inevitably 'degenerate'. However, after 1859 evolutionary theory

swept away the creationist rug that had supported the intense debate between monogenists and polygenists, but it satisfied both sides by presenting an even better rationale for their shared racism. The monogenists continued to construct linear hierarchies of races according to mental and moral worth; the polygenists now admitted a common ancestry in the prehistoric mists, but affirmed that the races had been separate long enough to evolve major inherited differences in talent and intelligence (Gould, 1981: 73).

At this time evolutionary theory entered an unholy alliance with 'the allure of numbers' – the amassing of measurements and the science of statistics (ibid.: 74). This alliance gave birth to scientific racism, the first and most astonishingly authoritative attempt to place social ranking and social disability on a biological and scientific footing. Scientists became enthralled by the magic of measurement. Anatomical criteria were tirelessly sought for determining the relative position of races in the human series (Morton, 1980). To an earlier assumption of cranial capacity as the primary stigma of racial and sexual ranking was now added a welter of new 'scientific' criteria: the length and shape of the head, the length of the forearm (the character of apes), deficient calves (also apelike), the shape of the ear (a stigma of sexual excess attributed to prostitutes), the placing of the hole at the base of the skull, the straightness of the hair, the length of the nasal cartilage, the flatness of the nose, prehensile feet, excessive wrinkles and facial hair. Most significantly, these stigmata were increasingly drawn on to distinguish atavistic 'races' within the European 'race': most notably prostitutes, the Irish, homosexuals, criminals, and the 'insane'. In the work of men such as Francis Galton (founder of the eugenics movement), Paul Broca (founder of the Anthropological Society of Paris), and Cesare Lombroso (an Italian physician), whose ideas seeped deep into popular thought, the geometries of the skeleton became the books of social difference from which one could read the psyche of the race.

What is of immediate importance here is that this welter of criteria for distinguishing the degenerate was finally gathered up into a dynamic narrative by one dominant metaphor: 'the family of man'.

Ernst Haeckel, the German zoologist, provided the most influential idea for the development of this metaphor (see McCown and Kennedy, 1972: 133–48).[4] His famous catch-phrase, 'ontogeny recapitulates philogeny', captured the idea that the ancestral lineage of the human species could be read off the stages of a child's growth. Every child rehearses in organic miniature the ancestral progress of the race. Recapitulation thus depicted the child as a kind of social bonsai, a miniature family tree. As Gould puts it, every individual as it grows to maturity 'climbs its own family tree' (Gould, 1981: 114). The irresistible value of the idea of recapitulation was that it offered an apparently absolute biological criterion not only for racial but also for sexual and class ranking. If the white male child was an atavistic throwback to a more primitive adult ancestor, he could be scientifically compared with other living races and groups to rank their level of evolutionary inferiority. A vital analogy had thus appeared:

The adults of inferior groups must be like the children of superior groups, for the child represents a primitive adult ancestor. If adult blacks and women are like white male children, then they are living representatives of an ancestral stage in the evolution of white males. An anatomical theory for ranking races – based on entire bodies, not only on heads – had been found (ibid.: 115).

Haggard neatly summed up this analogy in *Allan Quartermain*, the sequel to *King Solomon's Mines*: 'in all essentials the savage and the child of civilization are identical'.

Racial stigmata were now drawn on to elaborate minute shadings of difference in which race, class and gender overlapped in a three-dimensional graph of comparison. The English male aristocrat was placed at the pinnacle of the white evolutionary hierarchy, with the Irish working-class female in the lower depths of the white race. The white working-class prostitute was stationed on the threshold between the white and black races, sharing many atavistic features with 'advanced' black men. The Zulu male was regarded in turn as the 'gentleman' of the black race, while displaying features typical of females of the white race. Carl Vogt, for example, a pre-eminent mid-century German analyst of race, asserted that a mature black male shared his 'pendulous belly' with a working-class woman who had had many children (1864: 81).[5] More often than not the female Khoi or San was located at the very nadir of human degeneration, before the species left off its human form and turned bestial.

Instead of being seen as a changing social process, the monogamous patriarchal family of Western Europe was now vaunted as a biological fact, natural, inevitable and right, its lineage imprinted immemorially in the blood of the species – at just that precise moment in Western history when the social fabric of the family in its existing form had begun to unravel.

Degeneration: a biographical narrative

These debates are of great importance for an understanding of Haggard, for his fictional elaboration of these ideas in the arena of empire would cast a profound influence over an entire generation, affecting policies of social control not only in Britain but also in South Africa.

Henry Rider Haggard was born in 1856 into one of the few social scripts written for a Victorian of his birth. Son of a colonial mother raised in British India and a Norfolk Tory from the rural gentry, his life and work would take significant shape from the social contradictions embodied in his parents: the imminent fall of the ancient squirarchy (as national power shifted from land to manufacturing) and the rise of the new imperialism. He reached manhood during the Great Depression of the late 1870s – an era which saw both the calamities of poverty and the megalomania of the 'new imperialism'. Suspended as he was between a falling class and an ascendant imperialism, Haggard was in many respects peculiarly well-placed to produce, as he did, the narratives of male degeneration and restitution which were to become the most widely read novels of his time.

'A Tory to the backbone', Haggard's father, Squire William Meybohm, 'reigned at Bradenham like a king', living off the land in the patriarchal manner of the ancient squirarchy – the last of his family to do so (Haggard, 1926: 24). Haggard inherited from his father his own dynastic sense: 'To leave a son, and lands for him to inherit, to perpetuate his name, these were strong prepossessions with him' (G. Haggard in L. Haggard, 1951: 16). But the relation between male generation, naming, and the inheritance of land was peculiarly vexed for Haggard, a vexation he shared, as it turned out, with a whole generation of late-Victorian upper-middle-class men. Haggard was a younger son, disinherited from the patriarchal seat by the stern laws of primogeniture and entailment. His own son, Jock, was to die in youth, to Haggard's unstaunchable grief. At the same time the rural squirarchy as a class had begun to founder. Haggard started to write in the 1880s, during a period when the idea of paternal origins – instituting male power at the head of the family – had become increasingly problematic. Fervently attached to the dynastic ambitions of his family and class, but frustrated in these ambitions by historical change, Haggard took consolation in one of the few recourses available to a man of his generation: playing out his anachronistic phantasms of paterfamilial class power in the arena of empire. One might call the project which consumed his life and work the restoration of the father and 'the family of man'.

The poetics of male authorship is not just a poetics of creativity, but a poetics of possession and control over the issue of posterity. It involves the production of an order and a hierarchy of power. In

Haggard's case, the constellation of images of paternity, succession and hierarchy that informs the idea of authorship was particularly troubled and suggestive. Thwarted in his ambitions as a son and as a father, he became an 'increaser' and 'founder' by fathering an astonishing body of letters – 42 romances, 12 novels, 10 works of nonfiction, and a two-volume autobiography. He did thus succeed in perpetuating the male family name – not, however, through the medium of land or the succession of male offspring, but through authorship. 'There is what I shall be remembered by,' Haggard declared (1926: 64). Yet at once an anomaly emerges. As it turns out, Haggard inherited his literary authority, and hence his power to propagate the male family name, not from his father but from his mother. By Haggard's own account, his mother, Ella Doveton, 'possessed very considerable capacity for a literary career'. 'Had circumstances permitted I am sure she would have made a name,' Haggard recorded, but, he added approvingly, her life was 'all love and self-sacrifice' (ibid.: 18, 46). It is therefore fitting that Haggard should discharge the guilt he evidently felt for usurping his mother's generative authority by publishing, a year after her death, a memorial volume of her work entitled *Life and Its Author*. In short, the authority and continuity of the male family name and the male inheritance of property were secured at the expense of a repression: the repression of the mother as a source of life.

Haggard's well-nigh pathological anxiety about female generative authority is a thematic undercurrent coursing through most of his work. Yet it would appear to have derived much of its intensity from class as well as gender contradictions. For Haggard, as for so many others, the contradictions between the ideology of female idleness and the actualities of female manual labour, between paid and unpaid domestic work, between the sexuality of the Dresden china 'madonna' and the working-class whore, between vaunted female incapacity and the experience of female power, were most vividly and dangerously embodied in the living presence within the upper-class family of the female domestic servant. The story of middle- and upper-middle-class male anxieties about the working-class 'mothers' who bathed, fed, nursed, caressed and punished them, has only recently begun to be written. We know that Haggard recalled that as a child an unscrupulous nurse would terrify him into obedience with a disreputable rag-doll 'of hideous aspect, boot-button eyes, and hair of black wool' (Haggard, 1926: 56). Haggard called the doll 'She-Who-Must-Be-Obeyed', and this fetish symbol of an ominous and inexplicable authority, female and working-class, would haunt him until he was compelled to ward it off with an act of ideological exorcism in *She*. The astonishing popularity of this bestseller has led Sandra Gilbert to ask: 'What, after all, worried Rider Haggard so much that he was driven to create his extraordinary complex fantasy about Her and Her realm in just six volcanically energetic weeks? Why did thousands and thousands of Englishmen respond to his dreamlike story of Her with as much fervor as if he had been narrating their own dreams?' (1983: 449).

If, as Gilbert argues, the charisma of the book arose from its exploration of three nineteenth-century preoccupations, 'the New Woman', Egypt, and spiritualism, certainly much of Haggard's compulsion to create his 'ceremonial assertion of phallic authority' (ibid.: 444) also stemmed from his inability to resolve a social contradiction which marked his time and his class: the presence within the family of the female domestic worker.

Haggard shared with his upper-middle-class Victorian culture an unusually intense preoccupation with origins. He liked to view himself as the scion of an unbroken line of succession which stretched back to the ancient Danes. Yet to the evident discomfort of his daughter-biographer, Lilias Rider Haggard, the family stock on record was not entirely sound. Haggard's paternal grandfather had been a banker in Russia; his grandmother a Russian Jewess. His great-grandmother was an Amyand, whose 'accursed blood' had bequeathed the Haggard stock with 'more than a hint of mental instability' (L. Haggard, 1951: 24). The blood-flaw was betrayed in the features of the Haggard face by the faint but tell-tale stigmata of long nose, high cheekbones and tilted eyes – the inherited reminder of the seeds of debility that flowed in the family veins (ibid.: 25). But if the Amyand taint was evoked by Lilias Haggard within a well-established poetics of blood and 'degeneration', the family records reveal that the anxiety which underlay Haggard's childhood reputation as a dolt was more properly speaking the anxiety of class demise.

Arriving eighth out of ten children, Haggard lived in his family's eyes as an emblem of the possible lineal decline which the defiled Amyand blood foretold. Haggard's daughter recounts that as a child he was considered 'not to be very bright'. Significantly, his family reputation as a 'dunderhead' and 'as heavy as lead in mind and body' was figured not so much as a failure of mental vigour, but as a falling away from class. Squire Haggard bitterly derided his disappointing younger son as 'fit only to be a greengrocer' and predicted that his dullness of mind would find its more natural station with the lower orders (ibid.: 25, 23, 26, 27). In view of dwindling family resources as well as the boy's lack of promise and inconsequence near the end of a robust line of sons, Squire Haggard decided that Rider, alone of seven sons, would not be granted a public school education. Much has been made of Haggard's early stupidity – by himself, his family, his biographers and critics. Perhaps this was so because Haggard's early degeneracy became the indispensable narrative element in what would turn out to be an undeniably successful performance in pater-familial restoration.

This performance could best be played out at this time in the arena of empire. In the public and political debates of the late nineteenth century, the relentless superfluity of women and men was represented as a malady and contagion in the national body politic which could best be countered by leeching off the bad fluid and depositing it in the colonies. Not a few of the 'riddlings of society', as Haggard called them, came from the depressed gentry and the upper classes. In the colonies, urged J. A. Froude, Victorian historian and essayist, 'is the true solution of the British land question' (1890: 307). Much of this interest in colonial emigration was figured within the image of the family. In the words of Froude, 'The home of the French peasant is France.... The home of the Scot or the Englishman is the whole globe' (ibid.: 289). As he saw it, Britain's patriarchal order could be protected from civil discontent by packing the discontented off to the colonies: 'You who are impatient with what you call a dependent position at home, go to Australia, go to Canada, go to New Zealand, or South Africa. There work for yourselves. There gather wealth.... Come back if you will as rich men at the end of twenty years. Then buy an estate for yourselves' (ibid.: 306). 'People that country, people any part of any of our own colonies, from the younger sons who complain that there is no room for them at home.... Spread out there and everywhere. Take possession of the boundless inheritance which is waiting for you' (ibid.: 308).

Belated son, Haggard thus took his place in the Victorian script written for the younger or ill-begotten sons of good family, the male offspring of the clergy, and the swelling numbers of the unemployed and working-class poor. In 1875 Squire William wrote to his neighbour, Sir Henry Bulwer, newly appointed Lieutenant-Governor of Natal, and asked him to take the unpromising Haggard into his services. Bulwer agreed, and Haggard sailed as an obscure member of Bulwer's staff to Natal in August 1875. He was then 19.

THE REGENERATION OF THE FAMILY OF MAN

Regeneration through affiliation: an imperial narrative

Mediocre and disinherited in Britain, once Haggard stepped on South African soil he rose immediately into the most exclusive white elite of the country. His appointment to the colonial administration was nothing more glamorous than housekeeper to the largely male family of bureaucrats in Pietermaritzburg, the capital of Natal. But as general factotum to Sir Henry Bulwer, tasked with handling the 'champagne and sherry policy' (Haggard, 1926: 36) of Natal's small brass-band and cavalry administration, his prestige and self-esteem were enormously revived. Standing discreetly at the elbow of the paramount white authority in Natal, he was a far cry from the hapless dolt of his childhood.

Haggard's regenerative arrival in South Africa epitomises a critical moment in late Victorian male culture. In an important observation, Edward Said has pointed to the transition from 'filiation' to 'affiliation' in late Victorian upper-middle-class culture: how the withering of the 'generative impulse' – the failure of the capacity to produce children – took on the aspect of a pervasive cultural affliction. For Said the decay of filiation is typically attended by a second moment – the turn to a 'compensatory order' of affiliation, which might variously be an institution, a vision, a credo or a vocation, but which is always also a new system (1983: 17). Haggard's redemption in the colonial service vividly rehearses this transition from failed filiation within the feudal family manor to affiliation with the colonial bureaucracy. Through affiliation with the colonial administration he was quite explicitly compensated for his loss of place in the patriarchal family, and provided with a surrogate father in the form of Theophilus Shepstone, Natal's Secretary for Native Affairs. Haggard was in this respect representative of a specific moment in imperial culture, whereby the nearly anachronistic authority of the vanishing feudal family, invested in its sanctioned rituals of rank and subordination, was displaced onto the colonies and reinvented within the new order of the colonial administration.

This gives rise to a paradox. One witnesses in the colonies a strange shadow-effect of the state of the family in Britain.[6] The failure of the idea of filiation within the great landed and service families stemmed in part from the growth of the imperial bureaucracy, which not only usurped the social function of the service families, displacing administrative power beyond the network of the family, but also seriously undermined the image of the patriarchal paterfamilias as ultimate originary power. Yet if the growth of the bureaucracy unseated the patriarch as the image of centralised and individual male power, one witnesses in the colonies the reinvention of the tradition of fatherhood displaced onto the colonial bureaucracy as a surrogate, restored authority. In other words, the figure of the paterfamilias is most vigorously embraced in the colonies at just that moment when it is withering in the metropolis. The colony became one of the last opportunities for the reinvented authority of fatherhood, and it is therefore not surprising that one finds its most intense expressions in the colonial administration, in the very place which threatened it. Nor is it surprising that the reinvention of the patriarch in the colonies took on a pathological form.

Reinventing patriarchy in Natal

Natal, where Haggard found himself in 1875, was one of the most unpromising of British colonies. Lacking any vital raw materials for export and lying hundreds of miles from the markets of Cape Town, it was poor, isolated and vulnerable. Two paradoxes plagued Natal's white settlers: a shortage of land in a country of thousands of acres, and a shortage of labour in a land with a huge indigenous population. It was this which Haggard, in 1882, in his first published writing, *Cetywayo and His White Neighbours*, called 'the unsolved riddle of the future, the Native Question' (281; see also Guy, 1982; Slater, 1980; Harries, 1987; Atmore and Marks, 1975). And it is this unsolved riddle of land and labour, overdetermined by the contradiction between male land inheritance and female generation which Haggard faced in Britain, that *King Solomon's Mines* attempts to resolve. In the process the book reveals that the paradox of land and labour was rooted in the fundamental question of who was to control women's labour power – an issue being fought out at a number of levels: between black women and men within the Zulu homestead, among black men, and between white colonists and black men.

Many elements of the Zulu family drama are present in *King Solomon's Mines*. In 1856 a crisis broke out over the rightful heir to the Zulu king, Mpande, a struggle that prefigured the crisis of male succession which Haggard re-enacts in his novel. As in Haggard's tale, the blood-rivalry between Mpande's sons, Cetshwayo and Mbulazi, climaxed in a battle in 1856; an eyewitness account of the actual battle provided Haggard with many of the details he used for the battle scene in *King Solomon's Mines*. Haggard's depiction in his novel of the degenerate usurper king, Twala, is resonant of racist images of Cetshwayo as a gorilla-like monster in the popular illustrated papers. Furthermore, in both the novel and its historical counterpart, white men interfere in the crisis of male inheritance and arrogate to themselves the powers of white *patria potestas*. This gives them the authority to inaugurate what they believe will be a subservient black monarch, on terms favourable to the colonial state.

In the historical case, Cetshwayo emerged as victor in the succession struggle and Theophilus Shepstone visited the Zulu court to confer official blessing on him in 1861. However, instead of the adulatory welcome he confidently expected, Shepstone (like Haggard's heroes) only narrowly averted death. Nevertheless, the parties were reconciled and in September 1873 Shepstone proceeded to enact a pompous ceremony of monarchical recognition which he alone took seriously. Cetshwayo was proclaimed king with a great deal of pomp and ritual invented by Shepstone for the occasion, while Shepstone himself, 'standing in the place of Cetshwayo's father, and so representing the nation' (Haggard, 1882: 9) (or so he believed), enunciated four articles which he regarded as necessary for putting an end to 'the continual slaughter that darkens the history of Natal' (ibid.). These articles are strikingly similar to the articles of control Haggard's heroes would demand in *King Solomon's Mines*.

According to Haggard, Shepstone evidently felt he had been instituted as nominal 'founding father' of the Zulu nation, and he and Haggard made a good deal, both rhetorically and ritually, of his acquired status as 'father' of the Zulus. The coronation was not simply Shepstone's whimsy, however, but was a symptomatic replica of the neo-traditions of monarchical inauguration which inventive colonials were enacting all over British Africa. In what Terence Ranger has called 'the invented tradition of the "Imperial Monarchy"' (1983: 212), the colonists, lacking a single, centralised body of legitimating ritual, presented to Africans a dramatic effigy of tinsel and velvet royalty which bore little resemblance to the political reality of the British monarchy – by that time shrunk to a ceremonial figurehead (see Cannadine, 1983). In the African colonies, however, the withered figure of the monarch rose to its feet and walked abroad again. The anachronistic ideology of the imperial monarchy became a widespread administrative cult, full of invention and pretence, of which Shepstone's coronation of Cetshwayo, as Haggard's coronation of Umbopa, were symptomatic.

Nevertheless, when Ranger calls the 'theology' of an 'omniscient, omnipotent and omnipresent monarchy' 'almost the sole ingredient of imperial ideology as it was represented to the Africans' (1983: 212), he neglects what was arguably the most authoritative and politically influential of all the invented rituals in the colonies: that of 'the father', the patriarch. In colonial documents Shepstone is referred to with ritualistic insistence as the 'father figure' of Natal. Sir Henry Bulwer called him 'one of the Colonies' earliest fathers – the very Nestor of the Colony' (quoted in Gordon, 1968: 309). Shepstone was generally referred to by blacks (no doubt obliging his fantasy) as 'Somtsewu', which, according to Jeff Guy, 'notwithstanding much speculation on its meaning along the lines of "mighty hunter" … is a word of Sesotho origin meaning "Father of Whiteness"' (1982: 51n). Haggard, like Shepstone himself, took the name to carry the entirely unfounded implication that the Zulus regarded Shepstone as the originary potentate of the black people: Shepstone is 'par excellence their great white chief and "father."' In a message to Lobengula, chief of the Ndebele, Shepstone announced portentously: 'The Lieutenant-Governor of Natal is looked upon as the Father of all …' (Haggard, 1926: 9).

Shepstone took the title of 'father' and everything that sprang from it very seriously indeed, not only as a title but also as a political and administrative practice, with serious consequences for the history of South Africa. What is important here is that Shepstone manipulated the invented traditions of fathers and kings simultaneously, constructing a racial hierarchy of power in which he could mimic allegiance to certain customs of Zulu chieftainship, while retaining for himself the 'superior' status of father – the same ideological solution to conflicting patriarchies that Haggard rehearses in *King Solomon's Mines.* Most significant in terms of political impact was the hierarchical racial relation between white father and black king, superordinated over the gender relation between these men and black women, and figured within the overarching discourse of the racial 'family of man' in which the generative power of women is subordinated and negated. Thus Shepstone drew on an ideology of divine fatherhood as preordained and natural, the founding source of all authority. The black king, on the other hand, was his symbolic reproduction, mortal, invested and receiving authority only by virtue of his symbolic mimicry of the originary power of the father. For these reasons, I would argue, the reinvention of fathers and kings in South Africa can be seen as a central ideological attempt to mediate the contradictions operating at a number of levels: between the imperial bureaucracy and the declining landed gentry in Britain; between the colonial ruling patriarchy and the indigenous patriarchy of precapitalist southern Africa, and last, but most significantly, between women and black men and between women and white men. Here we come across the final, and most important, dynamic underlying both Haggard's tale and the emergent economy of the colonial state.

The invention of idleness

Shepstone's policy was based on an intimate sense of the precarious balance of power in Natal and Zululand. He knew that the frail colony could ill-afford to antagonise the Zulus and that it lacked both the military muscle and the finances to drive black men forcibly off their lands and into wage labour. As the missionary Henry Callaway asked ruefully, 'How are 8 000 widely scattered whites to compel 200 000 coloureds to labour, against their will?' (Callaway, 1896: 88). Out of this riddle rose the exceptionally vituperative discourse on the 'degenerate idleness' of the blacks. Of all the stigmata of degeneration invented by the settlers to mark themselves from the Africans, the most tirelessly invoked was idleness: that same stigma of racial unworth which Haggard saw as marking the Kukuana's degeneration and loss of title to the diamonds.

It is scarcely possible to read any travel account, settler memoir or ethnographic document without coming across a chorus of complaints about the sloth, idleness, indolence or torpor of the natives who, the colonists claimed, preferred scheming and fighting, lazing and wanton lasciviousness to industry. Very typical is Captain Ludlow's remark on visiting the Umvoti Mission Station: 'The father of the family leant on his hoe in his mielie garden, lazily smoking his pipe.... It is amusing to watch one of them pretending to work' (1882: 18). Haggard saw the racial hatred of whites rooted in this stubborn abstraction of African labour: 'The average white man ... detests the Kafir, and looks on him as a lazy good-for-nothing, who ought to work for him and will not work for him' (1882: 57).

The idea of idleness was neither descriptively accurate of the labouring black farmers, nor was it new. The arriving settlers brought with them to South Africa the remnants of a three-hundred-year-old discourse in Britain associating poverty with sloth, and put it to similar use. From the sixteenth century onwards in Britain an intricate and multifaceted discourse on idleness had gradually emerged, which served not only to draw distinctions between the labouring classes and the merchants and well-to-do artisans, but was also drawn on to sanction and enforce social discipline, to legitimise land plunder, and to alter habits of labour. The discourse on idleness can also be seen as a register of labour resistance, a resistance which could in turn be countered and lambasted as torpor and sloth, and as the mark of racial degeneracy. Colonists couched their complaints in the same images of degeneracy, moral belatedness, massing animal menace, and irrationality familiar to European descriptions of the dangerous urban underclasses (see Jones, 1971; Stepan, 1985). But the African pastoralists differed markedly from the uprooted and immiserated proletariat of Victorian Britain with which the settlers were familiar. Despite the large-scale plunder of their land, Africans still enjoyed a measure of self-sufficiency and were, on the whole, more successful farmers than the white interlopers. Thus settler fortunes were constantly imperilled by the coherence and self-sufficiency of black farmers. As in Britain, complaints about black sloth were often complaints about different habits of labour. If black people entered into wage relations for whites, it was often reluctantly or briefly, perhaps to earn money to buy guns or cattle, then to return home. Thus the discourse on idleness was not a monolithic discourse imposed on a passive people. Rather it was a realm of contestation, marked with the stubborn refusal of labour to alter traditional habits of work, as well as by conflicts within the white communities.

The assault on habits of native agriculture was not in fact an attempt to raise Africans to a more elevated state of labour, but an attempt to break habits of farming which were damagingly rivalrous to the whites. Most important, the assault on habits of black pastoralism was at root an assault on polygyny and the gendered division of labour in the precapitalist polity: the fundamental dynamic underlying both *King Solomon's Mines* and the emergent native policy of Natal.

One does not have to look far to find evidence that the root of the problem of black labour for the colonists lay in women's role in production. When Froude visited Natal, he noted grimly: 'The government won't make the Kafirs work.' Then at once he came upon the cause of the problem. Male 'indolence', he saw, was rooted regrettably but inevitably in the 'detestable systems of polygamy and female slavery'.

> My host talks much and rather bitterly on the Nigger question. If the Kafir would work, he would treble his profits.... It is an intricate problem. Here in Natal are nearly 400,000 natives.... They are allowed as much land as they want for their locations. They are polygamists, and treat their women as slaves, while they themselves idle or worse (1890: 370–1).

Missionaries and colonists voiced their repugnance for polygyny in moral and racial tones, locating it firmly within the discourse of racial degeneration. The practice of polygyny was seen to mark the male, as Haggard marks King Twala, as wallowing in the nether depths of sexual abandon: the 'African sin'. Yet colonial documents readily reveal that the attack on polygyny was an assault on African habits of labour which withheld from the resentful white farmers the work of black men and women. The excess labour that a black man controlled through his wives was seen as a direct and deadly threat to the profits of the settlers. As Governor Pine complained: 'How can an Englishman with one pair of hands compete with a native with five to twenty slave wives?' (quoted in Simons, 1968: 21).

Black women in Natal thus became the ground on which white men fought black men for control of their land and labour. As Jeff Guy has argued in chapter 1, precapitalist societies in southern Africa were organised around the creation and control of labour power, rather than the creation and control of products – fundamentally, the labour power of women. In *Cetywayo*, Haggard devoted a good deal of space to the question of polygyny, which he recognised as lying at the heart of Zulu power. In a metaphor which nicely expressed the relation between matrimonial and military power, he advised: 'Deprive them of their troops of servants in the shape of wives, and thus force them to betake themselves to honest labour like the rest of mankind' (1882: 54). Tampering with the circulation of women was thus tantamount to severing the jugular vein of the male Zulu polity's power and cohesion.

Indeed, this was the policy Shepstone attempted to follow. In the face of the bitter resentment and ire of the farmer-settlers, Shepstone doggedly pursued a policy of segregation, administration, and compromise. In the reserves, wretchedly apportioned as they were, blacks were allowed to retain access to land under 'customary law' (as were Haggard's Kukuanas in *King Solomon's Mines*). The communal polygynous household would have to be retained, since black resistance proved too tenacious, but the family would be gradually administered and modified by carefully diverting the surplus female labour from the homestead into the colonial treasury in the form of hut and marriage taxes. Knowing that an outright ban on polygyny was impractical, both Shepstone and Haggard favoured a hut-tax, a metonymic tax on wives rather than huts, as the surest method of driving men into wage labour. By legislating control of the rates of the hut taxes over the years, the Shepstone administration struggled to take control of the circulation of women out of black men's hands and simultaneously drive these men into wage labour. This put an administrative fetter on polygyny, even as it turned the women's labour power into a sizeable source of revenue for the dwindling treasury. Significantly, what this reveals is that there was no objection to drawing women's labour into a cash exchange and exploiting marriage as a commercial transaction, as long as white men and not black men benefited from it. At the same time, to administer this gradual process of cultural attrition, ductile chiefs would be appointed to supervise and implement the process.

THE REGENERATION OF THE FATHER: A FICTIONAL NARRATIVE

At this point we may return to *King Solomon's Mines*, for Haggard's knowledge that women's productive and reproductive power underlay the dynamics of the Zulu economy animates the entire narrative. A paramount concern of the book is the reordering and disciplining of two orders: female reproduction and sexuality within the black family, and labour in the production of mining. These two orders are reorganised within a narrative which takes the form of a journey, beginning with a mythology of racial degeneracy, reinventing the 'family of man' in the patriarchal cradle of empire, and culminating in the regeneration of the authority of the white patriarch in the specific class form of the landed gentleman.

The map

In the opening pages of *King Solomon's Mines* we discover a map. This map, we are told, is the facsimile of one that leads three white Englishmen on their journey to the diamond mines of Kukuanaland (a fictionalised version of Zululand). The original map was drawn in 1590 by a Portuguese trader, José da Silvestra, while dying of hunger on the 'nipple' of a mountain named Sheba's Breasts, somewhere in southern Africa. Traced on a remnant of yellow linen torn from his clothing, and inscribed with a 'cleft bone' in his own blood, Da Silvestra's map promises to reveal the wealth of Solomon's treasure chamber, but carries with it the obligatory charge of first killing the black witch-mother, Gagool.

In this way, Haggard's map assembles in miniature the three nar-

rative themes which govern his novel: map-making as a form of
military appropriation, the transmission of white male power
through control of the black female, and the plundering of the land's
riches. What sets Haggard's map apart from the scores of treasure
maps that emblazon colonial adventure narratives is that his is explicitly sexualised. The land, which is also the female, is literally mapped
in male body fluids, and Da Silvestra's phallic cleft bone becomes
thereby the organ through which he bequeaths the patrimony of
surplus capital to his white heirs, investing them with the authority
and power befitting the keepers of sacred treasure. At the same time,
male colonial inheritance takes place within a necessary economy of
exchange. Da Silvestra's death on the bad (frozen) nipple is avenged
and white patrilineal inheritance assured, only with the death of the
black witch Gagool, the 'mother, old mother' (74) and 'evil genius of
the land' (84). Thus the map hints at a hidden order underlying the
ritual of late Victorian male generation: the conquest of the productive
and reproductive labour of the black colonised woman.

There is a paradox in this map. On the one hand it is a rough sketch
of the ground the white men must cross in order to secure the riches
of the diamond mines. On the other hand, if the map is inverted it
reveals at once the diagram of a female body. The body is spread-
eagled and truncated – only those parts are drawn that explicitly
denote female sexuality. In the narrative the travellers cross the body
from the south, beginning near the head, which is represented by the
shrunken 'pan bad water' – the mutilated syntax depicting the place
of female reason as a site of degeneration. At the centre of the map lie
two mountain peaks called 'Sheba's Breasts' – mountain ranges
stretch to either side as handless arms. The body's length is represented by the right royal way of Solomon's road, leading from the
threshold of the frozen breasts over the navel *koppie* straight as a die
to the pubic mound. In the narrative this mound is named 'The Three
Witches' and is figured by a triangle of three hills covered in 'dark
heather' (118). These both point to and conceal the entrances to two
forbidden passages, the 'mouth of treasure cave' – the vaginal entrance into which the men are led by the black mother, Gagool – and
behind it the anal pit, from which the men will eventually clamber
with the diamonds, leaving Gagool lying dead within.

Haggard's map allows one to consider the colonial map as a document of pathology. The specific pathology it reveals might be called
paranoia, for it is only in the discourse of paranoia that one finds
simultaneously and in such condensed form both delusions of grandeur and delusions of engulfment. The colonial map is a document
that professes to convey the truth about a place in pure rational form,
and promises at the same time that those with the technology to make
such perfect representations are best entitled to possession. Marx's

dictum, 'They cannot represent themselves; they must be represented' (1969: 406), could hardly be more apposite. Map-making became the servant of colonial plunder, for the knowledge constituted by the map both preceded and legitimised the appropriation of territory. The map is in this way a technology of possession, operating under the guise of scientific exactitude, promising to retrieve and reproduce nature exactly as it is. Hence its megalomania, which it shares with the discourse of paranoia, for its delusions of grandeur are accompanied by delusions of engulfment. The edges and blank spaces of colonial maps are typically marked with visible signs of the failure of representation, symptoms of a collapse of mimesis and hence unbidden reminders of the illegitimacy and tenuousness of possession. The unrepresentable appears on the surfaces of these maps in the form of cannibals, savages, mermaids and monsters, threshold figures eloquent of the resurgent relation between sex, race and imperialism.

Haggard's map is no exception, for he represents the place of female sexuality as cannibalistic: the 'mouth of treasure cave'. The pubic mound is also called 'The Three Witches', and the 'Place of the Idols'. Yet if 'The Three Witches' signals the presence of an alternative female authority, this is denied by inversion and control. For on the map Haggard wards off the threat of the devouring female genitalia by placing alongside them the four points of the compass: the icon of rationality and possession of the earth. The logo of the compass reproduces the spread-eagled figure of the female body as marked by the two axes of global containment.

In this way Haggard's map depicts a fantastic conflation of the themes of colonial space and sexuality. The map abstracts the female body and reproduces it as a geometry of sexuality held captive under the technology of scientific form. Yet it reveals a curious *camera obscura*, for neither reading of the map is complete on its own, but each presents the shadowy inversion beneath it of its other, repressed side. If one aligns oneself with the authority of the printed page, the points of the colonial compass and the bloody labels, the map can be read and the treasure reached, but the female body will be stood on her head. If, on the other hand, one turns the male book upside down and sets the female body to rights, the crimson words on her body, in fact the male colonial adventure as a whole, become unreadable.

Crucially, the map represents King Solomon's mines as simultaneously the female source of life (sexual reproduction) and of the diamonds (economic production). In both the map and the narrative, the mineral wealth of the mines and the place of female reproduction are fused in a condensed, scatological image of particular neurotic intensity, which will be ritually conquered and reappropriated as white and male.

The narrative

Allan Quartermain, gentleman, hunter, trader, fighter, and miner (named, not accidentally, after a father-surrogate who had befriended Haggard as a youth), began to write 'the strangest story' that he knows for prophylactic reasons – as an act of biological hygiene. A confounded lion having mauled his leg, he is laid up in Durban in some pain, unable to get about. Writing the book will relieve some of the frustration of his impotence – it will return him to health and manhood. Further, he will send it to his son, who is studying to be a doctor at a London hospital and is therefore obliged to spend a good deal of his time cutting up dead bodies. Quartermain intends his imperial adventure to breathe 'a little life into things' for his boy, Harry, who will as a result be better fitted to pursue the technology of sanitation, the task of national hygiene, the restoration of the race. The story is thus a threefold narrative of imperial recuperation, embracing three realms and moving from one to the other in a certain privileged order: from the physical body of the white patriarch restored in the colonies, to the familial bond with the son in Britain, and from the son–doctor to the national body politic.

The task of paterfamilial restoration which motivates the narration of the journey to King Solomon's mines finds its analogue in the motivation for the fictional journey itself. Quartermain, Captain Good, and Sir Henry Curtis set out for the mines primarily to find Sir Henry's younger brother, Neville. Left without a profession or a penny when his father died intestate, Neville quarrelled with Sir Henry and set off for South Africa in search of a fortune – a small mimicry of the flight of so many of the distressed gentry to the colonies. At the end of the novel Neville is found in the wilderness, clad in ragged skins, his beard grown wild, his leg crushed in an accident – a living incarnation of the racial degeneration and wounded manhood thought to imperil the white race when abandoned too long in the colonial wilderness.

Thus at the level both of the telling of the story and of the story told, the narrative is initiated through a double crisis of male succession, and is completed with the regeneration of ruptured family bonds, promising therewith the continuity, however tenuous, of the landed patriarch. Yet as it happens, Haggard's family romance of fathers, sons, and brothers regenerating each other through the imperial adventure is premised upon the reordering of another family: the male succession of the Kukuana royal family and the obligatory death of the 'witch-mother' Gagool. Only with her death is female control over generation aborted and the legitimate king restored, in a ceremony presided over by the regenerated white 'fathers'.

In *King Solomon's Mines* we find figured the two theories of human racial development traced above. Both are intimately dependent on each other and both are elaborated within the metaphor of the 'family'. On the one hand, the narrative presents the historical decline from 'white' (Egyptian) fatherhood to a primordial black degeneracy incarnated in the black mother. On the other hand, the narrative presents the story of the familial progress of humanity from degenerate native child to adult white father. Haggard shared the popular notion that 'civilization' as embodied by colonials was hazardous to the African, who, 'by intellect and by nature ... is some five centuries behind.... Civilization, it would seem, when applied to black races, produces effects diametrically opposite to those we are accustomed to in white nations: it debases before it can elevate' (1882: 281). Crucially, the dynamic principle which animates the hierarchy of racial and gender degeneration, transforming a static depiction of debasement into a narrative of historical progress, is the principle of imperial conquest.

The journey to King Solomon's mines is a genesis of racial and sexual order. The journey to origins, as Macherey points out, is 'not a way of showing the absolute or beginning, but a way of determining the genesis of order, of succession' (1978: 183). Haraway (1984–5) has observed that the colonial safari was a kind of travelling mini-society, an icon of the whole enterprise of imperialism fully expressive of its racial and sexual division of labour. It is therefore fitting that Quartermain's party consists of three white gentlemen; a Zulu *keshla* (elder or 'ringed man') who lags nevertheless some five hundred years behind the whites on the evolutionary scale; three Zulu 'boys', still in a state of native immaturity in relation to the whites; and the racially degenerate 'Hottentot', Ventvogel. Thus we set out with the racial family of man in place, fully expressive of fixed divisions of class and race and with the female entirely repressed – a fitting racial hierarchy with which to reinvent the genesis of the species.

The journey into the interior is, like almost all colonial journeys, figured as a journey forward in space, but backward in time. As the men progress they enter the dangerous zones of racial degeneration. Entering the feverlands and the place of the tsetse fly, the men leave their sick animals and proceed on foot. On the edge of the burning desert that stretches between them and Solomon's blue mountains, they cross into the borderlands of pathology. Stepping into the desert, they step into the zone of prehistory. Their journey across the untenanted plain retraces an evolutionary regression from adult virility into a primordial landscape of sun and thirst, inhospitable to all except insect life. True to the narrative of recapitulation that underlies the journey, the men slowly slough off their manhood. The sun sucking their blood from them, they stagger like infants unable to walk and escape death only by digging a womb-hole in the earth in which they bury themselves. Notably, Ventvogel here enters his proper racial element. Being a 'Hottentot', and therefore untouched by the sun, his 'wild-bred' instincts awakened, he sniffs the air 'like an old Impala ram' and, uttering guttural exclamations, runs about and smells out the 'pan bad water' (39).

Again in keeping with the narrative of recapitulation, adult racial degeneration to the primitive state of the 'Hottentot' is accompanied by sexual degeneration to the female condition, while both states are attended by linguistic degeneration to an infantile state of preverbal impotence. As we know from the map, the 'pan bad water' represents the corrupted female head. At this point, just over the perilous threshold of race, the place of prehistory merges with the place of the female. The landscape becomes suddenly feminised – the sky blushes like a girl, the moon waxes wan, and at the very moment that Ventvogel smells the bad water, the men lay eyes for the first time on Sheba's Breasts. The prescribed narrative of racial, sexual, and linguistic degeneracy confirms itself here. At the sight of the mountains 'shaped exactly like a woman's breasts', their snowy peaks 'exactly corresponding to the nipple on the female breast', Quartermain plunges into the condition of reduced manhood and linguistic degeneration characteristic of the 'Hottentot'–female state. He cannot describe what he saw: 'language seems to fail me.' 'To describe the grandeur of the whole view is beyond my powers' (38, 39). This crisis of representation is a ritualistic moment in the colonial narrative, whereby the colonised land rises up in all its unrepresentability, threatening to unman the intruder: 'I am impotent even before its memory.' Yet this is a subterfuge, a pretence of the same order as writing 'cannibals' on the colonial map, for Quartermain contains the eruptive power of the black female by inscribing her into the narrative of racial degeneracy.

As the men leave the plains of prehistory and scale the sides of Sheba's Breasts, Ventvogel's racial debility begins to tell. 'Like most Hottentots' he cannot take the cold and freezes to death in the cave on Sheba's nipple, proving himself unfit to accompany the other men on their journey to the restoration of the paternal origin. At the same time, his death discloses a prior historical failing. In the cave where Ventvogel dies, they find, in foetal position, the frozen skeletal remains of the Portuguese trader, José da Silvestra. These remains are a memento of the racial and class unfitness of the first wave of colonial intruders in these parts, and thereby an historical affirmation of the superior evolutionary fitness of the English gentry over the Portuguese trader. To inscribe this liminal moment of succession into history, Quartermain takes up Da Silvestra's 'rude pen', the cleft bone, signifying mastery and possession: 'It is before me as I write – sometimes I sign my name with it' (45).

Standing aloft on Sheba's Breast, the men re-enter history. Monarchs of all they survey, their proprietary act of seeing inscribes itself on the land. Leaving Ventvogel and the tongueless zone of prehistory, they re-enter language. Nevertheless, this moment is not a moment of origin, but rather the beginning of an historical return and regression, for the journey has already been made. As Macherey has observed, the colonial journey 'cannot be an exploration in the strict sense of the word, but only discovery, retrieval of a knowledge already complete ...' (1978: 183). The landscape before them is not originary – it cannot find its principle of order within itself. 'The landscape lay before us like a map', written over with European history. The mountain peaks are 'Alplike', Solomon's road looks first like 'a sort of Roman road', then like St Gotthard's in Switzerland. The landscape is not properly speaking African, because it is already the subject of conquest. One of the tunnels through which the men pass is carved in ancient statuary, one, 'exceedingly beautiful, represented a whole battle scene with a convoy of captives being marched off in the distance' (48). Thus, 'the journey ... is disclosed as having ineluctably happened before.... To explore is to follow, that is to say, to cover once again, under new conditions, a road already actually travelled.... The conquest is only possible because it has already been accomplished' (Macherey, 1978: 183).

Macherey's observations are of great importance for Haggard's narrative, for if the narrative of origins is more properly speaking the genesis of an order and a hierarchy, and if the order the white men intend to impose is that of colonisation and the primitive accumulation of capital, their conquest finds its legitimacy only by virtue of the fact that the conquest had already taken place, at a previous moment in history. King Solomon, whom Haggard regarded as white, had already proved his titular right to the treasure of the mines, had already carved his road over the land. All that had to be accomplished to succeed to the treasure was to demonstrate family resemblance. A poetics of blood inheritance had to be written, whereupon the white gentlemen could succeed as rightful heirs to the riches.

As it happens, the Kukuanas are discovered not to be an originary people. They are the people of whom the character Evans had spoken: degenerate descendants of an ancient civilisation 'long since lapsed into barbarism'. Their ancestors had swept down from 'the great lands which lie there' to the north, identified as Egypt by the traces of 'Egyptian-like sculptures' that marked the terrain like signatures. These original people had been white, in keeping with the popular fantasy of Haggard's time that the Egyptian civilisation, the cradle of humanity, was not truly African. Possessed of the arts of mining, road-making, statuary, and writing, as well as a knowledge of the value of diamonds, these wanderers had built a city and put to work the servile black race living near the diamond fields. The Kukuanas, a hybrid racial mix, are lost in racial amnesia, having forgotten their august origins and the arts that flowed from them, and now reduced simply to protecting the treasure and keeping the roads clear of grass. Nevertheless, they are not entirely debased. True to the pseudo-scientific narratives of race, the women (typically thought to be the conservative element, retaining ancestral traces longer than males) reveal physiological features eloquent of their lost white ancestry – a certain dignity of bearing, their lips 'not unpleasantly thick', the hair 'rather curly than woolly', and an instinctive atavistic admiration for the 'snowy loveliness' of Good's skin (58). These atavistic traces of a superior founding race elevate them, we are told, above the Natal Zulus. Unlike the Zulus, who, we learn, are an even more degenerate offshoot of the Kukuanas, they do not squat near the ground on their haunches, but sit on stools (a recurrent measure of racial worth in travel writing of the time).

At once the family metaphor of recapitulation asserts itself. King Twala is descended from a patriarch with the name Kafa (a corruption of the generic term 'kaffir'). Infadoos, King Twala's brother, describes himself as 'but a child', a racial child bereft as much of the historical memory of his forefathers as of the value of the diamonds and gold, which are to him mere childish baubles, 'bright stones, pretty playthings'. Moreover, the Kukuana royal family is itself dangerously degenerate, offering a spectacle of familial disorder run amok. In the features of King Twala's face one reads the degeneration of the race. He is a black paragon of the putative stigmata of debasement, excessively fat, repulsively ugly, flat-nosed, one-eyed, 'cruel and sensual to a degree' (64). His degeneracy manifests itself most clearly in his indiscriminate sensuality. His is an unlicensed polygyny. 'Husband of a thousand wives', his access to women is unbridled, his family bears every mark of transgression and flaw, and the land groans under his 'red ways' (53, 69). The Kukuana royal family is in every aspect a family defiled.

Most significantly, the principle of disorder and familial defilement is female. It is immediately apparent that King Twala's reign is illegitimate, the source of corruption founded on a female presumption – the presumption of the mother to control the issue of generation and descent. Born a weaker twin (a sign of organic decay as Haggard saw it), Twala had usurped his legitimate brother's place with the connivance of his mother. According to ethnographic and popular lore of the time, the Nguni were in the habit of putting to death the second-born of twins. What seems to have caught Haggard's imagination in this notion was the direct threat which twins were thought to pose to the life of the father. As A. T. Bryant noted, it was believed that 'if both twins lived, their father would surely die' (1929: 640) or, as Josiah Tyler explains, 'if twins were born, one is immediately destroyed lest the father die' (1971: 104). 'This twin business', as Bryant calls it, served Haggard's interests by figuring a perilous threat to patriarchal continuity. With the help of Gagool, the *isanusi* (doctor), and Twala's mother, Twala assumed kingship in flagrant violation of the customs of the people. Thus female interference in the succession of male inheritance had plunged the land into chaos.

It is therefore not surprising that the *isanusi*, Gagool, represents the nadir of degeneration. Haggard's description of her, eloquent of a profound racial and sexual anxiety, is a thumbnail catalogue of the stigmata of debasement felt to attend the black female. Gagool is so old that she is barely human. Yet her age rehearses a regression, traversing time backward to a point where the human has become bestial. A 'wizened, monkey-like figure', she has lost the erect bearing of the adult and creeps on all fours. Everything about her is simian: her slit of a mouth, her prognathous jaw, her sunken nose, her bare, yellow and projecting skull, her deep yellow wrinkles, her gleaming black eyes, her skinny claw. Her racial regression to bestiality recapitulates the familiar regression to childhood: she is 'no larger than ... a year-old child' (67). The regression is complete when, after her prophetic announcement of the racial superiority of the whites, she falls into foaming convulsions, the condition of insane pathology most closely associated with the female.

Yet her preternatural knowledge places the men entirely in her power. Her merest touch during the 'witch-smelling' is equivalent to a ritual castration. Once touched, a man 'dragged his limbs as though they were paralysed, and his fingers, from which the spear had fallen, were limp as those of a man newly dead' (75). Repeatedly and ritualistically invoked by her attendants as the 'mother, old mother' of the land, Gagool holds all power of life and death. What appears to have appalled Haggard was the mortal consequences for men of the power of female generation. 'What is the lot of man born of woman?' the crowd chants. 'Death!' comes the reply. To compound matters, 'she and only she knows the secret of the "Three Witches"' (113). The last point is important for the clear impression it gives of the overdetermined sources of Haggard's profound anxiety, in which psychosexual, class, and racial paranoia fuse with an unbidden knowledge that the secret of the production of mineral wealth in South Africa, and thus the hoped-for regeneration of Britain, did indeed lie in the generative labour power of women.

The figure of Gagool recalls the dreaded ragdoll, 'She-Who-Must-Be-Obeyed', of Haggard's youth. Gagool also seems reminiscent of the alternative female authority of the female mediums at the London séances Haggard attended as a youth, which had so unnerved him that he had been forced to stop going. As Gilbert (1983) points out, the dark current of mysticism which flowed illicitly through the late nineteenth century, emphasised the link between alternative intellectual possibilities of female rule and misrule. It is no accident that Haggard embodied this frightful possibility in a South African *isanusi*. Colonial documents are eloquent on the unease with which white male administrators regarded the African diviners, who were predominantly female. What follows in *King Solomon's' Mines* is an elaborate narrative effort to ward off the implications of this frightful merging of mother, working-class domestic servant, and black woman by a massive reordering and disciplining of the female power of generation.

A crisis of inheritance in the royal family erupts and a blood-rivalry between brothers climaxes in a battle. Umbopa, who signifies his legitimacy by recognising the racial 'fatherhood' of the Englishmen, is at the same time revealed to bear around his loins the mark of a snake, the insignia of kingship. After the battle the white men settle the monarchical crisis through a ceremonial inauguration which places Umbopa at the head of the nation on two conditions: that he recognise their racial patrimony in the diamonds, and that he swear fealty to four edicts, which bear fundamentally on curtailing the right of the black monarch to unbridled access to the labour of the women. Twala had earlier justified the sacrifice of the women in terms of the continuity of the male house: 'Thus runs the prophecy of my people: "If the king offer not a sacrifice of a fair girl on the day of the dance of maidens to the old ones who sit and watch on the mountains, then shall he fall and his house."' In other words, the house of the father depended on the ritualised control of women – if this were halted, and with it the power of the female diviners, the power of the Kukuana monarch would be severely curtailed. Thus the ending of *King Solomon's Mines* is faithful to the political blueprint Shepstone had in mind for Zululand. Kukuanaland would remain territorially separate, but in effect a 'black colony' of Natal. A leader who swears fealty to the racial patrimony of the whites is installed. True to Shepstone's segregationist policy, white men would not be allowed to settle there. At the same time, true to Haggard's own class allegiance, though not to the outcome of history, the booty from the mines would be placed in the hands of the landed gentry, not in the hands of the mining capitalists.

The novel concludes with an extraordinary narrative effort to legitimise the reordering of generative authority in the black polity and the diversion of the surplus riches into the pockets of the white gentlemen. Only Gagool knows the secret entrance to the mines, a psychosexual image needing no elaboration. Entry to the narrow passage is guarded by huge, nude Phoenician colossi. Over the door of the treasure chamber the men read their racial patrimony, the title-deed to ownership of the diamonds. 'We stood and shrieked with laughter over the gems which had been found for us thousands of years ago, and saved for us by Solomon's long-dead overseer.... We had got them' (129). The patrimony is a found inheritance based on racial family resemblance to the 'white' Egyptians. Not incidentally, the patrimony is inscribed in Hebrew – Haggard was party to the common notion that 'Zulus resemble Jews in customs'. 'The origin of the Zulus is a mystery, nobody knows from whence they come, or who were their forefathers, but it is thought they sprang from Arab stock, and many of their customs and ceremonies resemble those of the Jews' (1882: 53). Haggard's anti-semitism, of a piece with his antipathy to mining capitalists and his conviction that imperialism should be guided and controlled by the landed gentry, placed Jews in a region of racial belatedness which they shared with the Zulus. (The Jewish Holly, in *She*, reveals a number of the simian stigmata thought to be shared by Jews and Africans.) At the same time, the labour of black diggers in extracting the diamonds is rendered invisible. Thus the first principle of repression is completed.

Immediately afterward, Gagool is crushed beneath the rock, and at once a ritualistic moment in the male colonial narrative asserts itself. With the death of the witch-mother, the men are reduced to a condition of prenatal infancy. They are plunged into darkness and are forced to crawl about on hands and knees. 'All the manhood seemed to have gone out of us' (131). What follows is an extraordinary fantasy of male birthing, culminating in the regeneration of white manhood. With great difficulty, the men find the entrance to the back passage to the pit. After hours of agonising labour and toil, they finally clamber out of the dark tunnel and tumble head over heels into the air, covered in blood and mud, crying for joy, unable to walk, but bathed in the rosy glow of dawn.

There is one final note to this story. In a burst of anal frenzy before leaving the womb–tomb, Quartermain stuffs his pockets with diamonds – diamonds, we are told, which are as large as 'pigeon eggs'. These pigeon eggs are fertile symbols of two new reproductive orders. According to this phantasmic narrative of white patriarchal regeneration, the white men give birth to the new economic order of imperial mining capitalism, while repressing the labour of black men and at the same time placing the process in the hands of the gentry. They have accomplished a new form of human reproduction, an autochthonous male birthing which annuls the mother. Finally, the pigeon eggs become the means for regenerating the declining gentry, for they allow Quartermain, like Haggard himself, to return to Britain and buy an estate. Thus the adventure of imperial capitalism restores the landed gentleman to the head of the family of man – which remains a pathological family, for it still admits no mother.

* * *

In this way *King Solomon's Mines* figures the reinvention of white imperial patriarchy through a legitimising racial and gender poetics. It asserts a regenerated white patriarch who institutes and controls a subservient and racially belated black king; he in turn grants white racial superiority and their patrimonial entitlement to the diamonds. It reorganises production and reproduction within the black family by usurping the chief's unbridled control of the lives and labour of women. And it violently negates the principle of black female generative power (both productive and reproductive). The fact that it is the labour of black women in homestead production that releases male labour in the mines is repressed, rendered as invisible as Gagool crushed beneath the rock. The Victorian obsession with treasure troves, treasure maps, and the finding of treasure may be seen as a symbolic repression of the origin of capital in the labour of people. Finding treasure implies that mineral riches can simply be 'discovered' – thus obscuring the work that is required to dig it out of the earth and, thus, the contested right to ownership. This represents a telling example of commodity fetishism, by which money is represented as able to breed itself, as the men were able to give birth to themselves in the mine–womb.

Thus the narrative of male phallic regeneracy is assured through the control of women in the arena of empire. The entire scenario of appropriating the land and minerals is given the legitimacy it so sorely lacks through the negation of the mother and the principle of female generation, and the reinvention of white patriarchy within the organic embrace of the regenerated 'family of man'. Fittingly, Haggard was himself enabled by the fantastically approving male reception of his tale of ceremonial phallic and racial regeneration to buy the landed estate from which he had been disinherited.

5

Family and gender in the Christian community at Edendale, Natal, in colonial times

SHEILA MEINTJES

The realm of the domestic has become an increasingly important focus of scholarship for those concerned to understand the continued and transformed nature of female subordination within male-dominated societies. This chapter takes the domestic as the starting point for an analysis of gender relations in Edendale, a Christianised, petty commodity-producing community in south-east Africa in the nineteenth century. Edendale became one of Natal's model mission stations, the object of scrutiny and admiration of colonial officials, settlers, missionaries and foreign visitors.

The chapter thus focuses on the social experience of a single mission. Yet although its history is in many respects a unique one, it may also be representative of other Christian communities in Natal and southern Africa. Its history embodies the effects of colonisation and missionary work on an African Christian community, and that is its value. This does not mean that these effects were not more widely experienced, but the most dramatic and intensive transformation in precolonial social practice occurred on mission stations, where mission control was immediate and direct. Whilst the colonial state provided the framework for the conduct of social relations and guaranteed social stability (so long as its subjects placed themselves under its law), the church was the major influence in the daily lives of the *amakholwa*, as Christian mission inhabitants were called.

From the very beginning of colonial rule all Africans were subject to the hut tax and *isibalo* (forced labour for the state). There was thus no escaping the need to engage in commodity relations. Missionary societies were of some significance in paving the way for these new social relations to take root, for they were in charge of institutionalised education, and provided models as well for new forms of social interaction on their mission stations. Their influence in imparting new agricultural skills percolated through to social groups not in direct contact with the missions, but it was on mission stations that it had greatest impact. Here the missionary wielded enormous control over the lives of inhabitants, particularly through the church and the school.

However, whilst the mission was vital in shaping a new normative approach both to production and to family life, one should not overemphasise its primacy. The transposition of the evangelical Victorian ideology of gender and sexuality and its assimilation by an African mission community was a complex process, and did not represent a mere imposition on a malleable and passive community. The community was not a *tabula rasa*, upon which missionaries could stamp whatever ideology and practice they pleased. The process involved interaction, compromise and synthesis. Significant customary practices were continued, often in conflict with what the missionaries were teaching. These shaped a cultural world which comprised a distinctive blend of its own, a synthesis of elements of custom from an African past, combined with Wesleyan and Victorian morality, bound together by the fundamental material need to produce for a colonial market in order to survive from day to day, and from generation to generation.

To penetrate the black Christian and colonial ideology of gender and sexuality which ordered relations between the sexes in Edendale is no easy matter. As already noted for the Eastern Cape, the voices contained in the extant sources are those of men, whether colonial officials, settlers, missionaries or members of the community itself. There are no women's voices, apart from an occasional woman visitor to Edendale, like Lady Barker in 1876. Even the voices of missionary wives are muted. This chapter attempts to probe the sources in a gender-sensitive manner and thus uncover the texture of gender relations at Edendale. What do the 'absences' in the sources tell us about the construction of relationships between men and women? What forms of the household and family emerged, and how were they tied to the materiality of people's lives, such as access to means of production, property ownership, the role of men, women and children in production and in the household? What composition did the household take, and how was marriage arranged and conducted? What determining role did Wesleyan Christianity and the colonial polity have on these relations and social forms?

EDENDALE: ITS ORIGINS AND DEVELOPMENT

The origins of the people who settled at Edendale in 1851 lie in the turbulent history of African societies on the highveld and in Natal in the 1830s and 1840s. Diverse forces of conflict and state formation were at work, operating in the context of the penetration of the region by merchants, missionaries and adventurers, the vanguard of colonial infiltration of southern Africa. A mixed community grew up around the missionary endeavours of James Allison, a Wesleyan catechist and later a missionary, who began working in Transorangia in the 1830s. These converts, the nucleus of the future Edendale settlement, were drawn from the diverse and often conflicting groups in the Transorangia region. They included individuals from the settlements abandoned by Barend Barends's Griqua band at Boetsap and Platberg on the Vaal, refugees from Boer apprenticeship in the northern Cape, and former Hlubi, Zulu and Taung clients of Sekonyela's Tlokwa, who had settled along the banks of the Caledon.

In 1844 this small band, numbering not more than 40 people, set out with Allison to establish a mission amongst the Swazi people, at the invitation of the Queen Regent, Thandile, mother of the heir-elect, Mswati, and her advisers. The mission established at Mahamba found itself drawn into the civil war following Mswati's succession, and within three years was abandoned as the community fled to Natal. They were accompanied by about 400 Swazi refugees, mainly from the Kunene people of Sigweje. In Natal the colonial state allocated to Allison's mission a tract of land on the Illovo River at Indaleni and provided a separate location for Sigweje. The majority of Allison's mission community now consisted of Swazi converts, although the original core remained.

In 1851, after a quarrel between Allison and the Wesleyan Missionary Society, the community, now numbering between 400 and 500 people, once more uprooted themselves. They settled on a 6 123 acre farm called Edendale, in a fertile valley watered by the Umsinduzi River, near the village of Pietermaritzburg, the capital of the struggling Natal colony. The farm was purchased by Allison and 99 members of his community on a share basis from the Boer leader Andries Pretorius. Not everyone who moved with Allison purchased shares; non-shareholders paid rent for the use of land. This was a unique experiment in land ownership in the 1860s and shaped the community's integration into the colonial polity and economy. The Edendale *amakholwa* spearheaded the acquisition by blacks of freehold land in Natal. This provided the foundation for the development of a family-based Christian communalism firmly identified with and located within colonial society. It also separated the *amakholwa* even further from their traditional roots.

The core of the community grouped around the church were Christian converts. When they settled at Edendale there were 150 full members of the church. The church gave a sense of communal identity to members of the mission, although not all who lived at Edendale, even from the beginning, were confirmed converts. Apart from members, there were some 270 'believers', who were not yet confirmed. There were also a fair number of non-believers, some 160 in all, who were allowed to purchase allotments and live among the rest, but were required to 'abandon their grosser native habits' (Colenso, 1855: 51–2; for figures of believers, see Garden papers 792). The overall population of the village did not change dramatically during the nineteenth century, remaining steady at between 800 and 1 000. But there was considerable migration both to and from Edendale, as families moved away from the 1860s onwards, seeking larger property holdings elsewhere in the colony or because they could no longer afford the rents at the mission. Indeed, the Edendale converts spawned a veritable colonising movement, creating new settlements in the Klip River district in the late 1860s and early 1870s, and in the 1880s purchasing farms in the Polela area in the Drakensberg foothills.

The language of community life reflected the people's origins: Zulu, Sotho, Seswati, and even Dutch. Church services were held in only three languages – Zulu, Dutch and English – and these were the languages used in the schools. The bible, hymns, catechism and other religious tracts were all translated into Zulu, which became the *lingua franca* of the community over time. Knowledge of Christian religious teaching and its social practices were, however, incorporated within a wider set of cultural traditions, bounded by customary law.

Colonial rule in Natal had not abrogated customary law and a dual system of law governed social relationships. All blacks, including Christian converts, remained subject to customary laws in so far as these did not conflict with 'civilised' notions of 'humanity' (Welsh, 1971: 17–18). As a result of missionary pressure, the colonial government did introduce legislation in 1865 (Law 28 of 1865), permitting exemption from customary law for individuals; women, however, could apply for exemption in their own right only with the support of their guardians, although wives and daughters acquired exemption through their husbands and fathers. This Act was vague as to what rights were conferred on exempted persons under colonial law. At first it was assumed that full equality with all white colonial subjects was intended. The exemption provisions were viewed with suspicion by Christian Africans because it allowed only for individual application. Their wish was for recognition as a group. However, changes to customary law following the Marriage Law in 1869 and the Administration Law in 1875, which in effect undermined the position of Christian marriage and removed the right of women to ownership of property, encouraged the *amakholwa* to seek exemption in the 1870s. As the century drew to a close, after the granting of responsible government to the colony, the interpretation of exemption from customary law gradually narrowed from near-equal status under colonial law, to a mere exclusion from the restrictive terms of customary law itself. Exemption never implied the acquisition of the vote – Law 11 of 1865 specifically excluded exempted Africans from the franchise, although it permitted Africans to apply for the vote after several years of exemption from customary law – and no more than three or four black people availed themselves of the right to the franchise throughout Natal.

At Edendale the community built a central village on plots of one acre or more, with outlying fields, individually allocated, and a commonage for grazing animals. Settlement in Natal brought the mission community directly into the nexus of the colonial economy and political relations. Proximity to Pietermaritzburg was significant in its successful establishment, for very soon members were supplying the town with fruit, vegetables and mealies, as well as poultry, cattle and other stock. Along with the inhabitants of the neighbouring Zwartkops location (an African reserve), the people of Edendale were the major suppliers of the Pietermaritzburg market during the 1850s and 1860s.

At that stage the African population in Natal were largely self-sufficient and engaged in market production only to meet the demands of the state for hut tax, to acquire ploughs or to pay rent. Neither wage labour nor sustained market production formed a major part of their activity. What distinguished the Edendale people from their neighbours in the Zwartkops location was their greater involvement in colonial property relations and commerce, particularly during the 1860s. Speculation in a prospective take-off of Natal's economy had created relative boom conditions, and large loans were taken out to finance trading ventures into the interior. In Natal land formed the basic security for loans. Edendale entrepreneurs took as much advantage of the economic boom as their white settler compatriots and, as much as they, felt the sudden effects in the mid-1860s of a severe economic crisis triggered by a world-wide depression. This was to last until the next decade, when the discovery of diamonds launched a second period of prosperity for Natal's entrepôt trade. Natal's economy was to remain dependent on this regional trade, its own productive base being left undeveloped apart from the growth of the sugar plantations from the late 1860s onwards.

At Edendale Allison was virtual overlord during the first decade of the community's existence there. In theory he was simply a co-tenant of the farm, but the farm was registered in his name and he used his special position to act in many ways like a lord with rights of demesne, although this was masked by his role as pastor, father, teacher and counsellor. This relationship was severed when a quarrel erupted over the granting of individual title-deeds once the farm was paid off. Allison was virtually hounded out of the village in 1861. Village elders then invited the Wesleyan Missionary Society to take over the pastoral affairs of the village. In order to put secular affairs on a proper basis, a trust deed was drawn up, embodying rules for the management of unallotted portions of the farm and common resources and facilities.

The original co-purchasers of the farm signed the trust deed.

Amongst those listed in the trust deed was one woman, Deborah Notese, whose name does not in fact appear on the register of title-deed holders. During the period 1851–1910, very few black women actually held land in their own right at Edendale or, no doubt, in the rest of Natal. This was largely because women independent of male guardianship were not recognised in customary law. Only one Eden-dale woman, Sarah Nyamtoli, held land in freehold up until 1887, but there is no evidence of either her or Deborah Notese's history in the mission or official records, or indeed from oral sources. It was only after the 1880s that a few more women acquired land, and then via inheritance from husbands or fathers. In 1887 Marian Dhlamini Mtembu became the second woman to be registered as a landowner when she inherited land from Joshua Dhlamini, her father. Mary Mini became a substantial landowner in 1891 when she inherited over 66 acres from her father, Nathanial Matebula (a member of the Swazi contingent who had joined Allison in the 1840s). She was married to Stephen Mini, who became headman of the village in 1893. By 1919 only 11 black women owned land in their own right in the village, out of a total of 205 landowners (of whom 30 were white and 40 Indian).

Under the tutelage of the Wesleyan Church a number of significant changes occurred at Edendale. Civil matters were more fully managed by leading elders responsible to an elected headman. The missionary was still expected to mediate on the community's behalf with the colonial authorities, as well as provide guidance and advice in village matters, but the Wesleyans were never allowed to wield the same authority as Allison had done. Their influence, however, remained a central force in village life, and in the chapel the missionary voice was law.

From the 1870s the changes in the political economy of the subcontinent initiated by the discovery of diamonds in the interior began to be felt at Edendale. The carrying trade offered profitable opportunities for those with wagons, and hastened a process of differentiation in the village which had already received enormous impetus from the depression of the mid-1860s. Only those *amakholwa* with some capital could afford to establish their own enterprises. Others were forced into wage labour, and many found it necessary to migrate to the diamond fields to gain adequately paid work. At the same time, the *amakholwa* in general became more conscious of a growing racism among white Natalians, who ignored their adoption of colonial life-styles and Christianity and blocked their incorporation within colonial civil society. Their competitiveness in the carrying trade and in the market place only gained them the name of thieves and rogues from envious and less successful colonists.

To counter the effects of these developments, *kholwa* communities strove to prove their worth as respectable and pious citizens. At Edendale this brought about tighter moral controls in the 1870s, as codes of Victorian rectitude were stringently applied in the village. In 1873 the most respected elder in the village, the headman Job Kambule, was forced to resign, for instance, when, following his wife's death, it was learned that he had harboured a second family in the village for a decade (NA, SNA 1/3/23, R1063/41, Bird to SNA, 31.3.1873).[2] At the same time, migrant labour had weakened the patriarchal controls of the elders, and young men were, according to the missionaries, being 'seduced into intemperate habits' (MMS 340, Edendale Circuit Minutes, 1874). Youth who transgressed the moral code of the community were severely punished. Christian children were not allowed to mix with non-Christian families. Young men were forbidden to drink liquor (MMS 319, Cameron to Boyce, 6.9.1872).

The Umgeni magistrate reported to the Secretary for Native Affairs (SNA) that the Edendale elders were disturbed by the independence of their offspring: 'the seniors complain that when their sons and daughters arrive at the age of 21 they believe that they can defy the authority of their parents, they make a very bad use of this imaginary liberty. The men drink and tamper with property entrusted to them by their parents, and both men and women indulge in promiscuous intercourse and they resent all interference with their actions from those who by law have full control over them' (NA, SNA 1/6/6, 455/1876, Clarke to SNA, 21.6.1876).

In 1877 the village elders asked the missionary Daniel Eva to refer their complaints to the Secretary for Native Affairs. The assistant magistrate sent out to investigate affairs reported that 'statements regarding the lawless and disorderly conduct of the young men on the station are exaggerated'. He considered that adultery, breach of trust and even crime, which the complainants suggested were common, rarely occurred at Edendale (NA, SNA 1/1/29, 57, Eva to SNA, 9.6.1877).

However, the unity of the community began to break down as economic depression, migration and the influx of new inhabitants altered the composition of the village. Edendale properties were let out or sold to newcomers. The authority of the elders was no longer as respected as before. Beer-drinking, which had been strictly controlled and vetoed by church elders and missionaries, became almost impossible to prohibit by the 1880s.

The people concerned in these practices disregard all counsel and defy all authority. It appears that the occupants of the houses reside upon their own land, and think they can act without any restraint. Drunkenness, immorality and abandonment of wives by their husbands, are some of the results which are taking place. The orderly and respectable people are greatly distressed at this state of things, but powerless to alter it (NA, SNA 1/1/40, 410/1880, Mason to SNA, 22.7.1880).

It is difficult to disentangle the roots of the disturbance. Partly, it was connected to attempts by the church-going village elite to break down some of the barriers to their advancement in colonial civil society. Temperance was one important route to respectability and thus acceptance; another was via exemption from customary law. The distinction between exempted and non-exempted introduced a new division into the community, and social differentiation among the landowners themselves increasingly became a feature of Edendale's social geography. The existence of a growing tenant class in the village from the 1870s added to the divisions and made it more difficult for church and village elders to control all members of the community.

THE MISSION HOUSEHOLD AND APPRENTICESHIP IN CHRISTIAN FAMILY LIFE

In Natal the missionaries mediated between the communal kin-bound, patriarchal household of the indigenous people, which the colonial state sought to manage and later recreate, and the rather different form of household developing on the stations. Missionary influence encouraged the formation of self-sufficient, petty commodity-producing units based on the nuclear household and on family labour. The nature of the productive process in these households made them resemble those of settler society, though they also shared aspects of indigenous, kinship-based households in the reserves.

Many of the original converts had been drawn directly into the mission household, where they served a kind of apprenticeship in the new material and ideological relationships involved in Christian household and family life. Boys and girls formally apprenticed by the Allisons boarded with them as well. Thus the mission household was akin to a boarding establishment, although the Allisons spoke in terms of taking youths into their family. This was the origin of what came to be called the 'industrial school', which later was separated from the mission household and acquired its own premises. At any one time the Allisons had between 23 and 30 children and youths boarding with them. It is not clear how many, if any, of these were girls. However, we do know that the school had an industrial department for girls, so at least a few girls must also have boarded with the Allisons.

Convert children were apprenticed by their parents to learn trades. In exchange for the labour of their children, parents were given five shillings a month for boys and one shilling a month for girls. The different prices allotted to the labour of the two sexes clearly reflected somewhat different values ascribed to the roles of men and women. What is significant about this is that specific attitudes towards gender divisions of labour were being inculcated. If gender is understood as the social construction of male and female identity, then what was learned in the mission household were the roles Christian men and women were expected to perform in social production and reproduction. Mrs Allison, like all missionary wives, was in charge of the domestic side of household management and also assisted her husband in teaching the young 'apprentices', whilst her husband managed the productive activities. In the mission household women had a subordinate and subservient position in relation to the male head. But at the same time, as wives, women were also valued as companions and 'help-meets' who commanded respect from society (*Natal Witness*, 17.10.1851). Their role was to care for and nurture husband and children with the domestic skills they had learned in their apprenticeship. This socialisation carried over into the school, when the latter replaced the mission household in the educational realm.

Within the framework of the Allisons' household there emerged certain kinds of productive relations, the exploitative nature of which were masked by the notion of 'the family'. The missionary was both 'kin' and 'employer'(albeit paternal in his dealings). What legitimated the new relationships was the notion of Christian kinship. However, the genuine ties of affection that developed within the mission household need also to be taken into account. The Allisons had no children of their own, so the African children they took into their home had no rivals against which to measure their experience. Mrs Allison said in one of her only surviving letters that she felt very close to those in her household: 'We have five native teachers in all that love us as tho' we were their parents' (C.T. Binns Papers, D. Allison to Anne, Mount Mahamba, 7.9.1845). Later missionary families at Edendale developed quite different relationships, because converts were no longer brought into the mission household except as servants. For them school and chapel discipline were to provide the material and moral training requisite for a productive Christian family life.

At Edendale, what were experienced as personal relations with Allison as patriarchal household head, teacher and magistrate, constituted at the same time new patterns of class relations for different categories within the family: adult men and women, young men and women, apprentices and younger children. Thus in the first few years of the mission's establishment, apprenticeship of converts in the missionary's household laid bare the fact that the private space of the household and family was also the arena in which the place, power and status of individuals in the hierarchy of mission and colonial society were defined. The mission household defined the class position of its inmates in such a way that the experience would not have been emotionally alienating. Yet notwithstanding the emotional bonds between missionary and converts, Allison's role was unequivocally that of a member of colonial society. As mediator between colonial civil society and members of the mission he acted as a kind of magistrate. As head of the mission, his moral position was that of a patriarch, which was matched in practice by the control he had over the secular affairs of the village.

WOMEN'S WORK

The mission household provided the first experience for black converts of new production processes. On the mission station, women's role was defined by the linking of new domestic duties to more traditional productive activities. New duties arose out of 'civilisation', like sewing clothes, making linen, and caring for new kinds of household dwellings with several rooms and furniture.

Although there was much to complement pre-existing relations, new tasks proclaimed new realms for the sexual division of labour. Artisanal work – carpentry, including wagon-making, shoe-making, hat-making and masonry – was only taught to men and boys. Most male members of the community combined artisanal work with their trading and agricultural activities. In the early years of the settlement they built houses for the white settlers while some of them worked on government building projects as intermittent wage labourers, and others worked as apprentices for settler wheelwrights. Women were taught different kinds of skills, including new methods of cooking, preserving, sewing garments in Victorian fashion from European cloth, and other skills appropriate to their becoming 'suitable wives'. These all formed part of what missionaries called 'household management'. The skills were also, of course, appropriate to women who might become domestic servants, which it seems many of them did before they married. In 1851 Edendale women were reported to be washing and ironing in town. Wealthier families in the village also employed servants, whose tasks were little different from those of family members, all of whom were employed in one way or another in the domestic economic cycle.

The early marriage register, for the years 1847–65, gives some indication of the domestic definition of women's work, at least prior to marriage. Some 56 marriages are listed. Out of these, only nineteen women were recorded as having any occupation: fifteen were maids, two were washerwomen, and one, Sarah Siljie, was a seamstress: all these were domestic tasks and show where women were being drawn into wage labour. Surprisingly, only one woman was listed as a labourer (suggesting field, rather than domestic, employment). It is highly probable that the remaining 37 women were engaged in domestic work at home. That this work was not recognised as productive says more about how little women's contribution was recognised and valued by the missionaries, than about what women were actually doing.

Their new tasks were combined with women's traditional role in African society – caring for small stock, as well as working in the fields, hoeing, weeding and harvesting. Women and children were traditionally considered productive members of the household unit. Men, women and children participated in preparing the food for storage. Women made huge baskets, *isilulu*, to store the cleaned and winnowed corn, sorghum (*mabele*), beans, monkey nuts, and jugo beans. A separate store-room or store-house was specially kept for these foods and pumpkins (*ithanga*) and melons (*amabhece*). Mothers and daughters prepared blocks of dung collected from cattle kraals for fuel. They collected mealie cobs and the dried stalks from the mealie fields and stored them for winter fires. Women also made clay pots for storing food or beverages. They cut thatching grass, wove mats and all manner of basketware for household use, and made brooms from *xema* grass. They made mattresses from soft grass cased in sacks, which were covered with sleeping mats, and pillows from poultry feathers or the soft fronds of grass collected by the riverside; these were seasonally replenished. Women also made patchwork quilts to cover the beds, and crocheted decorative doilies for tables and chairs. Men also had their special tasks to perform in the home. They made all the furniture: bedsteads, tables, chairs and benches. They carved drums to stamp mielies, and made pillows, *isigqiki*, from wood. They made big and small meat platters, and carved yokes for the oxen.

The introduction of the plough brought cattle – a male preserve – into the agricultural labour process in a new way and peripheralised the former dominance, though not the continued involvement, of women in agricultural production. Women's involvement in agriculture – not markedly different from that of settler women – was viewed with disapproval by the missionaries, for they believed it made slaves of them. Their main complaint was that agricultural activities kept women away from chapel classes (MMS 335, Imparane School report, 1845). Thus only men were taught 'European' modes of agriculture, although it was patently obvious that women's work lay at the heart of agricultural endeavour (MMS 335, Imparane School report, 1845; NWM 8/1, Allison to West, 29.5.1848). In the early years at Edendale, *kholwa* wives were consistently seen by the missionaries as inferior to their men. The missionary view was that the men were 'strong minded, and several of them very intelligent.... They are much in advance of the women who are what Kaffirs must be without education and training' (MMS 318, Pilcher to Hoole, 4.6.1864). This may have been precisely because of their participation in agriculture, which gave them less time to devote to furthering their education.

Yet despite missionary disapproval, women continued to be involved in agricultural production. Women worked in the fields, occupied in tasks defined as 'women's work' in African society, although strictly men's work as far as the missionaries were concerned. Many women sold poultry in Pietermaritzburg, for which they got 1s 6d a pair, and their domestic labour included field work. They also sold wood and corn (Mason, 1862: 19). Men and women went to market together, to sell their respective commodities. Missionaries were unable to comprehend the independent space which agricultural production provided for women. We cannot know whether women controlled their own income, but it seems possible, for they contributed money to the chapel independently from the men (MMS 318, Milward to Secretaries, 1 April 1864). The opinion of African women themselves about this labour is unknown, but agricultural activity would have provided them with a continuing role in production and hence some economic independence. By the early twentieth century some women had learned to plough. The breaking down of taboos about handling cattle which this presupposed may well have increased their importance in the domestic cycle of production (interview, Theodora Mngadi). One probably cannot infer from female participation in the early twentieth century that this was also true of the mid-nineteenth century. However, in the simple commodity economy of the mission community, men were frequently away on trading trips, and women would have been left in charge of the agricultural enterprise of their domestic unit.

The toil of men and women on the mission stations was not markedly different from that of colonial farming families. Ellen McLeod's letters to her sister in England between 1850 and 1880 portray a subsistence domestic economy in which the whole family was involved in ploughing and planting; surpluses were occasionally exchanged with neighbours or at the market in Pietermaritzburg (Gordon, 1970). However, missionary wives seem to have been less involved in agricultural activities on the mission and more involved in chapel and school. The missionary wife usually employed servants to do domestic chores and much of the child-care too.

Like colonial farmers' wives, the multiple duties of convert women made life one ceaseless round of hard work. Although women were kept busy with their own domestic chores, this does not mean that there was no communal sharing of work. Men and women combined together in work parties, *ilima*, to weed or reap as a group. This might include neighbours and friends, or even 'a poor person who has not got cattle, ploughs, etc.' who, in return, was granted the use of land (interview, Theodora Mngadi). The occasion of a work party required the preparation of food and beer by the women of the household whose fields were being worked.

Women were, of course, also the bearers and rearers of children, a long-term occupation. Analysis of the baptismal register gives an incomplete picture of the average size of families. The number of children recorded varied from four to as many as twelve per family. However, it is clear that less than half the number of infants born to Edendale women survived their childhood. It is unknown how many women died in childbirth and also virtually impossible to comment on life expectancy at this time. However, that women spent a great deal of time either pregnant or responsible for child-care did not lessen the burden of their other work.

SCHOOLING

The major emphases in mission schooling throughout the nineteenth century can neatly be summarised as 'discipline and order'.[3] This became particularly prominent in the late 1870s, when the emphasis on 'respectability' became a moral imperative, as settler racism began to limit the options and put a brake on *kholwa* achievement. The emphasis coincided, too, with signs of growing independence from parental authority on the part of the young men who plied their wagons between the diamond fields and Natal. Desire to reassert their authority increased parents' faith in the rod as a tool of discipline.

Initially, what little schooling took place occurred in-between the missionary's pastoral activities and comprised no more than learning the alphabet, the catechism and Wesleyan hymns, as well as 'European' agricultural and rudimentary artisanal skills. However, three schools were established at Edendale during Allison's time: an 'infant' school with between 90 and 140 pupils, a 'juvenile' school with an average of 40 children, and the industrial department, which by the end of the 1850s was in the charge of a wheelwright. The girls' industrial department ceased to exist after Allison's departure in 1861, although the boys' industrial school continued. Girls were still taught to sew, however, in the course of ordinary school instruction. (Only at Verulam, a Wesleyan mission station near the coast, were girls still apprenticed formally, though unlike with the boys, contracts were verbal.) The first two schools were coeducational and taught by the same young English woman in different sessions. In the 1850s Allison's niece taught in the school; when the Wesleyans took over the mission, young women were sent out from England by the Wesleyan Missionary Society Ladies Committee.

The content of education was limited largely to basic literacy and numeracy skills, the three Rs, singing (mostly of hymns, though also English nursery rhymes), a good dose of 'sectarian religious instruction', with some geography and history (mainly scriptural) (MMS 338, school reports 1866–8; NA, SNA 1/1/34 1271/1879, Russell to

SNA, 26.6.1879). The government provided grants to cover the salaries of the teachers. These were supplemented by Wesleyan Mission Society grants and, in theory, by fees – but these were only reluctantly paid by the community.

As we have seen, women's work was both onerous and multifarious, and child-care often devolved upon young girls. Mothers carried their infants on their backs but toddlers were given to young girls to manage and they took their charges to school. At one point the day-school mistress, Elizabeth Rowbotham, complained that their 'occasional crying is not only disagreeable but greatly obstructive of school operations' (MMS 318, Cameron to Secretaries, 27.4.1866). Attempts to get rid of 'this evil' led to a struggle with the parents which threatened the very existence of the school and provides a clear indication of the importance of young girls in relieving their overburdened mothers in the task of child-care.

An examination of mission education is important in giving some indication of how gender differentiation was constructed. We have already considered the way in which apprenticeship in industrial training accorded different status to boys and girls. Whilst education for boys was at the forefront of both community concerns and missionary educational enterprise, interest in girls' education reflected the bounded role anticipated for women in the community and in society at large. The Inspector of Schools, Robert Russell, maintained that industrial education for women was simply a euphemism for the training of domestic servants (NA, SNA 1/1/34, Russell to SNA, 26.6.1879). Mrs Blencowe, the wife of the missionary in charge of Edendale during the transition from Allison to the Wesleyan Missionary Society, remarked that although the men built good houses, the women did not know how to keep them clean and tidy (Findlay and Holdsworth, 1922: 29). In 1869 no less a person than Theophilus Shepstone, Secretary for Native Affairs, had suggested to a Methodist deputation that a separate girls' school be started. 'What is the good of educating a young man and then marrying him to an ignorant half heathenish girl,' he remarked (MMS 319, Barton to Boyce, 21.12.1869). The education and training of young girls was primarily aimed at filling this gap. Thus the cult of domesticity was developed to legitimate a subordinate place for women in the productive and reproductive relations not only of the household, but of society as well. This was buttressed by the desire of Edendale elders themselves, who 'wanted their daughters to grow up women capable of being good wives, able to sew, make garments etc etc' (MMS 337, Pilcher to Hoole, 14.6.1864).

In the 1860s the view predominated amongst Edendale parents that education should be useful but should not interfere with the productive tasks of their children. As with European youth, schooling was a short affair, not more than three or four years, and children 'are seldom allowed to remain long enough to acquire a good education; boys and girls are usually taken away for hired service or work at home, at the age most suitable for the acquirement of knowledge ...' (MMS 333, Pietermaritzburg Circuit Report, 1865). The Wesleyans tried to improve the quality of education in the 1870s, but their resources were limited. Even so, the government school inspector, Robert Russell, was able to report: 'The natives of Edendale are considerably advanced in civilization, and their children are nearly equal to the average of English children in regard to these matters' (NA, SNA 1/1/29, R567/1877, Russell, Native School Report, Edendale).

The content of education differed little from that in colonial schools elsewhere in Natal. This did not mean that Edendale parents were satisfied with their children's education. They were critical of the calibre of the women teachers sent out from England and in the 1860s refused to pay fees unless they were consulted over the appointment of teachers. The village notables set up a committee to monitor classes and examinations, much to the resentment of the incumbent resident missionary, who had married the school teacher. So dissatisfied were they with the standard of education compared to that at the American Board mission stations, that at one point they boycotted the mission school and hired a young African teacher trained by the American missionaries (MMS 318, Roberts to Secretaries, 7.5.1867; Cameron to Boyce, 5.7.1867). Indeed, by the end of the 1860s there was a general belief that the Anglican and American missionaries offered better educational opportunities than the Wesleyans, and by the mid-1870s boys spent no more than a year or two at Edendale schools before being sent away to boarding school in the Cape, at Healdtown or Zonnebloem in Cape Town.

The attitude towards education amongst the *amakholwa* altered during the course of the second half of the nineteenth century. As changes in the political economy in the 1880s affected the competitive advantage of *kholwa* traders and transport carriers adversely, so education began to assume more importance to the *kholwa* community. It was now recognised by the community that some form of commercial knowledge was important. Industrial education was still favoured but it became increasingly clear that colonists were unlikely to engage skilled *kholwa* labour in their workshops. Women's education became more important, too, as an element in fostering domestic respectability. In 1878 the Rev. John Allsopp urged the establishment of a separate girls' school. The American Board had already established a flourishing girls' school at Inanda in 1868 (see chapter 8), and the Verulam industrial school catered for girls' 'industrial' education from the early 1860s. In the late 1860s a school that had been run in

Pietermaritzburg by a 'coloured woman', with special classes for young women which were 'very much respected', ended upon her death. During the 1870s, the Edendale leaders were demanding a high school for boys in the village, but girls' schooling was still not considered a matter of great moment. However in 1880 a separate girls' school for the 'Mental, Moral and Domestic Training of Native Girls' was established (NA, SNA 1/1/71, 31.5.1883). Although some subjects taught were the same as those in the boys' school, the emphasis was on training women as elementary teachers or domestic servants (ibid.). The realm of the domestic remained the focus of women's education.

SEX AND MARRIAGE

In the mission household a new definition of acceptable relations of intimacy between men and women was learned. Missionaries considered public display of emotion 'lewd' and unchristian. Sexuality was also redefined. Men and women clothed their nakedness and what had been culturally acceptable in non-Christian societies became 'unnatural'. Privacy and delicacy, silence even, developed as the hallmarks of the sexual and sensual relationship between husband and wife. Daywear and nightwear hid men's and women's bodies from each other, and helped privatise human sexuality (see Davidoff, 1983). Intimacy between husband and wife occurred behind the closed door of the bedroom. Physical intimacy was hidden even from the children begotten from such sexual union. All this contrasted markedly with precolonial society where sexuality was proclaimed in public ceremonies of puberty rites and was also displayed in the open physicality of bodily functions and nakedness.[4]

Marriage as a property relation permeated both colonial and precolonial society but was based on quite different social relations in each. As discussed in chapter 1, women in precolonial Nguni society formed the major source of labour power, both as bearers of children and as the main agricultural workers. This made marriage the key institution for the reproduction of society as a whole, and thus the most important institution to be controlled by the precolonial state. In colonial society the marriage contract had its roots in the disposal of private property and the accumulation of profit. The history of the privatisation of the bourgeois household is complex, but the gradual confinement of women in an unproductive household, as part of the growing separation of production from the domestic realm, was also tied to the process of subordinating wives to husbands, and gave content to the notion of 'patriarchy'.[5] In marriage settlements women came to be regarded as a form of property. The ideology of women as 'angels of the house', which developed *en passant*, played an important part in legitimising the subordination of women. In the marriage contract, the unity of husband and wife gave legal capacity to men alone.

African marriage in colonial Natal, even if celebrated according to Christian rites, was legally still governed by customary law. This was true of all civil interactions between black people in Natal, including inheritance. In 1869 a law was passed (Law 1 of 1869) which purported to give greater freedom to women in the choice of partner but was largely a means of increasing revenue (NA, SNA 1/3/22, R738/99, 24.6.1872; MMS 320, Akerman to Boyce, 25.6.1874; Welsh, 1971: chapter 5). It required the registration of all marriages, introduced a marriage fee of £5 and limited the number of cattle for *lobola*. Perhaps most significant of all was the regulation which prevented the recovery of *lobola* by the wife's family on dissolution of the marriage, and abrogated any paternal right to protect the interests of a daughter upon marriage. These aspects were particularly unpopular. Christian converts argued that marriage now became a 'sale', rather than a compact binding both parties to honourable behaviour as in former times.

Christian marriage unions thus became superimposed on a customary exchange. There was also a realistic fear that women married without *lobola* would be unprotected should their husbands take other wives. This became common in the 1870s, in Edendale too, as the experience of colonial society and its contradictions drove even converts of long standing to return to customary unions. The practice of *lobola* served to draw families into a network of mutual obligation which even the new marriage law could not destroy. As one missionary pointed out, the terms of the law were simply avoided as marriage gifts took new forms. Depending on the wealth of the prospective in-laws, money, cattle, saddles, bridles and horses were given to a prospective bride's parents even before the question of *lobola* was negotiated (NNC, 1881–2: 27). *Lobola* remained an important element in cementing relationships between the families of the bride and groom. In practice this meant that the choice of marital partners was closely monitored by the fathers of both men and women on mission stations (interview, Walter Msimang).

As we have seen in chapter 3, missionaries believed that the dependence of women was compounded by the maintenance of *lobola* and other customary practices. Missionaries consistently urged the colonial state to legislate against *lobola* and polygyny, or else to release all Christians from the operation of customary law. They believed that *lobola* in particular encouraged polygyny and the practice of young women being forced to marry older men. They argued that this discouraged people, particularly men, from becoming Christians, and thus civilised. They argued, too, that it encouraged women to abscond to the towns, where, separated from the authority of their homesteads and families, their lives became polluted and degenerate (MMS 319, Barton to Boyce, 14 April 1869; MMS 320, Eva to Boyce, 21.8.1875; NNC, 1881–2: 27).

The reaction of women to the regulations of 1869 is hard to assess, though the fact that women took the opportunity to move to towns suggests there was some truth in the view that the new law gave them a modicum of independence not experienced before. However, the degree of independence for women in towns is even harder to determine. That women inevitably became prostitutes, as claimed by the missionaries, does not follow, for some may have found respectable employment as domestic servants, or even as beer-brewers. It is not clear to what extent mission station elders were expressing fears of what might happen, or the reality.

The maintenance of customary practices in marriage amongst Christian communities had important implications for the position of women. It perpetuated their status as minors in law, and prevented them from inheriting immovable property on the death of their husband. Instead, they were subject to the controls of their own sons, or their husband's brothers. For converts this might be a particularly precarious position if the rest of the agnatic family was not Christian. The retention of these aspects was crucial in establishing particular patterns of gender power relations on the mission stations. Christian women remained under the power of men, as did their children, in ways that were significantly different from settler society, where another set of laws governed familial relations.

The significance of continued customary practices for the position of young girls, and even of married women on mission stations, suggests that the freedom they had gained in the new society was a matter of form. According to the conventional view, missions provided a place where women could escape the controls of tradition and kin. For individuals this may have been the case, but the evidence in support of this view from Edendale is scanty. Analysis of gender and generational ratios amongst church members shows that new converts joined only sporadically. The numbers of hearers at church services exceeded the numbers of full members, and there does not seem to have been any great influx of outsiders until late in the century. Those who joined the mission, or became converts after the initial settlement in 1851, were apparently relatives or servants of the original settlers. Freedom and independence are relative concepts. How much women on mission stations were free to choose their husbands is a moot point where *hlonipha* (respect for parental authority and decision-making) was as strong as in African society. There may have been new areas of independence – for example, women's participation in the market on their own account – but it is equally true that on the mission stations women's domestic role involved new forms of confinement and control.

WOMEN'S INDEPENDENT CULTURE

As we saw in assessing the nature of education at the mission, new kinds of interrelationships between men and women were being forged which maintained the asymmetry between their respective status. This does not mean that women felt themselves to be subordinate. There was a good deal of scope for expressing their individual talent and creativity within their homes, and in the new collective experience which church membership entailed. Moreover their role in agricultural production did not confine them to the home but brought them into contact with other women. Many women became important class leaders in church. They were also Sunday school teachers. Formal *manyanos* did not emerge until the twentieth century (see chapter 10) but the women of the village did come together in church groups, where, no doubt, they shared their problems and were subject to group discipline.

There is clear evidence that in the early twentieth century women had developed important secular networks of support but it is virtually impossible to know how far back these go in time. At Driefontein, a farm settled by a community of former Edendale notables in the early 1870s, women formed a club called the 'Daughters of Africa' in the 1920s: 'All the women gathered together and taught one another how to sew, how to cook. And they used to say "We are Royal, Royal cooking, genuine Royal cooking", because they used Royal baking powder, which was their pride and joy. Baking all different kinds of cakes and scones' (interview, Theodora Mngadi).[6]

Such a club did not simply enable women to share recipes and support, but was also an important means of extending the cult of domesticity. The pleasure of sharing their knowledge at the same time involved a measure of social control. These were acceptable social events. Informal visiting, on the other hand, was not considered respectable; it provided opportunities for gossip, and a woman who did so acquired the reputation as *uyazula*, a woman with a long foot (interview, Walter Msimang). Few women had the leisure to visit their friends informally anyway. Sociability was associated with church gatherings or family celebrations, such as weddings and funerals. Communal and familial activities at Christmas and New Year were times of great ritual and feasting. Easter was a more sober and reflective time.

In spite of the continued observance of older cultural practices like *lobola*, Victorian Wesleyanism became an overriding element in the new cultural forms emerging on the mission stations. Modes of dress, for instance, were those of Victorian England. But the flamboyance of its expression came from the irrepressible vitality of the African imagination. This was true, too, of home decoration – cottages were painted in vibrant colours, whilst interiors expressed women's delight in decorative arts.

From the early days at Edendale, missionaries and visitors commented on the gaiety of women's fashions; even at church tea meetings, 'the ladies among the native tribes exhibit the same general tendencies as their sisters of fairer hue. Among them was a profusion of red, in the shape of dresses, ribbons, trimmings and such like' (MMS 317, Mason to Secretaries, 6.1.1859). One missionary commented, 'the people came, male and female, dressed cleanly and respectably. If there was room for complaint it was that some were too grandly attired, the females especially.' Years later Lady Barker hinted at the same preoccupation with fashion, when she noted with some surprise, and perhaps a little confusion, that a 'native' should dress with such grandeur:

I was specially invited to look at the contents of the good wife's wardrobe hung out to air in the garden. She was hugely delighted at my declaring that I should like to borrow some of her smart gowns, especially when I assured her with perfect truth, that I did not possess anything half so fine. Sundry silk dresses of hues like the rainbow waved from the pomegranate bushes; and there were mantles and jackets enough to have started a second-hand clothes shop on the spot (Barker, 1877: 205).

Missionaries disapproved when women of the lower orders dressed in the finery reserved for women of rank. In another context, Gill Burke has written about similar reactions to the fashionable dress of the Bal Maidens, Cornish women mine-workers. She suggests that it was their employment outside the home, their independence, which lay behind the criticisms. She argues that social control by class, religion and gender was threatened by this fashionable display of independent earning (Burke, 1986). In Natal missionaries were concerned to inculcate modes of subservience in a life devoted to labour for Christ and the mission community, where sobriety and pious respectability were the hallmark of the new Christians. Hence their attention to the flamboyant dress of *kholwa* women. Indeed, one missionary serving at Edendale even forbad his wife to wear anything but sombre black after their marriage (interview, Dr Unity Lewis).[7]

CONCLUSION

The tensions reflected in some of the conflicts in the Edendale mission in the latter part of the nineteenth century were symptomatic of the influence of a contradictory and syncretic mission culture. This incorporated some of the moral strictures of Victorian rectitude yet also saw value in customary practices construed as 'evil' in mission morality. *Lobola* was one of these practices; another was the role of women in agriculture – both of which gave value to women in ways not understood by stern Victorian missionaries. Beer-drinking, too, was not a loose moral activity if seen in terms of the web of customary hospitality and reciprocity surrounding it. Indeed by the 1920s, *kholwa* women were brewing beer to provide sustenance for communal work parties.

From the example of the first mission household, that of the Allisons, converts learned about the 'proper' relationships expected between Christian men and women, the hallmarks of which were privacy, discretion and female subservience. The very geography of the house inculcated a new kind of privacy, which was matched by the way people dressed and, more broadly, by the introduction of private property ownership. Life became formalised. At the same time, powerful countervailing tendencies pulled the *amakholwa* in the direction of traditional practices. First-generation converts were often more sensitive to the discipline of Christian and Victorian morality than their offspring, many of whom returned to polygamy, though taking with them new consumption patterns and lifestyles based on their mission existence.

Mission education was central in defining the separate spheres and roles of men and women, in that it trained women for domestic labour, whether for wages or at home. The cult of domesticity drawn from Victorian middle-class life was thus adapted to the needs of the mission station. In turn, the lives of mission-educated women tended to incorporate elements of traditional norms and practices as well. For women on the mission station the household and family were not as enclosed a space as they were for settler women. In this women drew somewhat on precolonial culture in which women's sphere was more communal. Work in the fields, beyond the village, was healthy if arduous. Women could work together, or at least accompany one another to their fields. Church and Sunday school provided opportunities for communal female interchanges to occur. Women's space created an arena for female solidarity, although at the same time it constituted a formidable means of social control for any woman who might balk at the constraints.

6

Women under indentured labour in colonial Natal, 1860–1911[1]

JO BEALL

To Protector of Indian Immigrants,
27th June, 1916.
  Dear Sir,
Bearers wish to be registered as man and wife. Will you please fix
them up today as we cannot afford to let them off two days, the
cane is so dry.
  N. Sykes and Sons,
  Trenance Estate (NA, Indian Immigration Files,
  1/191 416/1916).[2]

INDENTURED LABOUR IN NATAL

During the late nineteenth and early twentieth centuries, Indian
women were at the very bottom of the class–race–gender hierarchy
in colonial Natal. As workers they were ultra-exploitable, being used
for the most arduous and least skilled tasks in a forced labour system;[3]
as Indians they were regarded as unwelcome additions to the already
complex social make-up of the colony and, what is more, the persons
responsible for the increase of this despised and resented group; as
women they had to struggle against two separate but convergent
constructions of gender relations, both characterised by male domination.

According to Brookes and Webb, Indians were 'the only part of the
population of Natal which came by special and urgent invitation'
(1965: 85). For it was on the backs of Indian indentured immigrants
that the sugar industry of Natal was built. The invitation, however,
was not extended to Indian women. They were imported into the
colony only grudgingly. Whilst the industry wanted labourers, it
wanted only adult male labourers.

Women were deemed of little use in the sphere of sugar production,
for which indentured immigrants were introduced to Natal in the first
instance. Furthermore, their role in the sphere of reproduction was

regarded with suspicion and resentment. Rather than seeing women as a means of reproducing labour, the planters saw the system of indentured immigration itself as the way in which the labour force would be replaced over time. Moreover, the presence of women underscored the potential permanence of the Indian population, and other colonists felt that the introduction of Indians on a permanent basis was an unnecessary complication in Natal's social fabric.

Unfortunately for the planters, the government of India, which had allowed the system of indentured emigration to develop through the British Empire from 1830 onwards, had evolved a network of rules and regulations to govern the export of labour from India. These came to include the provision that for every 100 men that left India for a colony, so too had 40 women to go (or a female quota of 29 per cent) (Tinker, 1974: 89). The Natal government had no option but to comply.

Sugar was grown in Natal on an experimental basis from as early as 1848. What prevented immediate success, however, was lack of capital and a shortage of labour. Sugar production was labour-intensive and the planters were unable to induce the local African population to work on the plantations for a wage and under contract. The problem of capital was overcome largely by attracting funds from overseas investors (Richardson, 1981: 37). The problem of labour was solved by importing indentured immigrants from India.

The first shipload of 341 indentured immigrants arrived in Durban on 17 November 1860. This first phase of immigration continued until 1866 when it was terminated for eight years, partly because of economic recession in the colony and partly because by this time complaints of ill-treatment and employer violations of the terms of the indentured contract had reached the attention of the government of India. In response, a commission of enquiry was appointed in Natal in 1872, to look into the conditions of Indian immigrants. As a result of its report, the Natal Legislative Council passed Law 12 of 1872, which introduced some improvements, including the appointment of a Protector of Indian Immigrants. From 1874 immigration entered a second phase which continued unabated until it was terminated by the Indian government in 1911.

Through immigration and natural increase, the Indian population of Natal grew. Between November 1860 and July 1911, when the last shipment of Indians disembarked, 152 641 indentured immigrants landed on Natal's shores – 104 619 men and boys and 48 022 women and girls (Beall and North-Coombes, 1983: 67). This population was reduced by deaths and departures from the colony, which together exceeded births over the period as a whole. Altogether 42 415 immigrants and their children, some of whom had been born in Natal, returned to India in this time. Nevertheless, by 1897 the Indian population had surpassed the white population in Natal, confirming the worst fears of many of the white colonists.

Indentured labour contracts were initially served for three years, extended to five in 1864. After ten years under contract, immigrants were allowed to remain in the colony as 'free' Indians or were entitled to a free passage back to India. Alternatively, their passage could be commuted into a grant of Crown land equivalent in value to the cost of the journey back to India. In practice, however, only 53 Indians ever received these grants (Pather, 1961: 52). Instead, 'free' Indians tended to continue working on the sugar plantations or in other sectors which employed Indian labour, such as the coal mines and the Natal Government Railways (NGR). Some made an independent living as fisherfolk, agriculturalists and market-gardeners but, for the period under review, opportunities outside of contracted wage labour were limited.

This was particularly so after the passing of Act 17 of 1895, which came into effect in 1901. Introduced in the wake of complaints from white settlers (but not plantation owners) who objected to the continued importation of Indians, this Act attempted to reduce the level of importation and promote reindenture. It penalised Indians introduced to the colony after 1895 by imposing an annual tax of £3 on them (men and women alike), at the termination of their five-year contracts. It was extremely successful in its aims, forcing those who could not afford the tax (and this was the vast majority) either to reindenture or to return to India. From the late nineteenth century reindenture came to supplement to a significant degree the importation of indentured immigrants as a source of labour on the plantations (Beall and North-Coombes, 1983), reaching its peak in 1912 when the rate was 95,25 per cent (Report of the Protector of Indian Immigrants, 1912). Moreover, after 1901 nearly 30 per cent of the immigrants introduced after 1895 returned to India at the end of their contracts.

In addition to the indentured immigrants, a smaller number of Indians, referred to as 'passenger Indians', came to Natal at their own expense. The indentured immigrants came from eastern India, near Madras and Calcutta, and spoke mainly the Tamil and Telugu languages. They comprised 12 per cent Moslems, 5 per cent Christians and 83 per cent Hindus (Brookes and Webb, 1965: 85). The 'passenger Indians', on the other hand, were predominantly Urdu-speaking Moslems, from the Bombay area or from Mauritius, but included some Gujarati-speaking Hindus and Moslems as well. They came to form a relatively distinct and comparatively privileged trading community in Natal. Engaged in importing and retailing, they catered not only for the Indian immigrants but also in time competed with white merchants and African traders. This earned them a great deal of hostility, from the white settlers in particular.

Thus Indians in the colony differed among themselves in language, religion and class position, and did not form a homogeneous group. The main focus of this chapter will be on indentured women, the largest category of Indian women in Natal at this time.

THE INDIAN HERITAGE

In order to understand the organisation of gender relations amongst the Indian population of colonial Natal, it is necessary to understand something of the organisation of gender and the position of women in nineteenth-century India. Indian immigrants brought with them from India a culture which differed considerably from that of both the African population and the white settlers. It contained within it an expression of gender relations that was also distinctive.

India's history until relatively modern times was characterised by successive invasions of people with varying social and cultural backgrounds. External threats served to reinforce indigenous customs but also led to the assimilation of new social practices. Around 1500 B.C. the invading Indo–Aryans introduced Vedic culture and the pervasive Hindu religion and also developed the enduring caste system. In more recent times the invading Moguls – Moslem people who ruled much of India from the early sixteenth to the early eighteenth century – have had a marked impact on Indian culture. The British Raj which followed introduced another era of foreign penetration, characterised by both assimilation and resistance on the part of the Indian people. The dual process of cultural exclusiveness and cultural assimilation can be seen very clearly with regard to the position of women in the nineteenth century. Polygyny, for example, although a Moslem custom, was practised by Hindu and Moslem alike, as was child-marriage (a Hindu custom) and the Moslem practice of *purdah* (seclusion of women and the wearing of the veil).

Both in the Quran and the holy Sanskrit writings, women are not only respected but revered, particularly as mothers, and the mother-cult survives strongly even today. Nevertheless, 'In the role of wife, women are inevitably subordinate. A wife becomes merged on marriage into the persona of her husband, and this merging lasts beyond death. A dutiful wife (*patrivrata*) worships her husband, regardless of his worth or character, as if he were a god' (Caplan, 1987: 280).

The Indian family was a sternly patriarchal one. The degree of oppression to which women were subjected, however, varied according to class or caste. Polygynous marriage and the custom of *purdah*, for example, were features of the wealthier groups. Less privileged women who had to work in the fields or move about as migrant workers or who went to the cities in search of a living could not be so secluded. By the same token, polygyny was more usually associated with men of wealth and status whilst the monogamous state was more common amongst the Indian masses.

This is not to suggest that Indian women in general were emancipated. The most oppressive of the customs to which they were subjected were *suti* or widow-burning (outlawed by the British in 1829) and the prevention of widow remarriage. In 1856 the British legalised widow remarriage but, for all practical purposes, this Act remained a dead letter throughout the Raj and beyond (Thomas, 1964: 299). The life of Hindu widows was hard, living as they did in the households of their late husbands, under the jurisdiction of their mothers-in-law. The prevention of widow remarriage was all the more oppressive given the Hindu custom of child-marriage, which meant that girls could be widowed as very young children and condemned to a life of servitude in their dead husbands' households. In 1929, when legislation was introduced to prohibit the marriage of girls under the age of 14, there were some 140 000 widows ten years and younger in India (Thomas, 1964: 340).

Despite legislating against what they perceived to be the most horrifying forms of women's oppression, the British did little to enhance the position of Indian women. In some ways the condition of women even deteriorated. Poverty and the dislocation of village life ensured that vast numbers of women, many of them widows and some still children, were forced to abandon their homes in search of employment. Many resorted to a life of begging and prostitution in the cities. Some found jobs in India itself, for example on the tea plantations of Assam. Others were forced further afield into neighbouring territories or under indentured contract to far-flung corners of the British empire.

It is against this background that the efforts of the recruiting agents of the indentured emigration schemes to acquire the 29 per cent quota of women for each shipload should be viewed. Undoubtedly many women made the decision to emigrate of their own volition, a decision often signifying courage and independence. Nevertheless, many of the female emigrants fell prey to the recruiters and their touts, who lured them into indentured contracts by means of misrepresentation or coercion. Whereas the men had to undergo fairly strict medical inspection and the most sickly of them were turned down, the women received a more superficial examination and virtually all were let through, even when infected with cholera, typhoid, dysentery or venereal disease (Tinker, 1974: 138).

INDENTURED WOMEN AND PRODUCTION IN NATAL

Indentured women were drawn into production in a number of different sectors of the Natal colonial economy. Though it is not possible to generalise too broadly about their role in production or the extent of their exploitation, it is clear, however, that under the indentured system, within the different sectors, women workers were subject to greater exploitation by their employers than were men.

The sugar estates

The conditions of indentured labourers in general and of women in particular were at their very poorest on the coastal plantations. These estates also employed the greatest number of indentured labourers. According to the Wragg Commission of 1885–7, five times more indentured Indians lived in the coastal districts than inland (Meer, 1980: 309–14). The sugar-belt was dominated by a tiny minority of seventeen large planters, and they, together with the Natal Government Railways, employed 64 per cent of the indentured labour force on the coast, though constituting less than 10 per cent of the employers in the area (Beall, 1982: 173).

These plantations which dominated the economic landscape of Natal were organised along quasi-industrial lines. Workers were accommodated in rows of huts or in 'lines', long buildings constructed of corrugated iron or built of masonry and roofed with iron. They were poorly ventilated, badly lit and appallingly overcrowded. The unhealthy living conditions, when combined with the rigours of labour on the plantations, gave rise to a high incidence of occupationally and environmentally related disease and a high mortality rate. In 1904 the Protector of Indian Immigrants observed that the mortality rate on the large estates was far higher than in other areas of employment (NA, Protector to Colonial Secretary, II 1/2/1904). The Tuberculosis Commission of 1914 noted further that 'the extent of the sickness and death rate has proved a most reliable index of the conditions and treatment of coolies by different employers' (UG34–1914: 92).

When indentured labourers were first introduced to the sugar estates, the female quota was regarded as dead stock, the planters wanting only strong, healthy men to establish massive and orderly plantations out of the virgin subtropical bush. This attitude was reflected in the haggling by planters over the 'price' to be paid for each labourer. In terms of the original system, employers were to pay two-thirds of the cost of their labourers' immigration, the remaining one-third deriving from the colony's general revenue. By the end of the nineteenth century, however, as a result of their persistent and vociferous complaining, employers were no longer required to bear the cost of the quota of women assigned to them directly (NA, II, 1/53/1890).

In time, however, the planters came to see the value of women on their estates and for a period women formed an important component of the plantation labour force. Employers were thus able to benefit not only from female labour, which was very poorly remunerated if at all, but also from not having to bear the direct cost of introducing this labour supply.

According to Law 14 of 1859, remuneration for men was to be fixed at the rate of 10s per month for the first year of indenture, rising by a shilling a month for each successive year of the contract. Women who worked were to receive half the amount paid to men, and children were to be paid in proportion to their age. These rates, for first indentures, did not change for the half-century of indentured immigration to Natal. The law also provided that married women were not obliged to work and that employers were nevertheless still required to provide them with accommodation, rations and medical care. No mention was made of single women or women whose unions did not conform to the legal definition of marriage in the colony. As the majority of women fell into the latter categories (marriage by Indian religious rites was not recognised in colonial Natal), sufficient confusion existed to allow for a system of abuse by employers which was never eliminated.

In the second phase of indenture, from 1874 onwards, there was even greater confusion about the regulations governing the employment of women, and great capital was made of this by the planters. There was no blanket ruling enforced as to whether or not women were compelled to work, although significantly, the words 'if employed' that had appeared opposite each women's name on the old indentured contracts were omitted from the post-1874 contracts. This led to rulings by magistrates that women could be compelled to work unless protected by a medical certificate.

By the end of the first phase of indenture (1860–6), it was already clear that on many estates *all* women and older children were denied rations if they did not work. In 1866 Government Notice 34 was passed, stating that women and children under 10 years were entitled to half-rations if they were unable or unwilling to work. This represented clearly a compromise between the colonial authorities, who were responsible to the government of India for the welfare of the immigrants, and the planters, who refused to pay for or even feed anybody not engaged directly in production.

It was not long, however, before planters discovered the value and uses of women's productive labour. On the plantations a clear sexual division of labour was established. Field tasks regarded as suitable for women included hoeing, weeding, planting beans and cow-peas between the cane rows, and cutting plant cane (Meer, 1980: *passim*). Weeding was conducted along the lines of task work and, although classified as light labour, was a back-breaking and extremely monotonous task. Cutting plant cane, which was used to establish new cane-fields, was a semi-skilled occupation as the pieces to be used for plant cane had to be carefully selected and handled so as not to damage the eyes from which the new shoots would grow. In Natal the planting and harvesting seasons overlap to a considerable degree, and as the new fields were planted every year in rotation, this work engaged women on a fairly regular basis.

For their work women were supposed to be paid 5s a month with full rations, but from the evidence given to the 1872 commission of enquiry and the Wragg Commission of 1885–7 (Meer, 1980) it is clear that there was no uniform pattern of employment or payment for women on the estates or the other sectors of the economy. Many women found themselves on an estate which provided no rations and which offered them only task work at 6d a day during the season. Others were provided with full rations and the statutory 5s a month but only if and when they worked.

The unstated but very clear view of the planters, that women should only be paid if they worked, assumed both that women would be catered for within a family set-up (whether or not this was the case), and that the 10s monthly wage paid to male workers constituted a family wage. These were clearly unrealistic expectations and had severe implications for gender relations within the indentured labour force.

The tea estates

The most intensive use of women's labour on plantations was made by the tea estates in the Stanger district on the north coast. Mechanisation was not possible on the steep slopes where the crop was grown, and the profitability of the industry was too slim to sustain high production costs. Tea planters invariably placed requests for families of immigrants and attempted to import people directly from the Indian tea-growing area of Assam (NA, Liege Hulett to Protector, II, 4/1/1876).

In contrast to other sectors, women on the tea estates were assigned to relatively skilled tasks. It was they who were used to pluck the tender tips of the tea plants, their particular skills in this regard being explained in terms of gender stereotypes such as their greater dexterity or their capacity for work that did not require great strength but considerable powers of endurance. Men were used for clearing the fields and in factory work. Children were put to work at light factory tasks such as sweeping.

During the picking season, which lasted for nine months of the year, women laboured in the fields for eleven to thirteen or even more hours a day. For the rest of the time they were engaged in cultivation tasks such as hoeing and weeding. Despite their skills they were still paid half the male wage rates and received half the male rations. They faced the same control mechanisms and wage deductions as men, such as for illness or absenteeism, but they were refused rations when they were not at work. This led women to push themselves to work, whether sick, pregnant or even in labour. The worst time for them was the six weeks following the long picking season, when their labour was not required. In a complaint to Hindson and Company Limited, the Protector wrote of such women: 'Those who are without husbands or men to look after them are compelled to beg for food, which they do, or obtain food by more objectionable means' (NA, II, 1/130/1904). Hindson eventually agreed to give the women a fortnight's break with rations following the picking season (NA, II, 1/131/1904).

Apart from the cheapness of their labour, the great advantage of women workers to the planters, therefore, was that they could be drawn into the workforce when their labour was required and sent back to the barracks when it was not. With regard to male workers, the planters were more strictly bound by the conditions governing indentured labour contracts. The confusion surrounding female conditions of service gave employers great latitude to do as they pleased.

This is not to exaggerate the advantages men enjoyed or the extent to which planters abided by the rules in any case. In a letter to J. H. Hulett & Sons, lambasting them for their treatment of their indentured workers, the medical officer of Stanger, Dr H. W. Jones, fumed:

Well, I happened to ride round the corner of the old Factory – when lo and behold there were five Indians – who were very ill. One woman had her womb right out.... Now why were these people hiding there?... During the summer months you make your Indians toil in the blazing sun from sunrise to nearly sunset.... How would you like it yourself?... You may say perhaps that the *Industry* would not thrive unless the coolies were *sweated* to the tune of 3 or 4 hours per diem. Very well then. Let the Industry go to the devil. It benefits no one but yourselves (NA, II, 1/98/1900).

For his trouble Dr Jones was dismissed from his post by the Colonial Secretary, on the grounds that he was not in a fit state of health to continue his duties!

Other sectors of the economy

The largest official employer of indentured labour was the Natal Government Railways, which ran its construction and maintenance gangs along the lines of a mobile army, with no place for women. Women assigned to the NGR were not provided with work and received no wages or rations. In some of the smaller towns, where there were no other work opportunities for women, the situation was so bad that it led 'in some instances men to send their wives away from the line – as they plead (and rightly) that a 12 lb ration is insufficient for two people to live on' (NA, Report of the Deputy Protector, II, 1895).

A small but not insignificant number of indentured Indians were allotted to farms and smallholdings in the Natal Midlands. Here women were particularly welcome. They were most often used as domestic servants, although they had to engage in farm work alongside the men as well. In this sector women were subjected to the long hours and isolation which characterise domestic service. There is ample testimony to their poor working conditions in the complaints they put forward to the Deputy Protector of Indian Immigrants. Apart from having to work long hours, they were often treated with great harshness. One woman, for example, was made to stand on a barrel all day, for refusing to work because she was in an advanced state of pregnancy (NA, II, 1/191/1916).

The coal-mining industry also used Indian workers, but these were mainly ex-indentured or reindentured workers; between 1903 and 1913 these men averaged 37,3 per cent of the labour force on the collieries (Beall and North-Coombes, 1983: 54). Because 'free' Indians did not arrive in Natal with a statutory quota of women, the number of indentured women on the mines was therefore comparatively small. The women who were employed were engaged in surface work such as picking and sorting the coal. More important than their role in the labour process, however, was the way in which mine managers and owners used the scarcity of women to control the labour and mobility of the male workers, a practice by no means confined only to the mines.

There is ample testimony in the records to confirm that both Indian men and their employers regarded women as property, to be bought, sold or given away. Women were most commonly used to punish or reward workers on the sugar estates. This practice was less common on the NGR, because women's labour was not needed there. Instead, women consigned to the railways were often sold by managers to 'free' Indians wanting wives. In the case of the coal mines (as with the estates), women were valued both as labourers and as a means of social control. A *Natal Witness* report of 9 December 1904 carried a story headlined 'Amazing Allegations Against Mine Officials – Indian's Strange Story – Wife Bought for £10', which illustrates this point. The incident referred to had taken place on the Ramsay Colliery near Ladysmith and came to light in a court case. An Indian man whose indentured contract had terminated, had been forcibly prevented from leaving the colliery and from taking his wife with him. The mine manager, a Mr Thomas, assaulted both the man and the woman and instructed the clerk at the nearby Wessels Nek station not to issue the couple with travel tickets. The Indian worker was most indignant because, whilst working on the colliery, he had taken the woman, Mandaye, as his wife; in court he declared that 'he paid £10 for her, receiving a receipt for that amount from Llewelyn Davies, the secretary of the company.' It was not only the mine officials (who sold the women) and the male workers (who bought them) who conceived of women as property. In this case, when told by Thomas to go to work and take another man as her husband, Mandaye had refused, 'saying that she had been paid for by the complainant' (NA, II, 1/130/1904).

The ultra-exploitability of indentured women

Indentured labourers from India offered themselves for contract employment overseas in the manner of free labour. It was the employer, however, who had the upper hand in negotiating the contract with the British government of India. Although indentured immigrants attested to their contracts, they had no say over the terms of their employment. Once brought to the colony, they became a captive labour force. They were tied to their contracts for a period of five years, and sometimes longer when forced to reindenture (for instance through the £3 tax). They were unable to renegotiate wages regularly and suffered long hours of work. They had no control over the terms of their contract being upheld, enjoyed inadequate legal protection and were denied the right to organise. Furthermore, the opportunities for work outside of indentured labour have often been exaggerated, as the high rate of reindenture, particularly from the late nineteenth century, testifies.

For all these reasons indenture in Natal can be seen as a system of forced labour, which rendered the workers ultra-exploitable. Under this system, women were even more exploited than men. Indentured women were the lowest-paid workers in the colony, when they were paid at all. Their powerlessness stemmed largely from the system of labour regimentation and control which applied to the indentured labour force as a whole. But in addition women endured another set of restrictions that derived from their position as women in Indian and colonial society. In general their role in the labour process precluded them from tasks that might enable them to develop skills or experience and, in turn, bargaining power. (Tea-picking, which went into decline after 1911 anyway, and cutting plant cane were the only exceptions in this situation.) Furthermore, familial resistance to anything that was thought to challenge women's domestic role in life prevented Indian girls from being allowed to acquire an education when this became a possibility for male immigrant children in the early twentieth century. Finally, responsibility for child-bearing and also for child-rearing (the latter unquestioned by employers and the Indian community itself) further reduced their mobility and thus their potential for finding alternative forms of employment. The only choices facing women when phased out of indenture were repatriation, marriage, or some other form of dependence on a male partner or relative.

The question arises as to whether indentured workers resisted their exploitation. While there is ample evidence that they did, the extent of collective resistance amongst the indentured labour force has been widely debated.[4] Resistance by women does not seem to have taken an overt or demonstrably collective form, but more often found expression in individual acts such as desertion and arson, which increased the woman's vulnerability. For instance, one woman, Sornam, who was accused by her master of not working fast enough, in protest and desperation 'flung down her hoe and also threw herself on the ground', whereupon she received a beating from the estate manager (NA, II, 1/131/1904). In the case of one woman who set fire to cane-fields on the Natal Estates, repatriation was recommended on the grounds that she was suffering from a weak intellect (NA, II, 1/191/1916). To resist meant risking physical assault, deprivation of wages, the withholding of rations or dismissal.

The phasing out of women from the indentured labour force

It is revealing, given the importance of women to the labour process on the estates and their role in reproducing the labour force, that they were the first to be phased out of the plantation workforce. In time, African men, with their families, came to be seen by the planters as a more appropriate and potentially plentiful source of labour than Indian women, and replaced them. Indian men, however, maintained their place in the estate labour force, mainly in skilled work, particularly in the mills. In this way the male–female hierarchy that had been originally established in the labour force was later restructured along racial lines, to the detriment of Indian women.

Even during the period of indentured immigration, African daily or *togt* labour was used. Generally, however, the African population was able to resist long-term labour contracts during this time because of their access to land as well as the availability of *togt* work to meet their cash requirements. Around the turn of the century the pace of African proletarianisation quickened somewhat and there was a greater availability of African labour for the sugar estates. The expansion of the sugar industry into Zululand after 1905 took place on the basis of African labour.

African labour was more attractive to the planters because it was now cheaper than Indian. The African wage rate had dropped from around 10s a month at mid-century (the same as for indentured men) to around 9s a month by the end of the nineteenth century. Moreover, under the provisions of the Masters and Servants Act of 1894, Africans could be employed under twelve-month contracts on the estates, while Section 19 of the Act provided that their wives and children under 16 years were also bound by these contracts. Thus 9s a month bought the planters a labour force of some size.

What underpinned the cheapness of African labour was not only the unpaid family labour of contract workers on the estates, but also subsistence production in the reserves, which supported both contract and *togt* workers. In the reserves it was African women who were primarily responsible for this production and thus for the maintenance of the cheap African labour force. African men and women came to form another captive labour force and, in time, to replace indentured Indian workers.

Indian women were the first to be replaced in this way. As early as 1902 it was reported that Indian men 'were found very handy at the mill, to be good cane cutters, and very useful in making drains and roads, but the kaffirs were found best for ordinary field work' (*South African Sugar Journal Annual*, 1920–1: 181) – in other words, at tasks previously performed by Indian women. The one area of employment where Indian women had held some advantage by virtue of their relatively skilled status – the tea industry – failed to survive the ending of indentured immigration in 1911. Although it had been confidently argued that the labour question on the tea estates could be resolved by the employment of African labour, as in the case of sugar production, this did not prove possible: only an ultra-exploitable, captive labour force could be induced to perform the skilled but back-breaking work required on the tea estates for such minimal reward. With the demise of the tea industry went an important employment area for Indian women.

INDENTURED WOMEN AND THE REPRODUCTION OF THE LABOUR FORCE

As well as being directly exploited as workers, indentured women were also subjected to extreme forms of oppression in their capacity as reproducers of labour power.

Both women's productive and unproductive labour was harnessed by employers and served to hold down indentured wages generally. On the estates women laboured not only directly for the planters, but indirectly as well. Their cultivation of garden plots partly met their own subsistence needs, as well as that of their younger children and of the indentured men. This, together with their domestic work in the barracks, served to reproduce labour power on the estates on a day-to-day basis.

In the sphere of the proverbial double shift, indentured women were subject to extraordinary burdens. When not in the fields themselves, or during their breaks, they were required by their male partners or the men to whom they were somehow indebted, to take them their midday meal in the fields or at the mill. In the evening they prepared the meal and were expected to perform other domestic tasks such as washing and cleaning and to provide sexual services. Given the disproportion of the sexes, they were frequently required to perform domestic tasks on behalf of not one but several men. This was often done in return for rations or other favours, such as clothing or protection from other men. Their low reward for field work increased the dependence of women on men.

As already pointed out, the planters did not recognise women's value as reproducers of labour power on a generational basis at first, because they saw the system of indenture itself as replenishing their workforce. However, as reindenture came to supplement importation to a significant degree from the turn of the century, owing to the expansion of the economy and before Africans had become fully proletarianised, so the reproductive function of indentured women became more important to employers. This was especially so during the first decade of the twentieth century, at which time the system of indentured immigration was threatened with termination.

In the long term, however, the development of the sugar industry was carried out on the backs of African contract labour. That the value of indentured women's reproductive function was transitory is attested to by the fate of the women coming out of indentured contracts after 1911. The records of the Indian Immigration Trust Board reveal a host of cases of destitute women wandering around without employment or support in the years immediately following the termination of indentured immigration. These women were classified as 'free' Indians because, according to the Protector, 'a destitute Indian cannot be under indenture' (NA, II, 1/189/1913). Employers were not interested in having them live on their premises if they did not work for them. Women in this situation were frequently repatriated to India.

INDENTURED WOMEN, SEXUALITY, MARRIAGE AND THE FAMILY

As suggested above, the Indian immigrants brought with them a culture with a different form of gender relations from those prevailing among the African and white populations of the colony. Whilst emigration constituted a break with much that was 'Indian' – it was difficult, for example, to maintain the elaborate rules of caste under the new circumstances – much of the Indian heritage was also retained. The retention of cultural values was often a defensive strategy in an alien and hostile environment, and found expression particularly in the sphere of gender relations. It is significant that the only feature of caste which persisted in Natal was that of caste endogamy, wherever possible (Kuper, 1955: 23).

Yet although the form in which gender relations were expressed was culturally specific, much of its ideological content was confirmed and reinforced by the dominant ideology of gender prevailing among the ruling settler class. At the workplace there was both conflict and collusion between male workers and employers for control over Indian women. At a more general level white colonial perceptions and Indian expectations of the proper ordering of relations between the sexes tended to coincide.

Struggles around sexuality under indenture

The ideology of extreme wifely subordination in marriage that was brought from India persisted amongst the immigrant population and was given a sharper edge under conditions where men outnumbered women by nearly three to one. Despite this, life on the estates denied immigrants the opportunity of customary marriage and family life. Relationships between men and women were often very unstable and many men abandoned their partners either during indenture or when moving out of it (NA, II, 1/52/1890).

Whilst many indentured workers arrived at the emigration depots in India single, they frequently established relationships with members of the opposite sex at the depot or during the journey and declared themselves married, a practice disapproved of but recognised by the authorities. As Tinker has pointed out: 'The advantage to the man was obvious: he had someone to cook for him and attend to him in a society where females were very scarce. But there was also advantage to the woman in securing a protector in a savage new environment, and in establishing some sort of recognised position in a social order which held no place for adult single women' (1974: 34).

The extent to which women were protected by these partnerships or liaisons should not be exaggerated, however, for even on board ship women were subject to sexual assault, not only by fellow emigrants but also by crew members; and furthermore the blessings of a conjugal relationship on the sugar estates were mixed indeed. Swan has described how women on the plantations were 'treated almost as chattels, and even marriage was regarded with contempt in some quarters. On one of the biggest plantations, women were routinely used to punish recalcitrant labourers ... thus a situation was created in Natal which permitted the whites to believe that Indians were incapable of sustaining bonds of mutual affection or responsibility' (1985: 37).

The indentured labour system undoubtedly deprived couples of the conditions suitable for sustaining such bonds (NA, II, 1/5/1890). Partners were often sent to different estates and could be fined for trespass for visiting each other. Even when employed on the same estate, men and women found it difficult to maintain intimate relationships in conditions devoid of leisure and privacy. In this respect the Wragg Commission noted: 'We regret to observe that too little regard is paid to this very essential requisite towards purity of life. There is a general huddling together of the sexes, of all ages, much to be deplored' (Meer, 1980: 302). Yet when single women did lay complaints about sexual harassment, the response was invariably that echoed by the Protector, who argued that there was 'nothing whatsoever to prevent the complainants from keeping themselves apart if they wished, from the single men' (NA, II, 1/197/1900).

However, life on the estates was not as simple as that, as the evidence led in a murder case, *Regina* v. *Mulwa*, demonstrates. This involved an indentured worker, Mulwa, who murdered his common-law wife Nootini, on the Blackburn Estate in April 1890. The case shows how little resemblance there was between the ideology of marital stability and the actual ways in which indentured workers were obliged to interact and live together. The couple had arrived in Natal on the same ship and been assigned to the estate in 1879. On arrival at the estate they had to negotiate a place to sleep and were taken in by a man called Poonie, in whose hut they remained for about four months, with Nootini doing the domestic chores. In his evidence Mulwa stated that they had not felt 'safe' there. Nootini was not given work on the estate and received no wages or rations. The couple and their young child were unable to survive on Mulwa's twelve pounds of rice a week. After a time they were offered alternative accommodation by Sahabdeen, a mill worker who saw in Nootini a potential cook, housekeeper and mistress. In his statement before being sentenced Mulwa described what followed:

I declined at first – he again asked me and as an inducement said I shall get free rations – I and the woman then went – the food we got from the estate was insufficient. Sahabdeen said if the woman would cook for him he would give her clothing – Sahabdeen gave me to the extent of 9s. I returned 8s. Sahabdeen asked me for the balance I owed and said if I did not pay I must leave…. I said where were we … to go…. Sahabdeen then said I want you to go away but not the woman and child…. I went to Mr. Townsend [and] … reported the matter and asked for a lodging – Mr. Townsend did not give us a house…. I killed her because she went with other men (NA, II, 1/57/1890).

On the morning that Nootini was murdered a witness heard her pleading with her sick husband to go to work, saying 'If you don't go to work who will give us food?' Later that same morning Mulwa found her sleeping with Sahabdeen and subsequently attacked and killed her.

As could be expected in a situation of such complete powerlessness, indentured women were very vulnerable to sexual harassment not only by fellow workers but also by sirdars (or overseers) and by their white male employers. While it is difficult to ascertain how indentured women themselves perceived their lives, as they did not often have the opportunity to speak for themselves, most of the surviving records of women informants refer to this gender-specific form of harassment. Very typical is the case of a woman called Vellach who, caught in a double-bind, complained: 'About ten days ago whilst in my master's bedroom regulating it, he came in, striking his pocket and saying that he would give me £3 if I were to lie with him, as the mistress and her family had gone to town. I refused saying that my husband would beat me. He said he would not tell him' (NA, II, 1/7/1880).

In his defence the employer, a Mr Hulley, used the gilt-edged excuse frequently favoured by men of the ruling class, that of the promiscuity of the woman involved and the fact that she had venereal disease. He managed to convince the Deputy Protector of his innocence by arguing: 'Putting aside her personal appearance which is not very attractive, is it likely that I a married man, knowing what had been the matter with her ... would be guilty of such a charge?' (NA, II, 1/7/1880).

In such cases the employer's word was almost always taken over that of the indentured woman, and women in Vellach's situation were invariably denied their requests to be transferred to other employers. Colonial courts took the part of the men not only because of their position in the white ruling class, but also because they were men in a male-dominated society.

Sexual harassment was not confined to employers alone. It was common for planters, for example, to rely on sirdars to oversee the women in the workplace and the barracks, and these men frequently used their position to their advantage, subjecting women to abuse and indignities (NA, II, 1/77/1895). It was also common for indentured men to buy and sell women for a shilling, with the tacit approval of the employers and sirdars and even of the women themselves. Given the marked sexual imbalance in the Indian immigrant population, the men were most vigorous in asserting their claims over women. Where possible, marriage was entered into, but this was not always feasible as legally recognised marriages required a £5 marriage licence, which was out of reach of most indentured immigrants. Moreover, marriage by customary religious rites, Hindu or Moslem, was not considered valid in the colonial courts. This did not prevent Indian men from recourse to colonial justice in their attempts to assert control over women. Cases of desertion, adultery and breach of promise to marry were brought before the Protector for trial.

Giving evidence to the 1872 commission of enquiry, an Indian hotel-keeper at Verulam, by the name of Rangassamy, outlined his views on the problems created by the scarcity of women and the need for legislation to control Indian women:

As to marriages, among the coolies we first imported too many males [who] were single and the scarcity of females causes many debauches, and in many cases they committed suicide: therefore I consider to stop this, when they agree to marry, the agreement should be drawn by the Coolie Agent, in the Coolie office. After they agree to marry, if either party refuse to marry, the Coolie Agent should punish the guilty person. If a woman commits adultery, she should be punished by cutting off her hair, and ten days' imprisonment and cautioned that if she goes to another man, she must pay to the first husband ten pounds. The adulterer should be fined five pounds, and be imprisoned for 20 days, and get 12 lashes. The wife should be imprisoned until she repaid the money, or went back to her husband (Meer, 1980: 139).

It has been argued in the context of other colonies which imported indentured labour that women's scarcity value gave them considerable bargaining power in relation to men, and that by moving from one partner to another women could not only remain independent but could benefit materially (Moore, 1984: 4–5). Whilst this viewpoint might have some application in Natal as well, it would have to be qualified by an understanding of the underlying powerlessness of indentured women. One would question, for example, the extent of the independence open to a woman like Nootini in her decision to sleep with Sahabdeen. One would also question the bargaining power of a little girl described by the Inspector of Nuisances in a 1904 report to the Protector. This child lived in one of the NGR barracks, was not permanently attached to anyone, and had 'no regular sleeping place but finds any place she can for the purpose' (NA, II, 1/126/1904).

Marriage and family outside of indenture

Marriage was of greater moment for Indians outside of indenture than for those within it. Thus in 1886, out of 4 7047 married Indian women in the colony, 3 182 were 'free' (the figure does not include passenger Indians) and 865 were indentured (Meer, 1980: 261). It seems that once Indians were free from their indentured contracts and the conditions of estate life, marriage and the creation of a stable family life became a priority. It was, perhaps, a response to their somewhat uncomfortable location within the social fabric of the colony, wedged between the politically and economically dominant minority of whites and the vast, subjugated African population.

The practice of child-marriage was given a particularly unsavoury edge by the situation created through the sexual imbalance amongst Indians in the colony. There is evidence that young brides could be purchased from their parents and that some unscrupulous guardians took away a daughter married by religious rites to one man and married her to another for an additional fee. In many cases the girls were below 13 years, the legal age of marriage. Nundy (1902) reported that in Verulam alone, in only two out of ten marriages solemnised in one month were the girls even approaching the legal age; the rest were between 10 and 12 years old.

Recent interviews with Indian women in Durban give some insight into how this practice was perceived by the girls themselves:

The practice of child-marriage, as practised quite extensively in India, was more characteristic of the period following indenture.... Of all the women interviewed all those who had been married had no choice or say in who their husband was to be.... Velimah: 'Father chose the husband, they won't let us go and choose, they'll give us a hiding.... If he feels it OK we got married, never mind if he's a drunkard' (Williams, 1986: 17).

Although the young girls acquiesced in the practice, it was nevertheless resented, if not construed as oppression.

The question of marriage formed a central issue in the 1913 passive resistance campaign waged by Natal Indians under the leadership of M. K. Gandhi. However, the issue mainly touched the trading class, among whom wives were generally sent for from India once their husbands had established themselves in the colony. At first it was the practice to admit a woman, if she was the man's only wife, to reside in South Africa. In 1910, however, Mr Justice Searle ruled that for the purposes of immigration, no marriage could be regarded as monogamous, and therefore legal, if it was celebrated according to the rites of any religion recognising polygamy. Indians argued that this reduced their wives to the status of concubines. The ensuing passive resistance campaign (in which women played a significant part) succeeded in winning recognition of existing monogamous marriages amongst Indians in South Africa and restored the position to that which had existed before 1910. Although important in the political awakening of the Indian community, and providing a useful counterpoint to the stereotype of Indian women as especially docile and submissive, the issue was only really significant for the wealthy trading class. Given the imbalance between the sexes amongst indentured workers and their offspring, the question of polygamy did not much concern them.

As Carby (1982) has suggested with regard to blacks in America and under colonialism, it is possible for the family to become the site of both political and cultural resistance. That the resultant emphasis on communalism can be a conservative or even reactionary force does not reduce the persistent potency of Indian cultural values, particularly in the sphere of gender relations, as a source of social cohesion in the community. Nor should it be allowed to obscure the fact that the Indian family has also constituted a site of oppression for women.

The attitude of the colonial state

The attitude of the colonial state towards Indian marriage and family life was inconsistent. At one level, it attempted to promote, somewhat incongruously, some sort of Victorian ideal of family life and stability amongst the Indian population. At another level there was a persistent belief that Indian women were promiscuous, and they were blamed for all manner of social ills, most notably the prevalence of venereal disease amongst the indentured population.

The colonial state intervened to confirm the proprietorial attitude towards women held by Indian men. Government Notice 84 of 1873 empowered the Protector to adjudicate in cases of 'seducing, or cohabiting, or committing adultery with the wives of others; or enticing or abducting unmarried Indian immigrant girls under sixteen years old from the custody of their parents' (Meer, 1980: 173). In his 1877 report the Protector stated that the punishments he handed out for such offences had proved a successful deterrent. By the same token, success was achieved (without any apparent protest from Indian men) by inflicting harsher punishments on the women than on the men involved in illegal liaisons.

Reporting on the registration of marriages amongst indentured Indians, the Protector noted in 1875:

Those entered as 'single' include many aged widows and respectable persons, but the majority are no doubt dissolute and abandoned characters. It is not, of course, supposed that registration has put a stop to adultery among the Indians, but at least it affords the means of establishing the validity of their marriages and thereby facilitates a prosecution for adultery if committed. The best effect, however, is that it has certainly raised the women as a class; it has given married women a proper status, making them respectable in the eyes of the men, and thereby raising their own self-respect (Meer, 1980: 261).

In reality, of course, prevailing conditions prevented the development of stability in family life and promoted the social ills complained about – conditions which the colonial state did very little to improve.

A debate which took place in 1899 in the Legislative Assembly on the Women and Children's Protection Bill provides a measure of the prevailing sexual morality amongst the white male settlers, and reveals its double standard not only in relation to men and women but in relation to blacks and whites as well. The bill was introduced 'in the interest of womanhood' – but for 'womanhood' read 'white womanhood' – and dealt with the raising of the age of consent. The all-male legislators were in no doubt about the importance of this step for white women. They had become a virtual symbol of white supremacy and were being increasingly sheltered and protected at a time when women in Britain were gaining more freedom and autonomy (Beall, 1982: 196). But the age of consent became a contentious issue with regard to African and Indian women. The legislators' main concern, it seems, was for the white man who might be convicted of intercourse with a minor African or Indian girl. It was argued that because black girls matured early, it was difficult for white men to determine whether or not they had reached the age of consent.

The hypocrisy of colonial morality is summed up in the words of the Deputy Speaker, who argued that if the proposals did not refer to white women alone, 'you place the life and liberty of every white man in this country at the mercy of every coolie girl, and let that be distinctly understood. Further than that you open the door to a system of blackmail; at which the Indians of India are past masters ... there are already ample provisions made in the Indian Code [*sic*] and the Native Code for the protection of Indian and Native women' (Colony of Natal, 1899, Debates: 617).

His colleague, Mr Greene, argued further that 'It is very nice – we are protecting the females ... but I do not know why males are not entitled to have some protection,' and suggested that men be entitled to plead that the girl was a prostitute if carnal knowledge was proved!

CONCLUSION

Indian women were brought to Natal with great reluctance. Their labour power was, however, harnessed in the development of Natal's economy, at a time when they were amongst the most exploited members of the colony's proletariat. Both their productive and their reproductive labour facilitated capital accumulation, particularly on the sugar estates. Throughout the period of indentured immigration, Indian women were located at the very bottom of the class–race–gender hierarchy in the colony. As workers they were ultra-exploitable. As Indians they were unwelcome and subject to obnoxious stereotyping. As women they had to struggle against two different but converging constructs of gender relations, in both of which women were subordinated to men – that prevailing within the immigrant population itself and the broader relations of gender that developed under colonial rule.

Some writers have argued that women derived benefits from indentured immigration, in that it offered them an escape from starvation, widowhood, prostitution and beggary – 'that the decision to emigrate was in itself a sign of independent character of these women and the decision to emigrate alone and as individuals was a sign of their strength' (Reddock, 1984: 13). But whilst it is undoubtedly true that indentured women did fight to maintain some control over their lives, at the same time it is difficult to conceive of them finding freedom and independence under conditions of forced labour and the undoubted collusion between employers and male workers to maintain male control.

This is not to deny that indentured women devised a variety of strategies for survival, often outside the bounds of marriage and the patriarchal family. Indeed, for many women marriage was not an option, particularly for widows and for those who had been passed around the barracks from man to man and bore the scars, both physical and psychological, of that experience. What is necessary, however, is to understand the constraints under which Indian women made their choices.

Moreover, whilst it is important to recognise the persistence of the form of the Indian patriarchal family in Natal over the past hundred years, it is equally important to recognise that it has not been a static, unchanging institution. A discussion of marriage and family form in India is beyond the scope of this chapter; suffice to say that these varied over time and place and according to caste. Under conditions of indenture the patriarchal family was little more than an ideological form to which people aspired but which they were unable to establish in reality. With the termination of indenture, and as the Indian population became more settled and permanent, so the Indian family reasserted itself in Natal, its significance within the community being enhanced by the experience of indenture.

For women this was a mixed blessing, as the family nurtured patriarchal values. A haven in a hostile environment, the Indian family has also enabled oppressive gender relations to persist and has been the site of gender struggles between men and women in the twentieth century.

7

Gender and the development of the migrant labour system c. 1850–1930: An overview

CHERRYL WALKER

The migrant labour system has long been recognised as one of the key institutions in the development of modern South Africa – a source of immense profits for a few and immense hardship for many. Its impact on African society has been profound. Forty years ago the anthropologist Isaac Schapera described 'the continuous flow of men and women to and from European centres of employment' as 'one of the outstanding features … in the life of Native peoples inhabiting Southern Africa…' (1947: 1). More recently Murray has stated that 'no aspect of contemporary village life can be understood without central reference to the dependence of villagers for their livelihood on earnings derived from the export of labour' (1981: xi). Although he was referring specifically to Lesotho, his is a comment that could be applied to all the communities that together constitute South Africa's 'rural periphery' – the African reserves or bantustans within the borders of South Africa as well as the politically independent, labour-exporting states of the subcontinent.

Murray went on to remark that the dependence of the rural periphery on migrant earnings must be understood in its proper historical context. This chapter examines the relevance of gender to an understanding of this context, and reviews the involvement of women from the rural periphery in migrant labour in the period before approximately 1930. The most pervasive image of women under the migrant labour system is as victims – those 'left behind', lumped along with children, the old and the sick into the emotive but blurry category of the 'dispossessed' or 'surplus'. This chapter attempts to sharpen the focus, drawing out the complicated contours of the impact of migrant labour on the position of African women in this early period. It argues that gender relations, more specifically the control of women in precolonial society and its subsequent restructuring by the colonial state, played a key role in shaping the migrant labour system; further, that the impact of the system on the role and status of women was extremely complex, opening up opportunities for increased personal autonomy and mobility at an individual level while radically undermining the security previously accorded women in precolonial society.

It is a vast field and I am conscious of relying heavily on secondary, rather than primary, material in traversing it. Furthermore, despite an extensive literature on the history of migrant labour, few studies look directly at gender relations and the role of women; those that do, lean more to the theoretical than the empirical. It is a frustrating experience working through the literature with questions about the historical position and role of women to the fore. Most of the discussion on women is contemporary, looking at the sufferings of 'women without men' or the destructive impact of migrant labour on family life. The anthropological material tends to subsume women within the family and to privilege kinship at the expense of other social networks and relationships. These texts often lack an historical perspective and treat 'tradition' uncritically – yet, as the chapter by Guy has already argued, the apparent surface continuity in institutions such as the family, bridewealth and marriage obscures significant changes in their functions over time. Contemporary concepts of 'the family', with their powerful normative associations, are also difficult for the student of history to transcend. Even while employing terms such as 'the traditional family' or 'the extended family', researchers often unconsciously assume the model of the Christian, nuclear family. This may apply not only to outsiders attempting to reconstruct the history of the family of a particular society but to the members of that society as well; they too are susceptible to viewing their past through the filter of contemporary familial ideology and practice.

This chapter is thus regarded as a preliminary investigation, sketching out major features of the terrain only. It is divided into four parts: (1) the development of the migrant labour system between approximately 1850 and 1930; (2) the significance of gender organisation in shaping the manner in which precolonial societies engaged with migrant labour, and the role of the colonial state in restructuring gender relations to secure the migrant labour system; (3) women as migrants; and, finally, (4) the multi-faceted impact of migrant labour on the position and status of women in the rural periphery.

Some of these themes are picked up in chapter 9, which looks specifically at the migration of Basotho women to the Rand in the first half of the twentieth century.

HISTORICAL OVERVIEW: MIGRANT LABOUR 1850–1930
In the early 1970s it was argued strongly that the origins of the migrant labour system lay in the functions it served for capital. Articles by Wolpe (1972) and Legassick (1975) were extremely influential in

formulating the theoretical underpinnings of this analysis, which came to inform many interpretations of South African political economy and history. In an article on 'Labour Migration and Peasant Differentiation' in Zambia, Cliffe summarises the main tenets of this argument:

The origins of labour migration in Southern and Central Africa were to be found in the need for labour power as capitalist farms, mines and industries were set up by the settlers.... The extraction of the necessary labour power for the newly imposed units of production of course necessitated some penetration of the existing pre-capitalist social formations and their subservience to the demands of capitalist production. But the institutionalisation of labour migration and the efforts to perpetuate what had previously been regarded as a transitional phenomenon had an evolving logic for the capitalists. The responsibility for providing for the long-term reproduction of the labour force – the social security, retirement provisions, the bringing up of the next generation and meeting the subsistence needs of the workers' families – did not fall on the employer nor on the settler state, but was borne by domestic production (1978: 328).

He goes on to note that this required the maintenance of 'elements of pre-existing relationships, in order to preserve their ability to reproduce the labour force' (ibid.). Thus elements of precapitalist systems of land tenure and production, family forms, legal systems and political institutions were maintained by the colonial state in the African rural areas, albeit in a restructured form, in order to preserve the migrants' 'subsistence base' and hold down the cost of labour and of social reproduction in general. Capital, in this view, emerges as the all-powerful and ever-rational motor of history.

Numerous twentieth-century policy statements from the mining industry lend support to this argument, for instance the following classic formulation of the 'cheap labour thesis' from the Mine Natives' Wages Commission of 1944:

It is clearly to the advantage of the mines that Native labourers should be encouraged to return to their homes after the completion of the ordinary period of service. The maintenance of the system under which the mines are able to obtain unskilled labour at a rate less than that ordinarily paid in industry depends upon this, for otherwise the subsidiary means of subsistence would disappear and the labourer would tend to become a permanent resident upon the Witwatersrand, with increased requirements (quoted in Schapera, 1947: 204).

More recently, however, the Wolpe–Legassick thesis has been criticised for its exaggerated functionalism, and greater attention has been paid to the active engagement of African societies in the shaping of the migrant labour system in the nineteenth century. While with time both mining capital and the settler state came to see the value of a labour force of 'single' men still tied materially and psychologically to a rural and 'traditional' base, the policy position articulated by the 1944 Mine Natives' Wages Commission did not leap full-blown into the pages of history with the discovery of the first diamond or even the sinking of the first deep-level gold mining shaft.

Initially the mining industry viewed migrant labour as inefficient and expensive, 'the outcome of the weakness of the colonial authorities, the continued access Africans had to the land, and the cohesion of precolonial social formations' (Marks and Rathbone, 1982: 18). For much of the nineteenth century the outcome of the struggles over boundaries, economic development and social forms of the future African reserves and territories of southern Africa could not be predicted. Marks and Rathbone argue that the 'characteristic nexus of South Africa's labour controls' – the compound system based upon cheap migrant labour, revamped masters and servants laws, pass laws and the colour bar – had only emerged by 1900 and, furthermore, grew out of a complex set of interactions between African societies in resistance to full proletarianisation, and the powerful but not all-powerful representatives of capital (ibid.: 14). Noting that 'causes are not necessarily found in consequences', they contend:

Proletarianisation was undoubtedly largely the result of the penetration of capitalist forces of production; that it was 'incomplete' and also took the form of labour migrancy was … related to the complex struggles between and within ruling classes over the disposal of the labour power of young men.... In terms of the historiography, what is significant is the growing picture of structural relations within African societies acting every bit as powerfully on the actions and consciousness of migrants as any 'pull' of market forces, growth of 'new wants', or voluntarist individual choice on the one hand, or the 'determining role of the South African state' on the other (ibid.: 19).

Integral to these 'structural relations', it is argued below, were the gender relations that operated in the precolonial chiefdoms of southern Africa.

Indigenous responses to new forces of production

One of the weaknesses of the Wolpe–Legassick thesis is that it glosses over the marked regional variations in the responses of the southern African chiefdoms to the new economic order. In some areas the development of labour migration predated the mineral discoveries. In the Eastern Cape, as the chapter by Cock brings out, the movement of Xhosa-speaking people backwards and forwards across the frontier, in search of work, was well established in the early nineteenth century. Certain other areas still largely untouched by white settlement were experiencing labour migration by the middle of the century. Thus among the Pedi of the north-eastern Transvaal and the Tonga of the Delagoa Bay region in present-day Mozambique, young men were moving south to seek employment several decades before Kimberley and Johannesburg featured on the map, and before the incorporation of either chiefdom under colonial rule. Delius (1980) dates the beginnings of migration among the Pedi as early as the 1840s, when young men, organised in large groups of 200 or more, began leaving the chiefdom regularly in search of employment in far-distant Port Elizabeth and in Natal. Similarly, Tonga migrants were travelling to the Natal plantations and even as far afield as the Western Cape as early as the 1850s (Harries, 1982).

Furthermore, the initial movement of these men into migrant labour was prompted not by external forces but by processes largely internal to their societies. The primary incentive behind Pedi migration was to acquire guns for hunting and for defence against the threat posed to their chiefdom by Trekkers, Zulu and Swazi. The men tended to work for as long as was needed to acquire a gun and then to return home. According to Harries (1982), among the Tonga the decline of the local economy lay behind the early phase of labour migration: the shooting out of game, the restructuring of trade opportunities and a decline in agricultural production as a result of warfare and ecological problems. A severe drought in the early 1860s, coinciding with the Gaza civil war, resulted in massive cattle losses and led to the substitution of, first, hoes and then sterling for cattle in bridewealth payments. At first, interestingly, whole families moved from the Delagoa Bay region, but this was stopped because of the disapproval of the Natal authorities and the Zulu king, and in the 1860s the typical Tonga migrant was a young single man in his teens or twenties. Until the end of the nineteenth century, the driving force behind Tonga migrant labour was the desire to accumulate hoes, and later sterling – not to invest in agriculture or to exchange for commodity goods, but to invest in bridewealth. The migrant, therefore, operated within the circuit of precapitalist rather than capitalist production.

While the discovery of diamonds at Kimberley greatly accelerated the external demand for African labour and drew other chiefdoms into the process, the early stages of migrant labour to the mines were organised largely on terms set by African societies themselves. The role of the chiefs remained important. The bulk of the Pedi migrants went shortly after initiation and the Pedi chiefs made use of the age-regiment system in organising and controlling their movement (Delius, 1980). Labour migration among the Basotho began on a significant scale in the 1870s and by the end of that decade some 15 000 Basotho men were estimated to be away, divided in roughly equal numbers among the diamond fields, the colonial railways, and a miscellany of jobs in the Free State and Cape (Kimble, 1982: 128). According to Kimble, the primary structural determinant in Basotho labour migration in this early period was the role of the ruling Koena lineage, who organised and controlled the movement of the majority of migrants with the aim of procuring guns. Among the Tswana, local chiefs also played an essential part in organising the flow of labour, using the age-regiment system; as in the case of the Pedi and the Basotho, the acquisition of firearms was a major attraction (Schapera, 1947).

In all these societies agricultural production, predicated on female labour, was still far more important than migrant labour for the reproduction of the homestead. Changes in rural production enabled individual homesteads to adapt to a reduced labour force and shrinking household size. One such development – organised if not initiated by women – was a widespread shift away from labour-intensive crops such as sorghum to the higher-yielding though less drought-resistant maize as a staple (Harries, 1982: 157; Beinart, 1982: 99). The practice of inter-cropping, for instance beans with pumpkins, also allowed for the more intensive use of available land.

The origins of migrant labour were thus rooted in processes and relationships that were largely internal to the labour-exporting societies. Because of the way in which the homestead economy operated, it was the young, unmarried man who could most easily be released by the homestead – and he, therefore, who was the first to be drawn into wage labour. Desirous of new goods such as guns or hoes and determined to retain control over the young men who earned them, chiefs and elders favoured a system that guaranteed that the workers would return to their rural homes after a limited period. They also jealously guarded their control over women, to ensure the continuation of homestead production and their dominance within rural society.

In areas favourably situated in relation to the mining and urban centres, the opening up of the mines also created new market opportunities, to which there was a ready African response. Thus the Thlaping of Griqualand West became involved in a short-lived but initially lucrative trade in firewood and grain on the Kimberley market (Shillington, 1982). The South Sotho living in the agriculturally favoured lands of the Caledon River valley responded even more vigorously, as the following report from missionaries of the Paris Evangelical Mission Society testifies:

Hitherto our Basuto have all remained quietly at home, and the movement which is taking place beyond their frontiers has produced no other effect than to increase the export of wheat and other cereals to a most remarkable degree. While the district in which the diamonds are found is of desperate aridity, the valleys of Basutoland, composed as they are of a deep layer of vegetable mould, watered by numerous streams and favoured with regular rains in the good season, require little more than a modicum of work to cover themselves with the richest crops (quoted in Murray, 1981: 11).

Beinart (1982) has documented a similar process among the Mpondo. While this trade drew these societies into fundamentally new relations of production, it also enabled the more successful farmers to resist external pressures towards labour migration. Thus among the Mpondo, labour migration was very rare in the 1860s and 1870s, even as the Mpondo were drawn more and more into the colonial market economy through the exchange of cattle and hides as well as grain in return for commodities such as blankets and ploughs.

Colonial controls

In the longer term, however, independent African producers were unable to sustain such production in the face of settler competition, land losses and legislative and administrative controls designed by the colonial state to force them into wage labour. The discovery of gold on the Rand in 1886 raised the international stakes in southern Africa dramatically, and the 1880s and 1890s saw the extension of British imperial power over most of the region. By the end of the nineteenth century, all the former independent chiefdoms had been brought under colonial systems of administration as a result of direct conquest, annexation or negotiated settlement. The development of deep-level gold mining, with its particularly stringent cost imperatives, intensified the mining houses' 'ruthless and insatiable' demand for labour 'at the lowest possible cost and in the greatest numbers' (Marks and Rathbone, 1982: 12). The expansion of the migrant labour system now became a major policy goal. In 1889 the Witwatersrand Chamber of Mines was established and during the 1890s it applied its considerable power towards centralising labour recruitment and agitating for a pass system. Frustrated in its efforts to force down wages, it looked increasingly to the state to assist in 'the creation, coercion and control of the black labour force' (ibid.: 18). It was, however, only after the defeat of the Boer republics by Britain in 1902 that the mining industry found the state both sufficiently sympathetic and powerful for its demands to be adequately met.

Among the welter of controls that were introduced in the last decades of the nineteenth century, the hut tax was a central device for drawing the homestead into the nexus of the cash economy. Guy (1982) makes the important point that, unlike the extraction of surplus from the homestead by the chief, in the form of tribute and labour, the hut tax was based not on the actual productive capacity of the homestead but on its potential capacity and had to be paid year in, year out, regardless of the economic circumstances wrought by drought or disease. The imposition of the hut tax created a new and inflexible cash need in African societies. While some African homesteads were able to meet this by increased market production, more and more were obliged to turn to wage labour. Pass and other mechanisms of labour control – service contracts, curfew regulations, residence controls, travel permits – ensured that for the most part this continued to take the form of migrant labour (see Hindson, 1987).

A series of devastating natural disasters – locust swarms, droughts and, most serious of all, a rinderpest epidemic which swept through much of southern Africa in 1897 – further aggravated the problems facing rural African producers and forced more men onto the labour market. However, as Guy (1982: 184) has pointed out with regard to Zululand, where 85 per cent of the cattle were destroyed in the rinderpest epidemic, these natural disasters were not the critical factor behind African proletarianisation at this time. In precolonial times similar disasters had occurred, which African societies had been able to weather, albeit with suffering and loss. Now, however, natural disasters took place in a colonial context – 'in a situation which demanded that every year, regardless of their economic well-being, 14s was collected from every house within every homestead in the country' (ibid.).

Thus by the beginning of the twentieth century the relative autonomy that had previously characterised African participation in migrant labour previously no longer operated; the balance of power had shifted decisively to capital and the new South African state. The impact and extent of migrant labour was, however, far from uniform throughout the region. Despite strenuous efforts by the Chamber of Mines to control recruitment, by 1912 some 70 per cent of South African mineworkers still arrived independently; labour supplies from neighbouring countries were, nevertheless, increasingly canalised through the Chamber's recruitment agencies (Hindson, 1987: 23). While by the 1890s over half the economically active population of the Delagoa Bay region was estimated to be working in South Africa (Harries, 1982: 154–5), in Mpondoland as late as 1911 only 9 to 10 per cent of the male population were migrant workers (Beinart, 1982: 95). At that stage the economic position of most Mpondo families was 'by no means desperate' (ibid.: 70) – herds had recovered, and in good or average years most homesteads could still produce enough for their own subsistence, a situation which continued at least till the 1920s.

In the Mpondo case one can still see an African attempt to manage labour migration in terms of internal priorities. Migration in Mpondoland developed under a system of cattle advances controlled by local traders, who acted as recruiters for the mines. Under this system, the trader advanced a beast against the future wages of the migrant to the homestead head, subsequently collecting the migrant's wages directly from the mine in payment. While the traders profited from this system – for invariably the wage collected surpassed the value of the beast advanced – the homestead head also regarded the system as beneficial. It guaranteed that the earnings of the migrant accrued to the homestead, rather than to the individual worker, and also made it more difficult for the wageless migrant to abandon his rural home at the end of his contract. Nevertheless, as Beinart points out, Mpondo homesteads were now locked into a very new set of economic relationships. A further series of natural disasters, including drought in 1911–12 and east coast fever, underscored their loss of economic self-sufficiency. The government refused to intervene to assist the devastated farmers by fixing grain prices and preventing profiteering by the traders. 'It emerged clearly that the central government saw the solution to the problems facing the rural population primarily in terms of increased rates of migrancy' (ibid.: 75).

The establishment of Union in 1910 cleared the way for that rationalisation of 'native policy' urgently sought by the mining industry. In 1911 the Native Labour Regulation Act finally put in place a comprehensive system of pass controls and recruitment on the mines. It was based on the principles already developed, premised on the single, male migrant who returned to his rural home at the end of a limited contract. Over the next two decades other laws were adopted, hammering the migrant labour system ever more firmly into place: the Land Act of 1913, which set the parameters of the South African reserves and sounded the death knell for independent African peasant producers; the Urban Areas Act of 1923, which introduced a more uniform system of urban pass controls and a segregated urban housing policy; and the Native Administration Act of 1927. Building on Shepstonian policies from colonial Natal, this Act made it clear that the all-white government intended to base its native policy on a reconstructed 'traditionalism', the aim of which was to shore up homestead production and, in the words of Simons, adapt tribalism into a 'bulwark against radical movements' (1968: 52). Chiefs were coopted as lowly functionaries of state, customary law was recognised in civil cases between Africans, and tribal marriage was sanctioned.

Thus by 1930 the migrant labour system was a dominant force in the social and economic life of the rural periphery of southern Africa. While the proportion of men away from their rural home at any one stage varied from region to region, all regions were heavily dependent on migrant labour as a source of cash. Even in those areas where the proportion of migrants was relatively low, most men could be expected to migrate at least once in their lives. Thus in Bechuanaland where, in the late 1930s, the proportion of migrants amongst men in the 15–44 age group was estimated at a little over a quarter (28 per cent) – compared to 50 per cent in Basutoland and the Transkeian Territories and as much as 70 per cent in some Ciskeian districts (Schapera, 1947: 38, 195) – there was nevertheless an unmistakable trend towards men staying away for longer periods, spending shorter periods at home, and, albeit on a small scale still, abandoning their rural homes altogether (ibid.: 61).

By this time an important demographic shift had become noticeable in the composition of the migrant labour force. Expanding cash needs and declining rural production were propelling new categories of people into wage labour. Now, increasingly, older, married men were joining the young unmarried men on the migrant labour market; women, too, were abandoning their rural homes in growing numbers. The repercussions on homestead organisation and production – on which the migrant labour system depended – were far-reaching. Already by 1920 the reserves were producing less than 50 per cent of the subsistence needs of their populations (Hindson, 1987: 33, citing Simkins, 1981). The onerous responsibility for food production under increasingly adverse circumstances fell more and more heavily on women. Landlessness, especially among socially disadvantaged groups such as widows, younger sons, and abandoned wives, was growing apace. Although the much-vaunted 'collapse of the reserve economy' is now put later than previously thought, in the 1950s, and the process of rural decline was uneven, both regionally and among different social strata, nevertheless the dependence of the majority of rural households on cash wages earned far beyond their social horizons was fixed.

GENDER AND THE SHAPING OF THE MIGRANT LABOUR FORCE

The composition of the migrant labour force was thus largely gender-specific. Although the increased migration of women from the rural areas during this period was a source of concern to black patriarchs and white administrators alike, for the most part this movement took place outside the organised migrant labour system. Furthermore, despite the rapid increase in the rate of female migration in the first decades of the twentieth century, in absolute terms the number of African women in the urban areas of the Union remained low. According to the 1936 census, 52,6 per cent of all African women were then living in the reserves, compared to only 11 per cent in the urban areas (with the balance living in the white-owned countryside) (Walker, 1982: 41). Thus until the 1930s and even beyond, the majority of African women remained tied to the rural areas, successfully locked into homestead production and the underwriting of a predominantly male migrant labour system.

In many historical accounts the maleness of the migrant labour force is taken for granted, while the rural homestead is presented as a harmonious unit in which all members were united in maximising resources and resisting threats to its integrity. Thus Slater, in his

'Peasantries and Primitive Accumulation' (1977), presents a view of the precolonial homestead that is quite undifferentiated with regard to power relations within it. It is seen as a single productive unit, standing in opposition to the 'emergent groups of political power-holders' who appropriate its surplus production. In Hindson's other-wise important account of the pass laws, 'African' and 'man' are used interchangeably at times, and the historical position of women is not always clear – for instance, in referring to the identification system that applied throughout Natal in the late nineteenth century, he describes how '*Africans* had to register at magistrates' offices and were issued with "identification" passes.... Employers had to keep regis-ters of each *man's* pass' (1987: 29; my emphasis).

Other studies have demonstrated a deeper appreciation of home-stead production and gender relations in shaping the migrant labour system. Thus Cliffe, in his Zambian study, states that 'The extent and forms of underdevelopment and the class formation patterns experi-enced in different areas can ... be only properly understood if the position of women and their labour is brought into the equation' (1978: 339). Similarly Beinart notes that in order to understand the effects of incorporation on rural society, one needs to analyse relation-ships within the homestead and the domestic cycle (1982: 4). Never-theless, the power struggles involved in this process, between men and women and between the colonial state and women, have not been studied in depth. Women still tend to disappear from the discussion – tucked into the family or 'domestic community', their concrete lives obscure behind abstract concepts such as reproduction and, even, gender. Even in more gender-sensitive studies, the agricultural labour performed by women and children in the homestead often slides into 'family labour', with its value-laden connotations of equality of effort and reward for all members, as in Beinart's assessment of the initial impact of migrant labour on agricultural production in Mpondoland: 'Despite the decline in family size and the withdrawal of male labour from the rural areas for long periods, it seems that the changes in cropping, which were integrally linked to migrancy, enabled each family to cultivate more land' (1980a: 88). In the new social history it is the struggles between elders and juniors, chiefs and commoners within precolonial society, as well as the struggles between these groups and the forces of capital and of the colonial state, which have assumed analytical priority.

In an important article, Bozzoli (1983) problematises the question of why it was that the first workers were male, pointing out that 'common sense' answers – mining was men's work, women were needed to look after the children and keep homestead agriculture going at home – lack explanatory power. For one thing, the arduous nature of the work has not precluded the use of women (and children) in mine labour in other situations. Furthermore, women's role in agriculture and childcare in the African chiefdoms – while indeed a significant factor in their exclusion from the early migrant labour force – was not an expression of natural law, standing outside of history, but the product of very definite social interventions in the organisation of relationships.

It was not simply the men's *absence* that placed the burden of domestic and agricultural labour on the women; nor is it just that male tasks had been undermined by the destruction of the African states; it was *also* that these societies possessed a capacity to subordinate women's labour. Indeed, one might even suggest that the giving up of migrant labour by these societies partly rested upon their capacity to subordinate women's labour; and that it is in this capacity, that the resilience of these systems to 'full proletarianisation' may have rested (Bozzoli, 1983: 151).

Clearly the early history of migrant labour in southern Africa did revolve around the competition for control over the young male's labour power among father, chief and would-be employer – but this competition was predicated on the continued ability of the homestead to control the productive and reproductive capacity of its women. Precolonial society could not cope with the prolonged absence of its young, unmarried males, but their short-term absence did not seriously compromise its ability to reproduce itself. The decline in importance of hunting, as more and more game was shot out, as well as the waning of the military role of the young men, contributed to their relative superfluity, while various strategies were adopted to retain control over the migrant – the raising of the price of bridewealth among the Tonga (Harries, 1982: 152), the system of cattle advances developed in Mpondoland, and the exercise of chiefly control over recruitment in a number of societies. Ultimately, however, what allowed these societies to export male labour was the system of homestead production in which women were the primary producers. It is this that explains the violent opposition of chiefs and men in general – actual and future homestead heads – to female migration. It is this that informs much of the opprobrium with which the 'town woman', widely stereotyped as immoral, irresponsible and shockingly independent, was viewed. (This stereotype was not confined to African society. Schapera notes with a tone of marked disapproval the emergence of a 'class of flappers' among Tswana women – the modern girl 'with her short European skirt and irresponsible behaviour' (1947: 87).)

That women were the ones on whom homestead agricultural production depended was the outcome of an historically wrought patterning of gender relationships that was internal to precolonial society. It would seem that at first African societies relied on internal structures of control – gender ideology, social pressure, as well as women's economic dependence – to uphold the sexual division of labour and keep women in the homestead. The literature is silent on whether the Pedi and Tonga resorted to more overtly coercive controls to keep women at home in the 1840s and 1850s, but it seems unlikely that would have been necessary. Women had scant options for making a living outside the security of their own social framework at that time. However, as the cohesion of precolonial society began to crumble and new possibilities opened for women outside the homestead, so external sanctions, building on these earlier relationships, became more important in counteracting the centrifugal thrust of rural decline and in tying women to homestead production. As the efficacy of internalised social sanctions began to break down, chiefs, fathers and husbands felt compelled to turn to more overt forms of control over women's mobility. In this process they frequently turned to colonial administrators for assistance, to form a curious alliance – an alliance based on very different objectives for the two parties but nevertheless threaded through with a unifying presumption of male power over women.

Here the gender ideologies of coloniser and colonised converged, the race attitudes of the colonisers adding a further twist to their exaggerated conception of the subordinate status of African women. What Bozzoli (1983: 158) has described as the 'social vision' of the mineowners led them to assume that the proper form for African proletarianisation to take in southern Africa was male. In the cosmology of colonialism black women, *par excellence*, belonged to the realm of the natural and the domestic. Simons (1968) has described the self-serving outrage of nineteenth-century white settlers, legislators and administrators at what they perceived as male indolence in African society, which they blamed on what they chose to interpret as the virtual enslavement of African women by their men. 'Civilising the native' meant forcing the men into labour – not, however, for themselves, nor to unburden African women, but to labour for whites. At first the thrust of colonial policy was to procure male labour, not to prevent female migration as such. Since, however, the availability of such labour depended on the continued viability of homestead production, it became politic for colonial policy-makers to intervene on the side of chiefs and homestead heads, against female migration. African women's 'enslavement' was to be turned to white benefit.

Some of the strategies used to prevent female migration involved direct prohibitions on the mobility of women through pass laws and restricted access to transport. Thus in Zululand women had to be identified by a man known to the pass officer before they would be given permission to leave the colony; after 1899 no woman was to be issued with a pass unless accompanied by her male guardian (Guy,

1982: 188). Bonner's chapter in this book describes the cooperation of chiefs and colonial administrators in Basutoland in the late nineteenth and early twentieth centuries to control 'runaway wives' and bring back those women who had successfully absconded. In 1915 the Basutoland administration approved the legally dubious Native Women Restriction (Basutoland) Proclamation on the grounds that 'it is expedient to prohibit native women residing in the Territory from leaving the Territory against the will of their husbands, fathers, or natural guardians' (quoted in Kimble, 1983: i). This proclamation provided that no Basotho woman could leave the territory without the consent of her husband, if she was married, or her guardian, if she was not, on pain of a £5 fine or 3 months' hard labour (ibid.: 9). The correspondence makes it clear that 'native opinion' amounted to male opinion: 'The determining factor must be the attitude of the natives themselves – and as they are anxious for the legislation, I do not think that we need hesitate to agree' (ibid.: 16). The power of female opinion in Britain, however, was not to be discounted – the despatch notes that the only problem was to keep news of this regulation from reaching Mrs Pankhurst! Kimble sums up her discussion of the debate surrounding these restrictions by noting that 'all sections of political opinion coincided on the question of women entering wage labour, or moving to the towns of the Union to engage in petty commodity production, independent of their men. The only debate was who should control the women – chiefs, the state, or husbands' (ibid.: 18).

Schapera (1947) has described similar efforts by the chiefs, with the support of the colonial administration, to control the mobility of women in Bechuanaland. Such controls began 'long ago', when the Ngwato chief introduced a law that no woman could leave the reserve by rail without the permission of the chief, who posted special representatives at railway stations to enforce it (ibid.: 90). Subsequently two sub-chiefs in the Tati district issued a declaration that any woman who had left her home without permission, in this case to go to the adjacent colony of Rhodesia, would not be allowed to return, so as to prevent her from 'enticing' other women to follow suit (ibid.: 91). In 1930 the Kgatla chiefdom only agreed to the South African Railways extending its road motor service into the reserve on condition that its own men be employed as conductors, to ensure that women did not make use of the new service as a way of 'escaping from home' (ibid.).

Another major form of control over women was supplied by the revised system of customary law adopted by the colonial authorities. The process of adaptation of customary law by colonial administrations was a complex one. It was not simply a Machiavellian strategy on the part of the state to impose an inferior legal status on African society. At first there was strong resistance to the recognition of customary law within colonial society, on the grounds that it was immoral, unchristian and, more self-servingly, supported male idleness by condoning the enslavement of women through such institutions as polygyny and bridewealth. Simons's classic (1968) study of the legal status of African women documents the inconsistent and contradictory positions adopted by governments and colonists in nineteenth-century southern Africa as they grappled with very alien systems of legal practice and thought. It has been argued for some areas that women were able to take advantage of a period of legal *laissez-faire* preceding the imposition of a centralised system, which favoured a more monolithic patriarchal authority. Writing about Abercorn (Northern Rhodesia) at the turn of the century, Wright comments:

The civil court cases obviously tend to reflect and treat the social elements that were already on the move, as opposed to the more stabilized and localized households and productive units. Within this category of mobile persons, the court supported male prerogatives but considered also the condition of women. It appears to have facilitated a flow from ethnic to polyethnic communities, from 'slavery' to 'freedom' and toward what seemed more permissive or at least initially less adverse conditions (Wright, 1982: 44).

By the early twentieth century, however, the arguments in favour of a staunchly patriarchal interpretation of customary law, as the foundation for the edifice of pseudo-traditionalism that was being constructed, had largely won the day and the earlier period of legal confusion and flux had come to an end.

More was involved in the adoption of customary law than just strategic planning or cultural bias on the part of colonial administrations, however. As with the institution of migrant labour, the various African societies themselves had an important part to play in preserving and defining indigenous legal systems in the form of 'customary law'. Concerned by the threat that Western marriage practices and legal principles posed to the homestead, African chiefs and husbands looked to a particular interpretation of precolonial legal systems to shore up their authority. Using Northern Rhodesia as a case study, Chanock has argued that the colonial system of customary law was the result 'of a process not only of selective understanding by colonial officials but also of selective presentation of claims' by African witnesses who were invariably male elders – chiefs and married men (1982: 66). Chanock notes how the colonial subjugation of African social systems had 'destroyed the mechanisms of power in local societies, and ... [thrown] into flux the ways by which men controlled women':

This alone might have been sufficient to bring forth a search for new ways of legitimating male control, but we must add to it the strains on relationships resulting from the demands of the colonial state and economy and the consequent development of a socioeconomic system based on migrant labor. Together with migrancy came the increasing penetration of rural communities by an economy based upon the circulation of commodities with its disruptive effects on relations between generations, and between men and women, and renewed the need for a way to legitimate the various new claims being made so vehemently. Conflicts over the uses and effects of money, and over control of the labor of others, were conducted in the language of an emerging customary family law (ibid.: 66).

What was bothering the 'customary authorities' in Northern Rhodesia at the time that customary law was being defined, was 'the context of marital breakdown and sexual indiscipline' (ibid.: 59). Male claims about customary controls over women were 'fed into the court system, where they were given in evidence and "proved" and from whence they emerged as customary law'. 'The groundswell of African male complaint about white leniency towards misbehaving women translated itself into the presentation of a "traditional" severity to adulterers and into a pressure that the colonial legal system abandon its initial practice of treating it as a civil offense, compensatable by a cash payment, and punish adulterers as criminals instead' (ibid.: 60). (Interestingly, in 1917 a new law on adultery was promulgated among the Lozi, which was 'very protective of the absent migrant's interests' (ibid.: 63). Here one can see a shift away from the social dominance of the chiefs–fathers to an assertion of the rights of the migrants, who were now trying to protect their place within rural society.)

Guy (1982) has described a similar convergence of interests of 'colonial state, chiefs, fathers, and husbands' in Zululand after 1879. The reconstruction of British Zululand was devised in a situation where the African population was still strong enough to resist outright dispossession. Administrators, therefore, turned to the methods of 'indirect rule' already developed by Shepstone in the colony of Natal. This policy depended on the incorporation of the chiefly stratum – purged of its uncooperative members – into the colonial administration, and the preservation of certain features of the past while radically restructuring their content. Homestead production remained fundamental to the system – 'It was upon this that the majority of the population depended between contracts' (Guy, 1982: 179) – and it was 'the need to ensure the adequate functioning of homestead production that determined the character of the Zulu administration, its laws and system of control' (ibid.). Chiefs, operating under the overall supervision of white magistrates, were granted restricted criminal jurisdiction and heard civil cases under customary law, the latter redefined to bind women more securely to their husband's homesteads while their sons went out as migrant labourers. As in Northern Rhodesia, Zululand court records dealing with cases of seduction, adultery and abduction show 'the severity with which colonial law treated actions which, in effect, disrupted the organisation of the homestead' (ibid.: 180). Although neither Guy nor Chanock makes the point directly, in the process the principle of male proprietorship over female sexuality was also underscored.

The colonial state presented its administration as based on the 'traditional' social structure, with the addition of progressive elements – a process of reform, not revolution. The apparent continuities with the precapitalist past were, however, superficial. Writing of Zululand, Guy notes:

> It is true that homesteads still existed and production took place within them, that chiefs were still local administrators who applied the customary law which controlled the polygynous homestead, kinship and the transfer of *lobolo*; but empirical examination indicates that the content of these forms changed rapidly. As each year passed, so more homesteads lost their self-sufficiency as productive units under the supervisory control of the homestead-head. The material basis of the chief's status had begun to change from the moment he was appointed, and he retained his rank only as long as he served the interests of the colonial state. Basic principles of marriage and homestead formation were altered almost as soon as the colonial state was founded. In the 1890s Zulu society had changed fundamentally, from a society in which man was the aim of production to one in which production was the aim of man (ibid.: 189–90).

The process of reconstruction was thus a 'facade' – only certain precapitalist features were selected, those which allowed the colonial state to extract surplus from the rural homestead.

One of the major innovations made in Zulu customary law was the practice of bridewealth. Henceforth, instead of being a protracted transfer of cattle between the husband's and the bride's father's homesteads, one that was contingent on the proper performance of their duties by both bride and groom, it now had to be paid in full on the wedding day. A maximum was set for the number of cattle to be transferred, which was higher than what had been customary before; over time this tended to become the conventional amount. In setting defined limits to bridewealth in this way, the state was trying to establish a rate that would require men to go out and work, to earn it, without being so high as to become impossible to reach. One of the consequences of this intervention was to commercialise the payment of bridewealth, with negative effects for women. According to one magistrate in 1890: 'The system of lobola as at present recognised is just tending to make the people look upon the woman as little more than mere chattels for trade & barter, which until the last few years was not the case' (Guy, 1982: 182). A similar process of commercialisation of bridewealth, and consequent commoditisation of women, has been described in Mpondoland (Beinart, 1982: 68), Bechuanaland

(Schapera, 1937: 381) and Zambia (Cliffe, 1978: 342).

The various forms of customary law that had been adopted by different white administrations by the end of the nineteenth century all had in common their divergence from the far more fluid and subtle systems on which they were supposedly based – they were, in the words of Hay and Wright, a 'particular blend of tradition and wishful thinking' (1982: xiv). Women were particularly disadvantaged in this process, the principle of their legal minority and dependence on male guardians being both confirmed and extended. The legal disabilities they suffered in precolonial society were considerably exaggerated while the protection offered them by former non-juridical social practices – for instance, community opinion – was weakened by the elevation of an unfamiliarly formal legal system over other methods of arbitration. At a time of rapid social change, their subordinate status was fixed in an inflexible mould.

The forms of control over women developed in the colonial period were extended by the South African state after Union. By 1927 any lingering suspicions within the white community about the morality and desirability of tribalism had disappeared. The 1927 Native Administration Act sanctioned tribal marriage and bridewealth and set up a separate court system consisting of chiefs', commissioners', appeal, and native divorce courts (Simons, 1968: 53). Women married under customary law – the great majority during this period – were regarded as perpetual minors under the guardianship of their husbands, without the legal capacity to own property, enter contracts or be guardians of their children. In Natal the legal position of African women was even worse, since the Act preserved the code of customary law that had been adopted in 1891, turning African women into perpetual minors, regardless of their marital status and age.

The government also attempted to impose direct influx controls on women in the first few decades of the twentieth century. A rapidly escalating movement of women to town threatened not only the migrant labour system but, as the chapter by Bonner makes clear, law and order in the country's urban locations as well. However, although local authorities agitated for stricter curbs on female urbanisation, the central government hesitated to impose a comprehensive system of influx control on women, and such measures as it did introduce failed to stop the flow of women from the reserves. Strong opposition to passes for women, which erupted into a militant campaign in the Orange Free State in 1913, enjoined a cautious and pragmatic approach (see Wells, 1982). In 1922 the Interdepartmental Committee on the Native Pass Laws detailed the history of opposition to passes for women and concluded: 'The beneficial results to be obtained did not counterbalance the deep-rooted objection of the natives to their womenfolk being subjected to any measure of interference and control by police officers of the government' (Wells, 1982: 138). Significantly, it was male objections to which the government was most sensitive – as in Basutoland in 1915, the principle of control over women was not at issue, rather it was the locus and form of that control. Rather than undermine the authority of African men over 'their womenfolk', the central government chose to hold back on state-imposed controls. With the majority of women still located in the reserves, it could afford this less confrontational approach.

Although women were accordingly excluded from the terms of the Urban Areas Act of 1923, subsequent measures did continue to address the problem of African women's influx to town. In 1924 regulations imposed in terms of the Urban Areas Act required single female workseekers entering town to stay in labour depots; if they failed to find work, they could be endorsed out. However, the wives and children of African men who qualified for urban residence were not affected (provided they were living with the qualified male) and since single women were not required to take out workseekers' permits, enforcement of this measure proved difficult (Hindson, 1987: 41). In 1930 the Urban Areas Act was amended to prohibit both African men and women from entering proclaimed (urban) areas to seek work without the permission of the authorities. Women were subjected to an additional constraint that underscored their legal dependence on men: in order to receive the necessary permission, they had to furnish proof that their husband or father had been resident and continuously employed in town for more than two years and that accommodation was available for them (ibid.: 44). According to the Minister of Native Affairs, these provisions were intended primarily to control the large numbers of women engaged in illicit beer-brewing in Johannesburg, not to prevent single women coming to seek employment, and women domestic workers were excluded (Wells, 1982: 143).

Given these exemptions and without an effective pass system for women, enforcement of these measures proved difficult. Thus in 1931 there were no arrests of women under these provisions in Johannesburg, which has led Wells to conclude that in practice the provision for women's permits was 'virtually meaningless' (ibid.). Until a uniform and national system of passes for women was hammered into place by the Nationalist government after 1948, women determined to move to town were able to take advantage of the central government's reluctance to intervene too decisively. The measures imposed before 1930 signalled the central government's commitment to the migrant labour system and to the principle that African women belonged in the rural areas, under the control of male guardians and chiefs, but their limited reach indicated that at that stage the state intended to rely mainly on indirect controls, in the form of a reinforced patriarchal tradition, to achieve this.

WOMEN AS MIGRANTS

Although involving a relatively small proportion of women, the movement of African women away from the rural areas did take on increasingly significant dimensions in the first decades of the twentieth century. Since it was both an outcome of and a challenge to the hold the migrant labour system had developed on the rural periphery, it is worth looking at this process in greater detail.

Albeit on a far smaller scale than, and qualitatively different from, male migration, women began moving from the rural areas as soon as the establishment of new economic centres opened up the possibility of making a living away from the rural homestead. In Kimberley in 1877 one out of every nine in the 'non-European' population was a woman (Shillington, 1982: 104). (It is not clear, however, how many of these women would have been African.) The following chapter by Hughes documents the influx of 'runaway daughters', fleeing unwanted marriages, to the Inanda mission station in Natal from the 1880s. The phenomenon of 'runaway wives', described in greater detail in the chapter by Bonner, first surfaced in Basutoland in the 1890s and became a major source of concern to both chiefs and colonial administrators in the early twentieth century. A similar phenomenon has been documented in Abercorn, in then Northern Rhodesia, in the late nineteenth and early twentieth centuries. There women took advantage of a shortlived but booming construction industry (based on the building of steam vessels for Lake Tanganyika) to run away from traditional marriages and unsatisfactory family situations to the 'mushrooming camps, administrative centres and commercial posts' (Wright, 1982: 37). Wright does not give the number of women involved, but her article indicates that the scale was large enough to alarm local chiefs and 'ordinary men' who were 'encountering difficulty and were unable to prevent women from gaining refuge in polyethnic, commercial, and colonial communities' (ibid.: 39).

Once Johannesburg was established, the Rand became a major target for emigrant women. Van Onselen notes that between 1906 and 1908 'a significant number' of African women abandoned the rural areas and moved to urban areas in search of a living, as a result of 'the prevailing economic climate, drought, a rebellion in Natal and a new round of cattle disease' (1982: 146). Many of these women made their way to the Rand, where they found the one avenue of employment open to them, that of domestic service, already occupied by men who had been 'forced out into migratory labour by the poll tax a decade earlier'; thus many of them turned to beer-brewing and prostitution to make a living (ibid.; see also chapter 9).

Despite the sanctions on women leaving the rural areas, the rate of African female urbanisation in the first few decades of the twentieth century was considerably faster than that of men – pointing to the erosion of traditional controls and suggesting that, in the absence of state intervention, the marked sexual imbalance in the urban areas would have quite quickly been redressed. According to the 1911 census, African women in South Africa's towns then numbered just under 100 000, or 19 per cent of the total African urban population. By 1921 the figure stood at 147 000, an annual increase of 4,1 per cent, compared to a rate of increase of 1,5 per cent per annum for the urban African population as a whole (Hindson, 1987: 33). Between 1921 and 1936 the number of African women in town increased by a further 142,3 per cent compared to a 78,4 per cent increase among African men (Simons, 1968: 278).

Several features are worth noting about female migration in this period. Firstly, because of their central role in homestead production, women migrants were not participants in the formally organised migrant labour system – neither recruited by outside employers, nor sent out by chiefs or homestead heads as part of a socially sanctioned and controlled process. Secondly, the move to town was far more likely to be permanent for women than for men (Wells, 1982; Schapera, 1947: 70). The reasons for this are not hard to find. Whereas men in the periphery looked to the rural homestead to provide them with security and status in the long term – and were, indeed, compelled by twentieth-century state policy to do so – women did not have the same stake in rural society as men, even while the burden of rural production came to rest more and more heavily on them. At a time when controls against their presence in town were less stringent and less effectively applied than in the apartheid era, urban life held out for the brave and the desperate the prospect of an alternative to the oppressive social relations and deteriorating economic conditions of the rural areas. And once women had made the break, which often necessitated a break with their rural families, it was more difficult for them to reintegrate into rural society.

This lack of an independent stake in rural society explains what Bryceson (1980) has termed, with reference to Tanzania, the 'voluntarism' that characterised the movement of African women off the land throughout the subcontinent. Bryceson has argued that it is incorrect to see the process of female proletarianisation as involving their separation from the means of production – for women never controlled these anyway. (The same, of course, would be true of the unmarried men who became the first migrants but they, unlike women, would expect, in time, to acquire land, cattle and wives in their own right.) Yet women were the primary producers, under the control of male homestead heads. For female migrants, therefore, migration was more likely to represent a means of escape than either a means to reinvest in the rural economy or a process of dispossession.

It was a personal choice, involving flight from the controls of pre-colonial society initially and the deteriorating quality of rural life under colonialism and settler rule subsequently. This is in sharp contrast to the pattern of male migration, which, especially at first, represented a societal response to new pressures and opportunities and was characterised by conformity rather than challenge to existing norms and relations of power.

Of course the degree to which rural women were engaged in active rebellion against their position should not be exaggerated. Clearly most women accepted, and many actively upheld, the practices and norms which structured their subordination. Furthermore, not all women who migrated to town broke their ties with their rural homes. It was not simply that they were socialised into accepting their role within a patriarchal order. As the chapter by Guy has already pointed out, precolonial society offered to women as a group both economic security and a clear social identity, one that was invested with a certain status and, as they acquired seniority within the homestead, even power. Nevertheless, the theme of women rejecting their allotted place – of women running away, abandoning their husbands, seeking new options on mission stations, white-owned farms and in town – sounds loudly and regularly enough through the literature to justify the use of the term 'escape' in describing a major component of female migration from the start.

The women most likely to 'escape' in this way were those who were least adequately accommodated by rural society – the women most disadvantaged socially and hardest hit by the destabilising impact of male migrant labour. The categories of female migrants described in the chapter by Bonner were all women who, in one way or another, were experiencing difficulties in their marital situation and were hence especially vulnerable to the forces of landlessness, impoverish-ment and marginalisation within rural society – women in unhappy marriages, widows, and women whose husbands (typically migrants themselves) had deserted them. Junior wives in polygynous house-holds – those with the smallest stake in the homestead and its future – featured prominently among the 'runaway wives' from Basutoland in the 1890s. In Schapera's sample of Tswana women in the 1940s, the group most likely to migrate were women who had never been married, followed by women who had been divorced or abandoned by their husbands. Almost 40 per cent of the unmarried women in the 30–44 age group in his sample were away, compared to a tiny 4,6 per cent of the same group who were married (Schapera, 1947: 67). Male migration and the decline of polygyny, he noted, meant that whereas in precolonial times virtually all women were assured of the relative security of marriage and a clearly defined place in society, this was no longer the case.

The unhappy irony was that town life itself offered scant security to most women migrants. A rigid sexual and racial division of labour – of which the migrant labour system was itself an expression – excluded African women from jobs in the formal, industrial sector and compelled them to look to domestic service and the informal sector (beer-brewing, prostitution, hawking, laundry work, etc.) for a living.[2] Unwanted by the urban authorities, handicapped by their inferior legal status, their housing options determined by their relationships to men, African women were thrust onto the margins of urban society. That urban life continued to hold any attraction for them at all was testimony to the strength of female dissatisfaction with their situation in the rural areas.

As in the case of male migration, the process of female urbanisation showed marked regional variations. The movement of African women to town in the late nineteenth and early twentieth centuries was not an undifferentiated flow from all corners of the subcontinent. As the chapter by Bonner shows, Basotho women formed a disproportionately large component of female migrants from the start, rapidly developing a lurid reputation for rebelliousness and immorality in the process. In other regions the migration of women remained rare into and beyond the 1930s. Mpondo women, for instance, seem to have been largely untouched by the phenomenon of migration during this period (Beinart, 1982; Hunter, 1979), remaining – or so it would seem from Hunter's account – deeply traditionalist. Similarly in Bechuanaland, only about 5 per cent of the adult women in the six southeastern tribal groupings and 4,3 per cent in the country as a whole were working outside the Protectorate as late as the early 1940s, according to estimates made by Schapera (1947: 66).

Clearly certain societies were able to retain control over women more successfully than others. The reasons for such regional differences must be sought in a complex interplay between economic and social factors. Of central importance, but poorly researched and understood, would have been the internal dynamics of gender and the degree to which a particular society was able to sustain this in a time of radical social change. While the sex–gender systems of the precolonial societies of southern Africa were similar in their broad outlines, they were not identical. Differences in their operation could, in part, have accounted for differences in the way in which these systems responded to the inroads of colonialism and capitalism. Part of the explanation for why some social systems were more resilient to external pressure can be found in the economic sphere, in the unevenness of the process of economic decline and impoverishment in the rural periphery. Thus Bonner's chapter emphasises the decline of the local economy as a major factor behind female migration from Basutoland. Similarly Kimble's 1983 study links the early movement of women out of Basutoland to a process of marginalisation and growing landlessness among women under colonial rule; the growth of a labour market as well as the presence of relatives on white farms across the border also opened up possibilities of escape for women dissatisfied with their marriages and their position within the homestead. Where the local rural economy was stronger – as in Mpondoland – the pressure on women to migrate took longer to develop.

Related to this was the degree of male migration in a particular society, itself an indicator of decline in the local economy. A high level of male labour migration exerted greater pressure on marriage and homestead organisation and encouraged female challenge to male authority. Contrasting the situation in the Ciskei, where the rate of male migration was very high, with that in Zululand, where it took longer to develop, Gaitskell and colleagues note that a 'viable rural economic base ... persisted longer in Natal and Zululand than in the Ciskei or Orange Free State' and that 'the control of husbands and fathers was perhaps more intact in communities which had not been disrupted like the refugee Mfengu' (1984: 99). It is significant that the bulk of the Rand beer-brewers described by Bonner came from Mozambique, Basutoland and the eastern Free State – all areas that had been engaged in migrant labour from an early date.

The relative accessibility of the particular rural area to urban centres must also have played a part. Schapera (1947) stresses that the female migrants in his Bechuanaland study came mainly from the border areas and were more likely to go to towns and farms in the nearby western Transvaal than to the more distant Rand. Accessibility, however, would seem to have played an ancillary rather than a major role in migration. As has already been described, men from the relatively isolated Pedi and Tonga chiefdoms took the lead in labour migration from an early period, while the distances between the border areas of Bechuanaland and the Rand, on the one hand, and Basutoland and the Rand, on the other, are comparable – yet female migration began far earlier and continued in much larger numbers from the latter area than from the former.

Non-economic factors to consider are the spread of Christianity and Western-style education, as well as the role of the different colonial administrations in reinforcing internal sanctions against female mobility and independence. Christianity, with its stress on individual salvation and denunciation of pagan practices such as polygamy and bridewealth, undermined the precolonial family and held out the promise, if not the reality, of greater personal autonomy for women. It is significant that in general women responded to Christianity more enthusiastically than men, and the bulk of church congregations consisted of women (Etherington, 1978). While the chapter by Meintjes cautions against too easy an association between conversion to

Christianity and female emancipation, it would nevertheless seem that at least part of Christianity's appeal to women lay in the prospect it offered of an alternative way of life. In this context it is revealing that missionaries had already made considerable inroads into Basotho society by the 1870s.

The regional contrasts raise interesting questions about differences in the operation of gender relations in the various precolonial chiefdoms and the interaction of gender with other factors. Unfortunately there is as yet little detailed comparative data on this for the period under review. It remains a major but difficult task for historical analysis.

IMPACT AND RESPONSES

The impact of the migrant labour system on the position of women and the organisation of gender in the rural periphery of southern Africa was very complex. As already indicated, the transition period itself opened up an initial period of fluidity, legally and socially, with new – but limited – opportunities for escape for women who were dissatisfied with their situation in precolonial society. Escape from one set of oppressive relationships did not, however, mean incorporation into a more egalitarian order. In colonial society women were enmeshed in new relationships of power in which they were disadvantaged by both their sex and their race; as black women they were incorporated into the very bottom layer of society. They were, furthermore, unable to assert an unambiguous independence and improved status in relation to African men, owing to the intervention of the colonial and later South African state on the side of 'tradition' and 'tribalism'. The reinvented ideology of female deference to men that characterised the new 'traditionalism' was reinforced by the assumptions of female inferiority and domesticity that informed gender ideology in white society.

The entrenchment of the migrant labour system put a heavy strain on rural society's internal relationships and social institutions, with uneven results for women. By the early twentieth century the rural family was clearly in a state of crisis, evincing unmistakable signs of instability and a weakened ability to order relationships between the sexes and between the generations. In the 1920s and 1930s social scientists such as Schapera (1933, 1937, 1947) documented the evidence of stress within the African patriarchal family and the emergence of new patternings of relationships within the household. This work highlighted the destabilising effects of migrant labour in the form of marital breakdown, rising illegitimacy rates and a loss of respect for their elders among the young.

Male migrants were now able to secure at least part of their bridewealth themselves, and thus could arrange their marriages as well as establish their own homesteads at an earlier stage than before. The institution of bridewealth was itself being transformed, becoming an increasingly commercial transaction, stripped of its former social and economic functions. The position of the migrant within the family was changing rapidly – now, very often, he was both wage-earner and head of the household, a head who was not present for prolonged periods, during which time his wife and dependants had to fend largely for themselves. Unmarried migrants, with access to an independent cash income, were less inclined to submit to the authority of their elders. 'The general tendency [is] towards individualisation', for young men and women to want to 'control and dispose of their own personal earnings irrespective of parental control or custom or house responsibility,' noted a Transkeian magistrate in 1932 (quoted in Beinart, 1982: 96). Relationships between the sexes were also in a state of flux. While the migrant labour system tied the male migrant's long-term security to his rural home, thereby increasing the importance of the marital relationship to him, the prolonged absence of men from their wives and children strained the emotional and economic bonds holding the family together. Women accustomed to fending for themselves were less inclined to submit to the authority of their husbands on his infrequent visits home. 'Labour migration, by drawing the men away from home for lengthy periods, has increased the domestic responsibility of the women as well as their spirit of freedom,' noted Schapera (1937: 384). New, female-centred family forms were beginning to emerge in both the rural and the urban areas.

Everywhere the old sexual morality was breaking down. The results could be seen in increased rates of adultery, divorce and desertion by one or other spouse, as well as in the rising rates of premarital pregnancy. Schapera (1933, 1937) noted a marked shift in attitudes towards premarital pregnancy during his fieldwork in Bechuanaland in 1929–31. Whereas in 'former times' there was strong disapproval, evidenced in practices such as the social ostracism and mockery of the woman, the thrashing of the father and the infanticide of the illegitimate infant, by the 1930s attitudes were much more relaxed. While some stigma attached to the illegitimate child, in general people's attitudes were characterised by a 'mild disapproval', coupled with a sense of resignation on the part of the older members of the society to the decline in moral standards. The greater independence of youth had led to a 'marked relaxation of the old sexual morality' and premarital intercourse was 'so widely practised as to have become almost customary' (1937: 382).

There are also some suggestions in the literature of an increase in sexual violence towards women, indicative of heightened tension between the sexes and the breakdown of older codes of behaviour. Wright notes cases of 'rape, enticement, sexual exploitation and harassment' coming to the fore in late-nineteenth-century court records in Abercorn, in a context of increased mobility and independence among women (1982: 44). Schapera's account of premarital pregnancy in Tswana society also suggests sexual violence. Although he does not make comparisons with the past, he does indicate that with the falling away of former sanctions against premarital intercourse, the attitude of the uncircumcised boys towards girls was extremely predatory, their sex relations 'sporadic and casual', consisting 'in effect' of 'the violation of a more or less unwilling girl' (1933: 70).

Migrant labour was, of course, not the only factor at work. Whatever form it took, the process of proletarianisation would have strained precapitalist social relationships and encouraged the erosion of old and the adoption of new values and attitudes. The migrant labour system had, however, a particularly pernicious effect in that, while it undermined existing systems of social organisation, it prevented the organic development of alternatives. Backed by deliberate state intervention, it upheld the form but emptied the content of precolonial institutions, thus destroying their ability to adapt to meet new social needs.

The relationship of migrant labour to rural African society was essentially parasitic, feeding on and eventually drastically weakening, if not killing, its host. This apparently contradictory process has often been noted – on the one hand, the conservation of traditional institutions as the basis of the system's reproduction, on the other hand the 'dissolution' of these same institutions and relations under the pressure of the prolonged absence of key members of society and the decline of the local economy. In fact, these twin processes constitute the two sides of the same coin. As Murray has pointed out, 'processes of "dissolution" and "conservation" are simultaneously at work in rural communities of the periphery; but ... since they are both rooted in the political economy of the labour reserve, identifying them as "contradictory" perhaps serves a merely rhetorical purpose' (1980: 144).

This conservation–dissolution duo can be seen at work in the apparently contradictory effects of the migrant labour system on women. In order to underwrite the system of cheap labour, the colonial state intervened to shore up – conserve – patriarchal authority over women. At the same time, the social and economic order of rural society was profoundly dislocated – dissolved. Thus the institution of migrant labour undoubtedly led to a decline in patriarchal authority within the family – to the advantage of formerly subordinate groups, such as women and younger men. On the other hand the decline in economic security of the rural homestead – without the corresponding opportunities for women in the new economic order – had particularly negative repercussions on women, who were the most disadvantaged in the former rural economy and thus least able to secure resources in the rural areas. Increased economic hardship for women and increased opportunities for autonomy within the household were two sides of the same coin.

The literature emphasises the negative impact of migrant labour on the family. One of the problems with this is the tendency to assume that what is bad for 'the family' is automatically bad for women – and thus the contradictory effects of the breakdown of the 'traditional' family for women are not brought sufficiently to the fore. Bozzoli makes a related point when she notes:

To understand who benefits from the penetration of exchange relations into the domestic sphere, or who gets proletarianised first, is to throw us immediately back to the question of household relationships and the form taken by their interaction with the wider system. In most cases it may be assumed that the household *as an entity* will adopt a defensive self-protective attitude towards external forces; but that different protagonists in the internal domestic struggle will adopt different *individual* attitudes (1983: 147–8; her emphasis).

Another problem lies in the conception of 'the family', which tends to assume the norms and values of the contemporary, male-headed nuclear family. This model is both narrowly culture-bound and oppressive to women. It neither corresponds to the 'traditional' family that has since 'broken down' nor allows for any creative agency on the part of African people in adapting to the changing circumstances and pressures. The process of change in African family structure has involved not simply the breaking down of former relationships, but also the adoption of new family forms and values. Prominent among them has been the female-centred household, consisting of a woman, her children and, often, their children, without a permanent male head. Undoubtedly, however, the decay of traditional structures of support and security imposed, and continues to impose, enormous stress on women – a stress that is severely compounded by the lack of social security provisions for the African population outside the family system, as well as by the discrimination against women inherent in the sex–gender system of the wider society.

CONCLUSION

From the material reviewed here, two main points emerge. Firstly, the organisation of gender in the precolonial chiefdoms of southern Africa did play a critical role in determining the nature of the migrant labour system that emerged out of the nineteenth-century struggles over land, labour and resources among chiefs, commoners, capitalists and settlers. In particular, the availability of young, unmarried men as the first labour recruits, and the ability of the various African chiefdoms to retain a truncated form of homestead production into the twentieth century, depended on their capacity to control the productive and reproductive powers of women. Secondly, while at first the growth of towns and the curtailment of the power of chiefs and homestead elders under colonial rule did open up possibilities of individual mobility and independence for women, any radical undermining of women's subordinate status in African society was blocked by the subsequent intervention of the South African state, once the advantages of the migrant labour system to capital had become established. The cost to women for the relative autonomy they gained out of the disintegration of precolonial relationships was the loss of security, both material and social.

Women were thus transferred from one system of subordination to another. The nature of this subordination changed, however. The transition from the precolonial to the colonial order saw a shift from the relations of production of the homestead to those of the market place. No longer at the heart of production, African women were relegated to a more marginal position in society. Linked to this shift went a shift in the locus of control over African women, from chiefs and husbands to a far more impersonal agency, the colonial state, standing beyond the homestead. The state was, nevertheless, careful to maintain the principle of patriarchal authority within the rural periphery, as the guarantor of the migrant labour system. In the nineteenth and early twentieth centuries a curious alliance developed between the representatives of the precolonial ruling group – chiefs and homestead heads – and the colonial state, to reassert control over women and tie them to homestead production. In this alliance the respective gender ideologies of coloniser and colonised converged.

In the period under review this convergence did not succeed in stopping the movement of African women to town, but it did succeed in entrenching the social and legal disabilities of African women in a more severe form than that experienced in precolonial society. The extreme oppression of African women that has characterised twentieth-century South Africa cannot be seen as an inevitable outcome of the logic of capitalist development. Like the system of migrant labour itself, it has to be seen as a product of struggle, negotiation, compromise and defeat, the outcome of which was not foreordained at the start – nor immutably fixed for all time to come.

8

'A lighthouse for African womanhood': Inanda Seminary, 1869–1945[1]

HEATHER HUGHES

Founded in 1869 by American Board Missionaries, Inanda Seminary was the first establishment of its kind in southern Africa, embodying a new concept of educational work among young African women. Mission institutions in the Cape such as Lovedale already accepted female students (see chapter 3) but the Seminary was the first all-female boarding 'high' school – 'a complete Christian home' as the missionaries thought of it – to be established specifically for the daughters of African Christian converts. It represented a model that was to be more widely emulated in the later nineteenth century and early twentieth century at rural missions in Natal and beyond, and was an important influence in the establishment of the Young Ladies' Collegiate Institution for whites in Durban in 1878 (Vietzen, 1980: 184–5).

This chapter traces the history of the Seminary from its foundation until the end of the Second World War, during which time it was gradually transformed from meeting the needs of a local mission into an elite institution, offering academic courses to the daughters of a rising African petty bourgeoisie. Correspondingly, the nature of the courses changed from an emphasis on an 'industrial', practical training to an academic one. While always gender-specific, stressing subjects that would equip students for a life of domesticity or the female professions (teaching and nursing), Inanda did not educate African women for economic subservience, for a life as house servant, for example. In this there is a sharp contrast with institutions such as those described by Cock and Chisholm in this book. Nevertheless, its students were being educated within a racially segregated social order, which its teachers and governors did not challenge. In fact, from the 1920s, there was general support among those in charge of the school for the liberal segregationism being preached by policy-makers such as C. T. Loram. Such policies were perceived to be consonant with the interests of the classes whom the school served.

EDUCATION IN NATAL

In the 1860s education in the colony of Natal was not compulsory for anybody, white or black. Such facilities as did exist were extremely rudimentary and erratic – even among the white settler population, schooling for all but the very wealthy lasted at most a couple of years and the few attempts at higher education were devoted to the education of boys. There was one contemporaneous effort to open a boarding school for white girls – St Mary's at Richmond, which opened in 1870, but closed in 1883 because of factionalism within the Anglican Church and financial difficulties (Vietzen, 1980: 94, 111–20). In this context, Inanda Seminary, which aimed to provide a thorough Christian education for African girls, represented not merely something new: for many, both approving and disapproving, it was nothing short of revolutionary.

The structure of Natal colonial society decreed that from the very beginning the provision of education was fragmented along racial, class and gender lines, not only in institutional terms but also in subject matter. The colonial state, churches and private 'academies' all contributed to white education, which was of very variable quality. In those institutions that offered elementary grades, there was little distinction between what was taught to boys and girls, according to Vietzen (1980: xii). However, 'higher' (a relative term, meaning anything above two or three years of primary schooling) education was different: boys and girls were separated – a legacy which continues in Natal to this day – and, generally speaking, only the upper echelons of colonial society educated their children at this level. Their options were to provide tuition at home; to patronise private 'academies' – and in the 'ladies' academies' education was intensely gender-specific, consisting of embroidery, dressmaking, music, drawing and some grammar (Vietzen, 1980: 17–18) – or sons could attend a local boarding school or be sent 'home' to Britain, to public school. Only after Natal was granted responsible government in 1893, thus giving the settlers greater control over their own affairs, was a more rigorous educational system developed for white children.

From the 1870s until the late 1890s, some Indian pupils were permitted to attend white schools. They were mostly from 'passenger' (non-indentured) families; Indian children from working-class families relied on missionary or private effort for a basic education. By the 1890s there were 28 schools for Indians in Natal, two of which were exclusively for girls: within the tiny minority of school-goers, girls were a tinier minority still (Maharaj, 1979). Instruction tended to be unashamedly functional: much attention was given to learning 'a number of English phrases in daily use between buyer and seller, master and servant' (ibid.: 343). However, attendance at schools was extremely poor, as a government commission in 1884 remarked:

'There is hardly a boy or girl of seven years of age whose earnings do not contribute some trifle to their parents' stock, or for whom employment as domestic servants in European families might not be obtained if desired' (quoted in Maharaj, 1979: 342).

Provision of Indian education grew very slowly, partly because, as already noted in chapter 6, many whites in Natal harboured the hope that all Indians would eventually be repatriated. Only in the twentieth century were the first state-funded high schools opened, and only after the 1927 Cape Town Agreement (according to which the South African government agreed to redress some of the deepest grievances of Indians) was Indian education taken more seriously by the state. The gap between male and female attendance was always particularly wide until the Second World War: for example, in 1936 under three-quarters of boys of school-going age were in classes, while the fraction for girls was under one-third (Maharaj, 1979: 349).

As far as Natal's African population was concerned, it was the mission churches which shouldered the bulk of educational work – indeed, as shall be seen below, education was the principal means of evangelisation. Many mission schools were provided with state grants-in-aid but these tended to be minimal. In the mission day schools scattered through the African reserves and locations,[2] the rudiments of the 'three Rs', as well as religious instruction, were offered to any who wished to attend. Generally, there was only one teacher for each school, classes contained pupils of all ages, and equipment, such as textbooks, was very basic. Again, it does not seem as if there was any distinction between what was taught to boys and girls at this level (Gaitskell, 1986) and the religious content was obviously very strong.

Considerable importance was attached to 'higher' education by missionaries, at least as far as their resources would allow. For their evangelical work to spread and bear fruit, they had to train locally most of the personnel they required: teachers, lay preachers, clergy, community leaders, all except the first-mentioned being male activities. The American Board – the most active mission body in Natal – founded its first higher boarding institution for African boys, the Amanzimtoti Institute, in 1853, some twenty years before similar schools were opened for white boys.[3] Its aim was to train African ministers and (male) teachers, although the number of boys completing the full course of instruction was very small. Adams College, as the institution was renamed in the 1930s, became co-educational in the early twentieth century, and all American Board teacher training, for men and women, was undertaken there after that. Right up until the 1953 Bantu Education Act, virtually the only secondary schools available to Africans in Natal were operated by the churches. One exception was Ohlange Christian Industrial School, founded in Inanda not far from the Seminary by John Dube in 1903. Inspired by Booker T. Washington's Tuskegee, it offered boys a practical training – wagon-making, saddlery, farming, and so on.[4]

Thus in the case of African people, it was more a religious impulse than a class one which opened the door to educational opportunities beyond the elementary years. However, it must quickly be said that it was from the small communities of *amakholwa* – 'believers' – clustered around mission stations all over Natal, that a well-to-do peasantry emerged from the 1860s and 1870s, so that class and religious factors were intertwined.[5]

Any case study of a single institution always throws up more complexities than a general sketch (such as presented above) can incorporate. Nevertheless, the foregoing discussion should help to sharpen awareness of some of the dynamics of educational change through most of the period under review, as well as provide some benchmarks by which to measure the innovatory approach to African female education at Inanda Seminary during its first eight decades of existence.

THE ORIGINS OF THE SEMINARY

The founding of the Inanda mission station

Although missionaries of the Board had been active in Natal since 1835, it was only after British annexation in the early 1840s that they were able to settle into station life and attract adherents around them. Two of the pioneer missionaries of the Board, Daniel Lindley and Newton Adams, were in fact closely associated with the elaboration of colonial relations in Natal. Both were members of the 1846 Locations Commission, which earmarked a series of large tracts of land or 'locations', for African occupation. They were representatives of the view that African producers should not be dislocated from their lands; rather, they should contribute to the development of a strong cash crop economy. For a time officialdom supported this option but with the emergence of sugar production and its possibilities of attracting white settlers, it was less than enthusiastically pursued. As Henry Slater (1980) has pointed out, at issue was the nature of the extraction of a surplus from the indigenous population: in petty-commodity production or labour power. The balance gradually tipped towards the latter as the century wore on.

Within each location a portion of land was set aside for a mission reserve and soon the American Board had established itself as the leading mission society in the colony, with a string of stations stretching from Umzumbe in the south to Mapumulo in the north. Inanda was, by the mid-nineteenth century, one of the most thriving of these. The Inanda reserve was some 11 500 acres in extent, situated in the location of the same name, some 70 kilometres north-west of Durban.

The lands of the reserve were mostly inhabited by Qadi people under their chief Mqawe, who was the most prominent chief in the district. Although the people were permitted to reside on this land free of charge, they were liable for payment of hut tax and for *isibalo* (compulsory labour) for the state. Residents moving into the reserve later on were charged rent. There is some evidence that by the 1890s men were widely engaged in wage labour in Durban (though usually this was for short periods only) (South African Native Affairs Commission, 1903–5, Natal Evidence: 418). This was not universally the case for all social groups: those associated with chiefly families, for example, used their position in the old order to launch themselves comfortably into the new by acquiring up-to-date farming equipment (having ready access to draught oxen and adequate land to bring under more extensive cultivation), engaging in transport riding, and by skilfully employing the influence of the local pastor, Daniel Lindley, to their own advantage (Smith, 1949: 381). Mqawe himself was on very good terms with the Lindleys and attended church services although he never became a Christian. He sent his heir, Mandlakayise, to America to study and several of his daughters attended the Seminary.

Then there were those living around the mission station itself, the hub of Christian life on the reserve. Together with seven local converts, Daniel Lindley and his wife, Lucy, had founded the church – and hence a small Christian community – in 1849. It is worth saying something about this small band, since they and their offspring were to become socially and politically very prominent, not only locally in Inanda but more broadly in Natal and South Africa too. The forebears of two of Natal's most famous African figures of the twentieth century were represented: George Champion, father of A. W. G. Champion, and James and Dalida Dube, father and grandmother respectively of John Langalibalele Dube. Dalida was the most senior female member of this early congregation, being the widow of a former chief of the Qadi. Her son James – who was Mqawe's uncle – was the first ordained African minister at Inanda, succeeding Lindley in 1873. There was thus a particularly close family connection between these leading members of the Christian community, active in the formation of organisations such as *Funamalugelo*,[6] and the tribal elite. Other founding members included Jonas Mfeka, the father of one of the staunchest Christians and most determined African farmers in Inanda in the early twentieth century, and John Mavuma, a veteran of Shaka's army who became a lay preacher and went to live at Colenso's station Bishopstowe in the 1870s.

Among them was also a most remarkable woman, Nancy Damon. A daughter of John Cane, one of the first white adventurers at Port

Natal, and Rachel, a 'coloured' woman, she was orphaned at the age of 6 and taken by Newton Adams to his mission station on the south coast. Thereafter she was 'adopted' by the Lindley family and became Daniel Lindley's interpreter: she was responsible for some of the earliest translations of the Bible into Zulu. One of the Lindley sons said of her, '[She was] one of the most refined and able women I have ever met' (Smith, 1949: 280). In 1849 she married a Sotho man, Ndamane (of whose name Damon is a corruption). Her younger brother, Charlie Cane, and many African people held her in awe; her achievement as perhaps the earliest black woman in Natal to become so highly literate seemed to set her apart from 'ordinary' people. Charlie once remarked admiringly, 'Nanise had a box full of books' (Webb and Wright, 1976: 77).

Early interest in the doings of Lindley's mission was deeper than the size of the founding group would suggest: in his 'Tabular View' of 1848, Lindley reported an average Sunday congregation of 300, and 22 boys and twelve girls in his school (American Board Papers, A608, file 1849, A/2/27).[7] A few became Christians, and over the next decade their number grew sufficiently to require the station to move to a site on the reserve more favourable to the use of ploughs (Smith, 1949: 314).

The establishment of the Seminary

Both Lindleys came to perceive the need for female training of a more formal sort than could be got in either Lucy Lindley's kitchen or the day school. Like their earlier counterparts in the Eastern Cape, described in chapter 3, their primary motivation was to mould female converts into Christian wives and mothers, in accordance with their own gender ideology. Accordingly, Lucy Lindley exerted much pressure on her husband for an educational facility, since wives had no 'voice and vote' rights in the decision-making forums of the Board. Lindley's attitude was summed up in an annual report: 'How many times have we sighed to see, on our several stations, even one intelligent native mother, with a good degree of womanly refinement; one who would be a pattern to others in the keeping of her house; one whose cleanly habits and proper bearing others would feel not to be above the attainment of a native woman' (cited in Wood, 1972: 22).[8]

The Lindleys were, by contemporary standards, progressive in their thinking as far as their mission work was concerned. Before her marriage, Lucy had taught slaves on a large Virginia plantation, treading the borderline between what was legal (teaching them about God) and illegal (teaching them to read and write) (Smith, 1949: 57). She had thus gained experience which, though very different from the African mission field, did develop in her a sympathy for those who were harshly subordinated and dehumanised on the basis of their colour. For his part, Daniel Lindley privately tended to adopt a conciliatory approach – approximating Bishop Colenso's – towards customs such as polygyny and *lobola*. Official Board policy was that these had to be discarded completely before eligibility for church membership could be entertained. In addition, Lindley was firmly opposed to the objectives of the white settlers who wished to turn as many Africans as possible off their lands and onto the labour market (Smith, 1949: 301).

From the early 1860s there was broader receptivity for the Lindleys' idea of a female training institution from other Board missionaries. Like their counterparts elsewhere in southern Africa, they had come to realise that training men for Christian roles, as was under way at Amanzimtoti, would produce only half of what was required to propagate a stable Christian community – the trainees were having to confront the problem of the unavailability of suitably trained young women as prospective marriage partners. One prominent missionary, Bridgman, expressed the hope that the intended institution would be 'modelled after Mount Holyoke Seminary as far as the case will admit' (Etherington, 1978: 28)[9] and a committee to plan it was set up in 1865 (Christofersen, 1967: 39).

From the missionaries' point of view, the principal aim of an establishment solely for girls was to prepare the daughters of the first generation of converts (and of future generations too) for approximately the same kinds of roles as those played by missionary wives. It was training for the kind of domestic work George Bourne (in a rather different context) has described so evocatively as 'the cooking and cleaning and sewing from which middle-class women seem often to derive so comely a manner' (1984: 21). Emphasis would be very much on the home, where a wife was to be helpmate to her husband as well as good Christian mother. In the missionaries' view, this was certainly not preparation for a life of servitude but rather a release from it. Control of her own domain would confer upon the women 'a social equality with our men' (Lindley, in Smith, 1949: 386).

But there was more to the investment in young women's education than the comeliness of homemaking. Firstly, since primary education was the main means of mission expansion, the success of winning converts was related to the availability of teachers for new schools. There were definite limits to the number that the Board could send from America, especially in the lean post-Civil War period, but in any case it was Board policy to encourage mission churches to become self-sufficient. Teaching was an occupation considered suitable for both women and men – women were often general teachers as well as sewing mistresses[10] – and an early purpose for Inanda Seminary was the training of teachers, which at that time meant passing one or two grades above those one would teach.

Furthermore, if the tasks of homemaking and teaching were to be properly learned, new codes, customs and a different consciousness had to be instilled in the girls. If 'traditional' social organisation, culture and habits turned largely on the roles played by wives, mothers and grandmothers in the homestead, as missionaries believed was the case, so too could and should the new Christian way of life revolve around Christianised women. This was more than simply an appropriation of what the missionaries understood to be indigenous gender relations, since an attempt was also being made to transform men's roles. The missionaries aimed to put an end to what they perceived as males 'sitting around under trees' and involve men far more directly in agricultural production. In this sphere, as already described by Meintjes in chapter 5, men were expected to be in control, especially since the arrival of the plough.

In order to effect the required transformations among the girls, there was to be no place for what Sean Morrow (1986), writing of another girls' school, at Mbereshi in Northern Rhodesia, has called 'neo-traditionalism'. Examples of such practices at that school included the use of ritual, the incorporation of elements of female initiation ceremonies, the organisation of the boarders 'along the lines of a village community' and the use of the mother tongue rather than English as the medium of instruction (an important factor in limiting the employment chances of girls as against those of boys) (Morrow, 1986: 619). As noted, the American Board had from the start of its work in Natal been 'austerely uncompromising' (Smith, 1949: 277) in its attitude towards the practices of *lobola* and polygyny, believing them to be at the root of African resistance to Christianity (Etherington, 1978: 60). The so-called Umsunduzi Rules of 1879 finally codified missionaries' repugnance into a strict set of rules governing admission into and exclusion from the church. This attitude was to be reflected in the Seminary code. Girls were not permitted to converse in their mother tongue (except for prayers and at weekends), and the taking of snuff and belief in love charms and bewitchment – indications of the stresses of adjustment from known to unknown but regarded by their teachers as 'lapses' – were frowned upon (see *inter alia* Tyler, 1872; ISP (ap)). The women missionaries in charge of the Seminary were looking for a profound reorientation in the girls' world-view, an exacting task for the teachers and a daunting one for their charges.

At the same time as pressure was mounting from local American missionaries for a girls' boarding school, moves were afoot in the United States to encourage greater involvement of women in the mission field, as women themselves came to realise that 'religion provided an outlet for female talent denied access to political and economic leadership.... [They] could assume positions of power and prestige, influencing not only children and other women but men as well' (Berkin and Norton, 1979: 13). Single women missionaries could undertake work which their male counterparts and missionary wives could not, by devoting their energies entirely to working with the women in local communities, untrammelled by the niceties of sexual decorum faced by male preachers or the usually onerous family responsibilities of missionary wives. There was an ambiguity in their position, however: while glorifying the roles of matrimony and motherhood as desirable for African women, they themselves had actively chosen to avoid these roles (Morrow, 1986: 611–12). (It is worth noting that in most years from 1869 until well into the twentieth century, women missionaries outnumbered their male colleagues in American Board employ in Natal (ABP, A608, V.51).)

The Women's Board of Missions of the Congregational Churches in the United States, a kind of auxiliary of the American Board formed in early 1868, undertook initially to support seven women missionaries abroad. The first one was Mary Kelley Edwards, the redoubtable head of Inanda Seminary from 1869 to 1892, who lived on at the school until her death at the age of 98 in 1927. In the face of family hostility, she had educated herself in Dayton, Ohio, to be a teacher. In 1856 she married a school principal; when he died in 1867, she investigated the possibility of mission work. In 1868 she was appointed the first head of the new Seminary at Inanda; she assumed her duties when she was 40 years old (Wood, 1972: 7–8).

For African Christians themselves, there was a far more pressing need for a girls' boarding school than suitable marriage matches or employment prospects. Jacobus Matiwane of Verulam (the nearest town to Inanda) told the Natal Native Commission in 1881: 'Our authority over our children is less than that of the raw Natives ... the younger branches of our families think they know more than we do' (150). Sons no longer deferred to fathers, and daughters' 'purity' was harder to preserve. In fact, where church parameters had taken the place of those of kin, sexual relations were altogether difficult to regulate, especially in view of the uncertain, twilight legal status of the converts' own Christian marriages in the eyes of colonial law (Meintjes, 1985). 'Mission' people complained from very early on of the ways in which time-honoured norms had been eroded. Parents recognised that their own upbringing was an unsuitable model for their children and did not always know how to fill the cultural gaps created by their abandonment of old practices and habits. In the words of James Matiwane, another witness before the 1881 Commission: 'We have given up Native dancing, and attend tea meetings and the like. We have no social gatherings except weddings and such like. The boys and girls have no games; the boys do play at marbles sometimes' (Colony of Natal, 1881: 387).

Though some Christian parents had reservations about the cost involved, in terms both of the fees and of doing without their daughters' help at home, Inanda Seminary was in general looked upon as a place where girls approaching puberty would be protected. Here was a happy coincidence between the rigorous routine deemed necessary by the mission and the control over their daughters' sexuality which Christian parents desired.

FOUNDING YEARS, 1869–c. 1885

The first nineteen girls to enrol at the Seminary in March 1869 were from American Board stations at Inanda, Imfume, Umvoti, Umsunduze and Amanzimtoti. All had had at least four years of schooling and were literate in Zulu (hence the title of 'high' school for the Seminary). The youngest, Talitha Hawes, was about 9 years old and the daughter of Benjamin Hawes, pastor of Tafamasi station, Inanda; Laurana Champion, an older sister of A. W. G. Champion, was 'one of the most advanced girls' (Wood, 1972: 18). Through the first year numbers fluctuated between 19 and 32 with attendance always much lower than enrolment – only in the twentieth century did these begin to coincide. At first there was one class in which the following subjects were taught: reading, writing, arithmetic, spelling, geography, Bible study, and sewing – 'much attention was given to teaching the girls sewing' (ISP, file 19a, Phelps, 'Inanda Seminary'). By 1875, the same subjects were taught to two classes at different levels and by 1878 the number of classes had increased to five (Wood, 1972: 23–37).

Initially Mary Edwards was the only teacher, assisted by Martha Lindley and Talitha Hawes. Two teachers sponsored by the Women's Board arrived in 1877, one of whom had been trained at Mount Holyoke. Fidelia Phelps, another Holyoke graduate who was to succeed Mary Edwards as headmistress, arrived in 1884. The longevity of service of early teachers provided a degree of continuity and stability in an otherwise very uncertain climate.

There was continual disagreement between Edwards and the mission fathers over how much Board funding could be devoted to her school. Fees, then £4 per annum, were irregular if they came in at all and the financial position was so shaky that it was never clear whether the Seminary would survive into the following year. The colonial government granted an annual sum of £100, after a visit to the school by the Secretary for Native Affairs in 1870. Edwards recalled: 'I sent two girls to the blackboard and gave them a rather long example in addition. The girls did the work so quickly that the visitors were much pleased, then my pretty schoolroom with its new American schooldesks and chairs made a good impression and as they were leaving the Sec said, "You shall have a grant"' (ISP (ap), ms attached to letter, Phelps to Lamson, 27.3.1927).

The grant helped to cover running costs but Edwards believed the Board was not supporting the school extensively enough. Lack of funds was partly the reason for the faltering growth of the early years. Between 1870 and 1876 only 60 new students were admitted; by 1884 some 60 students in all were enrolled, although average attendance stood at only 41 (Wood, 1972: 36).

One way in which costs were kept down, and which dovetailed well with the general training regime at the school, was the use of students' labour, in an effort at self-sufficiency. The girls grew their own vegetables and maize, tended the gardens, fetched water, ground maize, cooked, chopped wood, cut grass and cleaned the grounds, dormitories and classrooms.

Within the world of the boarding school, the daily demands of 'civilisation' were learned, both the physical tasks and the appropriate forms of interpersonal relationships, self-control and association. The education inspector's report of 1885 gives an idea of school life:

The scholars are neat and clean without exception. All are well instructed in Needlework and cutting out; they make clothes in aid of the Mission at Inhambane, wash, iron and receive special instruction in household duties. The school buildings are very suitable. An inspection of the dormitories showed them to be scrupulously clean, and affording ample room for the Boarders. The Inanda Training School may fairly claim to be a model institution (cited in Wood, 1972: 87).

Almost every aspect of the girls' lives was regulated; for example, Mary Edwards vetted all mail and once declared, 'I shall be able to take the degree of "Professor of Love Letters," instead of Belles Lettres' (cited in Smith, 1949: 386). Yet for all the internal control, the students were not cut off from the busy life of the mission station or the surrounding community: for example, they attended the mission church and helped with mission work in the area every Sunday.

Despite the efforts of the Lady Superintendent and her assistants, however, the girls seemed apathetic, some even actively uninterested: next to not a few names in early registers is written 'ran away'. This was the sticking point for Mary Edwards, which prompted several resignation attempts on her part. In March 1874, for example, she notified the American Board: 'It is with deep regret that I say it but there seems to be no spirit of the true teacher in any of the girls and I confess I have no power to put it in them' (ABP, A608, file 1874, A/2/28). Could this have been surprising? As Norman Etherington has pointed out, the children of converts 'were born into station life without experiencing the insecurity and desperate needs which had drawn their parents into the church' (1978: 140), and so did not necessarily display the same religious zeal as their parents. Apathy, however, indicated more than this: it was but the outward appearance of a deeper sense of inner disharmony, a reluctance to pick up and carry the missionaries' cultural baggage unquestioningly. We have a rare insight into the profound ambivalence students must have felt in a short series of essays – the authors' names sadly not recorded – presented to Mary Edwards in 1884. One, entitled 'English in Natal', exemplifies this point most strikingly, on a subject clearly of keen interest.

It begins by recalling an imagined past of serenity, disrupted by Africans' 'discovery' by Europeans:

Many years ago this land of South Africa was a quiet land, as I imagine, but it was not so very quiet for some time the people had wars among themselves.... They had no blankets to cover themselves, no bed to sleep on, no flour for bread, no tea, no coffee, no sugar, no whisky, no brandy, no rum, no wine, they had only native foods ... they were not troubled about what they should do with their money for they had none ... they [had] noone to tell them not to soil their clothes, or to trouble them by calling them in to school, in this way the abantu lived till 1498 (ISP, Book 86).

The writer complains bitterly of the grasping ways of 'English, Dutch and coolies'; she is slightly more welcoming of the missionaries, but with qualifications: 'I do not think the missionaries did wrong to come among us for they came to tell us about the Word of God, and they did not want our land, but they have brought the white people, and the white people trouble us' (ibid.).

Having begun by looking back to a reasonably untroubled past, the essay ends by looking forward to a more dignified, if dramatically altered, future. It offers some fascinating insights into the aspirations and expectations of a young woman student, displaying too an eerie prescience:

The time will come when there will be no difference between a black man and a white man, only perhaps in colour and language. Some few people have already left native law and turned white men, although this few are as black as ever, and their hearts are as black as their faces.... In years to come we may have a Zulu for our magistrate.... We have Zulu preachers now, and why should we not have Zulu lawyers as well. Then will come Zulu newspapers and history – when I think of all these things, it makes me feel first as if I had been born 100 years too soon, and that the good times are coming after my time is gone (ibid.).

Through the first two decades of the Seminary's operation, the vast majority of students came from Christian homes all over Natal. By 1885, 216 girls had been enrolled, 79 of whom declared themselves to be active Christians (Wood, 1972: 36). Perhaps it was this seeming lack of headway in instilling more than a 'passive' Christian culture that led to the missionaries' encouragement of the girls to stay longer: in 1881, the first certificates were awarded for five years' attendance.

THE SEMINARY AS LOCAL SCHOOL, c. 1885–1910

Runaway daughters

In the early 1880s the first students from 'outside' (as opposed to 'mission') homes enrolled at the Seminary. These were mostly young women from the Umzinyathi valley in the Inanda reserve, who were seeking refuge from unwanted marriages: the so-called 'runaways'. Many were under 15 years of age and came with stories of bitter battles with their parents (see ISP, file 1a, KCM 52091).

In the 1870s Mary Edwards had begun to devote her attention to 'the hundreds of children in the Location who are yet to learn the Alphabet but who in reply to my salutation say, "Good morning"' (NA, SNA, letter to SNA, file 112, 1879, 1/1/33).[11] She had collected money for books to take into the Umzinyathi valley and received a government grant in 1879 to build two schools there. From 1882 to 1884 she temporarily gave up her duties at the Seminary to devote her energies to establishing more day schools in the location. Clearly, by the mid-1880s, missionary teaching had spread far enough to enable at least a questioning of existing marriage arrangements; the very existence of the Seminary enabled girls to exercise a greater degree of choice over their lives, presenting them with an avenue of escape from oppressive social expectations and sexual relations.

From the earliest phase of their operation, missions had attracted not only the displaced and rejected, but those adversely placed in relation to the faultlines of the 'traditionalist' order (Etherington, 1978: 59–60), which missionaries and colonial officials consciously or unconsciously widened. The late 1870s were a time when officials were trying very actively to loosen the bonds of polygamy and *lobola*. The Natal Code of Native Law of 1878 permitted women to sue for divorce on the grounds of ill-treatment by husbands. It also strengthened a provision contained in Law 1 of 1869, that women could not be married against their will, by requiring the presence of an official witness at all marriage ceremonies (Welsh, 1971: 84; Beall, 1982: 80). (It should, however, be noted that these provisions allowing greater freedom for women were more than offset by others which kept them always minors, under the guardianship of a male, either father or husband, and by sections of the Code which reinforced patriarchal control and hierarchical authority.) While some brides made use of this system, it was open to abuse. At marriage ceremonies, a bride's silence could be interpreted by the witness as consent, and in view of the ignominy suffered by a bride who refused to marry, it was extremely difficult for a girl to go against the wishes of her kin. Many who had said 'no', or had not answered at all when asked by the official witnesses whether they wished to marry, were among the runaways.

Among non-Christian communities there were also social and economic changes under way, more profound than those in the legal sphere. In 1874 the number of ploughs in the Inanda location was 48; by 1884 this had risen to 89 and a decade later to 500 (Natal Blue Books, 1874, 1884, 1894). The new technology enabled those homesteads with access to the necessary resources – draught oxen and ability to purchase or hire implements, for example – to bring more land under cultivation. This led not only to increasing pressure on land and to border disputes and 'faction fights' (including a major dispute between the Qadi and Tshangase in 1892), but also to increased demand for cattle. Additionally, there is evidence that at least some homesteads parted with cattle as payment for taxes. Yet others attempted to accumulate more cattle as an insurance policy against uncertainty. Furthermore, after the devastating rinderpest epidemic of the mid-1890s, homesteads had to build up cattle herds almost from scratch. One way to satisfy these various demands for cattle was through the marriage of daughters. This of course had always been the case but from the 1880s there was a way out for girls who did not want to marry according to their fathers' wishes. To some extent, age constrained choice: running away was far easier for women who had not yet borne children, for example.

One might note that the introduction of the plough had much broader implications for gender relations, as officialdom was quick to notice: 'Men and boys work the plough and this is in itself a great revolution of the old idea that cultivation of all necessary crops is the work of the woman, and woman only' (Inanda Magistrate's Report, Natal Blue Book on Native Affairs, 1894). Against this observation, it is interesting to consider Absolom Vilakazi's description of early Christian conversion among the Nyuswa, further up the Umzinyathi valley: 'A peculiar feature of the early Christians was the fact that they were all women. The men did not join them and the preachers were the only men in the congregations' (1965: 11). We do not have complete data on the composition of other early congregations, but it is possible that one of the ways in which women responded to displacement from the process of production and also to escape restrictive social relations was to join the church.

Whatever had set in motion the far-reaching changes which resulted in ever-increasing numbers of runaways at the Seminary, one must treat the missionaries' accounts of the phenomenon with caution, since they had a vested interest in stressing the excesses of 'woman slavery' in African society. One of the less dramatic accounts, taken from a signed deposition by Susiwe Bengu, nevertheless gives some idea of the dilemmas facing a runaway. When Susiwe was a young girl, 'a very old man' named Chief Bulushe negotiated with her father, Chief Dhlokolo of the Ngcolosi, for one of the latter's daughters, and she was the one chosen. She 'refused and kept refusing', and eventually Bulushe died. However, his son Sidada, 'who had several wives and was old', continued negotiations for her. Reluctantly she went to his homestead but 'I did not stay in his hut'. When she was sent back to her father's homestead with the *lobola*, she refused to return to Sidada: 'when they wanted me to go back with the beer, I refused till at last my mother went and took it for me.' Her father was by now extremely angry, and fearing the consequences of his wrath, she ran away to the Seminary (ISP, file 1a, KCM 52091).

Susiwe had attended church and school for some time before seeking protection, and the missionaries felt an obligation towards her. They were in a weak position vis-à-vis the law, which expressly attempted to bolster the authority of chiefs and (male) homestead heads. Already in the year of Susiwe's arrival, 1892, Mary Edwards had to surrender four runaways and she was determined not to lose another. It took three visits to the Secretary for Native Affairs in Pietermaritzburg, considerable publicity and, finally, a reluctantly sympathetic local magistrate before Susiwe was permitted to remain at the school (Wood, 1972: 49).

The issue of runaways was a delicate one, somewhat contradictory in its effects, for it threatened to upset relations with local community leaders: it was, after all, at their pleasure that evangelical work could proceed unhindered. On several occasions angry relatives arrived at the school demanding the runaways back. Fathers seldom came; usually the mothers (who clearly also had some interest in their daughters' social conformity) and sometimes the brothers were sent. One belligerent mother once threw a stone at Mary Edwards but generally family members tried verbal persuasion and, if they succeeded, a runaway was free to leave with them. But it was school policy never to 'give up' a girl against her will, unless of course forced to do so by the local magistrate.

What minimised the risk of local tension in Inanda was the unusual goodwill expressed towards the mission by the chief, Mqawe. As already noted, his own family straddled the divide between 'mission' and 'outside', and he looked favourably on the work of the mission. Several runaways from among his people sought protection at the school, but he blamed the law rather than the missionaries for the ensuing tension in and between the families concerned: 'The Law says a girl shall not be compelled to marry against her will. Formerly we could marry our daughters where we liked but now all has gone wrong. It makes our daughters wander about as prostitutes' (Colony of Natal, 1881: 221).

Not all the girls from non-Christian homes were at the Seminary against their parents' wishes, although one can imagine how strange was the idea of daughters spending so much time removed from kin, in a large single-sex institution which expected payment for the privilege of keeping them there. There were limits to family's forbearance, however, and the school had to compromise to some extent with local demands: girls were permitted to leave at hoeing time, for example (ISP (ap), Report from Inanda Seminary, 1900–1901).

The incorporation of 'primaries'

To cater for the girls from non-Christian homes who had minimal or no experience of schooling, special primary grades were created. The teacher in charge of them, Miss Price, developed textbooks which were widely used in day schools in Natal for many years after (Christoferson, 1967: 154). In 1886 altogether 12 out of some 60 students were so-called 'primaries'; by 1895 their number had swelled to 125, constituting 70 per cent of the enrolment of that year. Their numbers peaked around the turn of the century – it is noteworthy that this coincided with attempts to rebuild cattle herds in the aftermath of the rinderpest epidemic, when pressure on daughters to marry could have been intense. In 1901, of 312 students, only 72 were not primaries (ISP, file 1b).[12]

Some attempt was made to direct the primaries to Umzumbe Home, founded in 1873 on the American Board station at Umzumbe, some way down the south coast. It too was funded by the Women's Board but had been aimed specifically at girls from non–Christian backgrounds, admitting only a few Christian girls in the higher grades. Its philosophy of education was almost identical to that of the Seminary: 'From early morning till bed-time, all through the school term the girls are kept busy in useful and healthful occupations,' noted a visitor to the Home (ISP (ap)). At one point, in 1916, there was talk of turning the Home into a purely academic school, while the Seminary would offer 'industrial' courses only (ISP, file 1b, Committee notes). It was not as well endowed as the Seminary, however, and being far down the coast from Durban, was never the centre of activity that Inanda was. It finally closed in 1919.

The large number of primaries at the Seminary strained the staff's resources to the point where Edwards had to turn herself into something of an entrepreneur, initiating money-making schemes for the support of the school. Cash crops such as maize and beans were planted and a successful chicken business and unsuccessful venture with silkworms were launched (Wood, 1972: 56). By far the most ambitious scheme was a laundry, opened in 1888. 'Commenced originally for the benefit of married native women on the station' (ABP, A608, file 27, 189, 1/1/12), the transport costs entailed in the enterprise soon grew too burdensome for the women themselves. The laundry buildings were moved nearer to the school, seven women were employed to oversee the work, and the heavier manual labour was performed ('cheerfully', we are told) by the primaries, each of whom was paid one shilling daily during her turn. They worked for two months at a time, in relays of eighteen, for three hours at a stretch. In addition, every week 50 girls carried eight buckets of water each from the stream half a kilometre away.

Laundry was processed on a weekly cycle: on Saturday *togt* (casual) workers collected clothes from customers in Durban and put the bundles on the train to Duff's Road. They were collected and taken the rest of the way by wagon. On Monday the clothing was sorted, on Tuesday and Wednesday washed and dried and on Thursday it was ironed. It was then ticketed and packed on Friday, ready for the return journey on Saturday. In the ten months from July 1889 to April 1890, a total of 30 568 articles were laundered. A government grant of £150 yearly was approved on the basis of the Native Education Inspector's report that the laundry would qualify girls 'for an especially useful branch of service' (ABP, A608, file 27, 189, 1/1/12). Through the 1890s the laundry showed a modest profit and in some years brought in more money than did fees. After 1900, however, support tailed off because of the growth of laundry businesses in Durban, and profit dwindled – only £29 in 1905, for example (ibid.). Finally it was incorporated into the Seminary as a non-profit training facility.

The attendance of large numbers of primaries turned Inanda Seminary into much more of a local school than it had originally been. Edwards, while always in favour of integrating the school into the local community, recognised that many girls came simply because, despite her efforts, there were not enough day schools. Of course founding more day schools meant training the teachers to run them and this remained an important focus for the Seminary until 1909, when all teacher-training was transferred to Adams College. By 1885 some 66 teachers had been trained. In the following year, an official, standardised syllabus was introduced, and teacher-training up-graded. However, it was not until 1900 that any Inanda Seminary students sat the Third Class Government Teachers Examination. One of the candidates, Evelyn Goba, went on to pass the Second Class Examination in 1903 and topped the list of candidates in the First Class Examination in 1904. She and three other Seminary student-teachers were the first fully trained African women teachers in Natal. By this time, mission day schools were no longer eligible for grants unless their teachers possessed government qualifications, an indication of the growing state control over African education.

A SCHOOL OF GROWING NATIONAL IMPORTANCE, c. 1910–45
By 1910 nearly 3 000 students had passed through the Seminary, according to Mary Edwards's calculations (ISP (ap), ms attached to letter, Phelps to Lamson, 27.3.1927). Fees were coming in more regu-

larly, attendance and enrolment had begun to coincide and there was a move away from the students performing the manual work of the school, a staff of cooks and groundsmen gradually replacing them. In 1912 all classes below Standard 4 were dropped on the grounds that these were now fairly widely available. While this meant that the Seminary was beginning to resemble what would today be recognised as a boarding high school, it also opened a gap between the school and local Inanda communities, which grew wider in the following decades. Several links with local people were strengthened, it is true; yet the requirement that girls should have passed Standard 3 before admission meant that, increasingly, local girls were excluded and pupils drawn from a wider geographical area. From 1923, under the principalship of Margaret Walbridge, the organisation of the Seminary was further modernised to cope with new needs and a changing student population. A house system and form of student government were introduced, an office staff employed, hobby clubs and sports begun, and 'wholesome' Friday night entertainment, such as debates, choral singing and 'moving pictures', laid on.

Industrial education, the good countryside and segregationism at the Seminary

From about 1915, the educational ideas of C. T. Loram began to influence teaching at the school. For a short time Chief Inspector of Native Education in Natal and an 'authority' on appropriate education for Africans, Loram was a friend of the Seminary and took an active interest in its welfare. He was a key segregationist in the educational sphere, believing fervently in 'industrial' – a synonym for 'practical' – education, an approach which Hunt Davis has shown rested on two premises: 'African education ... should be geared towards entrenching white control and a rural-oriented way of life' (1984: 113). The Seminary glided quite effortlessly into the era of industrial education; such had been the stress on the part of teachers for decades. Nevertheless, there were now some important differences from their earlier efforts.

As noted in chapter 7, in these years of South Africa's industrial revolution, missionaries and officials alike were growing increasingly alarmed at the apparent attractions of town life to African people, and the accompanying problems, as they saw them, of immorality. While urban-based missions did their best to encourage 'righteous ways', rural ones tried to discourage townward drift. As older networks and hierarchies within African polities began to disintegrate in the transformed conditions of industrialisation, missionaries saw cause to concentrate more on matters of social control. Correspondingly, the goals of education and proselytisation of the nineteenth century – the promise of liberation from oppression – mutated in the twentieth into the need for restraint and authority. Everything which happened at the Seminary in this period needs to be set against this overriding concern.

It is important to note that the tenets of segregationism (as applied at the Seminary) were not perceived as undermining the interests of the emerging African petty bourgeoisie, for whose daughters the school was beginning to cater. While the purpose of segregationist ideology was to suppress African aspirations for social equality with whites, it did not entail a levelling of class interests to the lowest common denominator.

Just as there had been an earlier congruence between the needs of parents and missionaries, so there was now (and both were aligned with Loram's philosophy): parents wished to keep the girls out of the city's clutches. John L. Dube himself addressed the school on one occasion, darkly warning the girls of 'what our sisters do in public in cities and towns, and cautioned us to lead upright lives' (*Torchbearer*, 1, 1, 1933: 42).

The corollary to presenting the town as evil was to present the countryside – not so much the natural phenomena as the social forms located in it – as good. Shula Marks (1986) has shown that the ideology of the African petty bourgeoisie in Natal embraced a strong royalist–traditionalist sentiment, which in turn was favoured by leading segregationists such as George Heaton Nicholls. In a period of massive social dislocation, especially in the 1920s, there were intense efforts at organisation, either to protect privilege (for example, the African National Congress in Natal, representing the interests of the petty bourgeoisie, particularly landowners) or to win the most basic rights (for example, the Industrial and Commercial Workers' Union (ICU), appealing to tenants threatened with eviction and to urban workers). African landowners and whites generally were particularly unsettled. by the activities of the ICU in Natal, and supported the programme of Heaton Nicholls to project the Zulu royal family and a revived 'tribalism' as the best defence against radical, destabilising influences. This will explain the significance of Seminary girls being expected to honour the Zulu king: Margaret Walbridge proudly declared King Solomon's picture hung in the dining room (Walbridge, 1978: letter 27.7.1930) and there was intense excitement when Prince Mshiyeni visited the school in 1936.

In line with efforts not only to reorganise the Seminary internally, but also to turn it into a community centre, 'focusing on the everyday problems of villagers' (Hunt Davis, 1984: 116), Margaret Walbridge employed a farm manager, Henry Ngwenya. The son of an ex-Seminary student, he was born in Inanda and attended Adams, Lovedale and Fort Hare. Not only did he oversee the Seminary's own fields and crops, but he also started tomato clubs among local boys and with the head of the Industrial Department, Agnes Woods, began a series of clubs for young women of marriageable age from non-Christian homes. They were taught homemaking and numerous rural crafts in the hope that so occupied, they would not be tempted to town.

Perhaps Miss Walbridge's most ambitious project for promoting rural values was the mounting of a local agricultural show at the Seminary (Hughes, 1988). As she wrote in a letter to her family in June 1925, 'it was the first thing of its kind here and forty whites and many Zulus came, even the local chief' (Walbridge, 1978: letter 30.6.1925). The shows, which were held at the Seminary every year in the decade after 1925, were immensely popular among local farmers – mainly but not exclusively from the Christian community – who were trying to maintain a foothold on the land but finding it increasingly difficult to do so.

Education for domesticity and purity

As far as courses were concerned, a more 'scientific' approach was adopted: the theory behind the practice, as well as greater attention to practice itself, and a few 'general knowledge' subjects. The Standard 5 syllabus for 1914–15, while including Zulu, English, geography, arithmetic and history – 'pupils to be told about AmaXosa, Moshesh, Lobengula, Dinuzulu, Cecil Rhodes, President Kruger, Lord Milner, General Botha, Diaz, Cook and Columbus, Victoria, Edward VII and King George V' (ISP, file 2a, KCM 53120) – also made provision for needlework, laundry work, housekeeping and cookery. A special industrial course was offered from 1917 to those already having passed Standard 5. Subjects included 'Plain Sewing, Dressmaking, Gardening, Poultry Care, Housekeeping and Cooking' (ISP (ap) Report for 1918–1919). An advanced Domestic Arts course commenced in 1919, in the same year that the new Edwards Industrial Building, containing kitchens and a model suite of rooms, was opened. The principal at the time, Miss Clarke, could record in her annual report: 'the whole school is now an industrial school' (ibid.). Clearly, 'industrial' meant a blend of academic and practical subjects, even if the emphasis tended towards the latter.

For all the emphasis on practical work, it still could not be said that the education on offer was for class subservience. Attempts to link Seminary training with jobs in domestic service met with little success. Miss Walbridge wrote home to America enthusiastically in 1923: 'Inanda plans to give more training in domestic service. Durban is the center of employment and our missionaries there will investigate the homes and look after the girls when they reach the city' (Walbridge, 1978: letter 18–23.2.1923). There were, however, objections from other members of staff on the grounds of the poor wages and miserable living conditions offered by white employers, and the scheme petered out.

Yet the numerous subjects in the industrial course were popular with the students, for reasons not to do with prospective employment but with women's expected role in the home. Miss Phelps wrote, 'The domestic science lessons are very popular with the girls, especially the cooking lessons ... even the sweeping and dusting lessons are very much liked' (ISP (ap) *Our World-Wide Work*, nd). This seemed to be confirmed by the students, although there is evidence that they themselves made a distinction in status between the industrial course and more academically oriented subjects. (An academic course, offering Latin, English, Zulu or Sotho, algebra, geometry, arithmetic and history, and leading to the Junior Certificate, was introduced in 1925, but the first results were so poor that few in those years were attracted to it.) The following extract from a student essay captures the patronising attitude towards the industrial course – as well as a home truth: 'I am proud of my course, the Industrial Course, though those who don't take it seem to despise it. I feel pity for those who despise it, especially our young girls. They say: "What is Industrial after all?" They can pass their B.A.'s or whatever degree they pass, but they will finally be what an industrial girl is. They will have to start learning to cook, sew, etc., but it will be too late' (*Torchbearer*, 5, 2, 1937: 41).

Some impression of what students did with their training can be gained from information culled from the 'old girls' section of the school magazine, *Torchbearer*. A survey of 70 ex-students who attended classes in the 1920s and 1930s reveals the following pattern: 'teacher 27; nurse 21; cook 4; waitress 2; storekeeper 1; office worker 1; dressmaker 1; 'at home' 13 (*Torchbearer*, 1, 1, 1933–6, 1, 1938). It is impossible to say how representative this sample is without a great deal more research. However, it can be noted that the employment prospects of ex-Seminary students appear to have been atypical of those for most black women in South African at the time.

The 'at home' category was composed predominantly of those who had married; conversely, the occupational categories mostly contained those who had not. To some extent, then, this distinction reflected different age groups. The evidence here suggests that married women generally gave up their careers, though they could possibly find some way of earning money from home, for example through dressmaking, and generally involved themselves in voluntary activities, such as church work or women's associations: a service ethic was deeply ingrained in them. There were perhaps more women who continued in their careers after marriage than this random sample would suggest, and there were also those women who chose not to marry. Yet a brief comment by one student of an acquaintance is telling of how natural the transition from career to matrimony was considered: 'From teaching she got married' (*Torchbearer*, 3, 1, 1935).

This explains the popularity of the industrial course: a domestic ideology was central to the identity of the 'new woman'[13] and assisted her, if not publicly and politically, then privately and domestically. The domestic domain was her first priority, in which she expected to find fulfilment.

There was more to the making of the 'new woman' than a knowledge of housewifery. Correct conduct in personal relationships was strongly stressed in voluntary youth organisations that started operating all over the country in this period, reflecting concern over women's ability to care for themselves after their departure from institutions such as the Seminary: Wayfarers, the Students Christian Association and the Purity League. (There were boys' counterparts to some of these, such as Pathfinders, where presumably some attention was paid to their moral conduct too.) The message being conveyed was broadly similar in all these organisations. In Wayfarers, for example: 'We are taught to be clean daily, and try to help others ... we are taught to be good in all things which we do; and be faithful because we are working for God who knows every secret' (*Torchbearer*, 3, 1, 1935).

The Purity League was formed in the early 1920s by teachers from the Seminary, Ohlange and Adams, and had as its aim to teach girls 'how to look after themselves ... how to nurse their lives ... instead of giving up their lives recklessly to boys and so on ... those who would choose to live clean lives' (Walbridge, 1978). A driving force in the League was Sibusisiwe Makhanya, who had been educated and subsequently taught at the Seminary until 1923, when she left to become the League's full-time organiser. From there she won a scholarship to study in the United States, where she qualified as a social worker (Marks, 1987: 31ff).

School visits by the Ohlange boys were also arranged, presumably to enable both male and female pupils to break their single-sex isolation under controlled conditions. Ohlange was for boys only and clearly their visits to Inanda were a social highlight of the year: 'As we entered the Seminary, A.1 second to none, we found our cousins lined up in front of the Stanwood Cottage, arranged according to the order of the different groups. They welcomed us by singing that soul-stirring song of welcome: "We cheer for OHLANGE." After which, we received sweet smiles that made our thoughts ... and began to build castles in the air' (*Torchbearer*, 1, 1, 1933, 27–8).

As the years wore on, the question of 'sex education' had to be addressed ever more explicitly: in 1935 the newly appointed Board of Governors at the Seminary dwelt on this matter in its first deliberations, alluding to the increasing number of student pregnancies occurring during school holidays. Subsequently they organised a series of talks for the students, delivered largely by African women.

Towards elitism

By the late 1930s, Inanda Seminary had become well known as a school 'where the "elite" of African society could send their teenage girls' (Wood, 1972: 102). This was one of the strongest reasons put forward by, amongst others, the new head, Lavinia Scott, for keeping the school open in the face of economic pressures as a result of depression both locally and in the United States. About one-third of the costs of the school, £1 700, still came from abroad. Many teachers' salaries were paid by the Department of Native Education and fees, at £8 per year, brought in some £1 500 (ISP (ap), letter L. Scott to South African Native Trust). Most students by now came from professional homes from all over the country, and some even from the then Rhodesias and Uganda. Most would have been the third generation to receive education.

The status of the school had gradually changed from a local institution to one catering for a national elite as a result of a conscious decision on the part of the missionaries in charge to provide African girls with the sort of educational opportunities which were unobtainable anywhere else. As industrial courses were now available at several institutions, the academic ones – not at all widely available – took precedence. From 1930 Seminary pupils sat the same external examinations in the academic courses as white pupils did (Walbridge, 1978: letter 26.1.1930). As already noted, they had a reputation for being more difficult. In the Junior Certificate, for example, there had been 6 passes at the school in 1930, increasing to 34 in 1939 (Wood, 1972: 104). However, results were always better than those from other African high schools in Natal. In 1944 a matriculation class was introduced – the first in the Union in a school catering for African girls, at a time when a minuscule percentage of schoolgoing Africans went beyond the Junior Certificate, of whom most were boys (Marks, 1978: 9). By this time there were a total of 304 girls enrolled at the school and the number of staff had risen to 24 (*Inkundla Ya Bantu*, 7.5.1949).

There was also a greater stress on professional training. As mentioned earlier, teacher-training had been moved to Adams College but the other profession considered suitable for women, nursing, was developed at the Seminary. Medical work had always been an important component of American Board work in South Africa – Newton Adams was himself a doctor. In the early years of this century, another medical missionary of the Board, Dr J. B. McCord, moved the headquarter of the medical mission in Natal from Amanzimtoti to Durban; this was the start of the McCord Hospital. Because of the close mission association, Inanda Seminary had long provided McCord with its trainee nurses. However, in 1936 specialised nurses' training was begun at the Seminary, in conjunction with the newly opened King Edward VIII Hospital. One probationer nurse explained that the course taught them 'the causes of different diseases, and also how to prevent them and how to cure them when they have already developed.... The girls are not only taught these things, but they are also taught to be the leaders of their own people' (*Torchbearer*, 5, 1, 1937: 35). (It might be noted that in the post-Second World War period, the emphasis shifted to the preparation of students for medical school: a large proportion of African women doctors in this country began their training there.)

Again, significant reforms were introduced in keeping with these developments: a school library was built, a school uniform was worn from 1938, a school magazine was jointly produced with Ohlange, and a school board was appointed. The last-mentioned put some of the most influential Africans in Natal, such as John Dube and Chief Albert Luthuli, directly in touch with the day-to-day running of the Seminary. They indicated that they wished the Seminary to apply strict discipline: that dancing ought to be controlled, the girls' letters vetted, and more attention be paid to sex education. In some aspects at least, in the preservation of daughters' purity, the role of the school had barely changed over eighty years. Located as it was in a rural setting, it was considered ideally placed to undertake this task, away from the pernicious influences of the city.

CONCLUSION

All these changes meant that the Seminary gradually lost touch with the communities surrounding it. This did not mean that relations were severed abruptly; however, particularly from the late 1930s, local girls were at an even greater disadvantage than before in the face of increasing national competition for places at the school. The Inanda communities were altering too, as the influence of towns such as Durban spread: a greater dependence on the sale of labour power rather than crops, and the increasing numbers of women moving to urban areas being but two examples reflecting the growing difficulties of survival for Africans as independent producers. Local mission people still maintained contact with the Seminary, and some sent their daughters there. On the whole, however, more of them attended the growing number of day schools offering a rudimentary education, beyond which few of them would ever be educated. Inanda Seminary had become the premier boarding school for African girls in South Africa, a position it maintained until white private schools began opening their doors to black students in the 1980s.

9

'Desirable or undesirable Basotho women?' Liquor, prostitution and the migration of Basotho women to the Rand, 1920–1945[1]

P. L. BONNER

On 19 September 1937 a violent collision rocked Vereeniging's Top Location. It occurred after a detachment of police conducted an afternoon raid for unauthorised visitors and illicit beer. A crowd of 200, who had previously gathered in the square for 'traditional dancing', was soon swollen by 1 000 to 1 800 more when the police converged on the square, driving location residents ahead of them. As the police swarmed into the square 'women started shouting' and the police were suddenly pounded by stones hurled from the crowd. In the ensuing mêlée two parties of police were cut off from the main force and were fiercely attacked by the angry mob. By the end of the afternoon two white constables lay dead and four other policemen had been seriously injured. Dozens of other demonstrators and police nursed less serious wounds, while 70 location residents ended up in gaol (CAD, NTS 6671, File 87/332: 49–53, 83, 115, 128, 142, 374).

The Vereeniging riots, as these clashes came to be called, gave a sharp jolt to both local and central 'native administrations' and sent a ripple of unease running across many sectors of white public opinion. Protest meetings were held in dozens of rural areas in the Orange Free State and the Transvaal (Rheinallt-Jones, 1938: 18), liberal and missionary opinion stood aghast (ibid.; *South African Outlook*, 1.10.1937: 282–3), while Prime Minister Hertzog professed to see in them at least a partial confirmation of 'the ominous prediction of an approaching clash which began to take root among the European population following on the many instances of robbery and other crimes of violence committed during the last few months by natives on Europeans' (Rheinallt-Jones, 1938: 18–19).

The widespread attention attracted by the episode led to the appointment of a commission of enquiry to investigate the causes of the clash. In its report, published in October 1937, the commission singled out rough handling by the police and the provocative timing of the raid as contributory causes to the clash, but its main criticisms were reserved for what it saw as the slack control exercised over the location by the Vereeniging municipality. Illegal entry into the location, the commission charged, had been allowed to go largely unchecked because of the absence of an enclosing fence and because of the serious undermanning of the location police. Still more reprehensible was the failure of the location administration to make use of even those resources it had at its disposal, to control the illegal brewing of beer and the massive inflow of its principal manufacturers – Basotho women. The location superintendent, the commission observed, had been conspicuously slack and inefficient in not using location police to raid for liquor, in not withholding lodgers' permits from the husbands of female brewers, and in not using the appropriate sanctions of the 1923 (Natives) Urban Areas Act to curb the entry of Basotho women (SA, Vereeniging Native Riots Commission of Enquiry, 1937: 8–27). So alarming did it consider the scale of illegal brewing, that it reiterated the recommendations of the 1937 Police Commission of Inquiry and called for the establishment of municipal monopolies over brewing or the legalising of domestic brewing of beer (ibid.: 31).

The Vereeniging riots were only one among many less publicised disturbances in the Pretoria–Witwatersrand–Vereeniging area which flared up in the late 1930s and early 1940s in response to police raiding for liquor. In a sense they stand at the juncture of two periods of black urbanisation. The mid-1930s marked the beginning of a sustained surge of black immigration to the towns that would carry on for another two decades. A central feature of this process was the vast numbers of black women who streamed out of the black reserves and white farms, many of whom could find no alternative occupation in town to the brewing of beer. Basotho women were the most conspicuous among this group, and were at the centre of numerous clashes with the police and between different sections of the black urban population.

It is with these women that this chapter is primarily concerned. It looks first at the extent of the conflict which erupted on the Reef around the municipal monopolisation of beer-brewing in the late 1930s. It goes on to examine the role of single Basotho women in these collisions. It then attempts to explain why so many women migrated from Basutoland in this period, and concludes by examining why the authorities were unable to halt this exodus and what this meant for relations between women and men.

BEERHALL RIOTS IN THE LATE 1930s
From the early 1930s tension mounted in many of the Reef locations over intensifying police raiding for beer. The problem stemmed, at least in part, from a successful police crackdown on the illicit traffick-

ing of various kinds of 'European' spirits and wines. After the depression of the early 1930s, returning prosperity caused the illicit liquor trade to boom. It reached its peak between 1933 and 1934, after which new legislation (the Liquor Law Amendment Act of 1934) and a police clampdown reduced the volume of the traffic to relatively insignificant proportions. Far from disappearing, however, the liquor trade simply reappeared in new guise. The gap in the market which had been left by the elimination of 'European' liquor, was filled by the brewing of various adulterations of indigenous beer, such as skokiaan and barberton, which had long been consumed in the slums and locations but on a somewhat lesser scale. As police switched their attentions to this sphere of illicit liquor production, points of friction multiplied rapidly and scuffles and affrays became increasingly common (SA, Report of the Police Commission of Inquiry, 1937: 37–8, 43, 72–3).

The discontents fuelled by such raids are suggested by the high levels, both absolutely and proportionately, of liquor-related convictions. In 1936, for example, 107 348 out of a national total of 344 710 convictions secured against blacks were for liquor-related offences, compared to a 'mere' 71 052 pass law and 21 584 location regulation offences (ibid.: 69). But while the quickening tempo of police raids generated considerable friction and ill-feeling, they did not generally provoke large-scale confrontations. The Vereeniging riots were in this sense exceptional. The Police Commission of Inquiry of 1937 gives a clue as to why this was so. 'As the possession of liquor by a native is an offence,' it reported,

the native brewer adopts the expedient of hiding the maturing liquor by burying it in containers in a yard common to several houses or in adjacent roadways or vacant ground. If discovered, the liquor cannot be proved to be in the possession of any particular person, and when in the course of raids the police do unearth a container they can only destroy the contents while the natives stand by and look on. The position is one of 'stale mate' (ibid.: 70).

The Vereeniging riots commission reached a basically similar conclusion. Police efforts were 'unremitting' but 'in the Vereeniging location, as in many if not most urban Native townships and locations in the country, the result has been rather to make the liquor trade hazardous than to prevent it or even sensibly to diminish it' (SA, Vereeniging Native Riots Commission of Enquiry, 1937: 16).

A new twist to the screw was given in 1938. In the previous year the 1923 Urban Areas Act had been amended to compel local authorities to establish municipal monopolies over beer, or to permit domestic brewing. The measure was part of a wide-ranging programme to slow the pace of black urbanisation, which was steadily depleting the white countryside of black labour (Koch, 1983: 206–9).

are women
to the town
prevent
act urban

The liquor clause was aimed not only at stemming the flow of black women to the towns, by closing down access to incomes from beer-brewing, but also at providing the revenue to house and regulate the much-expanded urban black population. The first objective was quickly frustrated, but the second soon proved to be spectacularly successful. After 1938 the Johannesburg City Council was able to stop subsidising the Native Revenue Account from ratepayers' pockets because of the massive revenues the municipal beer-halls produced, and the same experience was reported all over the Rand (ibid.: 209). Between 1938 and 1940 all of the Reef municipalities established municipal monopolies which, in the majority of cases, soon yielded rich profits (SA, Report of the Native Affairs Commission, 1942, Annexure A: 19).

The municipal monopoly over beer provided a new incentive to Reef and other municipalities for suppressing the domestic brewing of beer and created fresh sources of conflict between municipal authorities and the residents of black urban locations. From 1938 to 1940 the tempo of liquor raiding mounted steadily, as the municipalities sought to root out all rivals in the trade. In the first three months of 1938 police destroyed 60 000 gallons of liquor and made hundreds of arrests in Johannesburg locations alone (*Rand Daily Mail*, 4.4.1938). As beerhalls were constructed elsewhere in the Transvaal the same pattern of aggressive police behaviour was repeated there as well. In August 1938, for example, Benoni's location superintendent announced 'a war' with Benoni's skokiaan queens (ibid., 6.8.1938). Early in 1939 Krugersdorp municipality reported a 50 per cent drop in the production of illicit liquor, and claimed that many 'skokiaan queens' had given up brewing or had left the location (*The Star*, 11.1.1939). In June 1940 some 20 separate raids on Marabastad location near Pretoria netted 17 150 gallons of beer and 8 524 gallons of skokiaan (ibid., 3.7.1940). Between 1937 and 1939 the number of liquor convictions on the Witwatersrand climbed from 46 018 to 63 728 (*Rand Daily Mail*, 6.12.1940).

The heightened intensity of raiding detonated explosions all over South Africa. In Vereeniging and Johannesburg's Western Townships effective boycotts of municipal beerhalls were mounted (*The Star*, 3.8.1939; CAD, NTS 7032, File 31/322/6: 67, 85; CAD, NTS 7036, File 31/322/6, aanhangsel). Elsewhere ugly confrontations developed between location residents and the police. In February 1938 some 29 police carrying out 'the most extensive liquor raid … in years' in Middelburg location were attacked by 'a mob of natives' and one policeman was seriously injured (*Rand Daily Mail*, 21.2.1938). In April of the same year 100 Vrededorp residents retaliated against a police raiding party by belabouring them with stones and sticks (ibid., 12.4.1938). The following month several hundred Africans stoned police who were raiding for beer on a vacant plot near Johannesburg's Bantu Sports Ground (*The Star*, 23.5.1938). Two of the most violent centres of conflict were Benoni and Springs. In May 1938 arrests for permits in Benoni location led to a clash between a crowd of 800 men and women and the police. One person was killed and one other was injured before the incident 'resolved itself' into a factional dispute between Basotho and Zulu (*Bantu World*, 15.5.1937: 18).

This last detail hints at the real source of the trouble. The Basotho, at least, were almost certainly visiting migrant workers from neighbouring mines. Since migrant workers were one of the principal sources of patronage sought by beerhalls all over the Reef, this was a constituency that local authorities were particularly anxious to exclude from the clientele of the 'skokiaan queens' (CAD, NTS 7032, File 31/322/6: 69, 73, 125, 156). Permit raids on migrants hence became a major weapon in the arsenal of the municipalities in their quest to monopolise the consumption of beer. The permit raid on Benoni location thus affected mine labourers and women brewers alike, provoking them to combine in their assault on the police.

An even more serious clash took place in Payneville location near Springs two years later. Payneville's municipal beerhall was only completed in the middle of 1938. Soon after it was opened the Springs municipality expressed its intention of emulating the Boksburg municipality, which had built a beerhall as part of a major urban complex that included eating facilities and shops (*The Star*, 1.1.1938, 8.8.1939). To sustain such a project the illicit brewing of beer had to be ruthlessly stamped out, and in the second half of 1938 the police and the location administration mounted a determined assault on beer-brewers and illegal visitors to the location. The opening shots in the campaign were fired on 14 August when 100 armed men descended on Springs location at 4 o'clock in the morning, arresting 70 women and 360 men and confiscating 1 000 gallons of illicit beer in a four-hour raid (*Rand Daily Mail*, 15.8.1938). This was followed by a 'clean up' campaign inaugurated by the Springs Public Health Committee in September 1938, which netted 110 'unauthorised' persons in its first weekend. Twenty additional constables were drafted in from Natal to spearhead the campaign, and it was soon being reported that Payneville's 'liquor queens' were beginning to leave the location, and that the sale of municipal beer had doubled (ibid., 15.9.1938).

Payneville's liquor brewers were, however, tougher and more resourceful than the Springs municipality had anticipated, and when the twenty additional constables returned to Natal early in 1939, the trade seems to have picked up once again (ibid., 30.9.1939). For the next eighteen months raiding seems to have slipped back to somewhat lower levels but in August 1940 it re-engaged higher gear. 'Hundreds of natives' were arrested in Payneville location and the adjacent timber plantation for beer and permit offences, creating a smouldering resentment among miners and brewers alike. This burst out into open conflagration the following month. On Sunday, 15 September police were called into the Payneville location to stop a fight between about 100 Basotho and Xhosa miners, but as soon as they arrived the erstwhile combatants united and the police found themselves the target of attack. Women shouted 'attack the police' and a general offensive was launched by hundreds of visitors and residents. So fierce was the onslaught that the police felt compelled to shoot their way out, leaving two of the crowd dead and two wounded. Six white and one African policemen were injured in the disturbance (CAD, NTS 7676, File 110/332: SNA to DNL 18.9.1940, Statements Sgt Kotze, Const. Cloete, Lieut. Pretorius, Report of post mortem examination 16.9.1940, statements Botha, Moller 16.9.1940).[2]

Payneville was the scene of an equally fierce confrontation in July 1945, except that this time it was a more carefully orchestrated affair. In that month the Control Board informed the Springs Council that its supply of 'kaffir corn malt' would be reduced by 55 per cent. The quality of municipal beer immediately deteriorated and the women's leader, Dinah Maile, together with local Communist Party stalwarts, decided to seize the opportunity to demand domestic brewing of beer. A boycott of municipal beer was immediately started, leading to arrests and a brief altercation between location women and the police on 9 July. Over the following two weeks daily meetings were held in the location, culminating on Sunday, 22 July in the renewed picketing of the municipal beerhall. Police action to break the picket resulted in a violently hostile reaction from the residents of the location. The police were stoned by a crowd of 3 000 men and women and were then cut off in the location after a section of the crowd broke through a fence and attacked them from behind (CAD, NTS 7676, File 110/332: Acting Distr. Commandant SAP Springs to Dep. Commissioner SAP 10.7.1945, Distr. Commandant SAP Springs to Commissioner SAP 23.7.1945, Report NAM Payneville 23.7.1945). According to a *Rand Daily Mail* report of 23 July 1945, 'women fought as fiercely as men' and it was only after rifles were brought from a nearby police station that the bruised and beleaguered policemen were able to shoot their way out. The casualty list resulting from the shootings made grim reading. Six were dead and twenty injured, while 15 men and 62 women (among whom Basotho women figured prominently) were arrested as a result of the affray (CAD, NTS 7676, File 110/332: Town Clerk to SNA 25.7.1945). In Springs at least the municipal monopoly of beer was taking a heavy toll.

BASOTHO WOMEN AND ILLICIT LIQUOR
The common thread running through most of these clashes – certainly

those at Vereeniging, Benoni and Springs – is the connection between women, migrants and beer. This association goes back to the earliest days of black urbanisation on the Rand. It is now widely accepted that the brewing of beer by women was vital to family survival in the first four decades of the twentieth century, and that much of the income earned in this way was drawn from migrant labourers and domestic workers. Since black urban wages were pegged at what migrants could be made to accept, it was impossible for urban families to survive on the income provided by a single male breadwinner. Equally, since virtually all avenues of wage labour – including domestic service in Durban and most of the Rand – were closed off to black women, the brewing of beer was one of the few alternative income-generating strategies that they could employ. In Johannesburg, Koch argues, the brewing of beer became 'the kernel of urban culture', while the improvised marriage arrangement of *vat en sit* became 'the crucial means whereby the informal production of the [slum] yards and the income from formal employment were harnessed together to provide for working class needs' (1983: 139, 162). These conclusions have been echoed in a number of other studies of the Rand as well as further afield (Gaitskell, 1981; Gilfoyle, 1983; Minkley, 1985).[3]

Given the centrality of brewing to black urban life, it would be easy to depict the beer riots of the late 1930s and early 1940s as valiant defences of family life by wives and mothers who had been driven to their wits' end. The women's anti-beerhall demonstrations at Cato Manor and elsewhere have indeed often been cast in this mould (Ladlau, 1975; Yawitch, 1978). Yet the part played by women in these confrontations, as well as female roles in the wider process of black urbanisation on the Rand, was far more complex and contradictory than this. At the centre of each of these clashes was not an undifferentiated and anonymous group of black urban women, drawn at random from the whole spectrum of black urban households, but clearly defined social and ethnic categories who had become increasingly conspicuous in the business of beer over the previous two decades. These groups were comprised of single women migrants from Lesotho, the eastern Free State, and southern Mozambique, who brewed professionally or semi-professionally and were frequently involved in the most fleeting and transient of relationships with men (SA, Report of the Committee to Consider the Administration of Areas Which Are Becoming Urbanised, 1938–9: 19; SA, Report of the Native Farm Labour Committee, 1937–9: 80).

These women were, all too often, not brewing beer to sustain a settled family life but were, rather, refugees from marriages that had cracked under the strain of rural pauperisation and the migrant labour system. Women from Mozambique were initially the most prominent practitioners of the brewing craft. In mid-1920 H. S. Cooke, the Director of Native Labour, alerted the Secretary for Native Affairs to 'the considerable number of such women residing in mine and other locations or in slum areas [who were] in almost every instance engaged in illicit liquor selling or prostitution', and recommended their forced repatriation (CAD, NTS 7715, File 53/331 (i): DNL to SNA 20.7.1920). With the support of the Portuguese Curator in Johannesburg, this was embarked upon towards the end of that year but the exercise seems quickly to have spluttered to a halt. By April 1921 the Home Native Co-operative Society of East Africa, an organisation of Mozambican migrants to the Rand which had earlier complained about the large-scale movement of Mozambican women to the Rand, was urging the resumption of the programme of repatriation and complaining of the presence of 2 000 Mozambican women at Barberton, Breyten, Witbank, the Witwatersrand, Klerksdorp, Viljoens Drift and Bloemhof (*The Star*, 23.4.1921).

The issue seems to have slipped briefly from view until 1926–7, when concern was once again expressed at the presence of 'loose Portuguese East African women' on the Witwatersrand and other industrial and urban areas of the Transvaal. By then the women's major centre of activity seems to have been Witbank and other mining towns of the eastern Transvaal, although they apparently still maintained a strong presence in Benoni. A more vigorously prosecuted programme of deportation soon saw their temporary removal from both Witbank and the Rand (CAD, NTS 7715, File 53/331 (i): DNL to SNA 21.4.1920, DNL to Dep. Commissioner SAP 5.9.1927, Acting DNL to SNA 22.12.1927). By the late 1920s they were, in any case, being eclipsed if not supplanted by another group of women migrants who were to dominate this sphere of activity on the Rand until the legalisation of the private consumption of alcohol in 1962. These were unattached women from the tiny land-locked British colony of Basutoland. It is on this group of women that this chapter concentrates.

As already mentioned in chapter 7, the flight of Basotho women from Basutoland emerged as an issue as early as the late nineteenth century. A colonial report of 1892 observed that chiefs from the north-western area of Basutoland were 'sore' about seeing their wives seduced into the Orange Free State, and in 1898 a full-scale rebellion was triggered by the same complaint. On this occasion a son of the senior chief Masopha seized back a 'runaway' wife from the Orange Free State, which in turn provoked a British reprisal and precipitated the Masopha rebellion (Phoofolo, 1980). A change in the character of migration may have occurred during the Anglo–Boer War. The garrison town that was established in Bloemfontein attracted women in droves, as washerwomen and also for the sexual services they could provide. The 1903–5 South African Native Affairs Commission, perhaps myopically, blamed the origin of large-scale prostitution on the military presence during the war, and the massive increase in the number of black women in Bloemfontein in this period may at least partly bear them out (Wells, 1982: 64).

To begin with, the majority of women attracted to the city were probably refugees from Free State farms, where agricultural production was severely disrupted by the war, but since close relations existed between Basotho on both sides of the border, which was in any case only a notional barrier to them, a number of women almost certainly slipped out from Basutoland as well. In the aftermath of the war the growing numbers of women absconding from Basutoland became an increasingly contentious issue, and an arrangement was eventually reached in 1908 whereby Orange River Colony officials agreed to deliver runaway women to the Basutoland border police. This procedure was of highly dubious legality, and in 1913, following Union, the Orange Free State administration refused to persist with it any further. The Basutoland National Council, consisting mainly of chiefs, responded by taking a leaf out of the book of the Natal Native Code. In its 1914 session it proposed a law 'making it an offence for a girl or woman to leave the country without the permission of her father or husband', which would then enable men to get a warrant to secure any absconding woman's return. Despite certain reservations by the colonial authorities about the possible reactions of British public opinion, the measure was passed into law in 1915 (Kimble, 1983: 4–5).

None of these measures had any appreciable effect, at least outside of the small Free State border towns. In 1911 nearly 3 000 females were recorded as being absent from Basutoland, and this more than trebled in the following decade when a quarter of the total population recorded as being absent from Basutoland consisted of women (Murray, 1982: 4). To begin with, the great majority went to the various eastern Free State towns, where they greatly aggravated relations between the town councils and their black urban populations. Together with the large number of women displaced or escaping from white farms, they ensured that the Free State's towns and dorps enjoyed the most balanced black sex ratios of urban centres in the country. In 1904, for example, the black population of the towns of the Orange River Colony was 56 per cent male and 44 per cent female, with the growth of the female component accelerating at a much faster rate than that of men (Wells, 1982: 61–2).

The female exodus from Basutoland gathered pace in the 1920s. Women 'flock[ed] into [Kroonstad] by the thousands, mostly from the tribal reserves' and helped to double its population between 1923 and 1931 (UWL, 'Evidence to the NEC', Box 3, File Kroonstad: 4635–6; 4649–50; 4700; 4704–10; 4736–7). Bloemfontein likewise experienced a massive jump in its female population, which progressively outstripped the number of males after 1925. A great part of the increase was contributed by new arrivals from Basutoland, who soon busied themselves in activities for which they would become notorious elsewhere – liquor-brewing and other 'immoral' activities (ibid.: 5118–22; 5149–51; 5230).

In the course of the 1920s large numbers of Basotho women also began moving further afield. The late 1920s saw a great surge of immigration into virtually every urban centre in South Africa, with the rate of increase of women rising far more sharply than that of men. In the late 1920s, for example, most Reef towns experienced a phenomenal growth in their female populations. The percentage increase recorded for five Reef municipalities in this period was as follows: Brakpan (1921–31) 58,6%; Germiston (1921–31) 158,9%; Krugersdorp (1921–31) 99,0%; Roodepoort–Maraisburg, (1925–31) 84,7%; Springs (1924–31) 67,4% (SAIRR, 'The Urban Native', Memorandum: 11).

In a number of areas Basotho women were in the forefront of this trend. In September 1930, for example, the Director of Native Labour (DNL) was evincing serious concern in a report to the Secretary for Native Affairs (SNA) at the 'very considerable number of undesirable native women from Basutoland [who had] taken up residence in locations on the Witwatersrand, notably Benoni and Nancefield'. According to the Director, in Benoni location 250 or more out of 818 stands were by that stage occupied by women, many of whom hailed from Basutoland (CAD, NTS 7725 File 166/333: DNL to SNA 12.9.1930).[4] By 1932 Brakpan was likewise 'teeming with people, principally from Basutoland', while the greater proportion of the increase of Vereeniging's female population in the 1930s was made up of single Basotho women (CAD, NTS 6671, File 87/332: 18–21, 331–5; Sapire, 1987: 65–7, 76–8, 106). These new immigrants were soon identified as the principal source of a variety of social malaises, centering around the illicit brewing of liquor and widespread prostitution.

In Benoni, Basotho women 'affect[ed] voluminous skirts with numbers of petticoats which ... [were] frequently used for smuggling liquor into the locations' (CAD, NTS File 166/333: DNL to SNA 12.9.1930). It was also 'common practice for [these] undesirable native women to travel by cabs and taxis to the neighbouring mine compounds for the collection of their debts and the furtherance of immoral business' (ibid.: DNL to SNA 20.11.1930). In Springs, Basotho women waited outside the mine compounds on weekends to direct miners where to get liquor, while in Vereeniging several hundred Basotho women sold vast quantities of liquor to compounded workers and miners both inside and outside the location (CAD, NTS 6671, File 87/332: 353; SAIRR, Paper read by E. W. Granger).

These Basotho brewers also seem to have engaged widely in prostitution. From the late 1920s the phrase 'Basuto women' was almost invariably paired with the opprobrious epithets 'undesirable', 'unattached', 'immoral' and 'loose'. In 1929, for example, the Native Commissioner of Benoni was already noting their propensity 'to take to immorality and the illicit liquor and beer traffic', adding that 'after a while many of them become so abandoned and unsuitable for anything that they follow a life of vice and die of disease and neglect' (Sapire, 1987: 83). Similar charges were echoed all over the Reef (SA, Report of the Native Farm Labour Committee, 1937–9: 80). Native commissioners and police were not alone in these opinions. Many Basotho men shared them as well. Author Simon Majara addressed this issue in the opening pages of his novel *Liakhela*. Here Majara remarks quite matter-of-factly that 'It is common to say that the women of Basotho who are all over the Republic are prostitutes' (16–17), before going on to explain why this was so. Majara's view was not uncommon among Basotho men, and a mini genre of Sesotho literature (as indeed of African literature more generally) grew up around this theme – Majara's *'Makotulo*, Masiea's *Lisebo*, Matlosa's *Mola Weli*, Tjokosela's *Mohale o tsoa Maroleng* and Khaketla's *Peto ea Mouna*. A number of letters to the Paris Evangelical Mission newspaper *Leselinyana la Basotho* raised the same complaint (8.7.1936: 3; 20.2.1940: 4), while some of the distaste felt by Basotho traditionalists when confronted by urban Basotho women is powerfully conveyed in a passage from the autobiography of A. S. Mopeli-Paulus, himself the son of a Witsieshoek chief:

I saw my Basutho women dressed in print skirts an inch below the knee, their blouses an inch above the navel, bracelets round their legs, running in the streets, swinging their coloured blankets in the air shouting 'If you are a man, come let me tell you keep away my boy! Go to the Christians! Here is Benoni-Twatwa. We rule ourselves.' Then throwing their skirts above their knees and crying 'Take and eat' (*Drum*, December 1954: 65–6).

These provocative postures could have more destructive outcomes than drunkenness, debauchery and disease. Increasingly, escalating violence and crime were also associated with illicit liquor and Basotho women. Already by 1930 weekend disturbances at Nancefield were 'almost invariably' due to so-called 'tea meetings' given by Basotho women. In the first nine months of that year the number of cases tried at the Benoni magistrate's court jumped to 7 265, up from 5 900 for the same period the previous year (CAD, NTS 7725 File 166/133: DNL to SNA 20.11.1930). This prompted the Native Commissioner of Benoni to stigmatise Basotho beer-brewers as the 'root of crime' as well as 'a cause of disease' (Cohen, 1982: 53; BMA, NEAC meeting 9.6.1952). The same experiences were reproduced all over the Reef. The sale of liquor and other services to miners in and around Brakpan location produced a situation where by 1935 'fighting and rioting is almost continuous, and lives are frequently lost' (Sapire, 1987: 82). In Springs, a hapless traffic inspector was stoned by Basotho beer-brewers when he tried to arrest one of them for purveying illicit liquor, while Vereeniging saw an attempt by angry Basotho women to ambush and kill the location superintendent in 1933, after he had several brewers deported to Basutoland, as well as a large-scale riot in the Indian quarter in 1936 (CAD, NTS 6671, File 87/332: 14, 375–7, 288).

A sudden surge of Basotho women to the Rand in the latter part of the decade added further fuel to the flames. From about 1937 Johannesburg experienced an unprecedented influx of Basotho women, many of whom engaged in the brewing of beer (IA, 'The Municipalisation of Kaffir Beer'). Heidelberg, Nigel, Krugersdorp, Benoni, Germiston and Vereeniging reported similar experiences (CAD, NTS 7715 File 53/331 (i)), accompanied by mounting conflict over illicit brewing. Conflict intensified after the municipal monopolisation of beer-brewing, and had reached such a pitch by mid-1938 as to prompt an urgent appeal from the Witwatersrand Compound Managers' Association and Gold Producers' Committee. Conditions on the Rand, the compound managers complained, were now seriously 'prejudicial to the health and efficiency of the mine Native labourers as well as a menace to the Native population as a whole'. The uncontrolled supply of liquor and prostitution in these locations, the compound managers went on to assert, were the direct cause of 'considerable lawlessness during the weekends resulting in a large number of casualties'. Recent clashes between ethnic groups at Venterspos and Springs had led to loss of life and the serious disorganisation of mine production.

In the worst collision, which took place on 6–7 August, 24 seriously injured miners had to be sent to the nearest government hospital, while a host of others were treated for less serious injuries at mine hospitals. All these casualties were 'directly attributable' to the uncontrolled supply of 'skokiaan' and 'women' (ibid., Gemmill to SNA 8.11.1930). The Native Commissioner at Krugersdorp shortly afterwards substantiated at least one part of this claim, informing the Director of Native Labour that West Rand Consolidated Mine had recently established that no less than 1 200 of its employees visited outside liquor dens every weekend (CAD, NTS 7715 File 53/331 (i): Thompson to DNL 18.11.1938).

For the compound managers, unattached women were also having another subversive effect. Many miners were forming liaisons with women 'of dubious character' in the locations and moving to settle permanently in the towns, thereby 'becoming detribalised and of no further use as mine labourers': 'Bastard families [were] becoming a serious menace, forming the class known as "Amalaita" ... [who were] absolutely useless for mining or manual labour of any kind' (ibid.). Besides suggesting the more effective implementation of the (Natives) Urban Areas Act, the Compound Managers' Association and the Gold Producers' Committee made only one specific proposal – the debarring of Basotho women from the Transvaal, and the deportation of all single Basotho women and those living with 'unofficial husbands' (ibid.: Gemmill to SNA 8.11.1930). The Native Commissioners of the Witwatersrand, when canvassed for their opinions, largely endorsed the compound managers' claims. Although two tried to evade direct responsibility for the situation by suggesting (quite incorrectly) that the problem of uncontrolled brewing was primarily one of the outside brickfields, freehold townships and peri-urban areas, not of the municipal locations, all acknowledged the central role of Basotho women and heartily endorsed proposals for their forced repatriation (ibid.: Jenner 23.11.1938, Thompson 18.11.1938, Carinus 19.12.1938, Norden 30.11.1938, Cherrington 4.1.1939).

These qualifications were enough to allow the Director of Native Labour to ignore the main burden of the compound managers' representations and slip himself gently off the hook. 'In most of the municipal locations,' he informed the Secretary for Native Affairs, 'there is no problem of control.' Outside the locations the problem would have to be addressed by excluding women who could not prove they had been married by Christian rites or customary law, and by rigidly restricting the number of tenants who could live on peri-urban farms. Taking note of his caution, D. L. Smit, the Secretary for Native Affairs, penned a reply to the General Manager of the Gold Producers' Committee which was a masterly example of evasion and inaction. The position was being 'closely watched' by the Department and 'wherever practicable' steps were being taken to repatriate. Meanwhile the restriction of any further influx of women 'was a matter for the local authorities concerned' (ibid.: DNL to SNA 20.1.1939, Smit to Gemmill 12.2.1939).

Unencumbered by the responsibility for actually having to do something about the situation, a number of government commissions which enquired into a range of issues at this time took a less complacent view. Both the 1939 Farm Labour Committee and the 1938–9 Committee into Peri-Urban Areas spoke of the towns and their margins being swamped by Basotho beer-brewers, whom they roundly denounced as 'a menace to Bantu social life' and 'the greatest individual vitiating influence in the areas they frequent' (SA, Report of the Native Farm Labour Committee: 80 para 459; SA, Report of the Committee to Consider the Administration of Areas Which Are Becoming Urbanised, 1938–9: 19 para 74). The 1942 Native Affairs Commission of Enquiry into the Use and Supply of Kaffir Beer likewise reported that 'The majority of women professionally engaged in this traffic appear to be of Basuto origin and the evidence shows that they have drifted into practically all the larger urban centres (with the possible exception of Southern Natal) where aggregations of male labour are to be found (SA, Report of the Native Affairs Commission: 16 para 163).

In the 1940s and 1950s the situation, if anything, got worse. The number of female absentees from Basutoland, which stood at 22 669 in 1939, increased to 32 331 in 1946 and 41 992 ten years later (Murray, 1982: 4). So large was the exodus of women in this period that the drop in the population of Basutoland, which drew so much comment after the war, could be attributed almost entirely to it. Towns like Vereeniging and Benoni were swamped by this tide of women immigrants, and soon felt themselves sinking in a vast lake of illicitly brewed beer.

ELOPEMENT, THE LEVIRATE AND RUNAWAY WIVES

Both the scale and the character of Basotho women's emigration were unique. Only Mozambique and the Ciskei began to compare in either respect. How is it to be explained? Mopeli-Paulus, who was not otherwise the most sympathetic observer of Basotho urban women, offers this suggestive comment: 'Lack of land has driven the women to places like this for they once followed their husbands to the Reef' (*Drum*, December 1954: 66). What Mopeli-Paulus alerts us to here is the central role of rural impoverishment and labour migrancy in this massive flight of women. It is to some of the less visible and more insidious effects of these processes on Basotho family life that this discussion now turns.

M. B. Smith of the Basutoland Chamber of Commerce identified four main categories of Basotho women migrants to South Africa in his evidence to the Native Laws (Fagan) Commission of 1947. First were women who had had trouble with their husbands. Second were widows who 'very often have a very rough time'. Third were girls who had eloped and had then been deserted by their partners, and fourth were women who had been properly married with cattle but had also been deserted by their husbands (UWL, 'Minutes': 2140–1). Other commentators suggest a basically similar breakdown (Gaye, 1980a: 42–4). With the partial exception of the first group, the women in each of these categories were the victims of land shortage and the casualties of the migrant labour system. However, while each of these categories seems to have been present in the ranks of female migrants from the early days of this movement, their relative importance varied over time, since the ravages of migrant labour exacted its toll in different fashions at different times.

In the 1890s it was 'runaway wives' who captured most attention. Where identified, these came mainly from polygynous households and it is likely that it was their status as co-wives or junior wives that prompted them to leave (Phoofolo, 1980; Kimble, 1983: 14). When the Basutoland National Council proposed in 1914 that women be obliged to carry a pass signed by their husbands or fathers and chiefs in order to cross the border into South Africa, the commoner councillor Josias drew attention to their often unhappy position: 'Some will blame you, the sons of Moshesh, some of these women will say they have no blankets, they have no homes, or they are denied conjugal rights' (Kimble, 1983: 15). Chief Maama dismissed Josias's intervention with the curt comment, 'Wives of polygamists will always complain' (ibid.), but the actions of the women themselves could not be so lightly set aside, as the number of runaways multiplied in the face of such unyielding attitudes.

As rates of polygyny declined, mainly because of increasing land shortage and poverty, the flight of wives from polygynous households made progressively less contribution to the annual exodus of women. In 1931 a Maseru court interpreter could still inform a visiting delegation from the South African Institute of Race Relations that 'The National Council asked that wives should be compelled to obtain passes before leaving Basutoland ... because most of the members of the National Council are polygamists and some of their wives are deserting' (SAIRR, 'Notes of a discussion with native groups'),[5] but for the majority of the population polygyny was a thing of the past. The number of men with more than one wife, as a percentage of the number of marriages recorded, declined steadily from 18,7 per cent in 1911 to 8,4 per cent in 1946 (Murray, 1982: 127). Here, at least, was one burden from which Basotho women were gradually freed.

A second type of emigration, present from the late nineteenth century, was made up of women who eloped or were seduced and fled across the border with their lovers. In the 1910s and 1920s significant changes occurred in the practice of elopement, as it grew in scale and won a grudging social acceptance. Young women now commonly eloped to the villages of their lovers' fathers, the payment of six head of cattle being exacted in compensation by their families from the man. This payment, called *chobale*, could subsequently constitute the first instalment of a full *bohali* (bridewealth) payment (ibid.: 121–2; UWL,'Evidence to the NEC', File Rydal Mount: 4839), but in practice it all too often allowed marriage on the cheap and reflected the growing poverty of much of Basotho society.

In the mid-to-late nineteenth century bridewealth payments in Basutoland had been raised to exceptionally high levels, as a means of entrenching the predominance of the Koena chiefly lineage. While marriage payments varied according to a woman's status, 20–30 cattle were henceforth demanded to marry even a commoner woman (Murray, 1982: 125–8; Thompson, 1975: 52–69; Sanders, 1975: 43–59; Poulter, 1976: 90–5, 109). These levels were considerably higher than those prevailing in most other parts of South Africa, and placed severe strains on the resources of many commoner homes (Wilson, 1981: 133–47; Sansom, 1974: 161–2; Kuper, 1982: 136, 158, 167–8).[6] These grew as Basotho prosperity was systematically undercut in the late nineteenth and early twentieth century. The latter story is sufficiently well known to need only a brief recapitulation here. Land losses after the Free State war of 1867–8, population pressure as a result of natural increase and the eviction of sharecroppers from the eastern Free State farms, exclusion from markets for agricultural products, and natural epidemics and blights, all served to cripple Basutoland's previously thriving economy. Per capita incomes from agriculture dropped; levels of migrancy climbed. By 1911 approximately 25 000 Basotho nationals were working outside its borders. Despite this, Basutoland's economy retained a degree of viability until the late 1920s. Then depression and drought combined to break its back. In the 1932–3 drought between 30 and 50 per cent of cattle holdings were lost, and cultivation of maize was temporarily extinguished (Murray, 1982: 15). Virtually every bit of ground cover was destroyed and choking clouds of dust filled the air. Older Basotho still date key events in their lives by reference to the all-enveloping clouds of 'red dust', and many even identify them as a turning point in their ability to win a daily subsistence from agriculture (interviews, L. Sefako; A.B.).

For young men, especially those born into poorer households, the level of bridewealth demanded now became increasingly unrealistic: it required half a lifetime of migrant labour to pay it off. In 1931 witnesses from Rydal Mount told the Native Economic Commissioners in Bloemfontein that abduction and seduction were rife because *bohali* was too high and young men preferred to pay *chobale* instead (UWL, 'Evidence to the Native Economic Commission', File Rydal Mount: 4839; see also Poulter, 1976: 106). Complaints about elopement pepper the minutes of the Basutoland National Council, where occasionally the same connection is drawn. In its 1938 session, for example, one exasperated councillor argued that twenty head of cattle for *bohali* was too high. Young men without livestock were eloping with men's daughters, having children and then absconding to the mines: 'people's daughters' were 'turned into dagga' which, 'after smoking,' was 'simply abandoned' (LA, 'Proceedings of the BNC', 1938: 304–9; see also Poulter, 1976: 106).

Abandoned women were indeed an increasingly common outcome of elopement. Without transferring a large proportion of the bridewealth payment, men enjoyed only limited rights over their children and a much weaker bond was sustained between husband and wife. Men were encouraged to adopt a more casual and cavalier attitude towards their spouses, and were more inclined to disappear into

South Africa and never return. M. F.'s experience illustrates this pattern. Born in 1917, she eloped to her in-laws' homestead in the early 1930s. After she had spent two weeks with her husband, he had a violent quarrel with his father and left to find work in the Free State. M. F. spent two years in her father-in-law's homestead waiting for her husband to return. When her father-in-law proposed a more intimate relationship with her, she finally decided to quit. She headed first for the Free State in search of her husband, and then, when she failed to track him down, went on to the Reef (interview).

Chobeliso wives were, to some extent, a marginalised category in Basotho society. Worse off, very often, were widowed women. These were faced with two often equally unpalatable options: to be married to a male kinsman of their husband (the levirate system), or to remain perpetually vulnerable to men (Gaye, 1980: 81). Those choosing the latter option often fell prey to chiefly opportunism or to the greed of their husbands' kin. A combination of land shortage and a proliferation of chiefs in Basutoland had pushed widows into an increasingly exposed position in the 1920s and 1930s. Under the system of 'placing' chiefs, which had been started by Moshoeshoe, the number of chiefs had grown steadily in the late nineteenth and early twentieth centuries, each exercising authority over a steadily dwindling patrimony. As one Basutoland National Council member exclaimed in the early 1930s: 'There are now as many Chiefs in Basutoland as there are stars in the heavens' (LA, 'Financial and Economic Position of Basutoland': 48–9). Their continually narrowing jurisdiction encouraged the chiefs to exploit more intensively their rights over the areas that remained. Fines and tribute (*lira*) labour for the chiefs' fields were extorted ever more remorselessly, with much of the burden falling on women. Widows, who lacked the protection of husbands and adult male children, were particularly vulnerable to these demands. Worse still, since widows were exempted from the payment of tax and the chiefs took a cut of the taxes collected in their territories, widows often found themselves arbitrarily deprived of their lands which were then allocated to young male tax-payers (Edgar, 1987: 10, 130; LA, Box 71, item 44; Kimble, 1983: 15–18). Other pressures, including the levelling of witchcraft accusations, could be applied by jealous in-laws, until the hapless widow was ultimately forced to leave. Such women often fled to government camps in Basutoland, where they engaged in the brewing of beer; alternatively they might proceed to the Free State or the Rand (Kimble, 1983: 16–18). It is presumably to this category of person that the superintendent of Bloemfontein location was referring when he spoke of 'the Basotho woman who is ostracised by the tribe and driven out', in his evidence to the Native Economic Commission in 1931 (UWL, 'Evidence to the NEC', Box 3, File Bloemfontein: 5150).

While these groups of, in one way or another, marginalised women made a significant contribution to the mounting exodus of Basotho women, by far and away the largest component of this movement consisted of women properly married by cattle and living with their children in monogamous homes. It is here that the callous destructiveness of the migrant labour system is most plain. Commonly husbands returned to their jobs in South Africa within a couple of months of marriage and were almost always away for considerable lengths of time (Gaye, 1980: 109–11, 122–3). Some never came back; others returned intermittently and in the interim neglected to provide their wives with adequate support. Many women were thus condemned to live lives of profound insecurity and poverty, never knowing when their husbands would come home or where their family would get their next meal. The records of the only surviving district archive for the post-1930 period in Lesotho are littered with the pathetic appeals of women to have their absent husbands tracked down. A few excerpts give some sense of the strain under which many Basotho wives lived:

Motsarapane Molapo to District Commissioner (hereafter DC), Leribe, 8 May 1954: 'I have been asked by Anna Lesaoana that her husband John who has been away for the last 6 years be repatriated. She says 10 cattle were paid for the marriage.'

J. D. Elliot, DC, Leribe, to Native Commissioner, Pretoria, 26 November 1955: 'I have received a report that Teboho Mpho Linakane of Thaba Phatsoa is not supporting his wife and 6 children. Please persuade him to support them.'

Elliot to Native Commissioner, Germiston, 23 December 1955: 'I have a complaint of non-support on the part of Elliot Thoahlara of the South African Repairs Shops, Germiston. He has been away from home for nearly 8 years.'

Acting DC, Leribe, to the British Agent in Johannesburg, 7 June 1956: 'The Chief reports Moleleki Mohale has been lost on the mines. His address is supposed to be the S.A. Railways and Harbours Compound, Germiston, but his wife says she has been there and he is not there. He has been missing for 10 months.'

DC, Leribe, to Manager, Eclipse Engineering, Benoni, 18 October 1958: 'The Bearer of this letter is Tomothea Malao, wife of Paulus Malao who is working in your firm. His wife complains her husband is not supporting her and also his children. Please persuade him to support her' (LA, Box 39, 57).

The problems experienced by the wives of absent husbands were often compounded by friction in their new homes. Upon marriage a young woman was obliged to live at her in-laws' homestead and it was often some time before her husband established a fully separate home (Gaye, 1980: 109–11, 122–3). In the meantime, especially if their husbands were absent, young brides occupied an invidious position. They were obliged to observe rules of respect and avoidance (*hlonepho*) with regard to the senior male agnates of the husband, there were tight restrictions on whom they could meet, and they could easily be scorned or frozen out by the other women of their new home. In these new and often alien surroundings potential for conflict abounded, particularly over the distribution of the husband's remittances or the allocation of work (ibid.: 99–101, 120, 122–3). 'Me Likeleko, for example, married with cattle in 1932 and went to stay with her in-laws, where she worked in their fields. Her father-in-law 'hated her very much', and she was forced to go back to her home. Her husband followed her to her parents' village but then began 'to beat her every day', until in 1942 she absconded to South Africa without his consent (interview). 'Me Mmatuku Ramatuku experienced similar problems. She was married in about 1940 and soon bore two children. Her husband was recruited into the Basotho contingent fighting in the Second World War and did not return for five years. In the meantime tensions mounted between Mmatuku and her mother-in-law, who was 'jealous of her possessions' which she bought with the money remitted by her husband. When her husband returned from the war he found his elder brother had died. Encouraged by his mother, he took over his dead brother's wife and family, abandoning his own (interview).

In every way migrant labour profoundly warped marital relations. The protracted absences of men predisposed women to extra-marital affairs. As P. M. Maguta, a Lesotho resident interviewed for this study, observes: 'These women were immediately left after marriage by their husbands. These men would remain with their wife for about two or three months and would join the mines leaving the woman still young and fresh and anxious for their husband'.

Extra-marital affairs in these circumstances were less the exception than the rule, inspiring intense jealousy among husbands who often resorted to beatings and abuse (interview, 'Me L.; ISAS, interviews; Gaye, 1980: 166–7, 126, 159–61). These pressures often so embittered relations between husbands and wives that one or other party would desert. Herein lies the background to Theko Bereng's lament to the Basutoland National Council in 1952: 'At the moment whenever we travel by train we see many women travelling to Johannesburg. Whenever I ask them myself why they are running away from the country, they tell me about the cruelty which is practised on them by their husbands in Basutoland' (LA, 'Proceedings': vol. II, 464–5).

What is most striking about the movement of Basotho women to South Africa is the overwhelming preponderance of married women in their ranks. Occasionally unmarried women would leave, usually those who had been 'spoilt in the yard' (that is, had fallen pregnant) but these were comparatively rare. 'Me M. P. was one such case. She fell pregnant while still at school and since she was alone with her mother and there were financial problems at home, she decided to look for work on the Rand. Although her initial impulse for leaving was unusual, her subsequent experiences find echoes in the histories of countless other women. A friend had a boyfriend in Germiston, who wrote to tell them that it was possible to find work in South Africa. The two women left for the Reef by train in 1944 but after they had tracked down the boyfriend at his place of work, he refused to see them – evidently because he was living with another woman. The women were thereafter directed to Masakeng (Mpanza's shanty town), where they were able to find accommodation. 'Me M. P. eventually found work as a domestic worker, entered a relationship with a Nyasa man and fell pregnant once again (interview).

The part of 'Me M. P's experience which is so reminiscent of that of other married women who set out for the Rand is the attitude of the man she went to find. In many cases women who went in search of their husbands would find they had disappeared without trace (interview, S. M. Majara). In cases where the husband was still at his last-known place of work, he would often refuse to see his wife. If he was living in a mine or factory compound this effectively closed off the desperate woman from any access to him. Simon Majara claims that *Makotulo*, his cautionary tale of the life of a migrant Basotho woman, was inspired by observing one such harrowing scene. A stereotypically beautiful young Mosotho woman came to the mine where Majara worked in search of her husband, only to be spurned and sent away. Rather than return to Basutoland, she took up the life of a brewer and semi-prostitute, being much fought over by rival Basotho men (ibid.). This seems to have been the characteristic response of wives rejected in this way. Overnight, 'respectable' married women thus became transformed into the notorious unattached and undesirable Basotho women so reviled by white administrators at the time.

Not all Basotho women migrants endured such unhappy experiences. A number interviewed for this study succeeded in re-establishing fairly harmonious marital relations after joining their husbands in the Free State or on the Rand (interviews, 'Me R. O. T.; 'Me M. M.; 'Me M. Ma; 'Me M. Me). Almost as common, however, was for the reconstructed marriage to collapse. Janisch and Shropshire estimated that the average period of cohabitation of black men and women in Johannesburg at the end of the 1930s was two years, and while traditional marriages by cattle were probably more durable than this, the volatility and flux of the urban environment seem to have exacted a heavy toll on these relationships as well. The marriages of two of the women interviewed for this study collapsed while they were living in the towns (interview, 'Me M. Mo; ISAS, interviews BWM 2), and the district archives of Leribe reverberate with complaints from indignant urban-dwelling husbands whose wives had vanished from their homes:

Native Commissioner (NC), Vereeniging, to DC, Leribe, 17 November 1954: 'Ntepe Jackson Mosala complains that his wife Matomasa Mosala deserted him on 8 November 1954 when he was at work taking her 11 month old baby. There was no reason.'

Moss Friedman & Co., Attornies, Vereeniging, to DC, 25 January 1956: 'Augustus Semena states his wife and 2 children have left him and are at Peka. She has written to him refusing to go back. He wants you to order her to go to his home at Fobana Leribe and lay any charge she has against him.'

NC Pretoria, to DC, Hlotse, 13 July 1954: 'Piet Malelane lodges complaint that his wife Christina Malelane has maliciously deserted his home and is now staying with her elder brother ... in your district. He asks she be prevailed upon to return home as he has nobody to look after the minor children' (LA, Box 57, File 1218).

Since these files refer only to women who had gone back to Basutoland, it is clear that desertion by women was taking place on a fairly substantial scale. Urban women were refusing to submit to the demands and caprices of their men. Men were losing control of their women. The same trend is evident in relation to the state; indeed, men's loss of control was partly premissed on the incapacity of the state to direct the movements and activities of women. It is to this subject that this chapter now turns.

STATE LOSS OF CONTROL

The loss of control over Basotho women can ultimately be traced back to the failure of the South African authorities to install an effective system of pass controls over South African women as a whole. The root of this failure can itself be tracked down to the campaigns against women's passes which burst out in a number of Free State towns between 1913 and 1923. In these campaigns, as Wells (1982) shows, a respectable middle-class women's leadership, linked to the equally respectable and middle-class African National Congress (ANC) and African People's Organisation (APO), played the most conspicuous role. Less visible but, if anything, even more important in provoking the conflict were poor, uprooted Basotho women from Basutoland and eastern Free State farms, who had been driven by a combination of economic and family pressures to seek refuge in the Free State towns. As Wells observes, 'it was no accident that the conflict [over women's passes] first emerged in the Orange Free State. The political economy of the region incorporated black women earlier and more extensively than any other in South Africa' (1982: 15). What Wells is referring to here are the women of sharecropping families who were being extruded from Free State farms in the 1900s and 1910s. Her comment could equally appropriately be extended to Basotho women on the other side of the border, of whom she is largely unaware.

Women arriving in the Free State towns in the 1900s, who were not already members of middle-class families, had two basic options: they could work as domestics, or they could engage in informal income-generating activities such as beer-brewing, petty trade or prostitution. Herein lay the source of the women's agitation. From the Anglo–Boer War onwards, most Free State towns experienced persistent shortages of female domestic labour. Women either refused to present themselves for such low-paying work or were unreliable and undisciplined, flitting between jobs. The reasons for their ability to withhold labour varied with their social class. Women from the more prosperous *oorlams* (deracinated groups that grew up on Boer farms) and Baralong families were freed very often from the economic compulsion to seek work and could devote their attention to their families and their homes. Women from poorer, farm-labouring stock or from Basutoland, on the other hand, engaged in a whole range of informal-sector activities in order to escape domestic work.

The first pass laws were thus framed with the related objectives of suppressing beer-brewing and prostitution, and forcing women onto the domestic labour market. As more and more Basotho women flooded into the Free State towns and the domestic labour shortage persisted as acutely as ever, local pass laws against women were enforced with renewed vigour. In Bloemfontein, Winburg and Jagersfontein their application was particularly indiscriminate and severe. In contrast to Heilbron and Kroonstad, where married women were exempted from pass controls, the police harassed staid middle-class matrons as well as younger unmarried women. A sudden burst of particularly strict enforcement in May 1913 provoked the first passive resistance to women's passes. Its leaders, as Wells (1982) stresses, were women from middle-class Baralong, *oorlams* and coloured households, and it was their efforts, along with the political and propaganda campaigns of the APO, which secured first the relaxation of pass controls over women, and then the exclusion of women from the provisions of the 1923 (Natives) Urban Areas Act. Without this leadership it is highly unlikely that this concession would have occurred, but this should not blind us to the context out of which the anti-pass movement emerged. It was this early large-scale proletarianisation of women which provided the context for the first women's anti-pass campaign, and it was this, in turn, which shaped the application of the pass laws for the next thirty years.

The accelerated influx of women to the Rand in the latter part of the 1920s led to renewed efforts to give the existing influx control legislation more bite. A 1930 amendment to the Urban Areas Act provided for the issuing of special permits to African women, conditional upon their joining a husband or father who had two years of continuous employment in the town, while the 1937 revision provided that a woman entering an urban area for the first time should have a certificate from the authorities of her home district granting her permission to leave (Wells, 1982: 258, 261–5). The 1930 amendment turned out almost immediately to be a dead letter. Several witnesses told the 1937 Vereeniging Riots Commission how easily this provision was evaded. As Albert Mduli put it, Basotho women came to Vereeniging and 'got a man around the compounds' in order to get a lodger's permit (CAD, NTS 6671, File 87/332; see also evidence of J. M. Simpson). When it came to policeman G. C. van der Merwe's turn to give evidence, his frustrations bubbled over: 'We have made a plan to get them out of the location', he told the Commission, 'but each one of them has a man, and you can do what you like, but they have got a man…. Unless I could show you 2 or 3 previous convictions you could not get them out. If you arrest a girl with the name Maria, tomorrow she is Jane. Consequently, unless you go to court and swear there are previous convictions you cannot get a sentence imposed' (ibid.: 150–1).

R. W. Norden, the Native Commissioner of Johannesburg, put the matter a little more dispassionately. Since irregular unions could be claimed as customary marriages, women could not be expelled under the 'habitually unemployed' clause of the legislation (17(i)(a)), or for not having sufficient honest means of livelihood (section 17(i)(b)). Deportation orders were difficult to secure even if the marital status of women was in doubt, and where attempts to check this were made, women frequently presented chiefs' certificates that were forged or simply unintelligible (CAD, NTS File 7725 File 166/333: NC to Chief NC 13.9.1937; CAD, NTS 7715 File 53/331 (i): Norden to DNL 30.11.1938; CAD, NTS 6671, File 87/332: 336, 88). A further hedge against arrest under Section 17 was for a 'single' woman to get a job as a domestic in a white suburb, take up residence with a man in the location, and then engage in beer-brewing while taking in the occasional load of washing as a cover (CAD, NTS 7715, File 53/331 (i): NC Benoni to DNL 4.1.1939, NC Germiston to DNL 23.11.1938; CAD, NTS file 7725 166/333: DNL to SNA 12.9.1930). Action under subsections (c), (d) and (e) of Section 17 could only be contemplated if the woman had a criminal conviction or had been convicted more than once for the illicit brewing and selling of liquor. Convictions here were equally hard to obtain. 'Kaffir beer' was exempt from this provision till 1938, and women seldom allowed themselves to be convicted more than once. Aside from routine techniques of evasion, beer-brewers became increasingly sophisticated in their manipulation of the law. In Benoni, for example, 'reprehensible' solicitors 'raised innumerable difficulties' to frustrate the efforts of officers of the law. Where all else failed, women facing conviction would simply estreat bail, and slip away to some other location (CAD, NTS 7725 File 166/333: NC Johannesburg to Chief NC 13.9.1937, Const. Snijman to Add. NC Vereeniging 22.9.1937, NC Heidelberg to Chief NC 30.9.1937, Barrett and Robinson to SNA 2.2.1931). Once convicted, offenders might still escape deportation. The hardpressed police on the Rand frequently lacked the time 'to search the voluminous records of the Reef courts', and as a result convicted women were free to resume their 'undesirable' activities again (ibid.: DNL to SNA 19.10.1937, Norden to Chief NC 13.9.1937).

Even once all these hurdles were cleared, other traps lay in wait for the unsuspecting Native Commissioner. Beer-brewers had to have somewhere to be deported to, and those not born on the Reef would simply refuse to disclose from which home district they came (ibid.: DNL to SNA 12.9.1930, 20.11.1930). The frustrations felt by many officials over their inability to deal with 'undesirable' women led a number to contemplate more radical solutions. Major Cooke of the Native Labour Department went so far as to recommend to the Native Economic Commission:

There certainly ought to be [a labour colony] for women, because one of the difficulties of dealing with a dissolute woman now is that she will not disclose the place from which she comes – which is the term used in the Act. Unless there is some other means of dealing with her, when it comes to the question of giving her the alternative of going back to the place to which she belongs, or being confined to a farm colony, then she makes no bones about disclosing where she does belong to. Similarly in regard to procedure about the Immigration Act, a woman may obviously be a Basuto ..., but she will allege she comes from Ficksburg or somewhere in the Free State and the Administration has the greatest difficulty in establishing whether she comes from this side of the border or the other side (UWL, 'Evidence to the NEC', Box 7, File Johannesburg: 7296).

Cooke's call was reiterated a number of times in the course of the decade as the rising tide of women and illicit liquor broke decisively through the banks of control (CAD, NTS 7725 File 166/333: NC Johannesburg to Chief NC 12.1935, Acting DP to SNA 1.1936, Acting DP to SNA 11.6.1937, NC Far East Rand to DNL 13.9.1930, DNL to SNA 17.10.1930, 20.11.1930, Sec. Justice to SNA 4.3.1931). Owing to shortages of funds a female section at the Prison Farm Labour Colony at Leeuwkop was not established until July 1937. However, even then similar problems bedevilled its operations. It was as difficult as ever to get convictions against 'undesirable' women, while the Supreme Court preferred warnings to immediate incarceration on the prison farm. As a consequence, over the next fifteen years the section often had as little as two inmates and sometimes none, and never housed more than fourteen at the same time. The Prison Department displayed predictable irritation at this low occupancy rate, especially since they had been bombarded with requests for the facility for over a decade, and the section's activities were first suspended in November 1951 and finally closed in mid-1954 (ibid.: Acting DP to SNA 15.4.1942, DNL to SNA 30.4.1942, Chief NC to SNA 11.2.1954, DP to SNA 18.3.1954, Gen. Circular 34 of 1954 issued by SNA).

The only alternative means of preventing Basotho women's entry to the Rand was to control their movement at source. This was attempted by both the Basutoland and the South African authorities, sometimes in unison, sometimes unilaterally. One of the earliest efforts was the Basutoland law of 1915 in terms of which no Mosotho woman was allowed to leave Basutoland without a letter signed by her husband or father and endorsed by her local chief and an officer of the colonial administration (Kimble, 1983: 9, 13–16). The system proved immediately ineffective. Women wishing to evade these pass controls could obtain a document to cross to the border towns of Ladybrand or Ficksburg, purportedly for shopping or medical purposes, and then simply entrain for the Rand (interview, 'Me M.; LA, 'Proceedings').

Attempts to breathe new life into the law were made after complaints by the South African authorities in the second half of 1930 about the 'steady migration of unattached Native women from Basutoland to the Witwatersrand where they form[ed] a most undesirable class which ma[de] a living by smuggling liquor into the locations and compounds and by immorality'. 'Crime' and 'disturbances' were the direct outcome of their activity, and the Basutoland authorities were requested to stem this flow at source (CAD, NTS 7725 File 166/333: SNA to GS 8.10.1930). Three months later the Government Secretary of the Basutoland administration was able to report that by arrangement with the Paramount Chief, all Basotho women would in future be stopped from leaving the territory unless in possession of a certificate from their local chief confirming that they had the permission of their husbands or parents to travel to the Union (ibid.: Foord GS to SNA 15.12.1930, 2.1.1931). This was the 1915 proclamation revived and it had just as little effect. Shortly afterwards the Secretary for Native Affairs was once again complaining to the Basutoland authorities that travelling passes were being issued indiscriminately to Basotho women to visit or find absent husbands on the Reef. The Government Secretary again assured the Secretary for Native Affairs that he would discourage this practice but only then revealed the limits of his powers. A major problem, he confessed, was the absence of colonial legislation restricting the movement of Basotho women,

246 Liquor, prostitution and Sotho women on the Rand

while the 'extensive nature of the border' made it easy for them to evade any proposed prohibition (ibid.: SNA to GS 5.3.1931, GS to SNA 24.2.1931, 24.3.1931). A further loophole was identified after a fresh batch of complaints in 1934: there was virtually no control over women visiting the border towns of the Union, from which they could entrain to the Reef.

The only solution proffered by the Basutoland government was that the South African Railways be instructed to refuse the issue of tickets to women not in possession of permission to proceed (ibid.: Acting GS to SNA 25.8.1934). They were conspicuously unresponsive to this appeal. Their General Manager replied that 'even if practical' they could not justify such action in view of the large number of women permanently resident in the Free State, whose movements were unrestricted by law (ibid.: Watermeyer to DNL 3.10.1934). The alternative of closing the border to Basotho visitors to border towns seems not to have been canvassed at all. An altercation which erupted some twenty years later probably provides the answer why. In September 1955, Secretary for Native Affairs Eiselen instructed the Native Commissioner for Ficksburg to apply the provisions of Section 12 of Act 25 of 1945 to Basotho citizens. This required that women wanting to enter South Africa obtain a pass from the Basutoland District Commissioner, who in turn was required to get the permission of the Native Commissioner or magistrate of the place to which the women were intending to go. A howl of protest went up from the Ficksburg Chamber of Commerce which was threatened with a dramatic fall in custom, and the Minister quickly backed off, claiming that the Native Commissioner's interpretation of his order had been an 'unfortunate misunderstanding' and that 72-hour visitors were always meant to be exempt (LA, Box 65: ? to DC Leribe 13.4.1956, Eiselen to Sec. for High Commission 8.12.1955, DC Leribe to GS 22.12.1955, DC Majara to all chiefs 9.11.1955). The ban would, in any case, probably not have made much difference. Even a pass to visit Ficksburg was superfluous if the Caledon River was not in flood. As Councillor Lepolesa reminded the 1952 session of the Basutoland National Council, 'women [could] just cross the river and go to the railway', thus making a mockery of the existing system of pass controls (LA, 'Proceedings': vol. II, 461–2). Women feeling they needed added security could simply go to the nearest farmer over the border. By the mid-1940s, and presumably earlier, 'some of the smaller farmers [were making] a kind of business of endorsing passes for women', for which they charged 2s 6d (UWL, 'Minutes': vol. 3, 2114).

The 1937 amendment to the Urban Areas Act represented a further attempt to regulate the movement of women. As in 1930 however, there was no proper mechanism of enforcement and it is difficult to escape the conclusion that the government was chary of any effort at compulsion following the resistance of the late 1910s (Wells, 1982: 258, 261–5). Women migrants were in any case quick to spot loopholes in the law. As the Native Affairs Manager of Benoni recorded ruefully in 1946, 'the average native has now got wise to the date of promulgation and when questioned he readily answers he came here before 1938'. In his view 'to all practical purposes the 1938 amendments were useless and obsolete' because women were not required to carry passes, which made prosecution 'extremely difficult and complicated' (BMA, NEAC minutes 11.1.1946, 9.4.1946). If anything, efforts to control the movements and activities of women diminished in the course of the Second World War, as the South African authorities relaxed the operation of the pass laws in an effort to ensure the loyalty of blacks, and this allowed Basotho women to flood into South Africa on an unprecedented scale. Not until the 1950s and early 1960s would effective measures be taken to curb this wholesale emigration, by which time a generation of Basotho women were securely ensconced on the Rand.

BASOTHO WOMEN AND BASOTHO MEN

The absence of state controls over the movement and activities of Basotho women seriously weakened the hold that men could exercise over them and created new tensions between the sexes. Across the African communities of the Rand, Basotho women acquired a reputation for being promiscuous and fickle. Questioned by the Vereeniging Riots Commission in 1937, Albert Mduli remarked: 'They do not stick to the men through whom they get their lodgers' permits. When a woman thinks she has sufficient money, she drives the man away and gets another' (CAD, NTS 6671, File 87/332).

Sotho migrant S. Pelanyane likewise recalls: 'Women at that time were enticed by money. If you had money you could have as many women as you wanted' (interview). The same stereotype recurs in the pages of Sesotho novels. Simon Majara writes in *Liakhela*, 'When a man is not bringing money home he is left and she goes to a new man' (17).

Of course what was promiscuity for Basotho men often represented independence for Basotho women. This independence seems in many instances to have been consciously asserted, and drew its strength from two principal sources. The first was Basotho women's experience of poverty, abandonment and neglect. The second was the independent income that could be earned from brewing and prostitution. Most Basotho women migrants had come to South Africa in a last desperate effort to save their marriages and find their men. Once finally rejected, many seem to have resolved never again to become wholly dependent on men. Beer-brewing and other informal income-generating activities provided this opportunity. Women made a point of keeping this money – which in the 1950s could amount to £10–£20 a week – for themselves; with this they could support their families independently of men. Thus one woman interviewed, M. F., saved money because 'in the end she knew she would come back to Basutoland'. Like most other brewers she also joined a *mahodisane* group (a rotating credit association). Three women participated in her group, paying £10 a time, which provided the necessary insurance against misfortunes like illness, arrest or deportation (interview). The grasping hands of men were kept well away.

A certain section of Basotho women were, nevertheless, on any reckoning, promiscuous. The experiences that had brought them to the town seem to have bred in them immensely contradictory attitudes and emotions. Despair and depression about the collapse of their marriages mingled with exhilaration at the new freedom of the towns. Men were alternately solicited and rejected, their company invited, their authority spurned. This behaviour and these attitudes were in a sense distilled in the *famo* dances that many urban Basotho women attended. Coplan writes:

According to numerous eye witnesses, the *famo* was almost defiantly suggestive. Women made shaking and thrusting movements with their shoulders, hips and bosoms, while lifting their flared skirts. The dancers wore no underwear but instead 'had painted rings around the whole area of their sex, a ring they called "stoplight"....' Men dancing alongside or seated against the walls chose the women they wanted and took them into the back for intercourse (1985: 98).

Maliehe Khoeli describes famo in similar terms: 'When women dance they jump and twist, lift their dresses about their waists and expose their underwear. Then men would come and produce their sexual organs which they called picks' (interview). M. R., a beer-brewer in Apex squatter camp near Benoni, likewise recalls: 'Women would dance around men, then lift up their dresses so that men would have sight of the panties or even their private parts.... Men would obviously be enticed. There would be hush-hush business taking place. Some would vanish as couples. Others would stand in the corners of houses in the dark. It was "Thagiso"' (interview). P. M. and C. Maguta, who lived in Benoni location in the early 1940s, remember miners from neighbouring mines outbidding each other to buy dances with these women, a practice which could easily degenerate into fights (interview).

Coplan describes *famo* as 'a cathartic moral comment on social problems' and cites the experience of Adelina who attended *famo* in Vereeniging and Kroonstad. She explained:

When I was deeply depressed and worried, in order to express myself and feel contented ... I went to the shebeen to sing these things. I had gone [to town] to visit my husband and I found him but we were separated. I suffered a lot because of that. So I had to go to these places and get some joy out of life and unburden myself. Others came for similar reasons, and to share their feelings with others (1985: 101).

Basotho men did not necessarily submit tamely to this provocative behaviour by women. Individual reactions would often involve assaults on women by their male partners, but there was also a more collective form of response articulated through the Ma Rashea gangs. This had an almost schizophrenic character. On the one hand the promiscuity of women seems to have been taken by gang members as justification for their simply seizing women by force. Simon Majara records in *Liakhela*: 'If they find a man walking with a beautiful woman they say "Here is the woman I have been looking for;" then they take her by force and sjambok her until she submits' (45). Ex-members of the Ma Rashea confirm the practice. Ex-gang leader Maliehe Khoeli recalls that 'The Russians used to say, "This is my wife of years that I have been looking for,"' adding that he himself prohibited the practice if the couple had been married by cattle (interview). Khoeli's attitude was nevertheless not shared by many Ma Rashea. When ex-member Nthodi was asked whether such treatment of women was an expression of moral censure against irregular marriages, he gave the purely instrumental reply that it was simply because Basotho women in towns did not enjoy the protection of a chief or male kin (interview).

On the other hand women living with Ma Rashea men were expected to conform to an entirely different code of conduct. If one absconded with another man she would be recaptured by the gang and mercilessly beaten. Again Majara writes: 'They seized women, but if your wife had gone with another man because of his wealth or something you could get them to go and get them back. By so doing they stopped prostitution. Many women began to stick to their husbands despite riches and wealth' (1972: 60–2). 'Me M. R. provides a somewhat different emphasis but makes a similar point: 'It wouldn't be defection as such, but I suppose love would be the cause, or at times a woman is not satisfied with the way she is being treated by the man.' Once caught: 'You will be ordered to take your belongings with you, and they will chase you all the way while beating you. At times you reach home dead. These men were terrible' (interview). S. Pelanyane confirms the reprisals in even more chilling detail:

She got beaten up by all the members. You see, I would be tightened with a band on my waist so that it tends to have a tail and be ordered to run and she runs after me and I must make it a point that she doesn't catch up with me while running. They would be beating her up so as to catch up with me and I wouldn't stop whatever. If I did I would also be beaten. But I had a whistle with me. If I felt she had had it I would then blow it and that would be an order to stop (interview).

Men went to extreme lengths to establish control over women, and still all too often failed. The efforts of the central government were likewise abortive until it resorted to draconian legislation to impose passes on women and deport illegal women migrants in the 1950s and 1960s. Only then was the rebellion of Basotho women temporarily and incompletely quelled.

CONCLUSION

This chapter has attempted to weave together a number of connected themes. It demonstrates that particular areas of southern Africa contributed disproportionately to the flow of women to the Rand. It suggests that this pattern was the product of the uneven impact of proletarianisation and labour migrancy and the specific constitution of the internal structures of the societies concerned. It also indicates the intimate connection between these groups of women and the illicit brewing of liquor, and focuses on the late 1930s as the time when the municipal and central authorities attempted to gain some control over the process of black urbanisation by controlling the brewing of liquor. The chapter suggests that control over women proved unattainable in this period, mainly because they were not obliged to carry passes, and that this freedom was the direct result of past struggles over passes and the potential for large-scale resistance revealed in other, contemporary collisions with women. Lack of governmental control over women in both Basutoland and South Africa also weakened the control of Basotho men over Basotho women, and had important repercussions on Basotho migrant culture in the towns.

10

Devout domesticity? A century of African women's Christianity in South Africa[1]

DEBORAH GAITSKELL

By at least the turn of the century, African churchwomen across the denominations and throughout South Africa were becoming active in distinctive, often uniformed, Christian female organisations. In the 1950s an important sociological study of these church groups, perhaps somewhat extravagantly, described them as 'the oldest, largest and most enduring and cohesive not only of all African women's organisations, but of all African organisations in South Africa' (Brandel-Syrier, 1962: 97). This early, widespread mobilisation and solidarity in *manyanos* (unions) – a Xhosa term for the Methodist groups and frequently used of the phenomenon as a whole – constitute an important part of the social history of African women's changing ideological, economic and religious roles.

African churchwomen's zealous evangelism and fundraising provided a critical back-up and growth point for local congregations, but by and large the women came together explicitly as *mothers*. Particularly in the eyes of missionary supervisors, such organisations had a vital part to play in safeguarding female chastity, marital fidelity, and maternal and domestic responsibilities. Accordingly these groups provide a window onto the ideological debates and economic conflicts that clustered around Christian concepts of sexuality, marriage and family as they were being imposed and self-imposed in the growing Christianised African community. As already pointed to in earlier chapters, obvious tensions emerge between the indigenous and mission sex–gender systems. In these organisations struggles over sexuality between older and younger African women can be discerned, together with conflicts over family life between the ruling and the dominated classes, mediated through mission and philanthropic activists.

The evidence strongly suggests, however, that these women's organisations, with their entrenched and fervent tradition of revivalist-style praying and preaching, must equally be seen as a demonstration of the enthusiastic, if necessarily gender-segregated, response of certain, mostly uneducated, African women to Christianity. Undeniably, of course – and here the spiritual and domestic aspects of *manyanos* reinforce one another – part of the appeal of the new message and the community it fostered was the priority and support it offered to motherhood in a time of economic and social upheaval (see Gaitskell, 1983: 249).

This chapter looks first, briefly, at African women's response to the coming of Christianity and some of the ways in which domesticity was enmeshed with conversion in late-nineteenth-century rural South Africa. The second section focuses on the growth of women's associations in the twentieth century in the very different urban setting of the Witwatersrand. In the third section, some ways in which Reef *manyanos* can be seen as subversive of domesticity are then suggested; while the fourth section points to the wider historical repercussions of such female mobilisation. The conclusion reasserts the importance of taking *manyanos* seriously as a religious phenomenon.

FEMALE CONVERSIONS AND CHRISTIAN HOMEMAKING: SOME BEGINNINGS

Missionaries to southern Africa settled first among the Xhosa and Tswana, in the 1820s; these were groups which eventually delivered a high proportion of converts. The southern Sotho and the Zulu, to whom the mission frontier advanced in the 1830s, likewise in time came into the churches in large numbers. From 1850 the Methodists were at work in the Orange Free State, while from 1860 German Lutherans laboured among the Pedi of the Transvaal (who remain the least Christianised today). By 1880 the new faith was relatively well established in most 'tribal' areas and still predominantly rurally orientated. Its literate African members were becoming teachers and, if male, pastors (Pauw, 1974: 416–21).

As regards the progress of different denominations of European origin, census figures from the twentieth century provide a rough guide to trends, although it has been suggested that such figures are usually inflated by about one-third for actual membership and one-half for active participation (De Gruchy, 1979: 240). (Churches vary in their understanding of membership, which makes the comparison of denominational as opposed to census figures unhelpful.) Thus just over a million Africans were reported as Christians in 1911, constituting just over a quarter (26,2 per cent) of the African population, whereas by 1946, over four million were enumerated as church members, more than half (52,6 per cent) of the total African population.

Whatever the admitted shortcomings of the census figures, the overwhelming importance of Methodists and Anglicans comes through: at a combined strength of 1 560 977 (over a million of them Methodist), they embraced well over a third of all African Christians (37,8 per cent) in 1946. The dominance of 'mission' churches of European and American origin also remains striking – despite the astonishing growth of the African independent churches in this century, they still accounted for less than a quarter of all Africans recorded as Christian in 1946.

What, regrettably, is not as easily uncovered is the gender breakdown of this church constituency. However, membership figures recorded by the women's groups (see below) give some idea of denominational and regional growth of committed adult women. What is also known is that with the increase in migrant labour from the late nineteenth century, laments at the depletion of male membership became a constant refrain from many rural churches. By the inter-war years Transkei Anglican missionaries were increasingly concerned at the disproportionate numbers of women and girls, as opposed to men and boys, who were being confirmed: 3 361 to 982 in that diocese in 1931, for example (SPG, *Report*, 1932).

The early stages of Christian missionary endeavour in South Africa have frequently been characterised as relatively unfruitful, with evangelists meeting indifference and hostility. Although far more detailed investigation is needed, in the Cape and Natal early converts were often already outcasts from 'traditional society' or came to mission stations because they offered a physical refuge or source of economic support away from the African community. Before the Cape and Natal Nguni were militarily broken and politically undermined, mission stations attracted, on the one hand, those seeking secular advantage in terms of employment, land, homes or material goods, together with outcasts, refugees and misfits on the other. It seems fair to say – though much more investigation is needed on this – that the self-improvers were mostly men, while, because of gender-specific life-crises, women featured prominently among the refugees.

It was aberrant for a woman in 'traditional' African society to live alone: as already described in earlier chapters, her productive labour and reproductive powers as daughter, wife or widow belonged to her father, husband or son. But the mission station provided an alternative set of protectors and an alternative economic base which made escape possible. The mission station was a magnet for young girls avoiding marriage (perhaps to rich old men, or pagans, or polygynists); for cast-off wives; or for widows escaping the levirate. Because on marriage Nguni women moved to live among their husband's kin, they were more isolated and vulnerable as strangers there, and mission stations could provide an escape from the malice of co-wives, accusations of witchcraft or the shame of barrenness (see Williams, 1959: 275–82 and Etherington, 1978: 95–9). It is important, though, to bear Etherington's point in mind – that it is often easier to identify why individuals came to a station than why they in due course sought baptism. It is also worth emphasising that the crucial generation of church expansion between the 1880s and the 1920s needs closer study, since school and church attendance spread far more widely then than in the pioneering conversion period (which hitherto has attracted most research).

Was it less threatening to African communities to lose their women, as opposed to their men, to the new faith? It could be said that while the conversion of runaway daughters posed a threat to paternal domestic control (and the gaining of bridewealth), male conversion – as anti-Christian chiefs well saw – constituted a greater political and military threat to chiefdoms. Further obstacles to male church membership were indigenous ideas of manliness associated with war and fighting, the herding activities of boys (which prevented them from attending Christian schools), and the strictures against polygyny. In addition, as household and community leaders, men were inevitably more involved in traditional ritual and ceremonial (Pauw, 1974: 422). So in a number of ways, women's relative powerlessness made them more open to conversion – and their Christianity might come under threat if it conflicted with traditional political and social mores and priorities.

This was exemplified in the life of one of the few early women converts who was not politically obscure and marginal, Emma Sandile. The daughter of a prominent Xhosa chief, she received Anglican baptism and education in the 1860s to prepare her for marriage to a politically important frontier chief sympathetic to Christianity, but pressure from his people, who refused to countenance his enforced monogamy, resulted in the marriage being called off. Sandile was furious that the new religion had stopped the marriage and eventually forced Emma to return to 'heathen' dress and marry a polygynist, rather than remain unmarried (Hodgson, 1987).

As other chapters in this volume make clear, Victorian Christianity offered a contradictory package to African women: a way of escape from some of the constraints of pre-Christian society and yet a firm incorporation into the domesticity and patriarchy of Christian family life. Nineteenth-century middle-class Christians from Britain and the United States were living through a revolution in and re-creation of their own domestic lives as a necessary basis for devout living (see Davidoff and Hall, 1987). The private female domain of the home, where women were dependent as wives and mothers, became increasingly separated from the public male world of work and independent citizenship. Viewed from this standpoint, African women seemed to be 'beasts of burden', 'slaves' working at their husbands' behest, because of their predominant role in agricultural production.

But it could be argued that there was an area of agreement between Victorian Christians and African communities as to the primacy of women's reproductive work. Despite the strand of mission thinking that stressed preparing girls for domestic service to settlers, a lifetime of wage labour seems not to have been the desired mission goal for female converts. African girls were seen as future spouses of Christian men, mothers of Christian children, makers of Christian homes. While not perfectly continuous with the precolonial economic centrality of women's fertility, as outlined by Guy in this volume, the mission emphasis on women as childbearers and homemakers overlapped in crucial ways with indigenous values.

Conversion was aimed at transforming the division of labour in African homes in order to fulfil these Victorian ideals of devout domesticity. As already described by Meintjes, when missionaries encouraged the adoption of the plough, the intention was that men should do far more of the 'heavy' farming seen as inappropriate for the more 'delicate' sex. This would free women to sew the clothes that betokened their new faith, and to create in exclusively monogamous homes a different, more 'companionable' type of conjugal relationship, one where the wife was 'helpmeet' rather than 'slave'. Thus Christian missionaries drew young African girls into their own domestic life, to learn about Christian womanhood and homemaking, both by hard work in service and by example. They set about eagerly encouraging their star pupils to pair off and fashion a new kind of marital companionship and Westernised home (Bean and Van Heyningen, 1983: 14, 25–7, 114, 125).

But the first women's prayer unions seem to have evolved not from explicit educational efforts through the schools but from regular devotional meetings held by missionary women with 'uneducated' adult African churchwomen. Sewing schools for adult women were a weekly feature of mission stations among the Tswana and Zulu, for example, from the 1830s, because to want to be 'dressed' or 'clothed' was synonymous with seeking Christian instruction or baptism. This widespread and significant emphasis on sewing probably acted from the first to bring women together in church groups – starting with the weekly sewing class – in a way that never happened to men. In this way, the gendered assumption that clothes were predominantly a female responsibility served to create a distinctive Christian female, as opposed to male, group solidarity across the denominations.

From meeting the practical need for clothing, women moved on to share their faith both with each other and with non-churchgoers. Already from at least the 1880s in the eastern Cape, missionary wives were bringing groups of baptised African women together in associations that met regularly for the sort of unstructured times of shared 'testimony', exposition of biblical verses and extemporaneous prayer that have been the life-blood of church meetings for thousands of African women over the past century. Such gatherings explicitly aimed by the early 1900s to help women in their new responsibilities as Christian wives and mothers. But they also seem, as in the case of meetings conducted by Mrs Waters in Engcobo from the 1880s on into the 1920s, to have acted from the very beginning as an outlet for energetic and successful female evangelisation of 'heathen' women, and to have been as well a vehicle for the denunciation of 'native beer' and exhortations to total abstinence. The women's help in reporting and visiting the sick has also long been an appreciated feature of such female bands. So while white supervisors compared these gatherings with 'Mothers' Meetings' back in England, which similarly provided tea and buns for refreshment after some uplifting home-related talk, their original rationale appears to have had four aspects: devotionalism (the prayer meetings), evangelism, temperance, and visiting the sick.

DOMESTICITY AND PRAYER UNIONS ON THE WITWATERSRAND

At the turn of the century, African Christianity was still predominantly rural. However, particularly once the Transvaal became a British colony after the South African War, urban centres like the Witwatersrand, with its large population of African male migrants on the mines, came to be seen as strategically important and potentially vital growth points for the church. By the 1920s, over twenty-six missionary societies were at work in Johannesburg.

Missionaries soon realised that it was not simply a matter of reaching male migrants. A few migrants had come with families while others had been followed to town by their wives; in addition, 'unattached' women increasingly came to the Reef seeking a livelihood. As a result, by the 1930s the male–female ratio on the Reef was 4,32: 1, whereas back in the 1890s it had been more like 10: 1. Of the 106 977 African females on the Witwatersrand in 1936, half those over 10 years old were officially returned as 'gainfully occupied'. Some 90 per cent of these 42 733 'employed' women were domestic servants (Union of South Africa, Sixth Census 1936: IX, xiii, xviii). The importance of this area of work for the churches is clear, and through hostels for domestic servants, which provided housework training and job placement, women missionaries attempted a Christian input (Gaitskell, 1979).

The two other major income-earning activities for African women in Johannesburg, especially in the inter-war years, were not recorded in the official statistics – though possibly some washerwomen were enumerated as domestic servants. They were laundry work brought home from white suburbs, and illicit liquor-brewing, particularly for sale to male migrants. Married churchwomen seem to have done the former and inveighed against the latter, as in this example:

It's almost impossible for us to live decently in Johannesburg…. The tempta-
tion to sell this stuff [beer] is too strong. All the women around here are
making a lot of money; buying pianos and gramophones and silk dresses.
Because I am a Christian and try to go straight, I have to stand here day after
day and kill myself washing (quoted in Phillips, 1930: 136).

The long-entrenched use of Thursday afternoons for *manyano* meetings may even have been related to the rhythm of the washing week:
bundles were fetched on Monday, washed on Tuesday and ironed on
Wednesday, freeing women for group prayer on Thursdays.

As already discussed in chapter 9, the beer trade was central to the
social and economic survival of many Reef African women (Hellmann, 1948). This gave the strong temperance strand in *manyanos* a
different twist from that in the rural areas. All three churches focused
on in this chapter forbade prayer women to brew, drink or sell 'native
beer' or other alcohol, and large annual interdenominational temperance conventions were held on the Reef under American Board
auspices in the late 1930s. Resolutions on liquor legislation were
passed by the Methodist *manyano*, which seems not to have taken a
stand on other inter-war questions of government policy.

But for both brewers and washers, a major incentive for working
from home in the yards and locations was that they could keep an eye
on their children at the same time, whereas female domestic workers
invariably lived on their employers' premises and were not allowed
to have their children with them. Given the poverty of African
families, a middle-class model of economically dependent Christian
wifehood was impracticable: without whatever earnings women and
children could make, families could not have survived on low male
wages alone. Many women on the Reef, of course, as in urban working-class Britain, moved in and out of various part-time and full-time
jobs as family needs permitted. Yet the temperance rule of prayer
unions certainly worked to reinforce the sexual division of labour
deemed appropriate in Christian families: no devout mother could be
a prosperous brewer – rather, husbands provided the main household
earnings for wives and children dependent on them.

As the mission apparatus of schools and churches spread in town,
the southern Transvaal began to see the emergence of the kind of
women's organisations recently started in rural areas, with similar
concerns for married women's domestic roles and responsibilities.
However, for the three most prominent prayer movements in
'mission' churches in the Johannesburg area in the first half of this
century (Anglican, Methodist and American Board), despite striking
underlying continuities, the domestic slant came in slightly different
ways.

Mrs S. Gqosho, wife of the African minister in Potchefstroom, started the Wesleyan Methodist prayer union in the southern Transvaal in 1907. She brought a small group of women together to pray 'for their families and for the common unity and for their sins', as well as for protection for husbands and sons working on the mines, and for the uprooting of witchcraft and superstition. The *manyano*'s basic objects were 'to cultivate the habits of praying and to consolidate Christianity among the folks' (*Manyano*, 1959). But after the wife of the white chairman of the District was brought in from 1910 as president, the focus on the domestic virtues of the devout wife and mother sharpened. Mrs Burnet urged the delegates at the 1915 convention to 'show the power of their religion in the way they care for their husbands – many of whom are not Christian – and in an increased effort to train their children for the Lord' (*Foreign Field*, February 1916: 133). Her concern for simple hygiene and propriety was reflected in the constitution in such elementary rules, later dropped, as:

(a) Sweep and clean the house every day. (b) Keep your things and your family clean and good. (c) If you have children teach them the Christian faith. Do not let them run naked (AP, 'African Women's Prayer Union (*Manyano*) Rules').

Clearly, more than a gender dimension is involved here – the patronising tone suggests a marked class and race divide. There are repeated instances in mission work in Johannesburg where the echoes of middle-class church activities and attitudes towards the urban working class in Britain can be heard. Mrs Burnet's daughter set out the Union's aims more formally in 1913, with a flavour of Victorian moral self-improvement:

1. To secure the due recognition of the place of a Christian home in a people's life.
2. The inculcation of the moral duties of industry, honesty, truthfulness, cleanliness and kindness by example and precept in the home.
3. The training of the younger women and girls to take their places as Christian in the national life.
4. The encouragement of individual Missionary effort among women not yet evangelised.
5. The consideration of any questions that affect the life of the native home and the morals of the people (*Foreign Field*, April 1913: 251).

Even at this stage, it was probably the fourth aim of evangelism, along with prayer itself, which was the most meaningful to the African members, as accounts below of zestful evangelisation and indefatigable praying at conferences seek to illustrate. Nevertheless, domestic education was a perennial emphasis, exemplified by the sessions at the 1923 conference on 'Health in the Home' and 'Duty of a Christian Mother to Her Children' (*Transvaal Methodist*, November 1923).

As for the second most important church on the Reef, work among Anglican women was pioneered by Deaconess Julia Gilpin from 1908. (She also started two other key female ventures in Johannesburg, St Agnes' School, Rosettenville, and a hostel for domestic servants.) After some preliminary weekly meetings – a short talk from her followed by some hymns and then prayers in which the women joined – she founded a society for communicants, to help them, she said, lead a better life. The stress was on building up regular devotional habits and a Christian standard of life, for conditions in the mine locations rendered it 'almost impossible for a decent woman to retain her purity and self-respect' since so many couples living there were in fact not married (USPG, WW Reports Africa, Dss Julia, 1908). (It must be remembered that before 1914 at any rate, the Witwatersrand seems to have had a number of relatively loosely controlled mine locations, as opposed to compounds proper, where some sort of 'family life' was possible: 53 mines had 3 784 women and nearly as many children in their married quarters in 1913–14, according to Moroney, 1982: 265.) In fact, with time, branches of the 'Women's Help Society' – they only linked up with the Mothers' Union from 1938 – existed in church congregations both on mine locations and in the variety of central town 'yards' and urban locations along the Reef as far as Springs, as well as in southern Transvaal centres like Potchefstroom, Vereeniging and Heidelberg. The majority of the early members had not been to school, and as the mission staff ended up too stretched to do more than visit most groups once every few months, these groups evolved in their own way under African leadership, replicating the revivalistic style of other churches.

As we have seen above, the Anglican women's society was meant to help married women 'retain their purity and self-respect'. The emphasis on 'purity', but this time in the sense of premarital chastity of teenagers, surfaced too in the third most important Protestant church in the Johannesburg area. The American Board Mission (ABM), which was Congregational, had its heartland in Natal among the Zulu. There, in 1912, a women's revivalist prayer movement called *Isililo* ('wailing') sprang up after African men at a church gathering accused their wives of being lax in supervising their children's courtship practices: gladly accepting gifts from their daughters' lovers and giving them 'opportunities for privacy' in return. Women admitted and repented of their shortcomings in this regard and then enlisted others on the new Christian basis that it was mothers who were responsible for their children's immorality (Mbili, 1962). The ABM's 'mothers' meetings' on the Reef, however, seem to have linked up with the Natal *Isililo* only in the early 1920s, and talks on 'purity' to Reef *Isililo* women were given mostly by women missionaries.

The other churches were also wrestling with the question of control of teenagers in the years before the First World War. Discussion about children at the 1912 Transvaal Methodist *manyano* convention, for instance, centred 'especially on the care of girls, who so often fall into evil ways' (*Foreign Field*, April 1913: 253). At this point the Anglicans were running penitents' classes for unmarried mothers. By the end of the war, their women's society was also trying to help mothers guide and direct their unruly daughters. In all three churches, special associations for unmarried girls were set up under the protective aegis of the mothers' organisations, to guard them from 'moral downfall'.

As more research is done on the beginnings of such associations in other regions of South Africa, this issue is bound to surface again. In Mothers' Union records for the Grahamstown diocese, for example, there is reference to a conference held in 1910, at the request of African women, to inaugurate the Union in Keiskammahoek. 'Very earnest was the Address about two weaknesses in Native Home Life viz, the lack of obedience among children, and of purity among the younger people.' The following year it was reported with satisfaction that the 'native people seem to have reached so simply and straightly the dominating idea of the Mothers' Union – united, prayerful guidance in the difficult task of the up-bringing of our children by precept and by example' (MU, 1910, 1911).

I have argued that, while the ABM women – uniquely, it seems – founded their movement on this issue, adolescent female sexual mores were not customarily the responsibility of mothers: it was the missionaries who preached that it should be. They themselves came from a culture which was laying increasing emphasis on female chastity and the almost exclusive identification of 'morality' with 'sexual purity'. There is plenty of evidence that while African mothers despaired of controlling their daughters and preventing premarital sex-play (allowed, even approved, among the non-Christian Nguni) and pregnancy in the very changed social and economic circumstances of the early twentieth century, they resisted being expected to give their daughters sex education and worse – having such matters talked about in church. But the burdensome and painful responsibilities of motherhood were at the heart of *manyano* spirituality (Gaitskell, 1982).

The *manyanos* are also well known for the distinctive uniforms members from different denominations wear. Although much more research is needed, the history of these movements makes it clear that the choice of outfit and the deep significance given to it, together with the complicated gradations of status denoted by small variations and additions to the official dress, are all traceable back to the women themselves.

By the first or second decade of the century each denomination was evolving its own uniform, which in many cases became standardised and more formally adopted in the 1920s. Complex cultural borrowings were at work: the Natal Methodist women from whom Mrs Gqosho of Potchefstroom took her inspiration, allegedly modelled their red, black and white uniform on British redcoats (just as the ABM Volunteers aped Boer War Volunteer dress). But later a more 'spiritual' interpretation of Methodist garb gained a currency it still retains: black skirts signifying sin, red blouses the saving blood of Christ and white hats the women's resultant purity. By the late 1920s, when the Anglican women had nearly 50 branches of their women's society in the Transvaal, they were bound to a uniform of black skirts and headscarves with white jackets (*TSR*, January 1927: 2). This seems to have originated in the eastern Cape and was probably influenced by the habits of the nuns who supervised some early groups there.

White mission supervisors tried to standardise dress – sometimes, as with the Methodists, in the teeth of opposition – and then found themselves vainly criticising the members for 'over-emphasis[ing] the non-essentials, such as badges, uniform, rules for absentees' (*The Watchman*, February 1946: 6). A Natal missionary primly observed, in a comment which underlined the domestic aim that was uppermost in white minds, 'Considering the multiplicity of "uniforms" seen in Native country, members of the Mothers' Union would be well advised to make their homes distinctive, and keep their clothes commonplace' (*SWM Journal*, April 1936: 8). Just as special church dress, I suggest below, marked out the devout at a stage when Western dress *per se* had lost its spiritual significance, so there were also periodic worries about prayer union sanctimoniousness – about a sense of superiority over other women which could lead to their being even stricter on one another than the general church disciplinary machinery provided for.

Among the first converts, the adoption of Western clothing signified commitment to new religious beliefs. As such clothing became more widely available, however, it could no longer be assumed to be an outward sign of inward spiritual grace. Categories blurred once more. For this reason church uniforms ought to be interpreted, perhaps, as the reassertion of a distinctive Christian dress, proclaiming the wearer's spiritual allegiance. Being 'bloused' by the prayer union was a solemn milestone of religious commitment and a reward for upright living. For women it also advertised marital respectability: membership and the right to wear the prized uniform could be withdrawn for marital infidelity. Hence those who were seen wending their way in crisply starched uniforms to Thursday afternoon meetings were proclaiming their conformity to the new ideology of Christian domesticity.

There is yet another way in which prayer unions and Christian notions of home life interacted. The sociability and mutual support offered by the prayer group should also be seen as a desired supplement to the isolation and monotony of responsibilities in the nuclear family that was propagated by the missionaries. The Christian idea of domesticity ensured that it was primarily women who would face all the difficulties of the home; but with its stress on individualism and monogamy, Christianity cut them off from older, communal supports. Although southern Africa has no tradition of formal women's groups of the kind that operated in West Africa, women in precolonial African society did perform many daily tasks – collecting wood and water, thatching grass, stamping mealies, etc. – in a group with other women and girls. They also came together in more formalised agricultural work groups and in leisure activities such as dancing or singing (which was sometimes combined with the praise poetry that, I suggest below, seems a precursor of the *manyano* style of oral testimony). In Nguni communities particularly, where women married out of their lineage and went to live with their husbands away from their families of birth, solidarity with other women was something of a necessity. Now, in changed circumstances, other Christian women substituted for kin at times of crisis, such as sickness and death, and provided mutual care. Hence the request of one *manyano* woman to her group to 'give me a hand to pick up the burden', and the resolve of another in trouble: 'I must get some strength from the mothers in this chain' (Pauw, 1975: 96).

FROM DOMESTICITY TO PRAYING AND PREACHING

But to portray these remarkable, long-lived prayer unions merely in terms of some normative Western family ideology or female group therapy is to risk missing the zealous and eloquent spiritual experience at their heart. That at least is what the historical record suggests. It is true that the accounts from the 1950s stress an atmosphere of weeping, sighing and mutual loud commiseration as women spoke about their troubles regarding children, family, sickness and death, as well as their struggle for survival. The impression created is of a cathartic 'self-induced frenzy of unpremeditated talking' (Brandel-Syrier, 1962: 15, 34–9; Brandel, 1955: 181–2). Insufficient evidence about weekly meetings prior to 1940 makes it hard to gauge how widespread such a style of lamentation was in the earlier period. However, reports of conventions convey, in contrast, a sense of vigorous enthusiasm and conscientious organisational upbuilding, even though women also wanted to be moved and inspired – which they frequently were, by each other's oratory.

The eventual routinised 'style' of *manyanos* across the denominations seems to have had its roots in late-nineteenth-century pietistic revivalist preaching, which sought to induce a kind of mourning in its hearers: they had to bewail and confess their sins, then publicly commit themselves to a fresh spiritual start. The African churches encountered this emotional type of service – highly participatory, preferably lasting all night – partly through visiting British and American evangelists in the Cape and Natal in the 1860s and 1890s (Mills, 1975: 25–7, 298 n.6; Christofersen, 1967: 93–4). As leading African Christian men translated the revivalist message into the vernacular, they picked up the oratorical style in the process. Medium and message took deep root in Nguni communities. In the last quarter of the nineteenth century, Scottish missionaries among the Mfengu found that 'from time to time a wave of spiritual conviction and surrender moved the district and swept considerable numbers in to the membership of the Church. These occasions often followed prayer meetings which were held by the people themselves and were carried on throughout the night' (Livingstone, 1918: 42–3). Fifty years ago, D. D. T. Jabavu characterised African Christianity in general as 'devoted to the simplicities of religion: prayer meetings, hymn-singing, assimilation of Scripture texts and the constant calling of others unto repentance' (1932: 112–13).

Whatever its exact diffusion, the all-night revival service-cum-prayer meeting spread widely, being reported as far apart as St Cuthbert's in the Transkei in 1896 and north-west of Pietersburg in the Transvaal in 1905. In the 1920s Transkei Anglicans used revival services as their main means of attempting to convert the 'heathen'. But wailing became entrenched in women's groups, it may not be fanciful to suggest, because weeping was deemed culturally more appropriate for women and wailing was how women behaved customarily at Nguni funerals. *Isililo* ('wailing'), the striking term the ABM women chose for their movement (and clung to when the activist American supervisors wanted them to call it the 'Women's Welfare Group of the American Board' instead), is used of the protracted ritual keening of women after the burial of the deceased. It is associated, reports an anthropologist, with the helplessness and submission expected of women at such a time of sorrow (Ngubane, 1977: 84, 93–4). (Men traditionally ended mourning by an aggressive act of ritual hunting.) Throughout black Africa, wailing is regarded as typically female, and women are invariably the singers of stylised funeral laments (Finnegan, 1970: 147–8).

But all was not submission and lament at the turn of the century, and it is in this respect that the curious subversiveness of the *manyanos* shows itself. Indigenous male revival movements sprouted in Natal among Methodists as early as the 1870s, in Edendale (*Unzondelelo*), and in the ABM in the 1890s at Umtwalume (the 'Volunteers'), and expressed a new, self-confident African Christian expansionism (Hewson, 1950: 76–80; Christofersen, 1967: 92). The desire for greater responsibility and autonomy led to breakaways into independency among the Cape Presbyterians and Anglicans. Some 15 to 30 years later, in a delayed echoing (it appears to me) of this demand for more evangelistic opportunity and autonomy, laywomen and ministers' wives held conferences and preached for converts. In a sense, prayer unions constituted a creative, self-confident impulse which generally stopped short of a breakaway into independence, partly because women could not found churches themselves if they wished to replicate mission models (which were heavily male-dominated), and partly because their leadership was generally not thwarted in the fierce way the new African ministry of the 1890s was. Women's marginality gave them a kind of freedom to experiment and learn from other denominations, making Christianity their own, because there was not such a fixed conception in each denomination of female as opposed to male ministry.

However, there were clashes between 1915 and 1930 with white women presidents and with white and black clergy and councils, who sought, with some success, to restrain what the African women would have liked to make a more unfettered autonomy. On the Reef, for example, white church leaders made sure they took titular and constitutional control of the unions. In 1915, in one location, Anglican women prayer-meeting members 'were reported to be praying that no white priest or white woman worker should come to them at all' (*Pilot Letters*, 1915: 32). Resentful African Methodist women were repeatedly reminded by their white president in the 1920s that each prayer group still came under the control of the local 'Leaders' Meeting' (*Manyano*, 1959).

The Transvaal Methodist *manyano* acquired its first African woman president by 1937, whereas the Mothers' Union, which had a small number of white members as well (in congregationally segregated groups), only obtained an African vice-president in 1948 and an African president in 1974. When examining the degree of organisational autonomy which African women were able to build up and retain despite the long-lasting presidency of white women missionaries, it is vital to bear in mind the growing number and geographical spread of these groups. Mission supervisors frequently commented that they could not possibly attend each weekly meeting personally, so in most cases these were left to the women to run themselves, under the leadership of the wives of the African clergy. In the case of the very active and well-staffed Anglican 'settlements' in Sophiatown and Orlando in the 1930s, the staff of white single women concentrated their efforts on children almost exclusively. In part this was because African wives did not see the unmarried among 'overseas' mission personnel as having much authority in what was still a very family-focused spiritual movement. Again, this served to reinforce African women's autonomy.

Considerable enterprise, vitality and self-confidence were involved in spreading the gospel, and the women's actions do not fit a cosy image of secluded homemakers. The *Isililo* grew because a group of women, led by a Mrs Gobhozi and a Mrs Kaula (though joined for part of the way at least by some men), walked, 'singing hymns and stopping for the night on the way ... like vagrant wanderers because of this great gospel of Isililo', to six ABM mission stations in turn (Mbili, 1962). Mrs Gqosho, founder of the Transvaal Methodist *manyano*, spread it by holding revivals throughout the District, followed by a convention in 1908 arranged (evidently to the admiring surprise of the white male superintendent) entirely by the women themselves. They brought 'their own food or money, and many of them slept on the floor of the church' (*Transvaal Methodist*, October 1938: 3–4).

The Methodist annual conferences continued to be impressively organised affairs, lasting a week at a time. They were only kept from growing beyond their peak of 600 women (at Evaton, in 1920) by the firm (and resented) hand of white supervisors, who introduced quotas to keep numbers down. Women, some with babies, travelled hundreds of miles, sometimes taking up to five days and using a variety of forms of transport – though the railways were vital to feasibility – to reach these gatherings. Mutual greetings provided 'a time of great hilarity, and of joyous, affectionate expression' (*Foreign Field*, September 1921: 233). The contagious enthusiasm of the large female assemblies, unattainable in small isolated church groups, the enjoyment of sociability, the sense of pride and freedom in setting off for conferences in style, as women together, all come through in the convention descriptions. As an ABM missionary wrote – somewhat patronisingly – of the *Isililo* annual gathering in Natal in the 1920s: 'This is their very first effort at self expression in the way of an organisation they have ever attempted you know, I am sure a lot of the delicious feelings of Woman's rights give spice to the occasion. You should see those Officers sitting up front, in their white caps and blouses and pink ribbon badges ...' (ABC: 15.4 v.48, Amy Cowles to Miss Lamson, 22.4.1926).

Although Anglican conferences on the Reef were never as big as the Transvaal Methodist ones (up to 200 women met for two days), in parts of rural Natal and the Transkei gatherings of a hundred or more women (who might walk 30 miles to get there) would meet in annual conferences for a couple of days.

In 1919 a group of seven Johannesburg Primitive Methodist women raised £25 and went by train to Aliwal North and Zastron – a round trip of a thousand miles – to thank the church for its support and hold revival services. The female secretary zestfully described the effective female preaching: Mrs Kumalo's exposition of a text 'became a very strong sermon', while Mrs Tsewo's the next day was 'a piercing sword to the people'. She also counted heads of the new members enrolled as enthusiastically as any male church leader with the Methodist obsession with numerical tabulation: 'Total from Saturday evening to Monday evening we got 33' (MMS 1180, A. A. Kidwell, unsigned letter 24.8.1919).

It was also crucial to *manyano* formation in the Transvaal that the number of ordained African ministers grew substantially among the Methodists after the South African War (from 17 in 1902 to 35 in 1908), for prayer unions have long been dominated by ministers' wives. Interestingly, colonial Rhodesia provides a comparable example of both the role of emotional revivalism and the importance of ministers' wives in the foundation of the equivalent female prayer unions there (Muzorewa, 1975). A growing number of ministers or clergy invariably meant a commensurate increase in spouses, who came to be regarded as 'ordained' themselves and found in *manyanos* a vital outlet for their new leadership status. (A Methodist history singled out and remarked on the 'uproar' from ministers' wives when the highest *manyano* office went to a 'lay woman'.)

This is one of many ways in which relatively high levels of female school attendance from the very start of mission education, plus intermarriage among pupils at elite schools, seem to have contributed to the scale of *manyano* formation. *Manyanos* also had committees, secretaries and treasurers, both locally and regionally; like church life everywhere for men, they gave women experience of more formal corporate organising and record keeping.

There are only scattered references to Methodist women wanting to preach to the church as a whole, but those who did faced opposition and lack of training until the 1940s; in contrast, thousands of men were able to channel their oratorical eloquence as 'local preachers', a vital arm of Methodist expansion. *Manyanos* provided a segregated sphere of female spirituality. It is frequently remarked that Thursday is the women's day, as Sunday is the preacher's. Women clearly *did* want to preach. As an Anglican nun wrote from the Transkei in 1916:

We have been making great efforts to guide and control the zeal of the Christian women who were described by one of themselves as 'thirsty for (the work of) preaching'. There is no need for paid Bible women here, for all the women want to preach, either to the heathen or to each other. Their zeal is excellent, but their knowledge is not always equal to it, and many of them are possessed by the idea that souls can only be won through noisy ranting (S. Cuthbert's Mission, 1916).

And yet even that supposedly safe separate arena of religious enthusiasm was regarded as unacceptable by African men. The fund-raising contribution of the women was much prized but their desire for financial and organisational autonomy was frequently viewed with ambivalence. In the early 1920s there was a sharp division of opinion among black Anglican clergy on the Reef as to whether women's all-night prayer meetings should be blessed or banned. (The men did not like their wives being out all night.)

The impropriety of the hour also perturbed women missionaries, for it did not conform to their view of appropriate female behaviour. 'Emotionalism' was an important bogey too: 'one hesitates to quench and discourage their eagerness to pray ... yet it is so much mixed up with a sort of excitement and it is so bad for women, mostly mothers of families, to get into the habit of being out all night' (USPG, E, 'Work amongst the native women in Johannesburg and the Reef', 1920).

White Anglicans (male and female) despaired at the African preference for praying 'corporately and vocally, not as we do, individually and silently' (*Cape to the Zambezi*, May 1937: 27). Activist Americans characteristically lost patience at times with the women's attachment to 'praying and preaching', because they wouldn't 'get down to business' and take '*definite* steps for bettering their home condition' (ABC: 15.4 v.48, Amy Cowles to Miss Lamson, 22.4.1926).

The appeal of 'praying and preaching', I argue, should also be seen in the light of the vitality of indigenous traditions of oral expression in which women shared – oratory, folk tales and praise poems vigorously 'performed' to a convivially responding group (Finnegan, 1970: 184, 91; Scheub, 1975; Gunner, 1979) – as well as of spoken, corporate, spontaneous prayer (Shorter, 1975: 8), and democratic public participation. What is vital to realise is that lively participation in a *manyano* meeting required no special church training, not even literacy. Women learnt their own hymns off by heart, spoke extemporaneously on biblical passages introduced by someone else and prayed spontaneously about immediate and personal needs. They did not need to be able to read or have formal educational qualifications to contribute. Their own eloquence and fervour could give them enough authority (although formal leadership was in later years invariably dominated by clergy wives). Indeed, the first women's groups began among an older generation which had lost out on school. As a woman testified at a convention in the 1920s: 'I cannot read the Book. I took the red blouse and daily I am out preaching to the heathen' (AP, Mrs Allcock to her family, 15.10.1924).

On account of the customary authority of grandmothers (and mothers-in-law, who prevented their young daughters-in-law from joining the Mothers' Union in its early days in the Transkei, for example), that age-group often dominated women's groups. Similarly, the room for acclamation as a good preacher, even if the woman was old and uneducated, helped entrench 'praying and preaching', so much so that by the 1950s Anglican disquiet, not only in Johannesburg as noted by Brandel-Syrier (1962: 92–5) but also in places like the Transkei, came to a head once more. Meetings teaching more 'practical' homemaking skills were widely introduced (not without difficulty), in part in the hope of attracting younger, 'more modern' women to the Mothers' Union, and uniforms were not to be worn (though in practice they were retained). Certainly the devotional style which I am enthusiastically characterising as the authentic appropriation of Christianity by African women in the early years of this century was being condemned by African Mothers' Union workers in the 1960s: 'they cannot read or write, the only thing they can do is to preach and pray', read a typical regretful report on one group in the Transkei (MU, 1962).

Despite the inter-war refrain from white missionaries about the Methodist *manyano* – 'The possibilities are great, but the need for effective and appropriate guidance is also great' – the response of white female Methodist supervisors to the uninhibited spiritual style of the movement was invariably enthusiastic, or at least tranquil in the knowledge that Methodism had a history of such emotionalism. It is certainly Methodist influence that has permeated the other denominations. At the week-long Transvaal Methodist conventions, prayer 'was the supreme business for which the delegates came' (*Foreign Field*, September 1921: 232). At the regular four services each day (ranging from dawn prayer through evangelistic, temperance and testimony meetings to memorial and communion services), women from more reticent English backgrounds were struck by the African women's eloquence: 'These native women have a wonderful power in prayer and they use it to the full. The meetings for testimony were also very striking' (*Foreign Field*, April 1913: 253). 'Unlike many Christian friends of a lighter hue, there was no unwillingness to speak. On the contrary, no sooner did one sister finish her story, than two or three were on their feet' (ibid., February 1916: 132). The singing, too, was 'indescribable' (*Transvaal Methodist*, November 1923: 30).

Dorothea Lehmann has aptly observed that life in extended family groups has trained African women to find organising social activities, catering for big festivals, and collecting money, very satisfying duties (1963: 65). All these managerial tasks were the women's in prayer unions, particularly at convention time. The Transvaal Methodist *manyano* and the Natal *Isililo* both showed great keenness in collecting funds over several years to advance their children's security, via, respectively, a Domestic Science School at Kilnerton (nearly £4 000 was given in annual shillings over 25 years) and a farm, which was bought at Umzinto in 1928 so that if their children became destitute they could live there (Mbili, 1962: 5–8).

THE MANYANOS IN THE CONTEXT OF
SOUTH AFRICAN HISTORY

By about the middle of the twentieth century, African women's prayer unions, particularly in the Anglican and Methodist churches, had built up a considerable membership. In 1940 there were at least 45 149 women in the Methodist *manyano* throughout South Africa, with numbers largest among the Transkei Xhosa (the Clarkebury District), the Sotho-Tswana of the Orange Free State and northern Cape (Kimberley and Bloemfontein District), and the Zulu of Natal.

Table I: South African manyano members by district, 1940

Cape	369
Grahamstown	4 060
Queenstown	5 453
Clarkebury	10 568
Kimberley and Bloemfontein	10 278
Natal	7 722
Transvaal and Swaziland	6 699

From *Minutes of Annual Conference*, 1940: 246–7

It is worth noting that the Transvaal Synod Minutes for the same year give an even higher membership for that District – 9 421 members, 2 567 of whom were in branches on the Reef. The *manyano's* growth in the Transvaal from seven members in 1907 to eight hundred in 1913 to nearly ten thousand by the Second World War is impressive – yet was being surpassed elsewhere in the country, as the table shows.

By the end of the Second World War the estimated African membership of the (Anglican) Mothers' Union in the Johannesburg diocese was around 3 500. By the beginning of the 1970s, for the continent as a whole, it was South Africa which provided the largest Mothers' Union membership, nearly 34 000. The all-African diocese of St John's (the Transkei) and in Johannesburg (though this did include some white and coloured women) had particularly thriving branches.

Table II: Mothers' Union membership, South Africa and Africa, c. 1970

	Branches	Members
Diocese of St John's	457	7,644
Diocese of Johannesburg	143	5 634
All South Africa	1 746	33 966
East Africa		19 462
Central Africa		11 229
West Africa		11 394
Uganda, Rwanda and Burundi		10 753

From *New Dimensions*, 1972: 198, 216

Lilian Ngoyi, redoubtable ANC women's leader in the 1950s, voiced what remains a standard complaint against the *manyanos*. Observing churchwomen weeping at Easter over Christ's suffering, she 'felt there was something very wrong, for after weeping nothing would be done. They all waited for some power from God' (Joseph, 1963: 165). Part of the argument of this chapter has been that these movements constitute an important and authentic female response to Christianity in their own right – they deserve to be assessed in terms of their religious origins and spiritual character. Nevertheless, historical research is uncovering ways in which condemnation of *manyano* reluctance to mobilise their considerable power for political or community purposes (Brandel-Syrier, 1962) may have been premature.

Julia Wells, for example, has documented how an active Methodist *manyano* member and the association's president were among the 'respectable' middle-class Christian housewives who led the 1913 female anti-pass demonstrations in Bloemfontein (Wells, 1980: 22–4). Her description of the mobilisation of Potchefstroom women in 1929 for protest against residential permits is strikingly reminiscent of, and I suspect may well have drawn on, typical *manyano* patterns of group revivalism: the women gathered through singing in the streets of the location, 'moving from street to street until all the women had been collected' and their meetings would last virtually all night (Wells, 1983).

The fascinating rural protest movement uncovered by William Beinart in Herschel in the 1920s likewise drew its strength from 'dressed' women who had come out of Methodist prayer unions. Their programme of defensive communalism came to entail 'an African Christianity, separate schools, a fight for "communal" tenure, and support for a restored chieftaincy' (1987: 262). Beinart suggests that the women's independent political action derived in part from an enforced independence, forged by the harsh social and economic circumstances in which they found themselves – alone in charge of homesteads for much of the year and bearing the brunt of economic pressures. These pressures were most acute for unsalaried 'progressives' who were expected to wear Western clothes and eat a more Western diet. But also important was that women retained separate administrative and financial control of their religious affairs: 'It seems to have been the *manyano* that provided the initial organisational core for the women's movement during the boycott. They were not explicitly directing their action against men, but increasing political independence was predicated on a challenge to male authority in which the *manyano* played some part' (ibid.: 239).

Beinart is then able to show that, unlike what we know thus far of other areas, by 1925 the potential for religious separatism in the *manyano* was being realised in Herschel, as Methodist women deserted to the ranks of a popular religious and political radical in charge of the local African Methodist Episcopal Church (ibid.: 245–7).

Those interested in exploring the history of African women's lives, or indeed social change and religious and political mobilisation of different African communities, cannot afford to ignore what was happening in the supposedly 'closed' world of the *manyano*.

CONCLUSION

In his masterly survey of modern African Christianity, Adrian Hastings (1979: 114–5, 265–6) remarks on how the ongoing contribution of female Christian associations, rather than the leadership of male catechists, has more often provided a 'dynamic core' to African church life. Furthermore, the spirit of these women's groups, 'with their concentration upon the small praying community, the confession of problems and failings, their emotional, even ecstatic prayer', was the spirit of the independent churches. Hastings suggests that when mission church leadership, preoccupied with school management, scientific medicine and printing presses, strayed from the 'central axis' of prayer, 'the independent churches were able time and again to steal their clothes and grow very effectively as just this and little else: churches of prayer'. This chapter has in part tried to show how *manyanos* provide virtually an independent 'church of prayer' for women within the mission churches. The emotional, participatory, expressive culture of the *manyano* was the choice and creation of the women themselves, as was its use as a vehicle of female spiritual leadership and church expansion. This was what they wanted from and valued in Christianity, even in the face of missionary misgivings. African women helped shape the new faith; it did not simply force them into a stereotypical mould.

What the *manyano* came to stand for as a whole was meaningful to many Christian women at the beginning of this century – spontaneous praying out loud about personal and family needs; extemporaneous evangelistic preaching to small and large groups; a leadership role for ministers' wives and older married women generally; a way of showing concern for one's children, especially wayward daughters, at a time when old controls were failing; a distinctive identity as devout Christian women, marked out by dress and expressed in corporate gatherings and fundraising.

Motherhood was central to African women's personal and cultural identity as well as their social and economic roles long before the advent of Christian missions in South Africa. But church groups served to transform, elevate and entrench the importance of marriage, wifehood and motherhood for women. They were among the powerful ideological forces contributing to the ongoing centrality of the notion of motherhood in African women's organisation in the twentieth century – although arguably the state's onslaught on their children has latterly been an even more powerful force mobilising mothers (see Beall *et al.*, 1987; Gaitskell and Unterhalter, 1989).

Just as organising on the basis of motherhood is a controversial area in feminist debate in contemporary South Africa, so is the question of the defence of family. Bozzoli has seen it as conservative, in the sense that *manyano* women seek 'to conserve and consolidate the family and the woman's position within it' (1983: 165). I would suggest it needs to be put in its wider historical context: who is defending the family against what and with what short-term implications for community solidarity and resistance, and what long-term effects (such as con- demnation of any who fall outside of a particular family model)? Certainly defence of family can be narrow, exclusive, inward-looking – and confining for women; but future investigation of gender re- lations in South Africa will have to pay sensitive attention to the changing ways in which dominant models of family life have been both valued and resisted by individuals and threatened by the state.

Like nineteenth-century maternal associations in America, *man- yanos* were 'grass-roots responses to the contemporary cultural and religious elevation of the mother's role' (Cott, 1977: 149, 156). Though likewise restrained in part by the very concerns which brought women into spiritual association – religious conviction and their family role – they exhibited, in their freedom from male and ecclesias- tical domination, an eloquent female solidarity and a fervently Afri- can Christianity.

11

Man-made women: Gender, class and the ideology of the volksmoeder

ELSABE BRINK

IDEALISED WOMANHOOD

One of the means by which men in male-dominated societies control women is by giving them a well-defined but circumscribed position within society, to which some status, honour and respectability are attached. The parameters of this position, within which may be found the notion of 'ideal womanhood', may evade exact definition but yet be widely acknowledged and accepted. Women who, even partially, begin to question society and their role within it, lose the privileges of this position, because, having questioned social norms and structures, they are no longer as controllable; society loses its power over them.

This chapter argues that the role allocated to women in Afrikaner society in the late nineteenth and early twentieth centuries was bounded by the notion of *volksmoeder* or 'mother of the nation'.[1] In terms of the *volksmoeder* concept, the Afrikaner woman was depicted not only as the cornerstone of the household but also as a central unifying force within Afrikanerdom and, as such, was expected to fulfil a political role as well.

This notion of an idealised Afrikaner womanhood, which had its origins in apologetic Dutch–South African historiography of the nineteenth century, is remarkable for its continuity until at least the mid-twentieth century. It came to form an integral part of emergent Afrikaner nationalism, and in addition, the white working class drew on its sub-themes of courage and resistance. It remained constant during a time of great industrial, political and social change in southern Africa, yet has been largely ignored, perhaps because 'Those studying the twentieth century find it difficult not to become so involved in the obvious and fundamental changes which have occurred in almost all aspects of social life that the continuities are neglected' (Roberts, 1984: 3).

In many respects the concept overlaps with notions of ideal

womanhood found in other societies. Recent research into the social position of women in nineteenth- and twentieth-century Britain (Davin, 1978), America (Ryan, 1981), France (McMillan, 1981) and Canada (Lewis, 1985) has identified a similar ideological framework, emphasising characteristics such as kindness, gentleness, care, frugality, discipline and conformity. The popular image of women in the late nineteenth and early twentieth century in Quebec for example contains particularly striking similarities with that of idealised Afrikaner womanhood.

The content of the image of idealised womanhood is usually not defined with any precision by society. Roberts, in her study of British working-class women during the late nineteenth and early twentieth centuries, concluded that oral evidence has shown that 'a large section of society [was] following and upholding a clearly understood, if *infrequently discussed,* set of mores. These produced women who were disciplined, inhibited, conforming and who placed perceived familial and social needs before those of the individual' (1984: 203, emphasis added). Victorian domestic ideology in Britain, which influenced Afrikaner notions of womanhood, contained clearly perceived yet not always clearly articulated notions of motherhood. In his study of the making of the British working class, E. P. Thompson argues: 'According-ing to conventions which were deeply felt, the woman's status turned upon her success as a housewife in the family economy, in domestic management and forethought, baking and brewing, cleanliness and child-care' (1978: 455). However, this notion was based on essentially middle-class mores and values, and was imposed on other strata of society. Hence a working-class mother who did not fulfil these criteria, however hard she struggled against the vicissitudes of poverty, 'would not appear as a model housewife, or as one properly dedicated to motherhood' (Davin, 1978: 33).

Over time, similar processes can be identified in the development of the image of the *volksmoeder* in South Africa. However, a distinctive role in the development and articulation of this concept was played in particular by the Anglo–Boer War and the emergence of Afrikaner nationalism during the early decades of the twentieth century. These developments contributed considerably to the 'style' with which the Afrikaner community was 'imagined', to use the terms employed by Anderson (1983: 15). After the Anglo–Boer War the concept of *volks-moeder* added a further dimension to Afrikaner nationalism and was propagated in a self-conscious manner by a new generation of Afrikaner nationalists who, in a manner reminiscent of the British pre-occupation with working-class degeneracy, concerned themselves with the ever-increasing number of poor whites and the so-called degeneration of the Afrikaner (Brink, 1986: 8). In this concern one can identify 'both a genuine, popular nationalist enthusiasm and a systematic, even Machiavellian, instilling of nationalist ideology through the mass media, the educational system, administrative regulations, and so forth' (Anderson, 1983: 104). For these cultural entrepreneurs the argument presented by Paul Thompson seems to have had validity: 'The unpaid labour of women within the household is not merely an essential contribution towards the maintenance of the existing structure at any time, but also, through the rearing of children, the foundation of the social economy of the future, and a mainspring of social change' (1981: 303).

In this chapter I describe the development of, as well as the content of and continuities evident in, the concept of the *volksmoeder*. I begin by analysing the emergence of the image of Boer men and women in the two Boer republics as a response to their negative portrayal in Cape colonial and European historiography at the time. I outline the impact of the Boer War and the experience of Afrikaner women during that war. Then I look at the way in which the concept of *volksmoeder* was propagated by nascent Afrikaner nationalism during the first decades of the twentieth century, and contrast this with contemporary research findings on the actual position of women during this period. Finally, I indicate how Afrikaner women, both middle and working class, identified with and internalised this idealised vision of Afrikaner womanhood.

THE NINETEENTH-CENTURY ORIGINS OF THE 'VOLKSMOEDER' CONCEPT

British colonisation and its positive, beneficial effects dominated nineteenth-century South African historiography written in English. Dutch settlement, as well as the Great Trek and the founding of the Boer republics, was regarded as peripheral to the saga of British settlement and government at the Cape. Works by Noble (1877) and Wilmot and Chase (1869) remained the standard source material on South African history until G. M. Theal began to publish research based more closely on archival material, during the latter part of the century. The writings of Noble and of Wilmot and Chase portrayed Boer settlers outside the Cape Colony as ignorant, illiterate and cruel, as 'living on the margin of civilisation', their 'moral condition ... scarcely higher than the Hottentots or slaves who were household companions' (quoted by Van Jaarsveld, 1974: 52).

During the last quarter of the century, especially after the mineral discoveries and the Boer victories during the Transvaal War of Independence (1880–1), such criticism began to be countered by an apologist approach to the Boers in both English and Dutch historical writings (the latter emanating from the Netherlands as well as the Boer republics). Historians such as Klok, Van der Loo, and Du Plessis took great pains to paint a positive picture of Boer society, drawing close parallels between the Boers and their exemplary European heritage (Van Jaarsveld, 1974; Du Plessis, 1898).

In the new historiography Boer women received greater attention. They were described as extremely courageous (Van der Loo, 1897: 143) and, owing to their sufferings in the past, were considered by some writers to be 'the greatest patriots'. 'Taking all the sufferings of mothers and daughters during the early days into account, it is indeed no wonder that it is amongst the female sex, especially amongst the older generation, that the greatest patriots are found' (Weilbach and Du Plessis, 1882: 22; translated). These authors painted a detailed picture of the simple and unassuming Boer lifestyle, which was presented as an overt sign of a classless and egalitarian society (ibid.: 23–4). At the same time, their ordered and structured society was emphasised, by way of countering the negative images mentioned above.

Van der Loo, in his work *De Geschiedenis der Zuid-Afrikaansche Republiek aan het Volk*, lavished praise on Boer women. Despite their contact with 'wild barbarians' and their isolation from civilisation, they remained true to their traditions of 'virtue, moral sensibility, political independence and free institutions' (1896: 63; translated). An added dimension was their purported racial superiority and purity. Symbol of her racial purity, the white complexion of the Boer woman – despite exposure to the African wilderness – was highlighted by Lion Cachet, who maintained 'a Transvaal woman is, for Africa, very white' (1898: 422; translated). This feature was likewise stressed by J. Klok in his description of Boer women. He also paid attention to their lips, implicitly contrasting them with Negroid features: 'thin lips, a round chin and a white neck…. Seldom does one see ugly, that is, really ugly women' (1901: 26; translated).

On the eve of the Anglo–Boer War, in his defence of the Boer republics, F. W. Reitz added to this image of Boer women by presenting historical evidence of their bravery and courage, which he had gleaned from the recently published work of Theal. Susanna Smit, the heavily built and well-spoken wife of the Reverend Erasmus Smit, the unordained minister of the Voortrekkers, was immortalised for her eloquent threat to the British Commissioner in Natal in 1843, that 'they had been deputed to express their fixed determination never to yield to British authority; that they were fully aware that resistance would be of no avail, but they would walk out by the Draaksberg [*sic*] barefooted, to die in freedom, as death was dearer to them than the loss of liberty' (Bird, 1965: 258–59; see also chapter 13). Smit's threat became part of the heroic vocabulary of Boer resistance to domination. Thus during the Anglo–Boer War, at a Day of the Covenant celebration, General Smuts used the heroism of the Voortrekker women to inspire male combatants: 'He reminded them how it was the Boer *vrouw* to whose heroism they owed so much. The women had insisted that the men should trek out of Natal, although they could have stayed there in peace and plenty; they preferred to go barefoot over the Drakensberg and endure nameless sufferings among the Kaffirs, rather than submit to the British flag. This must remain the inspiration of the men, the refusal of these heroines ever to submit' (Pakenham, 1979: 481).

THE IMPACT OF THE ANGLO–BOER WAR

The reputation which Afrikaner women had gained by the end of the nineteenth century was broadened considerably during the Anglo–Boer War (1899–1902). One of the most controversial and best-documented aspects of the war was the suffering of Afrikaner women and children in the field and in the British concentration camps (Warwick and Spies, 1980: 161). Their heroism, patriotism and defiance of the British enemy became bywords and were added to the already existent image of Boer women.

However, Boer women did not owe their celebrated status primarily to male politicians, apologists or cultural entrepreneurs, whether British or Boer. The prominence given to their sufferings during the war was largely the result of the work of a woman, Emily Hobhouse. She was an English philanthropist and pacifist, whose concern on learning of the sufferings of Boer women at the hands of the British military led to her active involvement in a campaign to improve conditions in the concentration camps.[2] Her revelations prompted an investigation of these conditions by the British War Office. When Hobhouse herself tried to return to the Cape in 1901 she was promptly deported. However, after the war she returned and continued assisting destitute Boer families. (Pakenham rather deprecatingly depicts her as a 'dumpy, middle-aged English spinster' (1979: 501). A more comprehensive and sympathetic picture of her emerges in Rykie van Reenen's 1984 collection of her letters.)

During her travels through war-torn southern Africa, both during and after the war, Hobhouse collected oral evidence of the war experiences of many of the Boer women she encountered. These she collated into an account of the war, published in 1902 under the title *The Brunt of the War and Where It Fell*.[3] The aim of the book, completed just prior to the signing of the peace treaty in May 1902, was to inform the largely ignorant British public of the treatment of civilians during the war. Making use of the testimony of the people involved, it traced the ravages of the conflict on their lives. The personal evidence of the Boer women herded into the concentration camps is interspersed with an exposé of the consequences of the British scorched-earth policy, which was based on Hobhouse's own observations during her visits to the concentration camps, as well as on those of other interested parties.

Hobhouse maintained that the book did not achieve its aim, for it was suppressed by the authorities in every way possible and barely found its way into bookshops in Britain and at the Cape (Van Reenen, 1984: 173, 180). Nevertheless, the book seems to have had a considerable influence on those who did read it – mainly patriotic Afrikaners. For example, Hobhouse once mentioned the positive reception of the book by an Afrikaner family, obviously members of the Orange Free State elite, who were all 'young, unmarried and full of vigour' (ibid.: 340, 201).

In 1924 she published another compilation, *War Without Glamour: or Women's War Experiences Written by Themselves, 1899–1902*. This appeared in response to the recent termination of the First World War, and in it Hobhouse stressed the universal plight of non-combatants during war. She also praised the specific qualities portrayed by Boer women during the Anglo–Boer War: 'The women maintained extraordinary composure and seldom lost mental control under this ordeal; a striking feature was their profound consciousness of the want of common-sense in those who initiated this movement against them' (1924: ii).

Public focus on the sufferings of the Boer women found expression in 1913 in the erection at Bloemfontein of the *Vrouemonument* (Women's Memorial), dedicated to the more than 26 000 women and children who had died during the war. The project was initiated in 1906 by the ex-president of the Orange Free State, M. T. Steyn, and enthusiastically supported by the Afrikaans poet Totius (J. D. du Toit), one of the main propagators of the Second Language Movement (which sought recognition of Afrikaans as an official language in the place of Dutch). Emily Hobhouse, a close associate of Steyn and his wife, was instrumental in helping to finalise the design of the statue at the monument and was asked to present an opening address. Because of ill-health she could not attend, but her address was read at the opening and subsequently published. In it she outlined a significant anomaly: 'I think for the first time, a woman is chosen to make the commemorative speech over the National Dead – not soldiers – but *women* – who gave their lives for their country' (Van Reenen, 1984: 402; her emphasis). To which could be added a further comment that it was an English woman commemorating the Afrikaner national dead.

This anomaly was carried still further by Hobhouse's eventual interment at the monument, ironically alongside mostly male heroes such as President M. T. Steyn, General C. de Wet and Dominee J. D. Kestell – 'the ideal of Afrikaner statesman, warrior and churchman respectively' (Moodie, 1975: 19). The only other woman interred at the monument is Rachel Steyn, the wife of the president, who was

honoured in this way because of this conjugal relation; she is universally hailed as a true *volksmoeder* in Afrikaner iconography – the
'hooggeagte en geëerde Volksmoeder' (highly esteemed and honoured *volksmoeder*), in the words of one biographer (Brink, 1986: 187).

Yet despite the prominence of Hobhouse's gravesite, she did not fit
comfortably into the general conceptual framework of Afrikaner
nationalists, who were to stress the racial purity and exclusivity of
Afrikanerdom in relation to the English. 'No mention is made [of her]
in any reported civil-religion speech during the 1930s and 1940s. Even
speakers at the Vrouemonument itself chose to ignore her' (Moodie,
1975: 407). Nevertheless, she did contribute considerably to the articulation and further development of the concept of *volksmoeder*. In the
published version of her speech at the opening of the *Vrouemonument*
she declared: 'Proudly I unveil the Monument to the brave South
African Women, who, sharing the danger that beset their land and
dying for it, affirmed for all times and for all peoples the power of
Woman to sacrifice life and more than life for the common weal' (Van
Reenen, 1984: 407).

The sufferings of Boer women and Emily Hobhouse's documenta-
tion of their travail considerably broadened the range of characteristics ascribed to the *volksmoeder* and tended in effect to substantiate
the claims made by nineteenth-century apologists for the Boers. In the
hands of Afrikaner nationalist ideologues Hobhouse's material,
which she had placed in the context of a broad and non-sectarian
vision of womanhood, was taken from its general framework and
applied parochially to the role of women in Afrikaner society.

AFRIKANER WOMEN, REAL AND IMAGINED

After 1902, Afrikaner women and their suffering during the war
remained in the forefront of popular consciousness, serving an important political function in the development and deployment of
Afrikaner nationalism. The glorification of Afrikaner women symbolised by the *Vrouemonument* served an overt political purpose.
According to Hexham, the opening of the monument on 16 December
1913 'gave the nationalist cause a symbolic victory over the advocates
of conciliation' (1980: 397). This victory was consolidated by the
steady literary production of the poet Totius and his brother-in-law,
Willem Postma, a Free State journalist and advocate of Afrikaner
nationalism. Together these two men developed 'their cultural nationalism and a sense of identity based upon Afrikaner traditions and
the Calvinist religion' (Hexham, 1980: 401).

In the projects of these men there is a clear convergence between
the development of the ideal of the *volksmoeder* and the rise of Afrikaner nationalism. In 1918 Postma (then retired because of ill-health)
was requested by two Afrikaner organisations, the *Nasionale Helpme-*

kaar[4] and the *Kultuurvereniging* of Reddersburg, to write a book entitled *Die Boervrouw, Moeder van Haar Volk* (The Boer Woman, the Mother of her Nation). The timing of this publication was important. It followed on the unveiling of the *Vrouemonument*, the Rebellion of 1914 and the termination of the First World War. The war was a significant event in the history of Afrikaner nationalism, for it was during this time that secondary industry, in particular labour intensive industries utilising mainly cheap female labour, began to flourish in South Africa. At the same time, a population explosion in the Afrikaner community, coinciding with the impoverishment of the rural areas, resulted in a massive influx of young, mostly unskilled Afrikaner men and women to this labour market in the urban areas (Brink, 1986). The presence of these unsupervised and unattached young men and women in the cities gave rise to grave concern for their moral safety in state, church and welfare organisations (ibid.; see also chapter 12).

In this social context, the characteristics of the *Boervrouw* as enumerated by Postma gained particular relevance for reformers, cultural entrepreneurs and concerned Afrikaners in general. His book was both an articulation of the already established image of the *volksmoeder* and a glorification of Afrikaner women, aimed at the instruction of Afrikaner youth and young girls in particular. In his writing the *volksmoeder* ideal was propagated as a role model for a new generation of women. This involved the emulation of characteristics such as a sense of religion, bravery, a love of freedom, the spirit of sacrifice, self-reliance, housewifeliness (*huismoederlikheid*), nurturance of talents, integrity, virtue and the setting of an example to others.

Of particular significance is that Postma extended the prevailing notion of ideal womanhood to include their nurturing of the *volk* as well. For the first time the Boer woman's role as mother and central focus of her family was expanded to include the concept of Boer women as mothers of the nation: 'The motherhood of the Boer woman extends itself to her *volk* just as it does to her child' (Postma, 1918: 164; translated). To substantiate his argument he cited the demonstration of Afrikaner women at the Union Buildings in 1915, when a huge delegation marched to Pretoria to protest against the capture and imprisonment of General Christiaan de Wet as a rebel. The idea of this demonstration had originated with women suitably connected to prominent men and thus well qualified to be regarded as 'mothers of the nation' – Mrs Joubert, wife of the famous Boer general, and Elsie Eloff, the daughter of the late President Kruger. Yet the way in which Postma saw the demonstration taking form portrays a revealing disregard for the women's initiative: 'In true womanly fashion the call was complied with, without delay, not taking account of expense or trouble. Love called, love obeyed' (ibid.: 164; translated). The limitations of Postma's perception of the women's action are evident in these words: women did not argue, they did not stop to consider the consequences and they did not calculate the cost or the trouble of their actions. They were motivated irrationally, solely by love. But having disregarded any political significance in the women's action, Postma proceeded to link the moral strength of the Afrikaner people to that of its women: 'A people are what its women are. The woman is the conscience of her nation as well as the measure of its values. The moral life of a nation is controlled by the women, and by the women can we measure the moral condition of the people' (ibid.: 179; translated).

While Postma's book represented an ideological glorification of Afrikaner women, a 1921 publication by the educationist and historian Eric Stockenström, *Die Vrou in die Geskiedenis van die Hollands-Afrikaanse Volk*, aimed to provide the historical context for this viewpoint. Stockenström set out to write a condensed history of the role played by Dutch women in South Africa from 1568 to 1918. His book was possibly more widely read and utilised by the Afrikaner elite and cultural entrepreneurs than by the general populace. In it many of the characteristics already outlined by Postma emerge: Afrikaner women had a purifying and ennobling influence on their menfolk; they would sacrifice much for their families and were loyal housewives and tender nurses, earnest in prayer, sage in advice, with a great love of freedom and steadfastly anti-British (ibid.: 38, 233). Stockenström maintained adamantly that Voortrekker women were aware of their calling as *volksmoeders*: 'The women profoundly realised that they were the mothers of the future Afrikaner nation, and they were fully conscious of the fact that their children and grandchildren could never develop into a virtuous and glorious nation unless they were absolutely independent and free' (ibid.: 232).

What is striking about this early period is the near-total absence of female voices, except that of Emily Hobhouse – an English woman – in the construction of the ideal of Afrikaner womanhood. In 1921, in contrast to Stockenström's rather stereotyped portrayal of women, Marie du Toit, sister of the poet Totius, published a book, *Vrou en Feminist – Of Iets oor die Vroue-Vraagstuk*, which was an attack on generally accepted notions of womanhood – she was an Afrikaans counterpart to Olive Schreiner, it would seem. However, Du Toit's book is virtually unknown, even today. It was not widely read at the time and has received little or no mention in subsequent literature on women in South Africa. This is hardly surprising, for unlike Postma's and Stockenström's work, it questioned the ideological parameters of their idealised notion of Afrikaner womanhood: 'continually we hear only of lesser, of lower value, inferior, weak, weak [women] yes, but we still have to carry most without complaining! We are reminded of duties, responsibilities, even recrimination comes ... and that is what the aunties call our position of honour. A beast-of-burden position of honour indeed!' (Du Toit, 1921: 138–9).

In the following two decades the position of white women did receive attention in three important studies conducted by women. These, however, were more concerned with the actual than the idealised lives of women. Du Toit's critical appraisal of women's role was overshadowed by a growing concern with the so-called poor white problem in South Africa: the social, economic and moral impoverishment or 'degeneration' of whites, mostly Afrikaners. This concern, which generated considerable academic and public interest, culminated in the investigation of the Carnegie Commission from 1930 to 1932. As the only female member of the Carnegie Commission, M. E. Rothmann (MER), a celebrated Afrikaans author, conducted a sociological study of the problems of mothers and daughters in the poor white family. In contrast to the writings of Postma and Stockenström, Rothmann painted a very realistic picture of the plight of impoverished white women in the rural areas, towns and cities.

In the initial conceptualisation of the tasks of the commission, the question of women did not feature as a separate category, but because of Rothmann's input 'her studies were considered so valuable that the Commission decided to publish her report as a separate whole' (Carnegie Commission, vol. 5, 1932: 2). It is not difficult to see why Rothmann's report merited separate inclusion. Albeit from a middle-class perspective, she approached her subjects with respect and sympathy, as is evident from her description of a widow, impoverished by drought and lack of education: 'She is careworn and slow of speech, so that it is difficult to keep one's attention fixed on her, but it is worth the trouble, for she thinks' (ibid.: 163). Rothmann did not fall into the trap of maintaining that these women 'do not ... feel the coarseness and roughness as we [middle-class women] do' (ibid.: 182). Instead, she quoted the pregnant wife of a shepherd: 'when I off-load the wagon and I know I must soon load it again with my things, and with such a burden to carry, then I think, why should I go on' (ibid.: 182). She did, however, accept the prevailing notion that women's primary responsibility was to fulfil a nurturing role centred on the family. Like her male counterparts, Rothmann showed great concern for the moral and social development of young girls, both in the rural and urban areas, and maintained that for them, 'the potential mothers of our nation, there is no normal social or home education' (ibid.: 198). Nevertheless, she also found that in the urban areas very few young girls remained unemployed; instead the young girl 'snatches at the chance of employment' (ibid.: 208).

In another contemporary study, Hansi Pollak investigated extensively the working conditions of white women in Witwatersrand industry during the Depression years from 1930 to 1932. In her thesis, completed in 1932, she found that some 90 per cent of the women employed in the manufacturing sector were located in the food and drink, tobacco, chemical, leather and clothing industries (Pollak, 1932: 572). Of these, the clothing industry was the major employer of white women. Pollak discussed matters such as working conditions in the factories, the place of birth, age and financial contribution to family income of these women, and was struck by both the extreme youth of many of them, as well as the financial burden they carried on behalf of their families. Like Rothmann, Pollak felt an empathy with the women she investigated, as emerges clearly in her notes describing their home circumstances. One respondent wrote to her: 'Often when I get home from work I feel as if I'm too tired even to lift anything. I know you won't think anything of me for writing all this, but the way you spoke to us this afternoon made me think I wouldn't be ashamed to tell you anything' (ibid., addendum: 56).

During the 1930s Erika Theron (supervised by Dr. H. F. Verwoerd, then professor of sociology at Stellenbosch University) conducted a similar investigation into the lives of 'coloured' and white women factory workers in Cape Town. She visited some 500 factory workers and analysed these women's level of education, their home and working life, as well as the recreational opportunities available to them. This third major academic study on the vicissitudes of women's working lives completes a picture, drawn from reality, which bears very little resemblance to the idealised and glorified portrayal of Afrikaner women by Postma and Stockenström.

However, the impact of these pioneering works on popular consciousness appears to have been limited. In the absence of publication and sales records, their impact can best be assessed by the subsequent use made of them. Rothmann's study, incorporated into the Carnegie Commission Report, has been widely available ever since publication and, it would seem, was used as documentary evidence to promote efforts to establish craft schools for young indigent girls. Pollak's research had a very limited impact, for her thesis was never published and only two articles by her appeared in academic journals at the time (Pollak: 1931, 1933). (During the past decade, however, her work has been regarded with renewed interest by academics researching labour history during the inter-war years.) Theron's study, published in Afrikaans, had an equally limited impact and was not generally known or used.

By contrast, the works of Postma and Stockenström were to exert a considerable and pervasive, though indirect, influence on the way the notion of an idealised Afrikaner womanhood was assimilated within Afrikaans popular culture. This is clearly evident when one considers how a refrain of ideas and notions formulated and expounded by them was echoed in the popular press and other publications, especially during the 1930s and culminating in the celebrations surrounding the Voortrekker Centenary in 1938.

These celebrations, which centred around symbolic ox-wagon treks across the country, culminated in a huge *volksfees* (people's festival) at the unveiling of the cornerstone of the Voortrekker Monument by three female descendants of the Voortrekker leaders. The ox-wagons represented the Voortrekker leaders and well-known Voortrekker women, such as Magrieta Prinsloo and Johanna van der Merwe. One wagon was called, significantly, *Vrou en Moeder* (Wife and Mother), and represented women's contribution to the Great Trek. Women also featured prominently during the celebrations and in the commemorative books published after the event. The process of glorification commenced by Postma and Stockenström was taken up and carried forward at this time, and their work provided the blueprint on which these writings on Afrikaner women were modelled.

Thus in a speech at the Voortrekker Monument on 14 December 1938, Judith Pellissier glorified the contribution of Voortrekker women in terms reminiscent of Postma. She felt that it was fitting 'to praise the honour and memory of the Mother of our nation' (Mostert, 1940: 26; translated). She suggested that one should listen to a song of 'mother-love that presents the nobility of her soul to her progeny … [in a] song that once again links her fearless courage, trust in God, her sorrow and her sufferings in a crying lament to the lament and groaning of the frail journeying little wagon' (ibid.: 26; translated).

The influence of Stockenström's book can also be seen in articles which appeared during 1938 in popular magazines such as *Die Huisgenoot*. J. Conradie, wife of the Administrator of the Cape, brought together the characteristics of Afrikaner women and their history in a speech presented to the *Afrikaanse Taal en Kultuurvereniging* (ATKV) and published as '*Die Bydrae tot die Geskiedenis van Ons Volk deur Suid-Afrikaanse Moeders en Dogters*' (The Contribution of South African Mothers and Daughters to the History of Our People) (*Die Huisgenoot*, 19.8.1938: 67). A speech by P. du Toit on '*Die Invloed van die Afrikaanse Moeder en Dogter op die Volkskarakter*' (The Influence of the Afrikaner Mother and Daughter on the Character of the *Volk*) was published in the following issue (ibid., 26.8.1938: 75). The historical role of prominent Afrikaner women was further elaborated in an article entitled '*Vrouefigure uit die Verhaal van Suid-Afrika*' (Female Figures from the Story of South Africa), by one Annette Jackson (ibid., 16.12.1938: 85).

On a more critical level, M. E. Rothmann, also actively involved at this time in the *Afrikaanse Christelike Vroue Vereniging* (ACVV), addressed the problem of the position of Afrikaner women (though she accepted its inherent limitations), by asking what they had achieved

during the past century. She argued that feminism, born from increased self-knowledge amongst women, manifested itself amongst
Afrikaner women in their involvement in various welfare organisations in the country. She saw these organisations as an 'education' for
the Afrikaner woman where she could learn 'to try to do for her *volk*
as a whole what every mother does for her children' (ibid., 2.12.1938:
105).

ASSIMILATION OF THE IDEAL

During the inter-war years the figure of the actual and the imagined
Afrikaner woman took literary shape. Postma and Stockenström
drew together the available historical material in an image which
glorified Afrikaner women, whilst Rothmann, Pollak and Theron
worked on a more scientific level, creating a picture of Afrikaner
women far removed from the heroic, rather one-dimensional rendering of their male counterparts. However, the former image was
more readily appropriated by various cultural and political agencies,
in order to woo their constituencies, whilst the latter was relegated to
virtual obscurity.

It is difficult to gauge precisely the extent to which Afrikaner
women responded to and assimilated the ideals upheld in the *volksmoeder* literature. Nevertheless, by considering two organisations in
the Transvaal, the *Suid-Afrikaanse Vroue Federasie* (SAVF) and the
Garment Workers' Union (GWU), whose constituencies were middle-
class and working-class women respectively, it is possible to assess
the impact of the concept of *volksmoeder* on two different but representative groupings of Afrikaner women. The SAVF can be viewed as
representative of middle-class women; in all four provinces scores of
middle-class women belonged to similar regional welfare organisations, for instance the *Oranje Vroue Vereniging* in the Orange Free State,
the *Afrikaanse Christelike Vroue Vereniging* in the Cape and the *Natalse
Christelike Vroue Vereniging* in Natal, to name but a few. The GWU can
also be used as an example because it included a considerable number
of urban working-class women, concentrated on the Rand. During
the inter-war years the clothing industry employed about half of all
white women in manufacturing industry, and some 90 per cent of
these women were Afrikaans-speaking (Pollak, 1932: 6). Furthermore,
recent research has shown that the majority of Afrikaner women on
the Rand during this period were economically active; they were not
housewives, but gainfully employed (Brink, 1986: 16–17).

The middle-class women of the SAVF, coopted into a more narrowly nationalistic ideological framework, used the term *volksmoeder* to
underpin their work on the welfare front with an ideologically acceptable base. At the same time, the GWU incorporated the ideal into a
wider working-class perspective, thereby giving newly urbanised

and exploited Afrikaner working women a firmer foothold in the industrialised society taking shape around them.

The SAVF

The SAVF was founded in 1905 by Georgina Solomon, yet another English woman, the widow of the Cape liberal Saul Solomon and friend of Emily Hobhouse. Inspired by Annie Botha, wife of General Louis Botha, who informed her about the destitution in the two Boer republics, Solomon returned to South Africa in 1904 to help personally with the rehabilitation of the Boers. With Annie Botha she visited the devastated areas and decided to found a women's welfare organisation to work towards the upliftment of impoverished whites.

The SAVF was an organisation of predominantly middle-class Afrikaner women who undertook numerous welfare functions on an entirely voluntary basis. They were actively supported by the state for the obvious reason that they fulfilled very necessary functions for which the state did not have to pay; their work also conformed to women's perceived domestic role. Their involvement offered them an outlet for work outside the home, at a time when it was still widely unacceptable for women who were not financially forced to do so, to enter paid employment. As Eisenberg (1987) has indicated, the SAVF inculcated a fierce loyalty amongst its membership, perhaps because it provided its constituents with a sphere of influence and some degree of autonomy and independence in a socially restrictive society.

Within this sphere, these women worked hard to provide a diverse number of social services, such as poor relief; hostels for unmarried mothers and young working girls; health-care and aid to poor whites. This organisation, along with similar organisations in the Orange Free State, Natal and Rhodesia, collaborated in the publication of a social work quarterly entitled *Vrou en Moeder*. Its slogan very aptly summarised both their energy and determination as well as the limitations under which they operated: 'Ons sien haar wen, want haar naam is ... *vrou en moeder*' (We see her win, because her name is ... *wife and mother*).[5]

The SAVF anchored its activities firmly on the principles of the Bible, the religious orientation of the organisation being clearly outlined in its anthem:

'Tis glorious to carry the name of daughters of South Africa
There's work, there's work, my sisters, work for women devout,
And free and strong! To serve her nation, honour her God,
O Lord, guide her Yourself, the woman, in service of her nation,
In honour of her God, guide her Yourself, the woman, O Lord!
(Eisenberg, 1987: 57; translated).

For the SAVF, of equal importance to the moral and economic

regeneration of Afrikanerdom after the devastations of war was its political regeneration. The organisation demanded 'freedom, true equality, self-government for our suffering *volk*' (ibid.). It found validation for its task of rebuilding the nation in the historical precedents so clearly elaborated by Postma and Stockenström. The history of Afrikaner women in South Africa as portrayed by these writers was often harnessed in the writings of the SAVF to inspire their members to greater effort. Their task was given a solid foundation by coupling it to the activities of the earliest female Dutch settlers and all their successors: 'Should we not take our children by the hand and together look for the spoors of our devout ancestors?' (*Vrou en Moeder*, March 1942: 3; translated).

As Eisenberg (1987) has indicated, during the inter-war years the organisation had strong links with Afrikaner nationalist organisations, including the Broederbond, the Dutch Reformed Church and its sister churches, as well as with the Smuts and Hertzog governments. During the 1930s the organisation came to espouse many of the ideals of the Purified National Party under Dr D. F. Malan, especially that of racial purity and the dangers of miscegenation: 'the failed poor white on his unhappily low standard of living can so easily become the companion and roommate of the non-white. Here, as well as at the communist meeting, the non-white learns to resist the idea of white guardianship and to regard himself as at least equal to the white [man]' (*Vrou en Moeder*, September 1943: 1; translated).

This middle-class perception of the 'degeneration' of the poor white and the imminent danger of fraternisation with non-whites coloured the attitude of the SAVF towards the recipients of its welfare activities. Eisenberg (1987) indicates an ambivalent attitude towards working-class women in the organisation. On the one hand the nobility of the suffering poor was praised, and on the other a hopeless picture was drawn of 'the shy, alienated, sensitive, poverty-stricken, sometimes backward and usually hopeless little woman with neither initiative nor ambition' (Eisenberg, 1987: 61–2, quoting *Vrou en Moeder*, June 1944: 14; translated).

Evidently SAVF members did not share the participatory empathy of researchers such as Rothmann and Pollak. While they strove to fulfil the demands made on them by male cultural entrepreneurs in the home and in the context of the *volk*, elevating the role of *volksmoeder* to a position of supreme service, they did not easily acknowledge the existence of *volksmoeders* beyond their own sphere of influence or work. The title did not extend to working-class women, even though the only criterion for membership was to be respectable (Eisenberg, 1987: 54). Indeed, very few working-class women ever bridged the gap between client and patron within the organisation, although in a recent interview Johanna Raath, president of the SAVF from 1947 to 1980, maintained that the 'most rewarding fruit of their work was seeing working-class women rise above their circumstances and aid the SAVF in their noble work' (ibid.).

Life-long work, valiantly and voluntarily executed amongst a constituency both idealised and patronised, was rewarded. After twenty years of service and loyalty, many members were awarded commemorative buttons – *volksmoederknopies*. These buttons, which were returned to the SAVF at the death of the recipient and placed in a commemorative album, symbolised the life-long commitment of members to the organisation (ibid.: 48). 'Once you become a member of the Federation you remain one. Yes, it's not easy to break away' (ibid.: 52; translated).

Besides being awarded these buttons, several prominent members of the SAVF were formally honoured with the title of *volksmoeder*. For example, when she died in 1944, A. Frost, who had chaired the SAVF branch in Krugersdorp for thirty years, was hailed as a true *volksmoeder*. 'Her *volk*, especially the poor were very close to her heart. Nobody ever left her empty-handed' (*Vrou en Moeder*, September 1944: 5; translated). Even greater praise was accorded to S. B. Broers, president of the SAVF during the 1940s. On her death she was conveyed to the cemetery in a Voortrekker wagon drawn by nurses employed at the SAVF Moedersbond Hospital in Pretoria. Her coffin was covered with the word *volksmoeder* written in flowers. The message which accompanied her to the grave was: 'Thus far has the Lord also helped us, by means of Afrikaner *volksmoeders* such as Mrs Broers' (*Vrou en Moeder*, November 1947: 6–8; translated).

The ideal characteristics of a good SAVF woman, of a *volksmoeder* – self-sacrifice, patriotism, religious commitment, moral conviction, determination, energy, courage, insight, desire to serve one's fellow beings, love and profound compassion – drew on strong historical precedents, rooted in the heroic ideology inadvertently created around the Boer women in the late nineteenth and early twentieth century. Their reproductive skills were utilised not only in the home but also in the nurturing of the *volk*: 'If it could ever be said of a nation that its women, alongside their menfolk, had brought about the growth and security of the nation, it can certainly be said of the Afrikaans woman' (*Vrou en Moeder*, June 1944: 3; translated).

The Garment Workers' Union

While social and economic obstacles prevented working-class women from becoming members of the SAVF and achieving the status of *volksmoeder* through voluntary community service, their enforced entry into the labour market did not prevent them from also laying claim to the title. This is clearly discernible in the ranks of Afrikaner women who were members of the GWU, one of the most militant unions during the inter-war years (Brink, 1986).

During the mid-1930s several Afrikaner women, including the Cornelius sisters (Hester and Johanna), Anna Scheepers, Katie Viljoen and Dulcie Hartwell, became prominent trade-union officials in the GWU, under the leadership of Solly Sachs, the union's general secretary. These female trade unionists worked at different levels. They extended the aid of the union from the factory floor, where it was successful in improving working conditions, to the home lives of its members. The union responded very positively to a wide range of personal demands and requests put to it by garment workers in need. In addition, on a cultural level, the *Garment Worker/Klerewerker*, official mouthpiece of the union, was issued as a bilingual publication that incorporated a wide range of literary efforts by trade-union officials, shop stewards and rank-and-file members. Towards the end of the 1930s the union also produced numerous plays, written mostly by Hester and Johanna Cornelius, for its members.

These writings, influenced by the 1938 centenary celebrations, laid claim to the common Afrikaner cultural heritage so enthusiastically espoused by Afrikaner nationalists at the time. However, the garment workers linked the struggles of the Voortrekkers with their own struggles in an industrial environment, developing a consciousness of themselves as women and their plight as working women in an alienating industrial environment. When the garment workers were derided for not being respectable, decent or virtuous, they adamantly claimed the contrary: 'In the factories there are just as many decent girls and women as in any other place' (*Garment Worker/Klerewerker*, October 1938: 9; translated). They were not ashamed to earn their living honestly in the factory: 'Amongst us factory girls there are many decent and noble daughters and we do not stand back for you. We are willing to do our work, but we demand to be treated with respect' (ibid., June 1939: 9; translated).

The garment workers were well aware of and mostly supported the prevailing view that a woman's place was at home raising her family. However, they also recognised that women confronted with financial hardship in their families were faced with a dilemma. When a garment worker, Anna Jacobs, was disapprovingly accused by a male opponent of the union of working outside the home, she retorted: 'Does it serve any purpose if we women work among the pots and the pans and these are empty? Must we fold hands and wait until food falls into the pots automatically?' (ibid., February 1940: 4; translated).

In the same article Jacobs linked the fortitude of the Voortrekker women and Susanna Smit's famous threat of 1843 to the struggles of working women: 'We, workers of our state and for all the women in our country, shall take the lead and climb the Drakensberg again.'

Her words were echoed by Anna Scheepers, who claimed in another article that working women had an important contribution to make, not only to progress in general, but to the trade-union movement in particular: 'In every country in the world and like the Voortrekker woman in this country, women workers contribute their share towards the progress of the trade union movement and of the nation as a whole' (ibid., October–November 1940: 10; translated).

The exploits of the Voortrekker women and of women in the Anglo–Boer War featured in the plays written by and for garment workers. Here this theme was used to rally the audience to greater effort and fortitude and to serve as an inspiration in their home and working lives (Brink, 1984: 41).

The garment workers, representative of at least part of the Afrikaner female working-class community on the Witwatersrand, did indeed see themselves as successors to the heroic tradition of Voortrekker women. As such they were hailed as *volksmoeders* and workers by Sachs in his open letter to them, written just prior to his departure from South Africa under a banning order in 1952. 'Hail, Mother of the Nation, Worker!... The Afrikaner woman has always played an heroic role in the history of the Afrikaner volk. Continue in this tradition' (*Garment Worker/Klerewerker*, May–June 1952: 3; translated).

During the 1930s and early 1940s, therefore, the notion of idealised Afrikaner womanhood became a contested idea. The image of *volksmoeder* found resonance and wide appeal, not only among middle-class Afrikaner women, but also among their working-class counterparts. The Afrikaner nationalists who aimed to gain the political support of these constituencies had succeeded in creating a role model to guide, instruct and appeal to Afrikaans women in general. However, its appeal was so widespread, particularly in the inter-war years, that a radical trade-unionist grouping within Afrikaner ranks, which from the nationalist point of view needed to be saved and brought back to the *volk*, also claimed this ideal to rally women to a wider cause.

CONCLUSION

Although the notion of the *volksmoeder* defies precise definition, it nevertheless incorporated a clear role model for Afrikaner women. It was a deliberately constructed ideal, the work of male cultural entrepreneurs who deliberately promoted a set of images surrounding women; these centred mainly on their nurturing and home-making roles. Even though some of the images were produced by women themselves, they were utilised in an utterly different context, and ultimately the *volksmoeder* became part and parcel of an Afrikaner nationalist mythology.

The idealised image of Afrikaner women and their role in the shaping of South African society was based on the exploits of Voortrekker women, as these were popularised in the late nineteenth century. The Anglo–Boer War of 1899–1902 and the sufferings of Boer women in the concentration camps provided further opportunity to flesh out this heroic vocabulary for political ends. It is ironic that it was through the efforts of an English woman, Emily Hobhouse, that the plight of women during the war was recorded and made public. However, whereas Hobhouse meant to demonstrate the universal plight of women, emergent Afrikaner nationalism appropriated her work to its own ends.

What lay behind the propagation of the concept of the *volksmoeder*? The early twentieth century was a time of intense social change. Against a background of Afrikaner youth flooding onto an ever-expanding industrialising labour market and the emergence of the poor white issue, Postma and Stockenström composed an historically based role model for young Afrikaner girls to emulate. In order to contain the impact of these developments, men presented – and women ultimately accepted – the socially sanctioned role embodied in the image of the *volksmoeder*. At one level, then, the notion represented the ideological incorporation of women into a male-dominated nationalism. In this way a socially, morally, economically and politically subordinate place was clearly defined for Afrikaner women within society. The *volksmoeder* ideal promoted a dependent position for women, as participants in the lives of their husbands and children rather than active in their own lives. Only within this circumscribed role could women achieve social recognition.

Both middle- and working-class women identified with the image of the idealised *volksmoeder*, but for different reasons. Marie du Toit's feminist voice was a lone cry in the dark, which did not take hold in either middle-class or working-class Afrikaner circles. The *volksmoeder* ideal found resonance among middle-class women because it gave legitimacy to their role in society as wives, mothers and voluntary workers. Equally, it gave them a sense of stability and purpose in a rapidly changing world. So strong was middle-class acceptance of the concept of *volksmoeder* that it placed working-class women on the defensive. Working-class women adopted the symbols and terms of the *volksmoeder* and then proceeded to redefine it for themselves. In so doing they claimed their own legitimacy, as valid members of society.

The union movement and especially the Garment Workers' Union of the Transvaal formed a bastion of alternative thought on the position of women in society for a short period before the Second World War. However, changes in the workforce undermined this alternative option. During the 1950s semi-skilled clerical work, which did not allow for a unifying union voice, superseded factory work for white women. This process dissipated any potential resistance to the ideology of the *volksmoeder*. Working-class women's identity was fragmented, and they succumbed to the powerful prescriptions of the *volksmoeder* ideology. In the second half of the century the image of the *volksmoeder* still remains deeply rooted in Afrikaner nationalist ideology.

12

Gender and deviance in South African industrial schools and reformatories for girls, 1911–1934

LINDA CHISHOLM

Between 1926 and 1934 waves of 'insubordination', 'defiance' and 'riots' surged through a girls' reformatory that was located first at Estcourt and then moved to Eshowe, both in Natal (TA, UED, a, b).[1] In September 1926 the Sub-Inspector of Police reported to the magistrate of Estcourt: 'On Sunday night the 12th inst. damage to the doors, windows and partitions of dormitories was done to the extent of many pounds and these dormitories are now totally unsafe to house the crowd. The European staff are in bodily fear and the position is such that I have arranged for a police guard to protect the officers and government property' (TA, UED, a).

Six ringleaders in this attack were identified, briefly imprisoned and later, on continuing to be refractory, transferred to Pietermaritzburg gaol. The reformatory itself was moved to Eshowe and housed in a building adjoining an adult male prison. These efforts did not, however, still the girls' rebelliousness. In March 1928 four girls ranging in age from 14 to 20 were reported to the Director of Prisons for 'making attempts to persuade [others] to disobey orders, to commit acts of violence and to destroy reformatory property' (ibid.). The day after they were sentenced by the magistrate, they proceeded to smash the doors, windows and furniture in their cells. More staff were appointed and discipline was tightened. Two years later, in October 1931, the 'non-European inmates, resenting the punishments inflicted upon them for misconduct' again 'assumed an aggressive and defiant attitude and endeavoured to create a disturbance among all inmates and to carry out assaults on members of staff' (TA, UED, b). In 1933 another 'wave of insubordination' racked the reformatory. Throughout the year there were attempted assaults on staff as well as hunger strikes and refusals to work (ibid.).

Two issues relating to these incidents are remarkable. The first is the way in which the girls' behaviour conforms to a general pattern – girls and women in twentieth-century prisons have been 'rowdier and more disorderly than young adolescent boys' (O'Brien, 1982: 141), or, put another way, 'although there was only a small minority of delinquent girls [in British reformatories between 1889 and 1939, as in South African], they were much more fiercely resistant to character reformation than delinquent boys' (Humphries, 1981: 237). The level of violence amongst these girls contradicted the societal view of females as normally passive.

The official reasons the South African authorities gave for this violence were that delinquent girls were feebleminded and thus prone to irrational, violent behaviour; that the absence of a punishment and reward structure in the reformatory encouraged collective resistance; and that the mental derangement which underlay violence also had its source in masturbation and lesbianism (TA, UED, a). The solutions they proposed involved testing by a 'mental expert' before admission to the reformatory, greater classification and segregation of girls, transferral of unsuitable or incorrigible girls to prisons or mental institutions, and the introduction of a properly graded punishment and reward structure.

The roots of these revolts are not the concern of this chapter; sufficient evidence for the specific grievances involved in each revolt is not available. What can be said with some certainty, however, is that the official construction of events reveals more about the assumptions and presuppositions underlying the approach taken to female crime and deviance in early-twentieth-century South Africa than about the causes of delinquent behaviour. The official reasons and solutions are thus notable not so much for their accuracy as for the correlation made by the authorities between female defiance and deviance, and between expressions of sexuality in young girls and mental deficiency. The process whereby criminalised black and white girls were constituted as both abnormal and defective forms part of the concern of this chapter.

Also noteworthy about the events recorded here is the institution in which the rioting occurred, an institution that, both in its structure and in the relationships between the girls resident in it, does not seem to have conformed to the more general ordering of South African society. The Estcourt (later Eshowe) reformatory was part of a national system of reformatories built after Union in 1910 and organised by colour, age and sex. By 1933 there were five reformatories for boys and the single reformatory at Eshowe for girls. The boys' reformatories were segregated according to colour and age. However, the girls' reformatory, by contrast, included girls of all ages and was not segregated, although African girls were in the majority. Yet if it was anomalous in this respect, it also formed part of a wider system of control for 'wayward' teenage girls that was indeed racially segregated.

Complementing the reformatory system was a system of industrial schools which had been established from 1909 onwards to 'rescue' the offspring of the white unemployed from indigence.[2] Two of these schools, one for boys at Heidelberg (Transvaal) and one for girls at Standerton, were specifically designed for youth in danger of falling into crime or prostitution or both, either through poverty or as a result of parental neglect. Despite its official designation as an industrial school, Standerton was, to all intents and purposes, a reformatory for white girls drawn mainly from the white manual working class. Whereas the reformatory was created for the rehabilitation of convicted juvenile offenders, the industrial school was intended for the 'protection of destitute [white] children and waifs and strays' (Children's Protection Act, 1913).

Within this dual system, the disciplinary regime of 'protection' and 'rehabilitation' as applied to the girls was informed by an ideology of femininity and domesticity common to both institutions. This ideology was mediated by a specific understanding of deviance, which cut across the lives of both black and white girls, affecting them differently. Thus an examination of the different social and ideological processes by which the girls were criminalised and institutionalised, the distinct futures for which they were prepared, as well as their responses to their situation, will help to cast light on the interaction of class, colour and gender in South Africa. This chapter will argue furthermore that social definitions of female deviance helped to shape 'normal' social and sexual relations in South Africa under segregation.

The institutions themselves, comprising one of the most hidden dimensions of the penal–educational nexus, made invisible a group of girls already marginalised by their sex and their class, even as they stigmatised and branded them on their return to society. It is important to note, however, that in taking the reformatory and industrial school as a case-study, I am focusing not on an 'abnormal' section of society but on what Michelle Perrot has called 'an exogamic aspect of ourselves, a broken mirror that reflects our image at the outer limits of experience … where we can read a culture differently but as clearly as in the accumulated mass of events' (1978: 213).

REHABILITATION: GENERAL THEORY AND POLICY

The immediate context for the expansion of the industrial and reformatory system was the development of an industrial social and economic order within South Africa in the late nineteenth and early twentieth centuries. New classes and social forces emerged at this time. On the one hand there had arisen a modernising indigenous ruling class, allied to British imperialism, that was intent on transforming social relations and creating a modern state with appropriate social institutions. On the other hand the process of primitive accumulation which this entailed had also created a new black and white proletariat. Neither section – black or white – was homogeneous. Within the white working class in particular a cleavage developed between the employed and the unemployed, what Victorian commentators would have referred to as the 'respectable' and the 'rough'. In South Africa this unemployed 'residuum' was discursively fixed, along with its rural counterpart, as the 'poor white'. It stood on the margins of the system of production: this marginality carried with it the menace of the unpredictable and the unattached. The destitution of this class was also its potential danger.

In the network of slums that grew up around Johannesburg and other cities, this class was thrown together with dispossessed blacks. A culture cutting across colour lines and marked by the criminality of the illicit liquor-seller emerged. As the number of poor whites increased nationally from an already high figure of 120 000 in 1922 to 300 000 by 1932, they became a matter of great concern to the dominant group: the potential effect on the dominated African people was considered to be catalytic (Davies, 1979). The response of South Africa's ruling class to this and other problems of industrialisation was the development of a segregationist policy (Marks and Trapido, 1987). A two-pronged strategy was adopted by the state towards the children of the white working class. Firstly, their incorporation into the established order was sought through free and compulsory schooling on segregated school benches. Secondly, the problem of the children of the rural and urban white poor and unemployed was addressed through industrial schools and reformatories, where they were to be trained and re-allocated to manual labouring and supervisory positions within the social and racial division of labour. This segregationist policy was legitimated by Social Darwinism and 'scientific racism', and it informed the official conception of delinquency that developed in the early twentieth century.

Two contrasting, although sometimes overlapping, approaches to juvenile crime unfolded during the first two formative decades of this century. The notion of rehabilitation was central to both. The one approach was represented by civil servants such as Jacob de Villiers Roos, Director of Prisons between 1908 and 1918 and architect of South Africa's criminal and juvenile policy after Union. For Roos, the threat and potential burden of crime to the state could be reduced first of all by empirically and scientifically demarcating and classifying the criminal population, and secondly by isolating different sections of this population in an institutional environment, such as a prison, reformatory or industrial school.

The classification and segregation of prisoners according to sex, age and race were fundamental to this notion of regeneration and rehabilitation. In the prison or reformatory, it was believed, the criminal could be converted, reformed and made useful. The prison or reformatory comprised 'one great reforming school' where the offender could be rehabilitated through work, religion and discipline (Roos, 1911: *passim*). Since criminality was viewed as a 'sort of moral illness', rehabilitation strategies were aimed at the 'moral reform' of the individual. In this way the individual could be reclaimed and public harmony and stability secured (Chisholm, 1988).

The rehabilitation of youth was integral to this approach. Its centrality was captured in the aphorism frequently repeated at this time: 'Save the child and prevent the criminal.' The industrial school would rescue children in danger of falling into crime and thereby becoming a burden to the state, by teaching them a trade and the 'habits of industry'. The reformatory would reclaim the 'fallen' juvenile offender by similar methods. This notion of rehabilitation was clearly founded on the belief that individuals could be saved through exposure to an environment away from the corrupting effects of modern city life.

The second approach to juvenile crime current in the early twentieth century was that held by a new generation of social workers, exemplified by the Christian socialist H. E. Norman, South Africa's first probation officer, who was appointed by Roos in 1916.[3] It was shared by welfare organisations such as the Children's Aid Society in Johannesburg, founded in 1908. Their welfare schemes differed from those of the philanthropists and missionaries of the early days of industrialisation in their emphasis on prevention rather than palliatives, education rather than charity and relief (Krut, 1983: 9). Although the welfare movement in South Africa was dominated by middle-class women, its key ideologist was Norman, who stressed the importance of rehabilitation, not in an institutional setting but in the community and family from which the offender sprang. The patriarchal family home provided the model for his rehabilitation strategies, which were at once an extension and a critique of the institutional model offered by men like De Villiers Roos. These reformers also advocated rehabilitation of the juvenile offender in an institutional setting, characterised by patriarchal relations, provided that probation work, aimed at reconstituting family life in civil society, was also involved.

Although penal and welfare ideologists differed over the meaning and content of rehabilitation, they shared a commitment to restoring social unity through the reclamation of juvenile offenders. Whereas the one sought to regulate social conflict through incarceration, the other sought to do so in civil society. Very early on, however, the contradiction between the repressive nature of reformatories and industrial schools and the expressed goal of humanitarian reform and rehabilitation was revealed. There was a public scandal in 1911 over reports of the prison-like atmosphere at the state institutions; inmates attempted to escape from them with disturbing regularity, and rates of recidivism remained high. All this seemed to testify against the reformative value of institutions. Nonetheless, they, and the goal of rehabilitation, remained fixed.

At this point we need to take a closer look at the concept of 'rehabilitation'. Three perspectives are relevant here, each of which informs, in different ways, the analysis that will follow. In the first place, there is the view that rehabilitation can be understood, as David Williams has argued, in terms of the way in which 'ideology mystifies the social realities of capitalist exploitation' (Williams, 1982: 34). Prisons, like reformatories and industrial schools, are only justified, he argues, by the ideological perspective which asserts that their aim is to reform offenders. This is part and parcel of a broad consensus perspective which denies any divisions or conflict in society: 'The assumption promoted ... is that society is essentially free from socio-economic divisions and crimes and that these must therefore be committed by people who are maladjusted deviants. Thus the consensus view of society leads to the conclusion that the maladjusted ought to be readjusted, i.e. reformed' (Williams, 1982: 34). The concept of rehabilitation in the consensus view thus displaces the blame for crime from particular forms of social relations to individual pathology. It justifies continued repression of the consequences of inequality.

Another view is presented by Michel Foucault (1977), that reform of the prison, and its discourse, are as old as the prison itself. This should be understood in terms of the role of the prison not in eliminating crime but, rather, of producing an autonomous sub-class of delinquents or habitual offenders, drawn largely from, but no longer belonging to, the working class. The creation of this sub-class draws a symbolic line, a boundary, between deviant and non-deviant. Its value for Foucault seems to be, above all, symbolic. The production of illegalities or delinquencies is achieved through specific mechanisms of inclusion and exclusion, and through the objectification involved in the processes of categorising, classifying, and institutionally segregating. The delinquent is thus 'placed in full light' and produced as pathologised subject. Simultaneously, those elements that are classically designated as part of a programme of reform – education and productive work – are, in Foucault's schema, part of the means by which the 'microphysics of power' productive of 'docile bodies' goes to work. In this sense, the practices of rehabilitation must not be taken at face value as constituting a new, more progressive and humane system of punishment: it forms a more finely calibrated means for both creating the disciplined body, the subjected individual, and for 'objectifying the delinquency behind the offence' (Foucault, 1977: 135–70, 257–93).

A further way of conceptualising rehabilitation is that which sees it as a means of defining social relations within the institution – as providing and creating the plan for all activities within it, the context within which institutional life takes place and the meaning given to the daily schedule (O'Brien, 1982). What happens inside these institutions, however, rarely corresponds to specific models or programmes. Institutional realities are shaped by the contextual, social reality of which they are a part, and with which they interact, and by the patterns of wider social relations brought into the institutions by the inmates. These help to shape and redefine the rehabilitative model within the institution. Thus the concept of rehabilitation should be understood contextually. The reality of rehabilitation is given its meaning through the institutional set of relationships defined by different models of rehabilitation, the social realities within which the institution is situated and which traverse its operations, as well as the wider set of social relations brought into the institution by its occupants.

THE CONSTRUCTION OF FEMALE DEVIANCE

The notion of female deviance developed in South Africa was shaped by an interrelated set of ideas about crime and mental defect. These ideas were generally applicable to girls, but also had a more specific racial component which was differentially applied to black and white girls. Its advocates were drawn from a new professional class in South African society. In the first two decades of the century the growing involvement of the welfare movement amongst urban 'poor whites', as well as the reorganisation of the education system for whites in general, brought in their wake a phalanx of educationists, psychiatrists, psychologists and social workers. Initially drawing on the same repertoire of ideas as Norman, they became increasingly receptive in the 1920s to the work on juvenile delinquency of psychologists William Healey in the United States and Cyril Burt in England. This approach readily segregated environmental from innate factors in the aetiology of juvenile crime. Whereas Norman and his co-workers tended to stress poverty as the major cause of delinquency, now, increasingly, psychology or intelligence was stressed, with delinquency being linked to behavioural traits and low intelligence. This shift had distinct implications for the content of rehabilitation strategies in South Africa.

By the beginning of the 1920s there was some overlap in penal and welfare–educational ideology. This was particularly evident in the official concern with the relative intelligence of black and white youth. It was an issue closely bound up with providing biological justifications for classifying inmates in the reformatories and segregating the races in the wider society. A virtual mania for testing and classification developed. Racist stereotypes were given a new, supposedly scientific legitimacy. C. T. Loram, Chief Inspector of Native Education in Natal, tested African children and 'discovered' that mental development was 'arrested' at adolescence (Loram, 1917 and 1927). Dr M. L. Fick, who studied at Harvard University and became an educational psychologist with the National Bureau of Educational and Social Research (predecessor of the Human Sciences Research Council), conferred further authority on these views by his tests, the results of which were published in 1939 in his book *The Educability of the South African Native* (see Cross, 1986; Dubow, 1987).

Fick's primary concern during the 1920s and the Depression years of the early 1930s, however, was mental deficiency amongst South Africa's poor and unemployed white population. This was the time when the 'poor white problem' was at the forefront of social and political thought. Reformatories and industrial schools provided an excellent laboratory for Fick's work and, accordingly, he and other doctors and psychiatrists conducted extensive tests in these institutions. The results were, not surprisingly, used to prove the connection between juvenile delinquency and mental abnormality (Moll, 1923).

Both classist and racist assumptions about the mental inferiority of blacks and poor whites, and the superiority of whites in general and of the middle classes in particular, underpinned the connection made between delinquency and mental deficiency. In the discourse of 'scientific racism', black juveniles were defined as backward because they belonged to an inferior race; black delinquency was, therefore, an expected rather than an abnormal state of affairs. On the other hand delinquency amongst whites, and in particular those seen as 'poor whites', was a sign of racial degeneration amongst the civilised races, a product of the uncontrolled development of a black and white proletariat thrown together in the cities (Dubow, 1987). Nonetheless, mental backwardness among 'poor whites' was not as irretrievable a phenomenon as among black youth. Many argued that the causes of white delinquency were different from those for black, thus guaranteeing at least the possibility of white educability and social mobility.

In 1928 Louis van Schalkwyk, Inspector of Industrial Schools for the Union Education Department, conceded that the 'great problem with which industrial schools have to cope is backwardness or mental retardation'. However, the cause of this backwardness, he argued, lay not in 'inferior mental abilities' but in an 'absence of parental responsibilities' and in 'psychopathic tendencies, that is tendencies towards conduct, character or personality difficulties' (TA, UED, b). In the case of both black and white youth, delinquency provided evidence of backwardness, but whereas defective home conditions, nonconformity and intractability were more often invoked as explanations in the case of white delinquents, in the case of black delinquents their supposed backwardness was explained on biological or cultural grounds. Degeneracy among whites was construed largely as a social phenomenon, a result of the corrupting effects of their environment. Degeneracy among blacks, by contrast, was construed as part of their biological constitution.

The Eshowe and Standerton institutions for girls developed within this general framework of thought about deviance. In addition, however, delinquency and mental deficiency amongst girls in particular were related to their gender and their sexuality. Young girls who were seen to be sexually active as well as rebellious were likely to be considered abnormal and deviant. The view expressed by Dr Moll, that 'the incidence of mental defect amongst sexually delinquent females [is] nearly always much higher than in any other group of wrongdoers' (Moll, 1923; see also Roos, c. 1920), was not an uncommon one. Here he was referring to the image of the white proletarian child, the potential prostitute, already congenitally disposed to degeneracy. These perceptions were reflected in the official reasons for the revolts at Eshowe, cited earlier. They embodied classic nineteenth-century stereotypes, translated into a colonial context. The distance of the white female deviant from the 'normal' woman was represented by her implied pathological predisposition to sexual delinquency, as well as by her feeblemindedness.

Any sexual flouting of the racial code reinforced the association of lower-class girls and women with degeneracy. As Gilman has pointed out, the term 'miscegenation', dating from the late nineteenth century and still in use at this time, embodied a fear not merely of interracial sexuality, but also of its supposed result, the decline of the white population. If such liaisons produced any children at all, these would be weak and doomed, threatening the white race with deterioration and ultimate defeat in the struggle for survival (Gilman, 1985: 107). On white women and girls, then, depended the survival of the race; theirs was the responsibility for keeping the race 'pure'.

The black woman or young girl stood at the opposite end of the scale of civilisation, of order and control. In late-nineteenth-century thought she was, as Gilman has shown, the source of corruption and disease, her sexuality an icon for black sexuality in general, black sexuality in turn being an icon for deviant sexuality as a whole. This representation of black female sexuality had a strong South African component. The 'Hottentot' woman, for example, during the nineteenth century became the epitome in European thinking of 'primitive' sexuality (Gilman, 1985). The black female represented in these terms society out of control.

Herein, perhaps, lies part of the explanation for the lack of a colour bar in the girls' reformatory. Placing white deviant girls in the same institution as black thus underlined their common lot as the dregs ('degenerates') of humanity in the minds of those shaping their lives. The white girls sent to Eshowe were girls who, through their close association with blacks and through their lack of feminine virtue, had abandoned their allegiance to 'civilisation'. They were the product of that moral decay attendant on race fusion and miscegenation which so obsessed the eugenicist-inspired social engineers of South Africa's racial order. As such, these girls were 'biological degenerates', deserving only of being cast out from white society. The black girls, by contrast, were present in the reformatories as exemplars of social disorder. Both groups represented that which the social engineers of segregation sought to isolate and identify as abnormal. It must be noted, however, that the numbers in the girls' reformatory were not very large. Between 1926 and 1934 an average of 8 white, 1 'Asiatic' and 77 'native and coloured' girls were sent to the reformatory per year (Prisons Department, Annual Reports 1926–1934).

In the segregated industrial school such girls could conceivably have contaminated those in whom the process of demoralisation was but embryonic. Standerton was established for white girls who had not crossed the boundary separating white from black, but who were living in circumstances or were developing habits which might help break down these social barriers. They could still be rescued and saved from this fate by removing them from an environment of vice and immorality to one of discipline and control.

These ideologies had material effects on the lives of the inmates of the institutions. Since their sexual deviance was held responsible for their aggression, they were punished for it with an equivalent psychological violence. If, as at Estcourt (later Eshowe), where the girls were already defined as deviant, their aggression and resistance to control appeared overdeveloped and could not be corrected by punishment, then they could be considered incorrigible, and so eligible for gaol, or certifiably insane. In 1930 a 15-year-old girl was sent for examination to a psychiatrist because she was 'very temperamental and quarrelsome [and] subject to violent outbursts of temper which were followed by prolonged fits of hysterical weeping' (TA, UED, c). In this case the medical officer found her to be sane and she was returned to her home. Others were not so lucky. Sophie K was transferred to a mental hospital in the same year, having caused 'considerable trouble and anxiety'. She had 'made no effort ... to reform herself. Her industry [was] very unsatisfactory. She [had] been the cause of many disturbances among the inmates. [She was] immoral in her conduct, very untruthful and dishonest' (ibid.). It was in this year, too, that the Board of Visitors of the reformatory recommended that the girls be examined by a psychiatrist every quarter

(TA, UED, d).

During 1933 and 1934, when the reformatory was racked by revolt, several girls were certified insane. One of these was Maria K, who had 'always been a most difficult case and [had] violent attacks of uncontrollable rage [which] were a danger to others' (TA, UED, a). Selina M was certified twice for being 'subject to periodical fits of violence and committing assaults on others' (TA, UED, e).

The proof of abnormality at Standerton was provided by regular mental testing. Here Dr Fick undertook testing with the clear intention of segregating and subjecting to sterner discipline those girls found to be 'feeble-minded' or 'sub-normal' (TA, UED, f). The more 'backward' a girl was, the more it was assumed she required strict discipline. Backwardness and abnormality were frequently linked to conduct, especially that regarded as defiant (TA, UED, f). After regular testing, the degree of sub-normality at Standerton was found to be high, and in July 1932 a special class was started, which subsequently grew into a separate school, Die Vlakteskool. The purpose of this segregation was to prepare 'sub-normal' girls for their expected restricted futures. While the prospective employment of a 'normal' delinquent was domestic service, sub-normal girls were not considered fit for this. 'The only avenue of employment for these misfits', Dr Fick intoned, 'appears to be work of a routine type in a factory with proper supervision in a hostel after working hours' (TA, UED, g).

Although special provision had thus been made for 'mentally sub-normal' girls, a need was still felt for a special institution that would cater for Standerton girls regarded as 'difficult' (Marks, 1987). Both the synod of the Dutch Reformed Church and George Hofmeyr, Secretary of the Union Education Department, took a special interest in establishing such an institution. Accordingly, in 1932 the Luckhoff Institute was opened in Durbanville, near Cape Town, to house about 40 girls defined as psychopathic. It was later renamed the Durbanville Institute for Girls. This Institute took in white girls only and resembled Eshowe in not including any instruction beyond drudgery in its programme.

The concept of female delinquency that gained currency during the first three decades of the century drew on and adapted wider ideologies of racial and sexual inferiority. It acted as a powerful legitimating tool for the isolation and differential treatment of a sector of working-class society seen as increasingly 'abnormal' in the eyes of a segregationist state-in-the-making.

REASONS FOR COMMITTAL: CLASS, GENDER AND RACE
The grounds on which girls were referred to the industrial school or to the reformatory underscore the argument that they represented a section of a segregated society 'out of control'. The legislative under-

pinnings of the industrial school–reformatory system were provided by two pieces of legislation. The Children's Protection Act of 1913, which was largely the work of the Children's Aid Society, provided several grounds on which white children could be removed to industrial schools, while the Prisons and Reformatories Act of 1911 specified conviction of a criminal offence as a precondition for committal to a reformatory (CAS, 1913). In the case of the industrial schools, white children under the age of 16 could be committed if their parents were found to have no fixed home, had been charged with a criminal offence or were living in circumstances likely to favour the 'corruption or seduction' of their charges. In addition to the grounds of destitution or neglect, children could also be sent to an industrial school for 'uncontrollability', such as playing truant from school or being engaged in begging or street trading. Almost without exception, it was poor or working-class children who were targeted by these criteria. The industrial school system also provided the state with a useful alternative to government schools for children from orphanages, and frequently orphaned children were automatically transferred to these schools upon reaching the age of 12. Magistrates, social workers and school boards were authorised to refer children to industrial schools.

There is evidence, however, that parents themselves often committed their children as well (CAS, 1909: letter to Rose Innes). The Children's Aid Society complained again and again that 'it would appear that the parents thought that the industrial school would be an easy way to get rid of their children' (CAS, 1909: letter to Rose Innes). At their congress in Johannesburg in 1912, the Zuid Afrikaansche Vrouwen Federatie called for penalties to be imposed on parents 'who were only too pleased to get rid of their charges' (CAS, 1913; Van Krieken, 1987). Often these parents had been forced to resort to this step because of their poverty. Thus Eleanor Shipley, herself a pupil at Standerton in 1926 and 1927, later committed her daughter to the industrial school, partly as punishment for the girl's 'cheek' and partly so that she could learn home-making skills. Abandoned by her husband, working long hours in a clothing factory and burdened with the care of five children, Shipley saw the industrial school as an option that would free her from her double burden as both a domestic and a wage worker (CAS, 1909; Krut, 1983; Eleanor Shipley, interview).

Undoubtedly many real cases of child abuse, neglect and incest came before the welfare community, and many of the girls who were institutionalised were very real victims of their home and living situations (see CAS, Minutes 1914; Krut, 1983). Nonetheless, the decision to institutionalise a girl often involved an official construction of her situation that reduced it to a question of morality and her conformity to the stereotypes of appropriate feminine behaviour. The

Children's Aid Society had the power to remove children from 'immoral' or 'unfit environments'. 'Immorality' when applied to parents usually meant that they were involved either in illicit liquor dealing or in racially mixed relationships (Krut, 1983: 27).

In the case of girls, immorality was also linked to their sexual behaviour. This is illustrated in the case of May and Winifred S (15 and 13 years old respectively), who were sent to Standerton during the 1920s on the grounds that they were destitute. Their parents, while in South Africa, had separated. Their mother had taken them with her to England, where she had placed them in a workhouse. Here they were found by a Mrs G, who had links with the Children's Aid Society and the girls' father in Johannesburg. May, then 11, was found 'covered in sores', 'suffering from a certain disease' and to have had 'immoral relations' with her mother's lover. Mrs G returned the girls to South Africa but found them 'more than she could manage' and so took them to the Children's Aid Society. What struck the Society was that 'May is most untruthful and disobedient and is not clean in her person and her morals are bad. The same applies to the younger girl Winifred…. The only thing to save them from becoming utterly bad is to put them in an industrial school where they can be under strict discipline' (CAS, Minutes 1914).

Comparison with the referral history of white boys helps to cast more light on the sexual construction of female crime. Two sources exist to examine this: the Annual Reports of the Department of Justice and Prisons up to 1918 and a Prisons Department file on 35 cases of children transferred to reformatories from industrial schools during 1932 (file 1/691/30, part 1). The former indicate that by far the majority of white boys committed to reformatory sentences at the Breakwater Reformatory in Cape Town during this period were convicted for illicit liquor-selling. White male youth criminality was mainly determined by their involvement in this trade. The problem amongst girls, however, was construed as one of immorality. In the file on 35 cases transferred to reformatories during 1932, two were girls, both of them classified 'coloured' (ibid.). The boys were all transferred on the grounds of 'destitution' and 'uncontrollability'. In all but one case, in which the boy was considered to be an 'absolute sex maniac', 'uncontrollability' referred to absconding from the industrial school at Heidelberg, theft, or having an 'evil effect' on other boys in the school. In the case of the two girls, 'uncontrollability' had a different connotation. Lucy L's crime (she was 15 years old) was that she had 'been keeping bad company and [was] immoral having had sexual intercourse with several men'. As a 'coloured' girl she could not be sent to Standerton, so was sent to the reformatory at Eshowe instead. In the case of Nettie S (also 15), 'uncontrollability' also referred to sexual promiscuity: 'The girl was working for Mrs W. P.

Mulder, but on several occasions ran away and had immoral relationships with coloured men. She was therefore brought under the provisions of the Children's Protection Act to place her under control and remove her from moral danger. She should be transferred to a reformatory where she can be under strict control and discipline' (ibid.).

Although these cases form a very small sample, the different interpretations of what constituted uncontrollability among the boys and the girls do illustrate a more general trend.

An analysis of the crimes for which black and white girls were committed to Eshowe shows, further, that the concern with sexuality and morality was most marked with regard to white girls. Between June 1927 and June 1934 there were some 268 girls in the reformatory. The vast majority of African and 'coloured' girls were committed on the grounds of theft, including stock theft, and house-breaking with intent to steal. The second most common reason for committal was poisoning and murder, with a few cases of assault, arson, desertion from employment and trespassing also reported. By contrast, just under half the white girls were sent to the reformatory because of theft. The rest had been institutionalised on various charges relating to 'immorality': prostitution, loitering with intent to solicit, and vagrancy. At a time when 'immorality' was often a euphemism for relationships across the colour line, interracial sex featured prominently as a reason for committal. A 1931 report of the reformatory stated unambiguously that 'many of the European inmates have been sentenced under the Immorality Act and for co-habitation with natives' (TA, UED, b).

Thus, whereas white girls were convicted mainly for offences of a social-sexual nature, black girls and white boys were more often charged for property offences. White girls, furthermore, were criminalised for transgressing not only the rules of socially acceptable feminine behaviour, but also those regulating relations between black and white. Black girls, in contrast, were criminalised for transgressing class laws and violating property relations in a colonial order. They were punished for crimes that represented a loss of control in society in general, whereas white girls were punished for their betrayal of white society in particular.

THE DISCIPLINARY REGIME OF EDUCATION AND REHABILITATION

Rehabilitation strategies at Standerton and Estcourt (Eshowe) were dominated by conventional notions of what constituted women's work and by specific structures of control. In this respect the two institutions did not differ from the girls' hostels established by missionary societies for black girls in South Africa's cities, or from the girls' industrial schools and reformatories in the United States, England and Australia. In all these institutions the curricular emphasis was on vocational training for domestic service, whether in the girls' own homes or in the homes of others (Cock, 1980; Brenzel, 1975, 1980; Gaitskell, 1979, 1983; Wimshurst, 1984; Hahn Rafter, 1983). Correctional education for girls was primarily meant to equip them for domestic service or motherhood. There were, however, differences in the way the ideology of domesticity was applied, as well as in the level of sophistication of control found in the two types of institution. In addition, the types of instruction the white girls received depended on assessments of their abilities through mental testing, and initially some were given the opportunity of limited academic work, if they were able to show the aptitude.

Thus some limited attention was paid to non-vocational education at the industrial school at Standerton, once it had been transferred to the Union Education Department in 1917. After 1919 outstanding pupils were sent to the local provincial school. At the industrial school itself, provision was made for schooling up to Standard 6 and for instruction in the National Housewife's Certificate once Standard 6 had been passed. Immediately after the school was transferred to the Union Education Department in 1917, moves were set afoot to ensure that 'a large number of pupils ... attain a better position in life' and be trained to become teachers (in housecraft schools), typists and nurses, but not much came of this initiative.

Apart from this scholastic work, the girls were also instructed in the following trades: laundry, sewing, cooking and upholstery. Courses offered in the boys' industrial school, on the other hand, included carpentry, joinery and cabinet-making, boot-making, tailoring and plumbing. The teacher of the upholstery class at Standerton was a man; in this class, girls made, amongst other things, bookshelves and cupboards, thus learning woodwork, a trade usually found only at boys' schools.

The main emphasis, however, remained on work qualifying girls for domestic service. This was underscored by the appointment of an Inspectress of Domestic Science for the school in 1921, one Miss Chattey, and by the apprenticeship of large numbers of girls as 'home helps' during the last years of their training. Their instruction thus provided the majority of girls for gender-specific, unskilled work in later life. Eleanor Shipley, for example, spent the greater part of her life washing clothes for others and working as a seamstress in a clothing factory. She was not unusual in this regard. A study of former pupils, conducted in 1931, showed that '50 per cent of the girls visited were with their families and of these 10 per cent were working for other people; the rest helped at home' (Albertyn, 1935: 93).

Before 1930 both the academic achievements of the girls in the provincial school as well as the instruction in woodwork were a matter of some pride to the school authorities. The former confirmed a belief in the educability of industrial school girls and in the possibility that they could be rehabilitated. Success justified the existence of the school. In 1929 an industrial school girl gained the highest marks for Form One in both her class and in the district as a whole.

Opposing notions about the backwardness of delinquent girls were, however, gaining ground by the late 1920s. Continual testing confirmed beliefs about their ineducability, and determined official perceptions about their future performance. In 1929 the School Inspector's report noted that 'About 70% of the pupils are of the mentally backward (subnormal) type. The quality of the schoolwork is thus of an elementary nature considered to be within the limits of the pupils' intellectual capacity and to make a certain degree of development possible' (TA, UED, f; translated). At this point the academic curriculum was modified: geography was dropped to allow for a greater emphasis on gardening and chicken-farming, and a special class and eventually a separate school, Die Vlakteskool, was started.

This was the time when concern about rescuing poor whites was at its height. Nationally, an inquiry into poverty (amongst whites only) was undertaken by the Carnegie Commission, its results being published in 1932. One of its key participants was the educationist and historian, E. G. Malherbe, who later observed that, because of their association with 'the destitute, the defective and the delinquent, as well as with manual work', which was generally seen to be the province of blacks, a permanent stigma became attached to the industrial schools: 'Though the Church baptized it and the Prisons Department nursed it for a time, it was begotten in shame. Placed later on the doorstep of the provincial education departments, this foundling was never happy. In fact, it was the Cinderella of the school system' (1925: 165).

If the industrial school was the Cinderella of the school system, the reformatory was its Caliban. At Estcourt (Eshowe) there was little, if any, academic instruction and domestic instruction was instructional in name only. Academic education involved gathering girls of all ages into one large room where the pretence was made of schooling them in the three Rs (Mrs Mpanza, interview). Most of the girls' time was spent in work designed to keep them busy and to supply other penal institutions and industries with various goods (UG36–18).

By 1934 some differentiation in the type of manual work undertaken by black and white girls at the reformatory had occurred. Even though both groups were occupied in unskilled work, the nature of the differentiation is suggestive of a racial hierarchy. For the black girls, 'industrial education' consisted of work done out of doors, in the gaol garden adjoining the reformatory. Here they gardened or beat sisal leaves for the making of mats and baskets (TA, UED, b). The white girls, in contrast, were generally employed inside the institution, making and mending inmates' clothing and working in the laundry. A revealing point of difference in status between the industrial school and the reformatory is that, whereas at the industrial school black women did the laundry for the white girls, at the reformatory the white girls did the laundry for the institution (including the black girls) as a whole. Thus at the industrial school, the hidden curriculum prepared white girls for a racial division of domestic labour within their future homes.

The subtle colour bar operating in the work the girls were given at the reformatory was more overt in the living arrangements, as well as in the privileges, limited as they were, that were eventually made available to white girls only. Thus the reformatory dormitories were segregated, while white girls whose conduct merited it were given permission to go on outings. The outings began to occur only after 1926, and took the form of invitations by the Board of Visitors to selected girls to attend Christmas picnics, motor outings, 'bioscope entertainments', lectures, swimming galas, sing-songs at the local school and theatrical 'entertainments' (TA, UED, b).

These discriminatory privileges can be interpreted in a number of different ways. They may have formed part of an attempt to develop a system of rewards and privileges for good conduct that was previously non-existent and strongly recommended after the riots of 1926, in which white girls had been involved. That only the white girls received this special treatment, however, reflects the racial form that charitable concern amongst the authorities took. The privileges may also have been part of an effort to try to heighten the white girls' sense of superiority over the black girls by virtue of their being white. In effect they operated as a form of social inclusion of the white girls and social exclusion of the black.

There were certainly grounds for official anxiety about the relative lack of colour consciousness amongst the girls themselves. Although there is evidence of racial insults being exchanged during fights, no doubt exacerbated by the differential positions occupied by the white and the black girls in the reformatory hierarchy, there is also evidence that black and white girls formed strong emotional ties of warmth and affection, frequently in active lesbian sexual relationships. Girls formed themselves into 'husband and wife' teams and could become so attached to their partners that if one partner found she was to be separated from the other, she would 'deliberately misbehave, regardless of any punishment to get back to her ...' (TA, UED, a). In these relationships no consideration was given to race. There was, indeed, considerable concern on the part of the authorities that 'European inmates encourage familiar behaviour on the part of non-European inmates towards them' (TA, UED, b). The relative privileges of limited social inclusion for the white girls may well have been a response to the social implications of this sub-culture. Whether it was a deliberate and conscious response or not, the process of discrimination, as well as its effects, expressed in microcosm the response of South Africa's dominant classes to forms of social organisation amongst the under-classes which threatened its racial authority and undermined the structures of control (see Davies, 1979).

The disciplinary regimes of the industrial school and the reforma-tory, while sharing certain features of 'the total institution' (Goffman, 1961), did evince differences in the way in which the girls were incorporated into the overall system of control. The structure of discipline and control in the reformatory corresponded to that of a prison. The institution, despite its location in verdant Natal, was itself housed in an old prison building after the move to Eshowe. Girls were locked into barred dormitories at night and were guarded by baton-wielding warders by day. Resistance between 1926 and 1934 thus took the classic form of prison riots. Doors, windows and dormitory partitions were smashed, dinner and work refused, and, at times, members of staff (all, apart from two black wardresses, white) were assaulted (TA, UED, a, b). When this happened in 1926 a police guard was called in, and those identified as the ringleaders were placed in solitary confinement in a small, dark and dank cell under the stairs, on spare diet, until their punishment had been decided upon by the local magistrate, in consultation with the matron.

In the industrial school discipline took a less overtly repressive form. The school was housed in military barracks dating from the Anglo–Boer War. These buildings were divided into 'cottages', each of which was run by an assistant matron, with the help of one of the 20 girls assigned to it. This girl was the patrol leader and was respon-sible for discipline, cleanliness and the tidiness in the cottage – a hard task, given the vermin-infested state of the buildings. The girls were under constant, albeit benignly expressed, surveillance – what one writer has referred to as 'affectional discipline' (Schlossman, 1977). By 1930 there were 29 members of staff as against 225–240 girls, giving a staff–pupil ratio of one to eight. An emphasis on personal loyalty to staff members was the chief mechanism for maintaining control; absconding, insolence and daydreaming were the main forms that 'counter-identification' with the institution took (Eleanor Shipley, interview; Haug, 1987).

At the industrial school the social exclusion of the girls was not as complete as it was, for the most part, at the reformatory. Girls were allowed to maintain greater contact with the outside world. As men-tioned earlier, after the Union Education Department took over the running of the school in 1917, some girls attended the local provincial school. Girls were also allowed to attend the cinema on Saturday afternoons, to receive visitors and parcels, to go camping during the holidays with the school, and to go home once a year, provided that their parents had made timely applications. They were constantly reminded, however, that these privileges depended on their good conduct, as well as on the material well-being of their families. The privilege of going home was frequently withheld, not because of the conduct of the girl, but on the grounds of the poverty of her parents (TA, UED, j). Several letters in the files testify to the often unsuccessful appeals by parents to see their children. A typical one reads: 'I have 2 daughters in the Industrial School at Standerton who have been there for seven years. I have applied for vacation leave before and got it; the principal now refuses because I am in arrears with fees (TA, UED, j). One mother who had been refused permission to take her daughters out, wrote back in frustration and with exquisite irony: 'If my home is not good enough for my own children to spend their vacation, I must point out that I have two more children in my custody, and they might just as well take these two from me' (TA, UED, j).

Thus both the reformatory and the industrial school operated as systems of social exclusion. Mechanisms did exist in each, however, to demonstrate to the girls that a measure of inclusion in the wider society was possible, though conditional. In the reformatory it was conditional on the colour of the girl's skin and very grudgingly granted. In the industrial school it was conditional on the girl's conduct and on the conduct of her family, this being associated with financial respectability. If a girl conformed, she was drawn into the embrace of respectable white society, redeemed despite the taint of blood and history. If she rebelled, however, she was cast out to the reformatory. Here the form of inclusion came as an act of charity once or twice a year. Its price and its purpose was the total social exclusion of the black girls in the institution.

CONCLUSION

From the mid-1930s onwards, conceptions of delinquency, the educability of girls and that of blacks began to change. Several factors combined to bring this about: the rise of manufacturing industry and its attendant segregationist ideology, the rapid urbanisation of blacks, and the emergence of a powerful class of professional child-savers. Amongst the new generation of liberal reformers, segregationist practices were increasingly justified on cultural rather than biological grounds, although beliefs about innate biological differences between blacks and whites and between males and females had become part of commonsense ideology and were firmly entrenched in educational practices such as regular IQ testing (which continues to this day).

In 1934 the administration of reformatories was transferred to the

Union Education Department. Colour boundaries became more rigidly fixed. After this period delinquent white girls were hardly ever sent to Eshowe but were more likely to be sent to the Durbanville Institute for Girls. Henceforward, although still marginalised, they were to be accommodated within the dominant racial hierarchy, through institutions whose social distancing from those for blacks was complete. Within this hierarchy, however, the reformatory and industrial school system continued to operate as a system of relative social exclusion for its inmates.

This chapter has shown how a notion of female deviance arose in early-twentieth-century South Africa which linked deviance to inter-racial sexuality on the part of white girls and the flouting of master–servant relations in a colonial order on the part of black girls. The girls institutionalised at Eshowe and Standerton represented a minute fraction of a larger section of society that was transgressing the sexual, racial and class codes of a segregated society. In criminalising such actions and defining them as transgressions, the new white middle and ruling classes were participating in the process of regulating and defining 'normal' social and sexual relationships in the society.

'Normal' social and sexual relations between black and white and between the white unskilled or labouring and middle classes were further enforced in the rehabilitative regimes of the reformatory and the industrial school. By contrasting the practice of rehabilitation in the reformatory and in the industrial school, and looking within the reformatory at the different treatment of black and white girls, the chapter has also tried to show how the practice (as opposed to the concept) of rehabilitation – in terms of training programmes and degree of exclusion from civil society – was contextually defined. The rehabilitation of white girls involved their conditional inclusion in the social and ideological structures of white supremacy, albeit as inferior members; the rehabilitation of black girls involved their incorporation as subject creatures into authoritarian domestic and unskilled wage relations. Yet, as the description of the riots which opened this chapter testifies, this strategy failed to produce unequivocally 'docile [female] bodies' or to control, within the institution, the growth of powerful networks of female solidarity (however temporary and flawed).

13

The women's suffrage movement: The politics of gender, race and class

CHERRYL WALKER

> *Question*: 'Do you favour votes for all women, irrespective of colour?'
> *Answer*: 'As a woman, sir, yes ... but as a South African born person, I feel that it would be wiser if we gave the vote to the European woman only' (from The Report of the Select Committee on the Enfranchisement of Women, SC12–1926: 51).

VOTES FOR WOMEN AND THE SOUTH AFRICAN 'BUT'

Women's suffrage was a minor but persistent issue in white politics between 1892, when a motion calling for a qualified franchise for women was defeated in the Cape House of Assembly, and 1930, the year when a racially exclusive Act of Parliament finally enfranchised all white women over the age of 18.[1] For the 4 000 or so members of the national women's suffrage body, the Women's Enfranchisement Association of the Union (WEAU), it was the culmination of many years of uphill work. White women had finally won their political majority and, the suffragists expected, would now take their rightful place as equals with men in political life.

It was a victory predicated on racial domination. It was not simply that black women were excluded from the vote. The enfranchisement of white women formed part of a much larger strategy of attack by General Hertzog and the ruling National Party on already enfranchised black male voters in the Cape Province. In the Cape, in contrast to the unambiguous whites-only policies of the three northern provinces, a formally non-racial but qualified franchise prevailed. Here, the small number of black men who met certain statutory educational and property qualifications were entitled to vote alongside their white counterparts, and this privilege had, after much wrangling, been specifically protected in the Union constitution of 1909: a two-thirds majority of both Houses of Parliament sitting together was required to amend it. A major political goal of Hertzog's government after it came to power in 1924 was to sweep away these rights and establish the unadulterated white supremacy of the northern provinces throughout the country. Thwarted in his efforts to abolish the Cape franchise outright, in the late 1920s Hertzog turned to women's suffrage to launch what Henry Burton, a former South African Party cabinet minister, described as a 'flank attack' on the 'fortress of the Cape franchise' (Molteno, 1959: 7). Less than 20 per cent of the Cape electorate in 1929, black voters amounted in 1931, once white women had been enfranchised, to just under 11 per cent of voters in the Cape and less than 5 per cent of the electorate nationally (Walker, 1979: 109).

The whites-only WEAU cooperated with the attack. Until the mid-1920s its policy was to secure the vote for women on the same terms as for men – that is, for white women only in the northern provinces and for those women who would meet the existing franchise qualifications in the Cape. The reach of its non-racialism was thus extremely limited, but even this came under fire. In the 1920s, under pressure to clarify its stance, the WEAU began to backtrack as self-interest and loyalty to the ruling white group became paramount considerations. 'We know in our hearts we shall not get all that we ask, but we are very anxious for the half-loaf,' said Lady Rose Innes of the WEAU in 1926. 'The other may come' (SC12–26: 17). Most suffragists resented having their own enfranchisement delayed by the haggling over the Cape franchise and ultimately identified themselves with the government's segregationist policies. In the long years of struggle leading up to the 1930 debate, white self-interest in the WEAU had never been seriously challenged by its commitment to women's rights anyway, since most members' understanding of 'women' did not extend to women of other racial groups. Sex loyalty stopped at the heavily guarded boundaries of white privilege.

In black politics before World War Two women's suffrage was barely an issue at all. Relationships between the sexes were not on the agenda. They were sheltered from critique behind the sustained assault of white power on black living standards and political status, and the further bulwark of the ideology of male superiority–female subordination within black society. The widespread assumption that politics was properly a male preserve went unchallenged while black leaders concentrated on more urgent matters.

The overriding concern of political organisations such as the African National Congress (ANC), formed in 1912, a year after the WEAU, was to defend the limited voting rights African people still enjoyed in the Cape against the rising tide of white segregationism. For most black politicians, campaigning to extend the franchise was beyond the bounds of feasible politics at that time. Campaigning to extend it to women, who were not even recognised as full members within the ANC, was even more of an irrelevancy compared to the central issue

– not till 1943 were women granted full membership, with voting rights, in the organisation.[2] A similar preoccupation with the prevailing politics of racial power characterised the South African Indian Congress and the African People's Organisation (APO).

This is not to say that black women were politically invisible. The vigorous campaign against municipal pass laws and permits for women, which began in the Orange Free State in 1913 and spread to the Rand, indicated that African women could be roused to public demonstration over certain issues.[3] Also in 1913, numbers of Indian women participated in the successful passive resistance campaign against a Supreme Court ruling which had invalidated the legal standing of marriages performed according to Hindu or Moslem religious rites (see chapter 6). Protests by African women in Natal in the late 1920s and on the Rand in the 1930s and 1940s, over a government crackdown on the home brewing of beer, were further evidence of black women's readiness to mobilise around issues that affected them and their families directly.

When measured against the political suppression of black people as a whole, however, as well as the traumatic dislocation of black social and economic life in the early twentieth century, the question of votes for women shrank into insignificance. For the average woman toiling to survive in the reserves and rural areas or in the burgeoning locations and shantytowns of the urban areas, it was far too abstract and narrow a demand. The handful of middle-class black women who recognised that women were discriminated against as a sex and who consciously challenged the assumption of politics as a male preserve, still identified themselves with the overall programme for black advancement espoused by male-dominated organisations. For them women's rights could not be separated from black rights; they formed only one strand in a much larger campaign for equality.

The operation of colour consciousness in the suffrage campaign is very clear. More difficult to measure is the operation of class interests. Certainly class was a factor. The WEAU was made up largely of middle-class women who were campaigning for all the privileges of their class denied them by virtue of their sex. The Cape franchise, the source of much of the controversy in the suffrage campaign and the rallying point for African nationalists, was itself based on class-bound qualifications of property and of education – and the suffragists' proposal to apply it to white women in the Cape was, in fact, attacked as elitist by white populists. For the most part, however, their class interests were not called into the open. Race and class consciousness converged, with the language of racial domination assuming ideological primacy.

White supremacy, black dispossession – it is impossible to discuss the history of women's suffrage in South Africa without becoming caught up in the racially charged struggle for control over resources and power. Overtly and covertly, this dictated much of the programme and the conduct of the movement before 1930, as well as attitudes towards the campaign then and since. Inasmuch as the women's suffrage movement has been critically analysed, this is the perspective from which it has most often been viewed – subsequent commentators reflecting the same preoccupation with the ordering of relations between black and white and, to a lesser extent, property and labour, as most of the actors in the suffrage movement itself.

Yet the history of the women's suffrage movement also has much to say about the politics of gender in the first decades of the twentieth century. In the suffrage debates spanning the forty-odd years of the movement it is possible to trace significant shifts in the dominant ideology of gender – that espoused by the white ruling class. These in turn related to a reformulation of women's roles in an industrialising age in which greater numbers of women were being drawn into wage labour, educational opportunities for women were expanding and the extended patriarchal family of the rural areas was being challenged by the new and unsettled conditions of South Africa's fast-growing towns and cities. The progress of the suffrage campaign was a particularly visible measure of the adjustment in attitudes towards women that took place in this time. By 1930 motherhood was no longer seen as incompatible with political equality, female virtue was no longer coterminous with staying at home all one's life. The tight controls on women's independent standing of pre-industrial white society had loosened considerably.

Yet if the suffrage movement has something to tell us about changes in the organisation of gender in the first part of the twentieth century, it also has much to say about continuity in the fundamental assumptions about women's role and nature. The granting of formal political equality to white women did not represent a revolution in male–female relations, not even within the white family. The principle of supreme male authority over the household, though less securely rooted than in the nineteenth century, was not overthrown. The persistence of the underlying principles of gender organisation, in a time of economic and social change, is a basic theme of this chapter. So too is the lack of commitment to any transcendent sex loyalty on the part of women – their primary identification lying with their own community, class and colour. Even among white women, ethnic loyalty to their own language group took first place, proving a major obstacle to the establishment of an organisation representative of both English and Afrikaner suffragists.

The discussion is organised in three main sections. After a brief look at the organisation of gender in settler society, the chapter outlines the history of the suffrage campaign and the underlying developments in the economic and social order. Thereafter it looks at the ideological underpinnings of the campaign, noting the shift in emphasis from a preoccupation with the proper ordering of gender relations to that of race relations on the part of the ruling class.

GENDER IDEOLOGY IN WHITE SETTLER SOCIETIES

The Boer tradition

The political culture that developed in the white settler societies of southern Africa was a thoroughly male one. From the earliest days of Dutch settlement at the Cape, government was seen as unquestionably a male responsibility. Settler society rested on a military foundation and war was the province of men. Throughout the eighteenth century there were fewer white women than men at the Cape, and competition amongst men for control over the fertility and sexuality of these women was fierce. Marriage and submission to the authority of their husbands, the supervision of the household, the bearing of children and the inculcation of the norms and values of their society into the next generation – these were the unquestioned duties of white women. If any justification of male political power were ever required, the Bible abounded with texts that confirmed it as fundamental to the God-ordained nature of the world.

The Boers took their guns, their Bibles and their large families into the polities they established in the interior. Yet although the place of Boer women was centred around the domestic, this did not mean they were unproductive members of society, or that they were excluded from community affairs. Farm and homestead, in which women's labour played an important part, formed the basis of the simple pastoral economy of Boer society. The feminine virtues emphasised on the frontier were not the passivity, modesty and decorativeness favoured in the Victorian drawing-room of metropolitan England. As elaborated in more detail by Brink in chapter 11, women needed to be strong and resourceful and played an important part in holding Boer society together. Spies notes 'a strong Afrikaner tradition of women's involvement in communal life and political affairs, although they were not accorded formal rights' (1980: 162).

Thus it is not that surprising that the first recorded claim for political rights for women in South Africa was made by a group of Voortrekker women in Natal in 1843. A deputation of these women scandalised Henry Cloete, British High Commissioner to Natal, by declaring: 'that in consideration of the Battles in which they had been engaged with their husbands, they had obtained a promise that they would be entitled to a voice in all matters concerning the state of this country. That they had claimed this privilege, and although now repelled by the Volksraad, they had been deputed to express their fixed determination never to yield to British authority ...' (quoted in Van Rensburg, 1966: 111). The women's claim for a 'voice' can be compared to developments in other nineteenth-century frontier societies where women's political rights were recognised long before they were conceded in the capitals of Europe. The first place where women were enfranchised above the local level was the American state of Wyoming, where women got the vote in 1869. This was followed by the enfranchisement of women at a national level in New Zealand in 1893 and Australia in 1902 (UNESCO, 1964). The exigencies of frontier life could create favourable conditions for the abandoning of gender stereotypes about women's capabilities and exclusively domestic preoccupations.

In South Africa, however, nothing came of the 1843 claim. Despite the historical precedent thus set, the suffrage movement that developed from the late nineteenth century drew its inspiration not from the conditions of frontier life but from the conditions of early South African capitalism and the example of the metropolitan, especially the English, suffragists. Its leaders were not rural or Afrikaner, but characteristically middle-class, urban and English-speaking. An ambiguous motion of the Transvaal Volksraad did go so far as to confer *burgherreg* (citizenship) on the wives of all burghers of the Republic in 1855, but there is no record of these women ever utilising the vote. While continuing to wield considerable authority in the community, most Dutch/Afrikaans-speaking women were content to exercise their power indirectly, without questioning the principle of male hegemony until well into the twentieth century. The hold of the Dutch Reformed Church, with its fundamentalist reading of the Bible and rigid adherence to patriarchal ideology, remained a strongly conservative force, strenuously opposed to more liberal attitudes towards women's public role in the Afrikaner community. So too did nationalist ideology, which, in a way reminiscent of later black nationalist movements, subordinated sectional demands within the community to the overriding struggle of the Afrikaner people against British imperialism.

The British legacy

The British, for their part, brought to southern Africa a sex–gender system that was also based on the putatively innate and unambiguous differences between men and women. The development of industrial capitalism in Britain during the eighteenth century was characterised by a fundamental shift in the social function of the home and family, away from its earlier importance as a site of production, to a site, primarily, of reproduction and consumption. This separation between what became the essentially private domain of the home, which was the proper realm of women, and the public domain of productive work and politics, the realm of men, was basic to the organisation of gender relations in Britain in the nineteenth century. In Britain in the age of Darwin, the theological justification for patriarchy favoured by the Boers played a less prominent role than naturalist ones, however. As described by McClintock (chapter 4), the sexual division of labour was seen as grounded in biologically conditioned differences in aptitude and temperament between men and women – though God did remain useful as the supreme arbiter of the British patriarchal order.

The fact that working-class women formed a significant proportion of the industrial labour force did not challenge the fundamentals of this formulation. 'At the present day, when probably more than half the world's most laborious and ill-paid labour is still performed by women … it is somewhat difficult to reply with gravity to the assertion "let women be content to be the divine child bearer and ask no more,"' commented Olive Schreiner ironically in *Woman and Labour* (1911: 81). Gender ideology was, however, riddled with precisely such class-blinkered doublethink. Female employment did not weaken women's reproductive obligations as wives and mothers, although the growing participation of women in wage labour did necessitate adjustments in its operation. Rather, their new responsibilities as wage-workers were simply added onto the old – doublethink flowing smoothly into the double shift – while in factory and office, gender biologism rationalised the channelling of women into certain sex-stereotyped areas of work, such as in the food and clothing industries or teaching profession, and justified lower wages for female workers.

The industrial revolution did, however, create the conditions in which a feminist movement to improve the social, economic, legal and political position of women could take root. The vicious exploitation of workers under early industrial capitalism, the appalling living conditions in working-class slums, which spawned not only physical disease but also social disease such as prostitution and alcoholism, spurred workers and middle-class sympathisers to agitate for reform. The suffrage movements that developed in the industrial world in the second half of the nineteenth century were originally linked closely to the major social and political reform movements of that time, in which middle-class women played an active part – temperance, prison reform, 'rescue work' among prostitutes, and, especially important in the United States, the anti-slavery campaign (Rowbotham, 1973; H. M. Lewis, 1949). In many respects these campaigns were infused with the sexual morality and gender ideology of the Victorian middle class, in which feminine modesty, domesticity and sexual purity were extolled. Yet in engaging in this work women reformers were forced to confront their societies' prejudices and prohibitions against female involvement in public life and thus to challenge in their own lives many of the social conventions that inspired them. Thus women campaigning against slavery in the United States 'found that in so doing they had to defend their right to do so, this leading to demands for their own political and legal emancipation' (T. H. Lewis, 1949: 36). The vote became seen not only as a means to a reformist end, but also as a way of enhancing women's status in society. The first society formed specifically to campaign for votes for women in England was established in 1867. Two years later a National Women's Suffrage Union was founded in the United States.

Gender and race relations in South Africa

In South Africa an organised challenge to women's subordinate status was slower to surface. Early-nineteenth-century ideas about female domesticity and submission to male authority were brought to the region by British settlers and adapted to the particular conditions of South African colonial life. Most women who immigrated to South Africa from Britain in the nineteenth century were not headed for a life of indolence. Like their Boer counterparts, the wives and daughters of the early settlers on the Eastern Cape frontier and in Natal were expected to pull their weight in housework and also farmwork.

She should know how to cook and bake and get up linen; she should be able upon a pinch to clean and place in order the sleeping and dwelling rooms of the house, and she should be well-skilled in the use of the needle. She ought to have energy enough to teach and rule the Kafirs entrusted with indoor occupations. Besides all this, she should have the temperament, and bodily strength which will enable her to find pleasure in these household engagements. The delicately nurtured lady, who can do none of these things, should on no account be transplanted to what must necessarily prove to her a sadly ungenial soil.

Thus Robert Mann, Superintendent of Education in Natal between 1858 and 1870 (quoted in Beall, 1982: 109–10). Also permeating British women's reproductive responsibilities in the colonies was the task of producing healthy babies and raising loyal subjects for the Empire.

Many British women who immigrated to South Africa during the middle and latter part of the nineteenth century came alone, as governesses or domestic servants, from a lower middle-class or working-class background (Cock, 1980). They saw immigration as a route to social advancement, benefiting from the relative shortage of white women to marry out of service and settle quickly into membership of the ruling racial elite. In this process the contours of their gender-defined subordination were altered by the infusion into their social relationships of a racially defined hierarchy of status and power, that elevated white women into a position of privilege and authority over blacks, both men and women. Much of the burden of white women's reproductive work was lessened by the presence of a vast underclass of black servants, male and female, to whom more and more of the onerous housework and child-care was directed (see chapter 3). White women's role in running the household became a supervisory one.

A similar pattern of white female 'rule' over 'the Kafirs entrusted with indoor occupation' applied in the Boer household. In the private domain of the white household, a distinctive patterning of gender and race relations developed, in which the institution of black domestic service played a critical part. The white home became the arena in which white children were socialised not only into their gender roles, as little men and little women, but also into their roles as members of the ruling group. While relationships between white mistress and black servant were characterised by a certain enforced intimacy, the social gulf between the two was enormous. In the home whites learned that blacks were 'other'. The racial attitudes reproduced daily in a domestic setting white women took into the world with them, and into movements such as the suffrage campaign. At the same time, white women's role as wives and mothers took on a new symbolic significance in the context of white supremacy – white women were custodians of 'civilised values', icons to the ideology of racial superiority, to be revered, protected and firmly controlled by their men. White male control over their sexuality took on an added dimension of racial hegemony. In her thesis on the political economy of colonial Natal, Beall quotes an extract from the 1913 Report of the Commission Appointed to Enquire into Assaults on Women, which brings out this point clearly: 'Violated chastity, especially where the offender is a male of inferior race, is keenly felt amongst white people as an irreparable wrong to the victim and her relatives and an outrage upon the white race ...' (1982: 133–4).

The origins of the South African suffrage movement

As in Europe, the movement to enfranchise women in South Africa took root and grew in the unsettled conditions surrounding the transition to industrial capitalism. While the ideology of female domesticity was never seriously in question during this time, the profound transformation of the region as a result of the opening up of, first, the diamond and, later, the gold mines compelled certain readjustments in the organisation of gender (and other) relationships in society. This did not happen overnight, but with time the spread of capitalist relations of production into the furthest reaches of the region did affect attitudes towards women at all levels of society.

As in Europe, although more slowly and on a smaller scale, the economic role of women began to expand beyond the overwhelming-

ly domestic, and to require redefinition. Although the mining industry in South Africa developed on the backs of male labour, the rapid
development of commerce and secondary industry that followed in
its wake drew directly on women as an additional source of labour,
with important consequences for their economic standing as well as
their perceptions of the world. While this process did not get under
way fully until after World War One, already in the late nineteenth
century new occupations were opening up for women in the towns,
especially for young, unmarried white women with some education.
Thus in the Cape Colony between 1891 and 1904 the number of
women of all races employed in the professional category increased
from 4 925 to 8 886. Of these, 83,1 per cent in 1891 and 82,6 per cent
in 1904 were white (G19–1905: 320–1; these figures have been adjusted
to exclude from account the African territories annexed to the Cape
after 1891).

Teaching was already a predominantly female profession. In 1891
almost 75 per cent of white teachers in the Cape were women, and as
the demand for skilled labour increased, so the regional need for more
women to train as teachers grew (ibid.: cxiv). In the period 1891–1904
the number of women working in 'Textile Fabrics, in Dress, and in
Fibrous Materials' in the Cape also increased, from 4 727 (of whom
3 671 were white) to 6 326 (of whom 5 177 were white), while the 1904
Cape census notes a 'striking' increase in the proportion of white
females in the category of 'Shorthand Writer, Typist, Reporter'. None
in 1891, they accounted for a remarkable 85,23 per cent of this category
of workers in 1904 (ibid.).

During this time opportunities for higher education for white
women began to expand beyond the private tutoring and finishing
schools for the daughters of the wealthy. The first university college
to allow women to enrol officially in its classes was the South African
College in Cape Town which, in 1886, nearly 60 years after its establishment, opened its chemistry department to women on a trial basis
for one year, before throwing open all its courses the following year
(E. A. Walker, 1929: 72). Many women graduates were destined for
marriage or for 'womanly' professions such as teaching – indeed, it
has been argued that in the United States the expansion of tertiary
education for women must be seen in relation to the need for more
teachers in an expanding economy (Simmons, 1976) – but a tiny
number of women now began knocking on the doors of previously
men-only professions such as law and medicine.

At the same time, the rapid growth of towns from the late nineteenth century introduced unsettling changes in all spheres of social
life. Over time the patriarchal family of the rural areas (both black and
white) underwent significant modification. The full history of this
complex and uneven process has yet to be written, but certain of its

components can be identified. Young wage-earners were no longer as economically dependent on their fathers as before; the extended family household of several generations made way for smaller, less uniform units, while the ideological norm of the two-generation nuclear family began to predominate. In the towns a new and more cosmopolitan culture emerged. The European immigrants streaming into the country in search of jobs and riches brought with them new ideas about relationships between rich and poor, men and women, parents and children, which fed into the ideological ferment. The influence of European and especially British social movements and ideas on South African intellectual life became stronger.

All this was beginning to apply pressure to the established organisation of relationships between the sexes, not only at work but in the home and family too. As early as 1883 Olive Schreiner's novel *The Story of an African Farm* raised a storm wherever it was read because of its outspoken criticism of women's subordinate status in society. 'I'm sorry you don't care for the position of women,' stated Lyndall, a central character in the book, on one occasion; '… it is the only thing about which I think or feel much' (1883: 197). Although Schreiner later distanced herself from the WEAU, because of the narrow and racist policies it adopted, she was an important source of inspiration for the South African suffrage movement, both through her writings and as a founding member of a Women's Enfranchisement League in the Cape in 1907 (Walker, 1979: 19–21).

The immediate impact of these developments on social attitudes in the late nineteenth and early twentieth centuries should, however, not be exaggerated; they were, rather, small pointers to what was to come. While a few radical thinkers dared to question old certitudes, they operated in a climate still very hostile to any suggestion of greater female emancipation. The 1904 Cape census concluded its discussion on the extent to which 'married women of the European Race are employed in occupations which are likely to interfere with the proper performance of home duties' on a cautiously congratulatory note: very few married or widowed women were thus engaged, it noted, the figures pointing to a 'not unsatisfactory state of affairs' (G19–1905: cxiv). In 1892 an attempt to introduce an amendment to the Franchise and Ballot Act in the Cape, to extend the franchise to suitably qualified women, was roundly defeated in the legislature. J. X. Merriman, arch-conservative on the issue of women's rights, drew cheers and laughter with a speech which mixed folk sayings and Scripture to condemn the proposal out of hand. Citing a 'good old Dutch proverb', he cautioned that 'women's counsel and brandy are two capital things but you must use them very cautiously', and invoked 'God Almighty [who] had made the sexes separate' (*Cape Debates*, 1892: 254).

Many of the themes of subsequent suffrage debates surfaced at this opening round in the discussion. Merriman also argued that 'in the last resource' men were duty-bound to take up arms to defend the country, and at times of war, women's counsel was brushed aside (ibid.). The Act itself raised the required property and education qualifications for male voters in the Cape and was introduced to prevent the 'swamping' of the voters' roll by black voters with the incorporation of the Transkeian Territories to the Cape. J. M. Orpen, who proposed the women's suffrage amendment, based much of his argument on the need to increase the 'civilised vote' by bringing in women of property and 'mental development'. 'The fundamental idea of our franchise was the representation of property, of wealth', he pointed out – so to exclude women on the grounds of their sex was 'to subvert the very principle of representation' (ibid.: 253). In his speech whiteness, civilisation and property blurred into each other. The injustice done to white women by denying them the vote was exacerbated by the subversion of the proper racial hierarchy as a result of the inclusion of black men: 'Imagine a gentleman visiting some lady who was, say, managing a farm ... and telling her that they had made provision for her own coloured servants in the franchise of the Colony, but that she alone – who possessed the whole farm – was excluded' (ibid.: 252).

Orpen also pointed to developments in other parts of the world where women's suffrage was making its way and condemned the 'brutal assertion of the inferiority of women' – if women were the weaker sex, then that was all the more reason why they should seek protective legislation through the vote (ibid.: 253).

HISTORY OF THE SUFFRAGE MOVEMENT 1895–1930

1895–1910

In South Africa the first organisation formally to espouse women's suffrage was the Women's Christian Temperance Union (WCTU), which was founded in 1889 to campaign against the trade in alcoholic beverages. Six years after its establishment it set up a Franchise Department because members had come to the conclusion that until women had the vote and thus exercised some political leverage over male legislators, their temperance campaign would be ignored. As in Britain, the first organised advocates of women's suffrage in South Africa were thus middle-class reformers, imbued with a strong sense of Christian duty and women's higher moral purpose. For them the vote was a means to an end which was not, in the first instance, connected to the status of women. The WCTU was to remain an important component of the suffrage movement, imparting its particular flavour of Christian reformism and sobriety to the subsequent campaign.

Women's organisations formed specifically around the issue of the suffrage first appeared in the early years of the twentieth century. The first Women's Enfranchisement League (WEL) in the country was established in Durban in 1902, the work primarily of an English couple, the Ancketills, who had emigrated to Natal in 1896 and quickly become active in labour and other progressive organisations in the colony. Following the establishment of the Durban WEL, suffrage societies were founded in all the major and several of the smaller towns – Port Elizabeth (1905), Cape Town (1907), Johannesburg, Pretoria and Bloemfontein (1908), Pietermaritzburg (1910) and Kimberley, Grahamstown, East London and Somerset East in 1911.

In the years after the Anglo–Boer War, however, the status of women in general and women's suffrage in particular remained side issues in white politics, completely overshadowed by the events leading up to the political union of the four British colonies in 1910. In 1907 a motion calling on the Cape House of Assembly to recognise that 'the time has come when the welfare of the people of the Cape of Good Hope will be most effectually conserved by conferring on women the privilege of voting' was soundly defeated by 66 votes to 24. For the most part it was a lighthearted debate. Once again J. X. Merriman drew cheers, laughter and applause in opposing the motion, rousing one legislator to protest indignantly at the injustice being done to women in making them the subject of such merriment (*Cape Debates*, 1907: 95–8).

Women's suffrage was raised, but only very briefly, at the National Convention. While controversy over the franchise raged at the convention, its concern was the status of the black voters of the Cape in the future Union of South Africa, not that of women. In December 1908 Prime Minister Moor of Natal moved that provision be made in the new constitution for the enfranchisement of women of 'European descent' – significantly, the first reference to women's suffrage on a national platform was in racially exclusive terms (Minutes of the National Convention, 1911: 133). Subsequently a Cape delegate, Colonel Stanford, moved to protect the Cape franchise by proposing that the words 'of European descent' be deleted (ibid.: 142–3). However, after the Christmas recess all discussion on women's suffrage ceased. Colonel Stanford's amendment had opened up 'new and alarming vistas to some of those present', wrote a contemporary commentator, and 'the advocates of Female Suffrage were brought to see the wisdom of leaving the question to Parliament' (Walton, 1912: 306).

The only white political organisations actively to espouse women's suffrage at this stage were a number of small, left-wing labour parties and debating societies on the fringes of the political establishment. In the late nineteenth and early twentieth centuries there was a flurry of trade-union and socialist activity amongst white workers in the urban centres, much of it organised by British immigrants. Women's suffrage was part of the package of ideas for political reform that these activists had brought with them. In 1910 these tiny left-wing organisations came together to form the South African Labour Party, which for many years was the only party in the South African parliament to include women's suffrage as part of its official platform.

In the early years the white labour movement's support for women's suffrage confirmed the fears of the establishment that the enfranchisement of women was a dangerous proposal, part of a larger revolutionary onslaught on the existing order of society. Ultimately, however, the significance of this alliance was minor. The larger political sympathies of most suffragists were moderate: they wanted women to be incorporated into, not to overthrow, the status quo. A comparison can be made with developments in other industrial countries, such as Britain, the United States and Germany, where over time the organised suffrage movement tended to diverge from more radical trade-union and socialist organisations and espouse essentially reformist rather than revolutionary politics. Those feminists who were socialists took their feminism into socialist organisations, rather than their socialism into narrowly feminist structures such as the suffrage societies.

There were, furthermore, very strict limitations to the radicalism of the South African Labour Party. It was a staunchly segregationist body, dedicated only to the cause of white workers in the struggle against capital. Black workers, in their numbers, the cheapness of their labour and the alienness of their culture, it perceived as a dangerous threat. In this regard it merely confirmed the racial prejudices already embedded in the thinking of most suffragists. The WEAU welcomed its support on the suffrage issue, concurred with its racism, but left its socialist ideas alone.

The WEAU: establishment and direction

The establishment of the Union of South Africa paved the way for the local Enfranchisement Leagues scattered across the country to form a national body. In 1911 the WEAU held its inaugural conference in Durban. Mindful of the bitter debates within the white community over the Cape franchise, the new organisation adopted a pragmatic, non-confrontational approach to the issue of black eligibility for the vote, one that accepted the parameters of the compromise already hammered out at the National Convention and would, it was hoped, appeal to as broad a section of whites as possible. Its aim was to work on 'non-sectarian, non-partisan lines', its objective to win the vote for women on 'the same terms as it is or may be granted to men' (Cross, 1913: 306).

Responses to its formation ranged from indifference to hostility.

Two public meetings held in conjunction with the conference were poorly attended while the *Natal Mercury* commented sourly in an editorial: 'We hope the women suffragists have enjoyed their picnic in Durban, but we do not think the political effect of their visit can have rewarded their endeavours, and we cannot pretend that we have any regrets at their non-success' (20.10.1911). For the next 29 years this organisation led the campaign to enfranchise women. Never a large movement, it grew in fits and starts to encompass 38 local leagues around the country by 1921. What the total membership of its affiliates was is difficult to say – not only are figures hard to come by, but many local leagues were often dormant or very inactive for long stretches of time. *Woman's Outlook*, the Association's monthly magazine from 1912 to 1922, estimated national membership at about 4 000 in 1918 (September 1918: 7) and there is little reason to believe that this figure would have increased much by 1930. In later years paid-up membership was not an accurate reflection of support for either the WEAU (which secured 54 500 signatures for a petition in 1921) or for the principle of women's suffrage, which during the 1920s began to gain new adherents among women who, for ideological reasons, would not identify themselves with the WEAU. Nevertheless, it is clear that the latter's organisational strength was always very limited. Communications between head office and branch organisations were poor, funds very limited and much of the workload fell on a few, hard-working members of the national executive.

The WEAU was, as has already been mentioned, exclusively white, predominantly English-speaking and urban, and thoroughly middle-class. Biographical information about its members is sketchy, but the available information on office-bearers confirms that they were women of standing – educated, civic-minded, many of them moving in the same social circles as the male legislators they wished to influence (Walker, 1979: 102–3). It does not appear to have been a particularly youthful organisation – its leadership, certainly, comprised older women rather than students and youngsters. Its first president, Mrs E. Macintosh, a child at the time of the diamond rush, had studied at the Huguenot Seminary in Wellington in the Cape, was married to a merchant and, in addition to the WEAU, was also active in the WCTU, the Guild of Loyal Women and the Empire League. Its second president, who held the position from 1916 till the WEAU disbanded after 1930, was Lady Steel, wife of a baronet and daughter of a minister, who included membership of the Maritzburg Croquet Club in her activities. Another prominent member, Julia Solly, born in 1862, was the daughter of an English university chancellor, had herself gone to university in England, was married to an engineer and farmer in the Western Cape, and was active in numerous organisations including the WCTU, the National Council of Women, the

Federation for the Abolition of State Regulation of Vice, and the Association for the Advancement of the Sciences. More unusual a member was Petronella van Heerden, one of the few Afrikaner women to join the WEAU. A child during the Anglo–Boer War, she had battled with her family to win permission to study medicine in Holland before and during World War One, finally qualifying as a gynaecologist and setting up practice as one of the first Afrikaans-speaking female doctors, in Harrismith.

Of fourteen prominent members on whom reasonably detailed biographies have been pieced together, at least seven are known to have had middle-class jobs of their own – admittedly a very small and not necessarily representative sample but suggestive of the relationship between women's economic independence and their commitment to women's rights issues. Three of these women were teachers or headmistresses; one was a farmer, one a botanist, one a journalist, and one (Van Heerden) a gynaecologist. Nine of the fourteen were married, with children (ibid.).

The establishment character of the WEAU shaped its programme and its politics. From the start it eschewed the confrontationist tactics adopted by Emily Pankhurst's suffragettes in England in favour of law-abiding methods such as petitions, public meetings, letters to the press and lobbying parliamentary support. The WEAU was, in fact, anxious to distance itself from the militant English suffragettes, whose campaigns received considerable, uniformly disapproving coverage in South African newspapers. It was by demonstrating their respectability and reasonableness that South African women could best persuade men of their fitness for the vote, it argued. A certain restiveness with their lack of progress did manifest itself from time to time – in 1921, for instance, *Woman's Outlook* concluded an editorial criticising General Smuts for refusing to sanction a government-sponsored suffrage bill, by making a vague threat of greater militancy: 'Does he propose that the women of South Africa should make their men "attend" by the drastic measures adopted by our forebears among the pedagogues and suffragettes?' (November 1921: 8).

Dissatisfaction with the rate of progress was deflected back into constitutional channels, however. In 1923 one member, an unmarried teacher by the name of Edith Woods, did adopt a more militant stance by refusing to pay her income tax, arguing in court that 'taxation without representation … is tyranny', but hers was an individual act of rebellion. Although other suffragists rallied to her support on the day of her trial, her demonstration was neither official, nor representative of WEAU tactics. Nor was it taken very seriously by the court, the prosecutor describing himself jocularly as a 'poor, humble bachelor' whose 'knowledge of the ways of women is very restricted' (*Cape Times*, 21.2.1923). An editorial in the *Cape Times* also trivialised the affair, denouncing Woods's actions as 'this silly business', but behind its scorn lurked a more serious concern. Passive resistance was 'a very perilous task for white women to take', the editorial warned: 'This is no country in which to refuse to pay taxes without direct parliamentary representation. The white women who can plead that injustice are an infinitesimal fraction of the inhabitants of this country who have it as a basic condition of their lives' (ibid.).

This was an argument which most of the suffragists would appreciate. The gulf between the WEAU and the black majority of the population was very wide. Few in the WEAU saw their campaign in other than racial terms. Even though the organisation had committed itself to the non-racial franchise in the Cape, this, as its subsequent history makes clear, was more a matter of expediency than inviolate principle. Making common political cause with black women was inconceivable to most members and no attempt was made to recruit black members or propagate suffrage ideas outside the white community. An article written in 1913 by I. K. Cross, a South African suffragist, illustrates this perspective neatly. Entitled 'The Women's Movement in South Africa – and Elsewhere', the article documents the worldwide awakening of women and then goes on to mention, in passing, the anti-pass campaigns that were then disturbing the Orange Free State (Cross, 1913). The account draws no links between this campaign and the WEAU's campaign for greater rights for women, nor does it take the Free State campaign seriously. Rather, Cross describes it patronisingly as 'a recent and rather amusing incident', evidence of the extent of the 'awakening' of women worldwide – even local 'native women' were stirring – but quite without further interest to South African suffragists (ibid.: 307).

At best the organised suffrage movement approached the situation of black women from the perspective of charity, not sisterly solidarity. Thus the only recorded time that the WEAU was addressed by a black woman was in 1921, when Charlotte Maxeke, a prominent social worker and founder of the Bantu Women's League, was invited to speak at the annual conference. The subject of her talk was not the suffrage, however, but the difficult, unstable conditions of life among African women in the towns – a topic of acute concern to her and other socially aware individuals but presented and received as a welfare, rather than a political problem (*Woman's Outlook*, August 1921: 5–6). Charity, welfare, concern about the breakdown of 'the family' and moral values – more particularly, the breakdown of 'traditional' values and controls within African society – these were areas where middle-class black and white women could meet, even agree, without serious challenge to white hegemony.

The campaign 1911–1918

Most of the energies of the WEAU campaign were directed at parliament. It worked hard to cultivate relationships with legislators, with at least some of whom its executive officers would have been acquainted socially. In parliament the Association relied heavily on a non-partisan House Committee on Women's Suffrage, which consisted of individual members who favoured women's suffrage and were prepared to liaise closely with the WEAU. In the early years of the Union parliament, however, such individuals were few and far between. Before 1919 the only party officially to endorse women's suffrage was the tiny South African Labour Party, with a mere five seats in 1910, reduced to four in 1915. A few legislators in the South African (SAP) and Unionist parties were sympathetic, but they operated as individuals, without the backing of their parties.

During the 1910s women's suffrage continued to be a side issue, eclipsed by other items on the white political agenda: the welding of a comprehensive 'native policy' out of the individual systems developed in each of the four provinces before Union; labour unrest amongst white workers on the mines; South African participation in World War One and, arising out of that, the 1914 rebellion led by former Boer generals dissatisfied with the pro-British policies of the governing SAP. Motions in favour of women's suffrage in 1913, 1917 and 1918 were defeated, while debate on the only suffrage bill introduced at this stage, in 1914, was adjourned during the second reading and never resumed. This bill adhered to the policy of votes for women on the same terms as for men, its sponsor, H. A. Wyndham, a Unionist, conceding that it would enfranchise a certain number of coloured women in the Cape but arguing that 'this was not sufficient reason to withhold the franchise from white women'. 'Were honourable members opposite so frightened of the coloured population that they would condemn their white women to be disenfranchised?'

During the war years the WEAU itself directed far less attention to its suffrage work than to the war effort. The majority of members were British loyalists who believed that women's first duty at this time of crisis was to lay aside their particular grievances and serve their government and king. Many prominent members had been born and raised in England and still looked to it as 'home'. At its 1915 conference the WEAU agreed to subordinate its suffrage campaign to war relief activities and to place the organisation at the disposal of the government (*Woman's Outlook*, February 1915: 4). It also passed a resolution protesting against 'citizens who have recently taken up arms in open rebellion being allowed to exercise their vote ... seeing that loyal women are still unenfranchised' (*Woman's Outlook*, July 1915: 5). Support for these resolutions was not unanimous, however, and their adoption sparked off a furious debate within the organisation. Critics charged that they conflicted with the policy of non-partisanship and would alienate Afrikaner support, while defenders maintained that the action was 'in the opinion of every loyal woman in South Africa, not only fully justified but a plain duty'. 'Surely we women of an Empire which gives liberty in its widest possible sense to its subjects are not going to stand aside at a time like the present?' was how one letter-writer to *Woman's Outlook* expressed it (March 1915: 12). So divisive was the debate that eventually the WEAU executive rescinded the war resolution. Nevertheless, the sentiments that had motivated it continued to inform the organisation and most branch activity reports in these years dealt largely or exclusively with war-related work, such as fundraising for the Red Cross, clothing collections and knitting drives. 'Propaganda work has been practically nil,' reported the Durban WEL in 1916 (*Woman's Outlook*, June 1916: 10).

New developments after the war

These years of relative stagnation in the organisation were, however, ones of enormous flux and movement in society at large. In Europe and North America the war is widely regarded as a watershed in the organisation of gender relations, drawing women into production on an unprecedented scale and dissolving many of the more rigid attitudes about sex roles from the pre-war period. Fifteen governments in Europe and North America enfranchised women between 1915 and 1921 (UNESCO, 1964), including Britain where women's suffrage was finally conceded in 1918, although for women over the age of 30 only. (Universal franchise was not established in Britain until 1928.) These developments, especially the enfranchisement of women in Britain, encouraged South African suffragists and introduced a new dimension to the local debate. No longer was women's suffrage an outlandish phenomenon confined to the dim edges of the European world; it was now an established principle of the 'civilised' centre.

In South Africa too, the war can be seen as a watershed in social and economic relations. It marked a major upswing in female employment outside the domestic sphere, which, in turn, worked to soften prejudices against female involvement in the public sphere and, thus, in politics. As secondary industry took off, a range of new jobs opened up for working-class women as machinists, packers, labellers, saleswomen and secretarial staff. The broad outlines of this process are by now well known and in many respects parallel developments in other parts of the industrialised world. Women workers became clustered in particular areas of employment, which could be seen as extensions of their domestic roles and did not conflict with established views about their 'natural' abilities. Thus in the professions, they were concentrated in the 'nurturing' realms of teaching and nursing; in business, in service and supportive roles as secretaries and saleswomen; in industry, in food processing and textile concerns, and, of course, in domestic service.

In South Africa the distribution of female labour was also informed by a very clear racial cleavage between black and white. Initially white women, young Afrikaner girls from struggling farm families on the *platteland* in particular, led the way onto the factory floor, followed only later, in the 1930s and 1940s, by black women, as white women as a social group began to move up into better-paying, 'pink collar' jobs as clerks, secretaries, etc. In production the systems of gender domination and of race domination interacted to produce a rigidly hierarchical patterning of employment distribution, in which both systems were reproduced – white male workers at the top, black female workers at the bottom, with black males and white females in separate and socially differentiated strata inbetween.

As in other parts of the world, these developments did not challenge existing gender stereotypes about women head-on. In many respects they worked to reinforce them in a new setting. Nevertheless, they did necessitate some adjustments in attitudes towards women, to the benefit of the suffrage movement. The growing numbers of women experiencing a new autonomy as wage-earners outside the confines of the home were becoming less inclined to submit unquestioningly to male control over their independence and their earnings, even if they believed, as most did, that marriage and motherhood were still their ultimate and preferred destination. A new frontier of tension in meeting social expectations, of contradiction between their reproductive and productive roles, was emerging in working women's lives.

The movement of university-educated women into the hitherto 'masculine' fields of science, law and medicine was an important marker of softening attitudes. In 1923, after a lengthy campaign in which the WEAU played an active part, the statutory bars against women entering the legal profession were finally removed by parliament. Although the number of women in 'masculine' professions remained tiny – a mere 4 research chemists and 8 dentists in 1926, and 35 attorneys, 5 advocates and 144 doctors and surgeons in 1936 (Walker, 1979: 63) – their social significance as alternative role models for women, visibly challenging the presumption of female intellectual inferiority and dependence on male breadwinners, was considerable.

From this time important sectors of the white political establishment began to relax their hitherto uncompromisingly hostile attitude towards the suffrage movement. In some ways the war gave them the opportunity to catch up with developments in gender relations that had already been set in motion beforehand. The question of women's enfranchisement had acquired an 'entirely new status' in recent years, editorialised the *Cape Times* in 1921 (30.4.1921).

In 1919 the principle of women's suffrage finally won a majority – albeit a very slender one of two votes – in the House of Assembly. In proposing the motion, long-time champion Wyndham used two main arguments: firstly, that state involvement in what was generally considered women's sphere – child welfare, education, health-care – was increasing rapidly, and made necessary some mechanism by which women could influence policy in these areas; and secondly, that women were being 'caught up in the industrial–economic system' (*Cape Times Debates*, 2.4.1919). Later that year the annual congresses of both the SAP and the Unionists also passed motions in favour of women's suffrage.

To the acute chagrin of the suffragists, however, majority support for the principle within the SAP did not translate into government policy. Prime Minister Smuts, who personally endorsed the principle – 'Since the war all values have changed,' he chastised anti-suffragists in parliament in 1920 (*Cape Times Debates*, May 1920: 91) – chose not to strain party unity on what he still regarded as essentially a minor issue. 'If it does not win this session, it may win the next session, or the session after,' he tried to reassure a WEAU deputation in 1921 (*Cape Times*, 11.3.1921).

In the early 1920s an important new front opened up in the campaign with the cautious exploration of the issue among women within the National Party. The movement of Afrikaner women to the cities and into factory employment put new pressures on the patriarchal controls of family and church, and opened up an important area of recruitment for the suffrage as well as the trade-union movement. The recognition that the eventual enfranchisement of women was now only a matter of time prompted Nationalist women to revaluate their former rejection of the issue – but in the light of party, rather than feminist, goals. Women were already playing a supportive role in the National Party but now they began to organise themselves more formally into women's branches. They were determined that any advance in the political status of white women be directed by Nationalist women to the benefit of their ethnic and party agenda. Thus Mrs E. G. Malan, step-mother of Dr D. F. Malan, argued at the inaugural meeting of the Cape branch of the Women's National Party in March 1923 that 'Women do not need to take fright at the word "politics".' Instead, 'With regard to women's suffrage, they must ensure that if they get it, the best men come to the head of affairs. Nationalist women must be organised. They must know on election day for whom they must vote' (*Die Burger*, 2.3.1923; my translation). Less positive about women's suffrage but equally determined to direct it to party purposes was a Free State member of the women's branch: 'The National Party is, as a party, against women's suffrage, but if women's suffrage is adopted by Parliament, it will be a disaster if

Afrikaner women do not do their duty' (*Die Burger*, 18.3.1923; my translation). The movement to win over rank-and-file Nationalist members to the suffrage cause finally bore fruit in 1927, when the party's Cape congress unanimously adopted a motion that it was 'high time' that women got the vote (Van Heerden, 1965: 24).

But while Nationalist support for women's suffrage brought the issue into the domain of feasible politics, it also increased the pressure on the suffragists' always fragile support for the non-racial franchise in the Cape. The new adherents to the cause were vehemently opposed to any proposal that would enfranchise black women along with white. That their definition of 'women' did not extend to black women was made emphatically clear by the Transvaal region of the Women's National Party in 1928, when it announced that '*Die vrou wil nie saam met die kaffer stem nie*' [Women do not want to vote with the kaffir] (Stockenström, 1944: 389).

The campaign 1924–1930

After 1924, when Hertzog's National Party took office with the electoral support of the Labour Party, such unabashedly racist attitudes moved into a position of greater dominance within the suffrage campaign. At this point the issue of women's suffrage became almost entirely an appendage to the battle over the Nationalist plan to wipe the Cape franchise from the Union constitution. An early indication of this came in 1925 when the Labour Party, now junior partners in a government intent on shoring up white supremacy before all else, failed to support a suffrage amendment in the House of Assembly. Its reasons were the imperatives of coalition which, its leader Creswell argued somewhat uncomfortably, necessitated 'putting in the background ... some of those points on which we do not agree, in order to carry points on which we do agree' (*Assembly Debates*, 1925: col. 2339).

By now the principle of women's suffrage had been conceded by all but the most die-hard of male supremacists in parliament, and it was the terms on which women were to be enfranchised, as well as the timing, that came under scrutiny. Evidence of both the new-found respectability of the issue and its subordination to the politics of white power was the appointment of a parliamentary Select Committee on the Enfranchisement of Women in 1926. Brand Wessels, a Nationalist member of the committee, spoke for many when he explained to a witness: 'After all, we who are opposed to women's suffrage are opposed to it not on account of the unfitness of women, but on the grounds of the difficulty in the coloured and native vote' (SC12–26: 3).

As the debate narrowed, so the WEAU itself began to vacillate on its superficially non-racial policy. In 1924 a motion calling for the vote for white women only was actually carried at its annual conference but subsequently not adopted as it was not ratified by a majority of branch leagues. Those who had actively supported the Cape franchise before began to talk in terms of 'the half-loaf', to adopt the phrase used by Lady Rose Innes before the 1926 select committee. 'We are so weary of fighting to get some recognition,' said Emily Solomon, another witness before that committee (SC12–26: 3). Although Solomon herself remained staunchly committed to the Cape franchise – so much so that after 1930 she refused to use her vote because she regarded it as compromised (Walker, 1979: 87) – her comment pointed to a loss of drive within the organisation. Now that a women's enfranchisement bill looked within reach, those who had previously gone along with the Cape franchise on pragmatic grounds began to chafe against its constraints and argue for a new pragmatism, more in keeping with their own political outlook. Thus Mrs Grant of the WEAU, before the 1926 select committee: 'Well, in this country it is no use talking of justice. If we talk of justice we are told we shall go under. Such native policy as we have is based on injustice.... Should we women be so wonderfully just, when after all, the white men in the country are not entirely just to native men?' (SC12–26: 42).

The suffrage journal *Flashlight* (established in 1927 to replace the defunct *Woman's Outlook*) commented in 1928: 'The W.E.A.U. has always asked for the vote on the same terms as it is or may be given to men. But it has always added that it is prepared to accept any measure of enfranchisement however limited which Parliament may wish to grant ...' (third quarter 1928: 5).

General Hertzog now emerged as the central figure in the campaign. His own position on women's suffrage had been spelled out in a 1924 debate on the subject: women (by which he referred only to white women) were qualified to vote but they would have to wait till the problem of the Cape franchise had been dealt with. He was confident that they would understand that their enfranchisement was not in the best interests of the country at that point and so accept the situation (*Assembly Debates*, 1924: col. 266). In the 1927–8 parliamentary session he intervened to prevent the adoption of a suffrage bill which looked set to pass – originally granting women the vote on the same terms as men, the bill had been amended at the committee stage to apply to white women only, in which form it enjoyed majority support. A general election was about to be fought and Hertzog was unhappy with the timing of the bill, even though in its amended form it met his criteria. By then several attempts to overturn the Cape franchise in parliament had failed for want of the required two-thirds majority, and it appears that while Hertzog had already decided to use women's suffrage to weaken its base, he wanted to ensure that his government's electoral position was secure before formally incorporating votes for women into his political programme. In return for the cooperation of the Assembly, he promised that he would personally introduce suffrage legislation if returned to power (*Assembly Debates*, 1927–28: col. 1657). Interestingly, Hertzog at that stage was prepared to include 'coloured' women with white – for him the threat to white supremacy came not from the 'coloured' minority, whose links with the white community he recognised, but from the overwhelming African majority, and it was against this group that his disfranchisement campaign was directed.

Having duly won the elections, in 1929 Hertzog introduced the promised bill which passed smoothly into law as the Women's Enfranchisement Act on 19 May 1930. Through it adult suffrage was extended to white women in all four provinces – the anomalous situation thus created in the Cape, where the qualified franchise still applied to men, being rectified with regard to white men the following year when universal suffrage was granted to them as well (thereby further diluting the value of the African vote). Despite Hertzog's earlier commitment to 'coloured' women, they were not included in the terms of the Act. Hertzog argued unconvincingly that this was because it was impossible to differentiate effectively between 'coloured' and African women. Since it was no more difficult to differentiate 'coloured' from African than white from 'coloured', it is apparent that his breach of promise was to assuage the total segregationists in his party. 'I was always in favour of the native question being settled first,' said Hertzog in introducing the bill. 'As however it is clear that the majority in this House wants us to go on with this matter before such time, I am not prepared to oppose it any longer' (*Assembly Debates*, 1930: col. 2265). In fact, as already pointed out, his decision to support women's enfranchisement was to bring him closer to his goal of settling 'the native question'.

Thus in mid-1930, 35 years after the WCTU had first established its Franchise Department, the WEAU finally won its half-loaf. Some voices were raised within WEAU circles to protest against the betrayal of the Cape franchise – Olive Schreiner's husband, for instance, asked that the dead writer's name not be associated with the suffragists' victory celebrations (*Flashlight*, July 1930: 47) – but these were drowned in the general jubilation. The victory issue of *Flashlight* tried to assuage consciences by arguing that enfranchised women would now be in a stronger position to fight for the rights of the unenfranchised:

The exclusion of the coloured in the Cape Province … has been severely criticised by some of the older workers. But those who have been actively engaged in the work during recent years realise that this was the only measure possible for many years and, as it has been pointed out by Lady de Villiers and others, enfranchised women will have far greater influence in matters affecting the interests of the non-European section of the population than they had when unenfranchised (July 1930: 1).

More to the point, however, was another article in the same issue, which made it clear that for the average suffragist the battle was over: 'Is success always mingled with regret? I wrote to Miss Dorman, when the Bill had passed the second reading, "Victory is in sight, what shall we do with our empty lives now?" ... her reply was a quote from a Gilbert and Sullivan song "They give me this and they give me that, In short I have nothing left to grumble at"' (ibid.: 35).

The effect of the 1930 legislation on black political consciousness was a radicalising one. At a huge protest meeting in Cape Town organised by 'coloured' organisations to protest against the discriminatory terms of the legislation, a youthful Cissy Gool declared 'I am afraid that I am slowly going Red' (Empire Group of South Africa, 1931: 5). The hopes of the black elite of a gradual incorporation into the institutions of political power had been firmly rebuffed. The fact that women were used to deliver the blow gave an added piquancy to the insult. 'Fancy the parliament of a civilised country doing such a low and mean thing as actually dragging their womenfolk and giving them the vote for the purpose of robbing the Native of his vote,' commented Dr Abdurahman of the APO bitterly (Karis and Carter, 1972: 276).

IDEOLOGICAL UNDERPINNINGS OF THE CAMPAIGN

Relationships between the sexes

What emerges from the history of the suffrage movement is the degree of unanimity within white society about certain principles of social organisation regarded as basic to its continued existence. The maintenance of white overlordship (in one form or another) and of the Christian family as the primary social unit were two such fundamentals of white political thought.

The suffrage campaign never represented a basic challenge to the prevailing organisation of gender relations in the country. Most suffragists and anti-suffragists were in basic agreement: they did not want to upset the existing division of labour between the sexes. Arguments for and against were riddled with naturalist assumptions about male and female identity. Both sides built on an essentially biologist view of gender, which ascribed gender identity to certain inborn differences between men and women. They were in broad agreement about women's 'natural' nurturing capabilities and greater moral purity – the socialisation theories of gender difference developed by modern feminists did not form part of the currency of debate.

Thus the suffragists did not challenge the view that women's primary responsibilities were domestic and that marriage and motherhood constituted women's most important achievements. While it is possible that more detailed biographical information would reveal a higher proportion of unmarried women among its members than the societal norm – women who had, by choice or circumstance, opted for career rather than marriage – the WEAU subscribed strongly to the viewpoint of the middle-class, nuclear family as the backbone of society. It recognised that not all women were equally 'privileged' to have a home and that increasing numbers of young women in particular were going out to work, but did not regard this as ultimately detracting from the centrality of women's reproductive role. Home values were stressed throughout their campaign. 'The home, as has so often been said, is the woman's sphere,' stated *Woman's Outlook* in 1913. 'We must show other women what we already know so well, that it is the very things pertaining to the well-kept, happy home that need their combined operation' (June 1913: 5). In 1926 Julia Solly argued before the parliamentary select committee that women needed the vote as a 'home-protection weapon' (SC12–26: 26).

Even in more radical circles, where women's suffrage was seen as but one component in a much larger process of emancipation from the shackles of class exploitation, conventional attitudes towards the sexual division of labour within both household and political organisation prevailed. Thus the responsibility of women activists at the 1919 May Day celebrations organised by socialists on the Rand was to make tea for the participants (Walker, 1982: 48). A joke about women voting, which appeared in a 1922 issue of the left-wing newspaper *International*, played on sexist stereotypes about women's preoccupation with physical appearance to the exclusion of more important matters: '"How did you vote?" a young girl was asked, to which she ingenuously replied, "In my brown suit and squirrel toque"' (ibid.: 48).

There were individual feminists who challenged the predominant viewpoint. One unorthodox contributor to a 1918 issue of *Woman's Outlook*, Ida Hyett, dismissed marriage as 'slavery tempered by chivalry' (June 1918: 7). 'The suffragist, eager to see women earning independent incomes, plays into the hands of the capitalists by encouraging an influx of cheap and unorganised labour into the market,' she had argued in a previous issue of the magazine (May 1918: 7). Such thinkers were a very small minority, however, and their arguments had little effect on the overall direction of the campaign.

A similar preoccupation with women's domestic and reproductive responsibilities characterised the other side of the debate. Anti-suffragists, however, used this to justify the exclusion of women from the political process and to warn of the dangerous consequences of tampering with the existing division of responsibilities between the sexes. In 1909 the poet C. J. Langenhoven wrote an article which encapsulated this viewpoint. The suffrage movement, he argued, was inimical to 'the divinest duty of all' of 'our women' – 'the duties of the heart'. Women's reproductive function and its value to men were extolled in glowing terms: 'We shall want a class to watch over the cradles of our young, to nurse our aged and sick, to brighten our homes with cheer and lighten our burdens with sympathy ...' (1909: 64–5).

Where the two sides differed was on whether women's domestic responsibilities were compatible with political rights or not. Suffragists saw no contradiction between running a home and voting. Further, they argued that because of women's particular role as homebuilders, they had a special contribution to make to the political process, as well as special needs which required representation in parliament. They did not argue against biology as destiny but incorporated biologism onto their side. Anti-suffragists, on the other hand, adopted a paternalistic view, arguing that as the weaker sex, women were quite unsuited for the hurly-burly of politics. In the years before World War One they were fond of pointing to the 'outrages' of the English suffragettes as proof of this thesis. Their vision of what would happen if women were to be granted the vote was apocalyptic: home life would be neglected and the family, the moral basis of society, would crumble. Thus Merriman in the 1918 Assembly debate described the enfranchisement of women in England as 'a case of democracy gone mad'; woman was a different creature from man, with different functions – hers was 'the great function of motherhood' (*Cape Times Debates*, 13.12.1918: 62). When pressed on the issue of representation, anti-suffragists claimed there was no conflict of interest between men and women and that women were already represented in parliament, through their enfranchised fathers, husbands and brothers. Typical of this position was a speech by a Cape legislator in 1907, in which he argued that if women did their duty in the home, then they formed the character of men, and thus, by providing the 'right sort of man' to govern and lead, influenced the country's welfare by their precept and example (*Cape Debates*, 1907: 98).

Over the years such arguments began to lose ground as the exclusive hold of purely domestic responsibilities on white women's time began to weaken. In response to the charge of revolution, proponents of women's suffrage were at pains to point out the essential conservatism of women. Thus in a debate on a women's enfranchisement bill in 1923, General Smuts, arguing in favour of the bill, emphasised that women were more cautious than men. He referred to Rhodesia where women had been enfranchised in 1919, arguing that the women's vote there had been the decisive factor in the Rhodesian electorate's decision not to join the Union (*Cape Times Debates*, 1923: 38).

Despite the forebodings of the diehards, the enfranchisement of women did not bring about the fundamental reordering of gender relationships that many male opponents had feared and a few female proponents had hoped for. In the years following 1930 very few women, white or black, entered national politics, which remained a male-dominated terrain. Those women who did, tended to devote themselves to backroom party work in a supportive, rather than a leadership role. It took another 23 years for even a partial curtailment on the marital power of men in marriage to be written into the statute books, and then it still did not apply to the vast majority of women who were black and married under customary law. The dire warnings of the anti-suffragists, that social chaos, family breakdown and immorality would accompany the enfranchisement of women, were exposed as gross exaggerations of the power of the vote. As the more pragmatic analysts of what female enfranchisement would actually mean had long pointed out, going out to vote once every five years hardly amounted to a fundamental disruption of women's domestic routine.

Relationships between the races

The range of arguments used for and against women's suffrage did not alter much over the years. Merriman speaking in 1918 sounded much the same as he had in 1892 – although with less effect. What did change was where the emphasis fell. As already pointed out, when the issue was first raised most observers saw it mainly in terms of a challenge to existing male–female relationships, and exchange over the proper ordering of gender relations formed the heart of the debate. As time went on, however, and support for women's enfranchisement gained ground, more and more of the debate, both inside and outside parliament, centred not on the principle of whether women as a sex were qualified to vote or not, but on the practicalities of which women should vote, and how their eligibility could best be measured. Concern with the implications for white supremacy came to the fore.

A content analysis of the parliamentary debates on suffrage between 1913 and 1930 reveals the shift in preoccupation very clearly. In the ten years between 1913 and 1923, the most frequent argument for women's suffrage was that women had a special contribution to make to the political process and that their enfranchisement would contribute to the general good. The next most frequently cited argument in its favour centred on the precedents that had already been set, for instance by women voting for school boards, later by the enfranchisement of women in other parts of the world. The third most popular type of argument referred to the changing position of women in the world. In the same period the most frequently advanced argument against women's enfranchisement was that women's place was in the home. The next most popular argument of the anti-suffragists was that most women did not want to vote; thereafter, that politics was a dirty business, and engagement with it would either 'cheapen' women or prove too much for them to take.

After 1923, however, suffragists and anti-suffragists alike dealt most extensively with the issue of race. While suffragists were at pains to defend the Cape franchise, or belittle the significance of the black vote, or argue that white women should not be penalised by the special circumstances of the Cape, anti-suffragists hammered on the dangers to white power of extending the franchise to black women. Often the ideologies of white supremacy and of male superiority fused to form a single, albeit convoluted argument, as in a remarkable speech by Heaton Nicholls, SAP member of parliament for Zululand, in 1923:

By all the canons of logic and reasoning, if we [white South Africa] were an aristocracy in this country, we should weaken in native eyes our rule if we diluted it with rule by women…. The effect upon the native mind throughout the country of granting votes to women would be to do infinitely more harm than any good we could get from it. It was contrary to all Bantu tradition for women to rule…. it was no reflection on white women to point out the facts existing here in our midst…. This country was unique (*Cape Times Debates*, 1923: 39).

Both sides were in broad agreement that radical change was not desirable in South Africa. Although in the early years the language of the campaign was superficially non-racial, the movement was in fact saturated with the ideology of white domination and superiority from the start. As already described, it was led by white, middle-class women who rarely questioned the unspoken assumption that the community of 'women' on whose behalf they laboured was a community of white women.

This is not to say that the suffragists were unanimous on the best way to approach 'the native question'. A few radicals were prepared to envisage the incorporation of more black people into the political process. A larger minority continued to support the concept of a qualified franchise based on property and educational criteria as a special case in the Cape, accepting that this would mean the enfranchisement of a small number of black women too. For them the more sophisticated and flexible criteria of class, rather than the crude determinism of colour, should form the basis on which the allocation of the privilege (never the right) of voting should be made. It was, of course, an understanding of class that never challenged the fundamentals of white domination – very few black women would qualify, supporters of this position were at pains to point out. The only parliamentary party to challenge the class-based elitism of the claim, the Labour Party, did so from a white supremacist position – white women were by definition 'civilised' and it was an insult to apply an eligibility test to them. For its part, the ANC of this period never publicly challenged the class basis of the Cape franchise either, nor the assumptions about 'civilisation' which informed the franchise debate and flowed from the ideology of white supremacy.

With time a more directly segregationist position grew stronger within the WEAU. In turning from its original, formally non-racial position, the WEAU attempted to justify itself on the grounds of expediency. It is probably true that even had the WEAU refused to cooperate with the Hertzog bill of 1930, this would still have been passed into law, although perhaps not that year. Nevertheless, more was involved in the WEAU shift to the right than a regretful bowing to the inevitable. Its readiness to ally itself with the maintenance of white supremacy made it easier for the issue of women's suffrage to become subordinated to the struggle within the white ruling group to devise an acceptable 'native policy' in the decades after Union; by not distancing itself from the 1930 legislation, the WEAU in effect legitimised its whites-only content. But more than that, the majority of suffragists – and the majority of white women – did not have any qualms about the manner in which they were enfranchised. Race consciousness, not gender consciousness, determined where their political interests and loyalties lay. The distinction Aletta Nel made in 1926 between 'woman' and 'South African born person', that is quoted at the beginning of this chapter, encapsulated very neatly their assessment of priorities.

The claim made by the WEAU in 1930, that white women would use the vote in the interest of the unenfranchised majority, was little more than a pious rationalisation and was certainly not borne out by subsequent voting patterns among white women. The history of the suffrage campaign had itself demonstrated how unwilling the enfranchised are to extend the vote without pressure from the unenfranchised. The Women's Enfranchisement Act widened the gulf between white women, now clearly incorporated into the institutions of white political power, and black women, unenfranchised not because they were women but because they were black.

The WEAU was essentially a middle-class organisation, dominated by women of education and, either as wives of professional and business men or as salaried women in their own right, of economic means. While the demand for women's suffrage was not in itself a middle-class demand, the priority accorded to it by suffragists, as the most important reform needed to improve the condition of women's lives, was a product of their middle-class position. Economically secure, well-educated, anchored socially in the upper strata of the ruling group, they looked to the vote to redress the discriminations they suffered by virtue of their sex. Although they used the growing participation of women in wage employment as an argument in their favour – and were often genuinely concerned about the exploitation of women workers – they made little attempt to recruit even white working-class women into their organisation. The underlying presumption of class was, however, overlaid by a political consciousness that was saturated with the ideology of white superiority. Ultimately most suffragists looked to race solidarity to protect their specific class interests.

The powerful pull of race and ethnic loyalty on female political consciousness was not just a feature of the organised suffrage movement. A previous chapter has demonstrated its effectiveness in mobilising Afrikaner women to the nationalist cause. For black women, too, any experience of gender oppression they might share with white women was rendered largely peripheral by their experiences as members of an oppressed racial group, an experience that was not only deeply felt but was also concretised – articulated and legitimised – in the political discourse, in a way that the experience of gender was not. Whether it was African women organising against passes or Afrikaner women mobilising for the National Party or British loyalists suspending suffrage work to knit socks for the troops during World War One, women's sense of community with other women, the basis of their perception of themselves and their political mobilisation as women, was circumscribed by sturdy boundaries of language, ethnicity and the broader race consciousness around which South African society was organised. While these boundaries were never completely sealed – and, witness ruling-class concern in the 1920s and 1930s about the development of a working-class culture that cut across colour lines, had to be constantly defended – for the most part female political organisation conformed to this mapping of the world.

It is useful here to place the South African suffrage movement in international perspective and to see how similar to movements in other parts of the world it was in many respects. Although the issue of race gave to the South African campaign its own peculiar flavour and set of locally structured imperatives, yet the parallels with certain of the European and North American organisations in terms of membership, political goals and identification with the ruling class are instructive. Thus in Britain, Emily Pankhurst's militant suffragette movement suspended its escalating civil disobedience campaign as soon as World War One was declared and committed itself wholeheartedly to support for the government with which it had hitherto been locked in conflict. In Wilhelmine Germany in 1908 the

Radical Union linked its support for more political rights for women to discrimination against ethnic minorities, by endorsing a 'language paragraph' which established German as the sole language of political debate (Hackett, 1976: 133). Other governments, too, were capable of turning to women's suffrage to achieve political objectives unrelated to women's rights: the first group of women to be enfranchised in Canada were those who in 1917 had husbands or close relatives in the armed forces – because the Canadian government was battling to pass a conscription measure that was extremely unpopular in Quebec and saw these women as allies (Lloyd, 1971: 100). Nor are the parallels confined only to Europe and North America. In a recent article on the implications of stratification for women's politics in contemporary Africa, Staudt concludes: 'While organizing in the name of women, women's politics operate like class politics to advance the interests of the already privileged' (1986: 203).

Yet despite the major limitations of the suffrage campaign as a women's rights movement, it is unfair to dismiss its achievements out of hand. Certain gains were made; certain barriers rolled back. After 1930 it was not possible for political parties, white or black, to maintain a males-only franchise for much longer – the principle of no gender discrimination in the franchise had been established, even if that principle was obscured by the race discrimination that was more firmly nailed in place. While white, middle-class women were the major beneficiaries of this development, its long-term effects could not be stopped at the boundaries which these women had themselves helped to consolidate. The cause for which the suffragists fought, to eradicate biology as a determinant of eligibility for political rights, was essentially a liberal democratic one. Its acceptance by parliament in 1930 represented a formal recognition of the principle of equality between the sexes. Formal recognition was not the same as practical application, and the enfranchisement of women did not signal a radical restructuring of power relationships between men and women or a fundamental redefinition of women's primary role as reproducers; nor was this what most women wanted. Nevertheless, it did constitute a limitation on exclusive male power, an enhancement of women's status and, as such, undermined the ideological underpinnings of unquestioned male supremacy.

This shift percolated, slowly and unevenly to be sure, through the entire society. The fact that in South Africa the suffrage movement was extremely undemocratic in its attitude towards and ultimate treatment of black people, did not confine the spread to the borders of the white community. In 1930 women's suffrage became an established principle in South African political thought and as such was incorporated into subsequent campaigns for political rights among the black majority as well.

Notes and References

WOMEN AND GENDER IN SOUTHERN AFRICA: AN OVERVIEW

1. The term 'patriarchy' to describe a system of male domination over women has been criticised for collapsing the distinction between the domination of the father within the household (over women but also over sons and junior male kin) and the domination of men over women more generally. Thus, according to Barrett, 'not only is it by and large resistant to exploration within a particular mode of production, but it is redolent of a universal and trans-historical oppression' (1980: 14). It has, however, become a widespread popular term for describing women's subordination to men (and not simply to fathers) and it is in that sense – as a convenient descriptive term for this social condition, rather than an analytical term defining the precise parameters of the relationship – that it is used here.

2. The term derives from Gayle Rubin's influential 1975 article in which she defines the sex–gender system as 'the set of arrangements by which a society transforms biological sexuality into the products of human activity and in which these transformed sexual needs are satisfied' (159).

3. Although 'women' are singled out as a significant category, worthy of special study, the aim of this book is not to delineate a separate 'women's history'. ... the task of women's history is more than to commandeer a few female public figures to be given positions of honor in the historical record. Instead, we employ gender as a category of historical analysis, and in so doing, we try to determine and to understand the systematic ways in which sex differences have cut through society and culture and in the process have conferred inequality upon women (Newton *et al.*, 1983: 1).

4. In the conceptualisation of this book, the geographical net was deliberately cast wider than modern South Africa. For the precolonial period modern political boundaries have no relevance and even in the modern period, when these boundaries do affect peoples' lives, the relationships discussed here transcend national borders. With the exception of the chapter on the Basotho legal system, however, most chapters do concentrate on developments within the boundaries of contemporary South Africa itself.

5. Some have argued against the search for origins, as fruitless. But while it may prove difficult, even impossible, to establish a precise chronology for

this process in southern Africa, yet the elaboration of a convincing theory of how it was that men came to exercise control over women would be a valuable exercise, if only to remind ourselves that female subordination to men is a socially and historically wrought phenomenon, not some inevitable, natural condition, standing outside history. In this regard, the transition to pastoralism and the establishment of cattle husbandry within southern Africa were clearly of great importance.

6. Bridewealth is the generic term used for this exchange. Individual chapters tend to use the appropriate vernacular term where relevant.

7. Sesotho orthography is favoured in the text, except in the case of quotations, where the original spelling is retained, and in the case of some personal names, where the historic spelling may be used in the interests of clarity and consistency with the documentary record.

8. Within their broad identity of purpose and belief, there were undoubtedly differences in how the denominations treated women which are not explored here. It would be an interesting topic to pursue. It does appear that the American Board allowed its female missionaries a more active role, one that was not necessarily dependent on their being married to male missionaries, as was often the case in other denominations.

9. This view is borne out by a recent account of precolonial society among the Tswana-speaking Tshidi, which points to a sexually determined division of the world into public and private domains, with the women and children assigned to the private, domestic space around the home and fields, and the men operating in the public domain associated with the political space of the chief's homestead (Comaroff, 1985).

10. Chodorow (1978) argues that gender socialisation has to be analysed not only in sociological but also in psychological terms – that the construction of gendered identities takes place at a far deeper, psychological level than explanations based on role training can account for on their own. Drawing on a psychoanalytic perspective, she points to the enormous significance of the fact that it is *women* who are the primary caretakers and nurturers of children in the construction of male and female identities and identifications, and suggests that until this responsibility is shared with men, gendered inequalities will not be eradicated. It would be a fascinating project to apply and test her thesis, clinically, to the gender socialisation of African infants and children.

Secondary sources

Barrett, M. 1980. *Women's Oppression Today. Issues in Marxist Feminist Analysis.* London: Verso Books

Bozzoli, B. 1983. 'Marxism, Feminism and South African Studies'. *Journal of Southern African Studies.* 9, 2

Chodorow, N. 1978. *The Reproduction of Mothering: Psychoanalysis and the Sociology of Gender.* Berkeley: University of California Press

Comaroff, J. 1985. *Body of Power, Spirit of Resistance.* Chicago: Chicago University Press

Harris, O. 1981. 'Households as Natural Units'. In *Of Marriage and the Market. Women's Subordination in International Perspective*, ed. K Young *et al.* London: CSE Books

Marks, S. and Trapido, S. (eds). 1987. *The Politics of Race, Class and Nationalism in Twentieth Century South Africa*. London: Longman

Newton, J. *et al.* (eds). 1983. *Sex and Class in Women's History*. London: Routledge and Kegan Paul

Nkululeko, D. 1987.'The Right to Self-Determination in Research: Azanian Women'. In *Women in Southern Africa*, ed. C. Qunta. Johannesburg: Skotaville

Qunta, C. 1987. 'Outstanding African Women, 1500 BC–1900 AD'. In *Women in Southern Africa*, ed. C. Qunta. Johannesburg: Skotaville

Robertson, C. and Berger, I. (eds). 1986. *Women and Class in Africa*. New York: Africana Publishing Co.

Rubin, G. 1975. 'The Traffic in Women: Notes on the "Political Economy" of Sex'. In *Toward an Anthropology of Women*, ed. R. Rapp. New York: Monthly Review Press

Stamp, P. 1986. 'Kikuyu Women's Self-Help Groups: Towards an Understanding of the Relation Between Sex-Gender System and Mode of Production in Africa.' In *Women and Class in Africa*, ed. C. Robertson and I. Berger. New York: Africana Publishing Co.

Walker, C. 1982. *Women and Resistance in South Africa*. London: Onyx Press

Wells, J. 1983. 'Why Women Rebel. Women's Resistance in Bloemfontein (1913) and Johannesburg (1956)'. *Journal of Southern African Studies*, 10, 1

1 GENDER OPPRESSION IN SOUTHERN AFRICA'S PRECAPITALIST SOCIETIES

1. An earlier and longer version of this chapter has appeared in the *Journal of Southern African Studies*, 14, 1 (1987), under the title 'Analysing Pre-Capitalist Societies in Southern Africa'.

2. In this chapter I use 'oppression' to refer to the social experience of 'exploitation', that is the dominance of one social group over another, based on the appropriation of surplus – in this case, the surplus of labour power manifested in and created by women. These are not definitions, of course, and have to be read within their specific contexts.

3. There has been much debate on the use of the terms 'production' and 'reproduction' in analysing gender. Here I follow commonsense usage: by production I refer to the production of material life – in this case farming and related activities – and by reproduction to the biological reproduction of the human species (although once contextualised, the implications of reproduction give the term much wider meaning).

4. This interpretation, while recognising the political authority of the chief and the tribute in labour and goods he exacted from his people, nonetheless does not see the chiefly stratum as structurally separate. The chief was the most powerful and wealthiest of men, but ultimately the foundations of this power lay, like that of all men, on his capacity to appropriate female labour power. This interpretation therefore differs from those which seek the existence of a 'tributary mode of production'. For more on this see Guy, 1987.

Secondary sources

Bozzoli, B. 1983. 'Marxism, Feminism and South African Studies'. *Journal of Southern African Studies*, 9, 2

Etherington, N. 1978. *Preachers, Peasants and Politics in Southeast Africa, 1835–*

1880. *African Christian Communities in Natal, Pondoland and Zululand.* London: Royal Historical Society

Fuze, M. M. 1979. *The Black People and Whence They Came. A Zulu View.* Pietermaritzburg and Durban: University of Natal Press and Killie Campbell Africana Library.

Gluckman, M. 1967. *Politics and Ritual in Tribal Society.* Oxford: Basil Blackwell

Guy, J. 1987. 'Analysing Pre-Capitalist Societies in Southern Africa'. *Journal of Southern African Studies,* 14, 1

Harris, O. and Young, K. 1981. 'Engendered Structures: Some Problems in the Analysis of Reproduction'. In *The Anthropology of Pre-Capitalist Societies,* ed. J. S. Kahn and J. R. Llobera. London: Macmillan

Huffman, T. N. 1986. 'Iron Age Settlement Patterns and the Origins of Class Distinction in Southern Africa'. In *Advances in World Archaeology,* 5

Kimble, J. 1985. 'A Case for the Defence'. In *Canadian Journal of African Studies,* 19, 1

Kinsman, M. 1983. 'Beasts of Burden'. *Journal of Southern African Studies,* 10, 1

Lodge, T. 1983. *Black Politics in South Africa since 1945.* Johannesburg: Ravan Press

Marx, K. 1976. *Capital: A Critique of Political Economy.* Harmondsworth: Pelican Books

Meillassoux, C. 1972. 'From Reproduction to Production: A Marxist Approach to Economic Anthropology.' *Economy and Society,* 1, 1

Meillassoux, C. 1981. *Maidens, Meal and Money: Capitalism and the Domestic Community.* Cambridge: Cambridge University Press

Preston-Whyte, E. 1974. 'Kinship and Marriage'. In *The Bantu-speaking Peoples of Southern Africa,* ed. W. D. Hammond-Tooke. London and Boston: Routledge and Kegan Paul

Sansom, B. 1974. 'Traditional Economic Systems'. In *The Bantu-speaking Peoples of Southern Africa,* ed. W. D. Hammond-Tooke. London and Boston: Routledge and Kegan Paul

Shaw, M. 1974. 'Material Culture'. In *The Bantu-speaking Peoples of Southern Africa,* ed. W. D. Hammond-Tooke. London and Boston: Routledge and Kegan Paul.

Simons, H. J. 1968. *African Women: Their Legal Status in South Africa.* London: C. Hurst and Co.

Walker, C. 1987. 'Review Article: Women's Studies on the Move'. *Journal of Southern African Studies,* 13, 3

Welsh, D. 1971. *The Roots of Segregation. Native Policy in Colonial Natal, 1845–1910.* Cape Town: Oxford University Press

Wright, J. 1981. 'Control of Women's Labour in the Zulu Kingdom'. In *Before and After Shaka: Papers in Nguni History,* ed. J. B. Peires. Grahamstown: Institute of Social and Economic Research

2 FIGHTING A TWO-PRONGED ATTACK: THE CHANGING LEGAL STATUS OF WOMEN IN CAPE-RULED BASUTOLAND, 1872–1884

1. Professor T. Bennett, Ms S. Frankental, Dr K. Hughes, Professor C. Saunders and Mr A. Spiegel provided helpful comments on a preliminary

draft of this chapter. I am indebted to them, to Mr J. Anderson for all his help, and to the Harry Oppenheimer Institute for African Studies, University of Cape Town, for providing a grant for research in Lesotho.

2. Basutoland was the official name of the kingdom from the time it became a British protectorate until its political independence in 1966, when it reverted to being called by its Sesotho name, Lesotho. Except where the context makes it appropriate to use the Sesotho name, I have used the colonial name in this chapter.

3. The following abbreviations are used for primary sources in the text:

CA   Cape Archives
CPP   Cape Parliamentary Papers
LA   Lesotho National Archives
UBR   Unpublished Basutoland Records

Letters of the alphabet are used to designate case volumes in the Lesotho Archives. For the sake of clarity the spelling of Sesotho names in the text follows that used in the original documentary sources, except in the case of well-known figures (such as Moshoeshoe and his wife 'MaMohato), when the Sesotho orthography is adopted (although the original spelling is retained in quotations).

4. The Cape ruled over Basutoland until the Gun War of 1880–1, which flared up in response to attempts by the administration to disarm the Basotho; eventually Britain resumed control in 1884. The political and legal history outlined in this chapter is discussed in detail in Burman, 1981.

5. Various magistrates and missionaries who knew the Basotho well referred to the high value they placed on children, while a search through all extant government records for the period 1871–80 and all extant court registers and records to 1884 produced references to a total of eight cases of infanticide and concealment of birth which came before the magistrates. Given the circumstances pertaining in the country, it is, however, likely that some cases did not reach the magistrates' courts. (See e.g. *Leselinyana la Lesotho*, no. 6 of 1875.) Ashton (1952: 255) says such cases were dealt with within the family.

6. The uncertainties which could arise when any of these requirements were not fulfilled are demonstrated by such cases as *In re Carlotta alias Malepolesa* v. *Tsita Moshesh or the heirs of Moshesh*. According to the evidence, Carlotta spent much of her life being repudiated as wife by both Moshoeshoe and his son Tsita, each claiming that she was the other man's wife (LA, Divorce Record Book, 2.8.1874).

7. This form of clientage resulted in the children of the marriage being counted as children of the chief rather than of their biological father.

8. This could give rise to such relationships as, for example, that between Bereng Molomo and Nthlakala, who were technically brother and sister but biologically cousins and who, as a result of the Basotho preference for cross-cousin marriages, then became husband and wife (LA, A, *Bereng Molomo* v. *Nthakala (his wife)*, 7.1.1875).

9. Women's opposition to polygyny could, however, spring from causes other than religion, as demonstrated by the wife who declared in court: 'I refuse to allow him to get married [to a second wife] because he has deceived me and said that he would never marry anyone else. It is a shame that he

should seek another wife before he has even built me a house. If he were to marry a wife now I should never have a house of my own according to Sesuto custom. I should be relegated to secondary rank. The house he is building, it is not he who is building it. I caused the foundations to be laid and carried the stone myself' (LA, A, *Bereng Molomo* v *Nthakala (his wife)*, 7.1.1875).

10. Magistrates' decisions were not always predictable however. In the case of *'Arone Mpatsa' of Korokoro* v. *'Ma-Mookho' of Raphuthi's village in Ramantso's Ward, widow of Ramarathanyane, deceased son of the Plaintiff*, a widow who had originally been awarded custody of her children (although married by customary law) lost the custody when her Christian father-in-law took her to court again on the grounds that she was now cohabiting with a man unrelated to the family. The magistrate, W. H. Surmon, added a note to the case that judgment was given 'on the ground that the defendant has lived and still intends to live an immoral life and in vice and is therefore unfit to be the guardian of her children by Ramarathanyane' (LA, D, No. 36 of 1877, 8.11.1877) – even though she was in fact in a stable relationship.

Primary sources

Cape Archives (CA)
> Colonial Office (CO) 3193, 3232
> Native Affairs (NA) 273–275
> Unpublished Basutoland Records (UBR) vi

Cape Parliamentary Papers (CPP)
> Report of Governor's Agent, G27–73
> Report of Governor's Agent on Working of Basuto Regulations, A23–73
> 1873, Appendix III: Report of Special Commission on the Laws and Customs of the Basuto
> Blue Book on Native Affairs, G21–75
> Blue Book on Native Affairs, G17–78

Lesotho National Archives (LA)
> Court of the Assistant Resident Magistrate. Thaba Bosiu District:

Civil Cases	A: June 1874–July 1875
	B: 16 July 1875–August 1876
	C: August 1876–May 1877
	D: June 1877–May 1878
	E: May 1878–November 1879
	F: November 1879–August 1881
Criminal Cases	AA: May 1873–December 1875
	BB: December 1875–May 1877

> Divorce Record Book, Divorce Court of the Chief Magistrate, Maseru, pre-1884
> S9/1/2/1: Governor's Agent to Secretary for Native Affairs, 1873–80
> S9/1/3/3: Governor's Agent Miscellaneous Letters Out, 1875–9
> S9/2/2/1: Chief Magistrate to Magistrates, 1871–5
> S9/2/2/3: Chief Magistrate to Magistrates, 1876–84
> S9/2/3/1: Resident Magistrate Maseru: Letters Despatched, 1876–83
> L2/1/1: Leribe: Letters Despatched, 1872–9
> MF2/1/1/1: Mafeteng: Letters Despatched 1872–80

Secondary sources

Ashton, E. H. 1952. *The Basuto: A Social Study of Traditional and Modern Lesotho.* London: Oxford University Press

Barkly, F. 1894. *Among Boer and Basutos.* London: Remington.

Burman, S. B. 1981. *Chiefdom Politics and Alien Law: Basutoland under Cape Rule, 1871–1884.* London: Macmillan

Casalis, E. 1889. *My Life in Basuto Land: A Story of Missionary Enterprise in South Africa* (translated from the French by J. Brierley). London: The Religious Tract Society

Ellenberger, D.F. 1912. *History of the Basuto, Ancient and Modern* (rewritten in English by J. C. MacGregor). London: Caxton Publishing Co.

Hadley, P. (ed). 1972. *Doctor to Basuto, Boer and Briton 1877–1906: Memoirs of Dr. Henry Taylor.* Cape Town: David Philip

Matthews, Z. K. 1934. 'Bantu Law and Western Civilization in South Africa: A Study in the Clash of Cultures'. M.A. thesis, Yale University

Sanders, P. B. 1975. *Moshoeshoe: Chief of the Sotho.* London and Cape Town: Heinemann and David Philip

Smith, E. W. 1939. *The Mabilles of Basutoland.* London: Hodder and Stoughton

3 DOMESTIC SERVICE AND EDUCATION FOR DOMESTICITY: THE INCORPORATION OF XHOSA WOMEN INTO COLONIAL SOCIETY

1. This chapter draws on the historical material presented in my *Maids and Madams*, 1980.

2. These clay pits were a source of clay used as a dye and for cosmetic and ritual purposes.

3 This was not always the case: in the diary of Thomas Shone, for instance, we read much about how he paid to have his washing done and his house cleaned, but this may have been because he was a widower whose domestic life required some organisation.

Primary sources

Cape Archives, Colonial Office papers, 51/15 A.5. Copy of the Register kept in the district of Albany of contracts for service executed from 4/7 to 31/12/1828 between inhabitants of the Colony and Caffres or other foreigners under the provision of Ordinance 49

Cory Library, Rhodes University: Mary Moffatt's Journal, MS 6027

Methodist Archives, Cory Library, Rhodes University: Mrs Mary Taylor's Journal, MS 15163

Secondary sources

Bean, L. and Van Heyningen, E. (eds). 1983. *The Letters of Jane Waterston.* Cape Town: Van Riebeeck Society

Branca, P. 1978. *Women in Europe since 1750.* London: Croom Helm

Bundy, C. 1972. 'The Emergence and Decline of a South African Peasantry'. *African Affairs* 71, 285

Butler, G. (ed). 1974. *The 1820 Settlers. An Illustrated Commentary.* Cape Town: Human and Rousseau

Cairns, H. A. 1965. *Prelude to Imperialism. British Reactions to Central African*

Society, 1840–1890. London: Routledge and Kegan Paul

Calderwood, H. 1858. *Caffes and Caffre Missions: With Preliminary Chapters on the Cape Colony as a Field for Emigration and Basis of Missionary Operations*. London: James Nisbet & Co.

Cock, J. 1980. *Maids and Madams: A Study in the Politics of Exploitation*. Johannesburg: Ravan Press

Donaldson, M. 1974. 'The Council of Advice at the Cape of Good Hope 1825–1834. A Study in Colonial Government'. Ph.D. thesis, Rhodes University

Fihla, P. 1962. 'The Development of Bantu Education at the St Matthews Mission Station, Keiskamma Hoek, 1853–1959'. M.Ed. thesis, University of South Africa

Fraser, D. 1932. *The Teaching of Healthcraft to African Women*. London: Longman

Hammond, D. and Jablow, A. 1970. *The Africa That Never Was. Four Centuries of British Writing about Africa*. New York: Twayne Publishers

Hewson, L. 1959. 'Healdtown, a Study of a Methodist Experiment in African Education'. Ph.D. thesis, Rhodes University

Hunter, M. 1933. 'The Effects of Contact with Europeans on the Status of Pondo Women'. *Africa*, vi

Keppel-Jones, A. (ed). 1960. *Philipps, 1820 Settler. His Letters*. Pietermaritzburg: Shuter and Shooter

Kitson Clark, G. 1967. *An Expanding Society. Britain 1830–1900*. Cambridge: Cambridge University Press.

Lennox, J. 1973. 'Noqakata'. In *Outlook on a Century: 1870–1970*, ed. M. Wilson and D. Perrot. Lovedale: The Lovedale Press

Long, U. (ed). 1949. *The Chronicle of Jeremiah Goldswain, Albany Settler of 1820*. Cape Town: Van Riebeeck Society

Long, U. 1947. *An Index to Authors of Unofficial Privately-Owned Manuscripts Relating to the History of South Africa*. London: Lund Humphries

Macmillan, W. M. 1963. *Bantu, Boer and Briton. The Making of the South African Native Problem*. Oxford: Clarendon Press

Macrone, I. D. 1937. *Race Attitudes in South Africa*. Oxford: Oxford University Press

Majeke, N. 1952. *The Role of the Missionaries in Conquest*. Johannesburg: Society of Young Africa

Marks, P. 1976. 'Femininity in the Classroom: An Account of Changing Attitudes'. In *The Rights and Wrongs of Women*, ed. J. Mitchell and A. Oakley. Harmondsworth: Penguin

Maxwell, W. A. and McGeogh, R. T. 1978. *The Reminiscences of Thomas Stubbs, 1820–1877*. Cape Town: Balkema

Maylam, P. 1986. *A History of the African People of South Africa: From the Early Iron Age to the 1970s*. London and Cape Town: Croom Helm and David Philip

Merriman, N. J. 1952. *The Cape Journals of Archdeacon N. J. Merriman 1848–1855*. Cape Town: Van Riebeeck Society

Moyer, R. A. 1976. 'A History of the Mfengu of the Eastern Cape, 1815–1865'. Ph.D. thesis, University of London

Peires, J. B. 1984. 'Sir George Grey versus the Kaffir Relief Committee'. *Journal of Southern African Studies*, 10, 2

Pringle, T. 1834. *Narrative of a Residence in South Africa*. London: Edward Moxon

Ralls, A. M. n.d. *Glory Which Is Young's: A Tribute to Pioneer Ancestors*. Pietermaritzburg: Shuter and Shooter

Shaw, W. 1860. *The Story of My Mission in South Eastern Africa*. London: Hamilton, Adams & Co.

Shepherd, R. 1940. *Lovedale, South Africa: The Story of a Century*. Lovedale: Lovedale Press

Slee, A. 1946. 'Some Aspects of Wesleyan Methodism in the Albany District between 1830 and 1844'. M.A. thesis, University of South africa.

Soga, J. H. 1931. *The Ama-Xhosa: Life and Customs*. Lovedale: Lovedale Press

Stewart, J. U. 1906. *Dawn in the Dark Continent*. London: Oliphant, Anderson & Ferrier

Van Allen, J. 1972. 'Sitting on a Man: Colonialism and the Lost Political Institutions of Ibo Women'. *Canadian Journal of African Studies*, 6, 2

Ward, H. 1851. *The Cape and the Kaffirs: A Diary of Five Years Residence in Kaffirland*. London: Henry G. Bohn

Whiteside, J. 1906. *History of the Wesleyan Methodist Church of South Africa*. London: Elliot Stock

Williams, D. 1959. 'The Missionaries on the Eastern Frontier of the Cape Colony 1799–1853'. Ph.D. thesis, University of the Witwatersrand

Williams, D. 1967. *When Races Meet: The Life and Times of William Ritchie Thomson, Glasgow Society Missionary, Government Agent and Dutch Reformed Church Minister 1794–1891*. Johannesburg: A.P.B. Publishers

Wilson, M. 1972. *The Interpreters*. Third Dugmore Memorial Lecture. 1820 Settlers Monument Foundation, Grahamstown

Wilson, M. and Mafeje, A. 1963. *Langa: A Study of Social Groups in an African Township*. Cape Town: Oxford University Press

Wilson, M. and Thompson, L. (ed). 1969. *The Oxford History of South Africa*, Vol. 1. Oxford: Clarendon Press

Young, R. 1902. *African Wastes Reclaimed: The Story of the Lovedale Mission*. London: J. M. Dent

4   MAIDENS, MAPS, AND MINES: KING SOLOMON'S MINES AND THE REINVENTION OF PATRIARCHY IN COLONIAL SOUTH AFRICA

1. An earlier version of this chapter appeared in *The South Atlantic Quarterly*, 87, Winter 1988.

2. Haggard was in South Africa from 1875 to 1881. In 1876 he personally raised the British flag over an annexed and disgruntled Transvaal.

3. *King Solomon's Mines* was reprinted four times in the first three months, sold 31 000 copies in the first year, and has never been out of print since its publication. *She*, too, was an instant bestseller, and has been translated into over 20 languages, made into numerous films and plays as well as an opera, and has also not been out of print in Britain in the past century.

4. For a detailed discussion see Gould, 1977, especially pp. 126–35.

5. For the analogy of the 'pathological' sexuality of 'lower races' and women, see Talbot, 1898: 18, 319–23. See also Ellis, 1974. For the working of the analogy in scientific discourse, see Stepan, 1986, 261–77. For the relation-

ship between female sexuality and degeneration, see Foucault, 1979; Gay, 1984; Conway, 1970: 47–62; and Harrison, 1977.

6. George Orwell once acidly described the British ruling class as 'a family with the wrong members in control'. Drawing on the by now well-established figure of organic degeneration, he had a vision of Britain ruled over by a decrepit family of 'irresponsible uncles and bedridden aunts' (1968: 11, 67). Yet, as Williams (1975) notes, what Orwell regretted was not so much the existence of a ruling family but rather its decay of ability. The image of the family as the model of social order had so powerful a hold over Orwell's imagination that he could not yet dispense with it in favor of a notion such as class, and he could express his unease only in terms of biological decay. At the same time, a family ruled by irresponsible uncles and bedridden aunts was for Orwell a pathological family, for the father was nowhere to be seen. It did not seem noteworthy either to Orwell or to Williams that the image also admits no mother. Here an important relation makes itself felt. Orwell saw the social group from which he came, the great service families, 'pushed down in importance by the growth of the centralized bureaucracy and by the monopoly trading companies' (Williams, 1975: 20).

7. In an interview with Foucault, the editors of *Herodote*, for example, note that 'geography grew up in the shadow of the military. A circulation of notions can be observed between geographical and strategic discourses. The region of the geographers is the military region (from *regere*, to command), a province is a conquered territory (from *vincere*). Field evokes the battlefield ...' (Foucault, 1980: 69).

8. Graham Greene, recalling that it was *King Solomon's Mines* that prompted him at 19 to study the appointments list of the Colonial Office, recaptures the overdetermined class and gender paranoia that infused the figure of Gagool: 'Didn't she wait for me in dreams every night, in the passage by the linen cupboard, near the nursery door?' It was the 'incurable fascination' of Gagool, her bare yellow skull and wrinkled scalp, that had lured him to Sierra Leone, and that he remembered when lying sick with fever in Liberia (1969: 16).

Secondary sources

Atmore, A. and Marks, S. 1975. 'The Imperial Factor in South Africa in the Nineteenth Century: Towards a Reassessment'. In *European Imperialism and the Partition of Africa*, ed. E. F. Penrose. London: Cass

Bryant, A. T. 1929. *Olden Times in Zululand and Natal*. London: Longmans

Callaway, H. 1896. *A Memoir*, ed. M. S. Benham. London

Cannadine, D. 1983. 'The Context, Performance and Meaning of Ritual: The British Monarchy and the "Invention of Tradition," 1820–1977'. In *The Invention of Tradition*, ed. E. Hobsbawm and T. Ranger. Cambridge, Mass.: Harvard University Press

Conway, J. 1970. 'Stereotypes of Femininity in a Theory of Sexual Evolution'. *Victorian Studies*, 14

Curtis, L. P. 1971. *Apes and Angels: The Irishman in Victorian Caricature*. Newton Abbot: David and Charles

De Kiewet, C. W. 1941. *A History of South Africa: Social and Economic*. London: Oxford University Press

Ellis, H. 1974. *Man and Woman: A Study of Human Secondary Sexual Charac-*

teristics. New York: Arno Press

Foucault, M. 1979. *The History of Sexuality*. London: Allen Lane

Foucault, M. 1980. *Power/Knowledge: Selected Interviews and Other Writings. 1972–1977*, ed. C. Gordon. New York: Pantheon Books

Frankfurt Institute of Social Research. 1972. *Aspects of Sociology*. Boston: Beacon Press

Fredriekse, J. 1982. *None But Ourselves*. Johannesburg: Ravan Press

Froude, J. A. 1890. *Short Studies on Great Subjects*. London: Longmans

Gay, P. 1984. *The Bourgeois Experience: Victoria to Freud*. New York: Oxford University Press

Gilbert, S. 1983. 'Rider Haggard's Heart of Darkness'. *Partisan Review*, 3, 1

Gilman, S. L. (ed). 1985. *Degeneration: The Dark Side of Progress*. Chicago: Chicago University Press

Gilman, S. L. 1985a. *Difference and Pathology: Stereotypes of Sexuality, Race and Madness*. Ithaca: Cornell University Press

Gordon, R.E. 1968. *Shepstone: The Role of the Family in the History of South Africa, 1820–1890*. Cape Town: Balkema

Gould, S. J. 1977. *Ontogeny and Phylogeny*. Cambridge, Mass.: Belknap Press

Gould, S. J. 1981. *The Mismeasure of Man*. Harmondsworth: Penguin

Greene, G. 1969. *Collected Essays*. London: Bodley Head

Guy, J. 1982. *The Destruction of the Zulu Kingdom*. Johannesburg: Ravan Press

Haggard, G. 1951. 'Foreword'. In *The Cloak That I Left*, by L. R. Haggard. London: Hodder and Stoughton

Haggard, H. R. 1887. *Allan Quatermain*. London: Longman, Green & Co.

Haggard, H. R. 1882. *Cetywayo and His White Neighbours*. London: Trubner & Co.

Haggard, H. R. 1926. *Days of My Life*. London: Longmans Green

Haggard, H. R. 1975. *King Solomon's Mines*. New York: Hart Publishing Co.

Haggard, H. R. 1888. *She: A History of Adventure*. London: Longman, Green

Haggard, L. R. 1951. *The Cloak That I Left*. London: Hodder and Stoughton

Haraway, D. 1984–5. 'Teddy Bear Patriarchy: Taxidermy in the Garden of Eden, New York City, 1908–1936'. *Social Text*, 11

Harries, P. 1987. 'Plantations, Passes, and Proletarians: Labour and the Colonial State in Nineteenth Century Natal'. *Journal of Southern African Studies*, 13, 2

Harrison, F. 1977. *The Dark Angel: Aspects of Victorian Sexuality*. London: Sheldon Press

Himmelfarb, G. 1984. *The Idea of Poverty*. London: Faber and Faber

Hobsbawm, E. and Ranger, T. (eds). 1983. *The Invention of Tradition*. Cambridge: Cambridge University Press

Jones, G. S. 1971. *Outcast London*. Oxford: Clarendon Press

Ludlow, W. R. 1882. *Zululand and Cetywayo*. London: Simpkin, Marshall

McCown, T. D. and Kennedy, K. A. E. (eds). 1972. *Climbing Man's Family Tree: A Collection of Writings on Human Philogeny, 1699 to 1971*. Engelwood Cliffs: Prentice-Hall

Macherey, P. 1978. *A Theory of Literary Production*. London: Routledge and Kegan Paul

Marx, K. 1969. 'The Eighteenth Brumaire of Louis Bonaparte'. In *Selected Works*. Moscow: Foreign Languages Publishing House

Mayhew, H. 1968. *London Labour and the London Poor*, ed. J. D. Rosenberg. New York: Dover

Morton, S. G. 1980. *Crania Americana*. Ann Arbor: University Microfilms International

Orwell. G. 1968. *The Collected Essays, Journalism and Letters of George Orwell*, ed. S. Orwell and I. Angus. London: Secker and Warburg

Ranger, T. 1983. 'The Invention of Tradition in Colonial Africa'. In *The Invention of Tradition*, ed. E. Hobsbawm and T. Ranger. Cambridge: Cambridge University Press

Said, E. 1983. *The World, the Text, the Critic*. Cambridge, Mass.: Harvard University Press

Simons, H. J. 1968. *African Women: Their Legal Status in South Africa*. Evanston: Northwestern University Press

Slater, H. 1980. 'The Changing Pattern of Economic Relations in Rural Natal, 1838–1914'. In *Economy and Society in Pre-Industrial South Africa*, ed. S. Marks and A. Atmore. London: Longman

Stepan, N. 1982. *The Idea of Race in Science*. London: Macmillan

Stepan, N. 1985. 'Biology and Degeneration: Races and Proper Places'. In *Degeneration: The Dark Side of Progress*, ed. S. L. Gilman. Chicago: Chicago University Press

Stepan, N. 1986. 'Race and Gender: The Role of Analogy in Sciences'. *Isis*, 77

Talbot, E. S. 1898. *Degeneracy: Its Causes, Signs and Results*. London: Walter Scott

Tyler, J. 1971. *Forty Years Among the Zulus*. Cape Town: Struik

Vogt, C. 1864. *Lectures on Man: His Place in Creation and the History of the Earth*, ed. J. Hunt. London: Longman, Green

Walter, R. D. 1956. 'What Became of the Degenerate? A Brief History of the Concept'. *Journal of the History of Medicine and the Allied Sciences*, 11

Williams, R. 1975. *George Orwell: A Collection of Critical Essays*. Englewood Cliffs: Prentice Hall

5   FAMILY AND GENDER IN THE CHRISTIAN COMMUNITY AT EDENDALE, NATAL, IN COLONIAL TIMES

1. Emma Sandile, daughter of Chief Sandile of the Ngqika people on the eastern frontier of the Cape Colony, was probably the first black woman in southern Africa to have a title registered in her name. See J. Hodgson's *Princess Emma*.

2. The following abbreviations are used in the text:

MMS   Methodist Missionary Society Records
NA   Natal Archives
NWM   Natal Methodist Missionary Society Records
NNC   Natal Native Commission
SNA   Secretary for Native Affairs Records

3. Theodora Mngadi used this term to refer to the quality of life at Driefontein (interview), but it epitomises the general attitude of the *amakholwa* (MMS 337, report 1862).

4. See the descriptions of daily life in Cetshwayo's *umuzi* in Bourquin, 1986. This is not to suggest that in pre-colonial society sexuality was less restrained.

Indeed, the relationships between men and women were strictly controlled.

5. This paragraph is based on a wide reading of European (mainly British) history. See, *inter alia*, Bridenthal and Koonz (1977), Prior (1985), Vicinus (1977 and 1985).

6. According to Mngadi the movement was initiated by a Driefontein person who had visited the USA. It became a Natal-wide organisation, with links to the African National Congress.

7. Her grandfather, Reverend John Allsopp, the missionary in question, served at Edendale during the Zulu War.

Primary sources

C. T. Binns papers. Copy in the possession of Mrs Sheila Spencer, Durban

Colony of Natal. Report and Evidence of the Natal Native Commission (NNC), 1881–2

Garden papers. Journal of Journeys in South East Africa. Captain Robert J. Garden, 45th Regiment. Natal Archives, Pietermaritzburg

Methodist Missionary Society Records (MMS). School of Oriental and African Studies, University of London

Natal Methodist Missionary Society Records (NWM). Natal Archives, Pietermaritzburg

Secretary for Native Affairs Records (SNA). Natal Archives, Pietermaritzburg

Interviews

Dr Unity Lewis, Pietermaritzburg, 1986

Miss Theodora Mngadi, Edendale, February and March 1986

Mr Walter Msimang, Edendale, February and March 1986

Secondary sources

Barker, Lady M. A. 1877. *A Year's Housekeeping in South Africa*. London: Macmillan

Bourquin, S. (ed). 1986. *Paulina Dlamini, Servant of Two Kings*, comp. H. Filter. Pietermaritzburg: Natal University Press

Bridenthal, R. and Koonz, C. 1977. *Becoming Visible: Women in European History*. Boston: Houghton Mifflin

Burke, G. 1986. 'The Decline of the Independent Bal Maiden'. In *Unequal Opportunities*, ed. A. John. Oxford: Basil Blackwell

Colenso, J. W. 1955. *Ten Weeks in Natal: A Journal of a First Tour of Visitation among the Colonists and Zulu Kafirs of Natal*. Cambridge: Macmillan

Davidoff, L. 1983. 'Class and Gender in Victorian England'. In *Sex and Class in Women's History*, ed. J. L. Newton *et al*. London: Routledge and Kegan Paul

Findlay, G. G. and Holdsworth, W. W. 1922. *The History of the Wesleyan Methodist Missionary Society*. London: Epworth Press

Gordon, R. E. 1970. *Dear Louisa: History of a Pioneer Family in Natal, 1850–1888*. Cape Town: Balkema

Hodgson, J. 1987. *Princess Emma*. Johannesburg: Ad Donker

Mason G. H. 1862. *Zululand: A Mission Tour in South Africa*. London: James Nisbet

Prior, M. (ed). 1985. *Women in English Society 1500–1800*. London: Methuen

Vicinus, M. J. (ed). 1977. *Widening Sphere: Changing Roles of Victorian Women*. Bloomington: Indiana University Press

Vicinus, M. J. 1985. *Independent Women: Work and Community for Single Women, 1850–1920*. London: Virago

Welsh, D. 1971. *The Roots of Segregation: Native Policy in Colonial Natal, 1845–1910*. Cape Town: Oxford University Press

6 WOMEN UNDER INDENTURED LABOUR IN COLONIAL NATAL, 1860–1911

1. This chapter is based on my paper, 'Indian Women under Indenture in Natal', which I delivered at the conference on South Asians Overseas, Oxford, 1987.

2. Hereafter, the Indian Immigration files in the Natal Archives are referred to as II, followed by the relevant file number and date.

3. The concept of ultra-exploitability is developed by Johnstone (1976) to describe migrant labour on the South African gold mines, and by Cock (1980) to account for the experience of domestic servants in the South African context.

4. See Bissoondoyal and Servansign (1986), Ginwala (1974) and Swan (1985).

Primary sources
Colony of Natal
    Blue Books 1852–1909
    Census of 6th April 1891
    Census of 17th April 1904
    Debates of the Legislative Assembly, 1899
    Indian Immigration files 1890–1913
    Reports of the Protector of Indian Immigrants, 1890–1913
Union of South Africa
    Census of 1911, UG32–1911
    Report of the Commission Appointed to Enquire into Assaults on Women, UG39–1913
    Report of the Indian Enquiry Commission. UG16–1914
    Report of the Tuberculosis Commission, UG34–1914

Secondary sources
Ballhatchet, K. 1980. *Race, Sex and Class under the Raj: Imperial Attitudes and Policies and Their Critics, 1793–1905*. London: Weidenfeld and Nicolson

Beall, J. 1982. 'Class, Race and Gender: The Political Economy of Women in Colonial Natal'. M.A. thesis, University of Natal, Durban

Beall, J. and North-Coombes, M. D. 1983. 'The 1913 Disturbances in Natal: The Social and Economic Background to "Passive Resistance."' *Journal of Natal and Zulu History*, 6

Bissoondoyal, U. and Servansing, S. (eds). 1986. *Indian Labour Immigration*. Moka, Mauritius: Mahatma Gandhi Institute

Brookes, E. H. and Webb, C. de B. 1965. *A History of Natal*. Pietermaritzburg: University of Natal Press

Caplan, P. 1987. 'Celibacy As a Solution? Mahatma Gandhi and Brahmacharya'. In *The Cultural Construction of Sexuality*, ed. P. Caplan. London: Tavistock Publications

Carby, H. V. 1982. 'White Woman Listen! Black Feminism and the Boundaries of Sisterhood'. In *The Empire Strikes Back: Race and Racism in 70s Britain*, ed. Centre for Contemporary Studies, Birmingham University. London: Hutchinson

Cock, J. 1980. *Maids and Madams*. Johannesburg: Ravan Press

Ginwala, F. 1974. 'Class Consciousness and Control: Indian South Africans 1860–1946'. Ph.D. thesis, Oxford University

Jayawardena, K. 1986. *Feminism and Nationalism in the Third World*. London: Zed Press

Jefferey, P. 1979. *Frogs in a Well: Indian Women in Purdah*. London: Zed Press

Johnstone, F. A. 1976. *Class, Race and Gold: A Study of Class Relations and Racial Discrimination in South Africa*. London: Routledge and Kegan Paul

Kishwar, M. and Vanita, R. (eds). 1984. *In Search of Answers: Indian Women's Voices from Manushi*. London: Zed Press

Kuper, H. 1955. 'Changes in Caste of the South African Indians'. *Race Relations Journal*, 22, 4

Kuper, H. 1957. 'An Interpretation of Hindu Marriage Ritual'. *African Studies*, 16, 4

Kuper, H. 1960. *Indian People in Natal*. Pietermaritzburg: University of Natal Press

Lal, B. V. 1985. 'Kunti's Cry: Indentured Women on Fiji Plantations'. *The Indian Economic and Social History Review*, 22, 1

Meer, Y. S. 1980. *Documents of Indentured Labour, Natal 1851–1917*. Durban: Institute for Black Research

Minai, N. 1981. *Women in Islam*. London: John Murray

Moore, B. 1984. 'Sex and Marriage Among Indian Immigrants in British Guiana During the Nineteenth Century'. Paper presented at the Third Conference on East Indians in the Caribbean, Trinidad

Nundy, E. 1902. *The Law Relating to Indian (Hindu) Marriages: Its Defects and Abuses*. Durban: International Printing Press

Pather, S. R. 1961. *Centenary of Indians (1860–1960)*. Durban: Cavalier Publishers

Ray, R. (ed). 1978. *The Role and Status of Women in India*. Calcutta: Ava Press

Reddock, R. 1984. 'Indian Women and Indentureship in Trinidad and Tobago 1845–1917: Freedom Denied'. Paper presented at the Third Conference on East Indians in the Carribbean, Trinidad

Richardson, P. 1981. 'The Natal Sugar Industry, 1849–1905: An Interpretative Essay'. *Collected Seminar Papers*, 12, University of London, Institute for Commonwealth Studies

Swan, M. 1985. *Gandhi: The South African Experience*. Johannesburg: Ravan Press

Thapar, R. 1966. *A History of India.. Harmondsworth*: Penguin

Thomas, P. 1964. *Indian Women Through the Ages*. Bombay: Asia Publishing House

Thomas, P. 1939. *Women and Marriage in India*. London: George Allen and Unwin

Thompson, L. M. 1938. 'Indian Immigration into Natal'. M.A. thesis, University of South Africa

Tinker, H. 1974. *A New System of Slavery: The Export of Indentured Labour*

Overseas 1834–1920. London: Oxford University Press
Williams, M. 1986. 'Echoes from the Past: Race, Class and Gender; Indian Women in the 1930s and 1940s'. History Research Project, University of Natal, Durban
Witz, L. 1980. 'Indentured Indian Immigration into Natal 1860–1885'. B.A. Honours dissertation, University of Natal, Durban

7 GENDER AND THE DEVELOPMENT OF THE MIGRANT LABOUR SYSTEM, c.1850–1930

1. This chapter does not look at migrant labour from white-owned farms, whether by sharecroppers, labour tenants, farmworkers and members of their families – an important area for research and analysis but beyond the scope of the chapter.

2. Bozzoli (1983: 163) has analysed African women's informal-sector activity in the urban areas in terms of their 'late' proletarianisation and ability to 'avoid' factory work: African women were the last to be separated from the means of production and leave the land, so by the time they entered the cities, jobs in the formal industrial sector were already monopolised by men and by white (and 'coloured') women, to the disadvantage of African women. However, the proletarianisation of African women cannot be linked simply to their movement off the land – clearly rural women's dependence on wages, in the form of remittances, predates the 1940s and was not contingent on their abandoning the rural areas and moving to town. Furthermore, African women were already present in the urban areas by the 1920s and 1930s, when secondary industry was expanding rapidly, yet they were not drawn into factory employment in proportion to their numbers even then. The degree to which African women actively chose informal-sector activity above formal employment, developing a new culture of female work in the process, needs further investigation. Certainly Bonner (in chapter 9) suggests that Basotho women chose informal-sector activity above domestic work in the Orange Free State in the early twentieth century.

Secondary sources

Beinart, W. 1980a. 'Labour Migrancy and Rural Production: Pondoland c. 1900–1950'. In *Black Villagers in an Industrial Society*, ed. P. Mayer. Cape Town: Oxford University Press
Beinart, W. 1980b. 'Production and the Material Basis of Chieftainship: Pondoland c.1830–80'. In *Economy and Society in Pre-Industrial South Africa*, ed. S. Marks and A. Atmore. London: Longman
Beinart, W. 1982. *The Political Economy of Pondoland 1860 to 1930*. Johannesburg: Ravan Press
Bozzoli, B. 1983. 'Marxism, Feminism and Southern African Studies'. *Journal of Southern African Studies*, 9, 2
Bryceson, D. 1980. 'The Proletarianisation of Women in Tanzania'. *Review of African Political Economy*, 17
Chanock, M. 1982. 'Making Customary Law: Men, Women and Courts in "Colonial Northern Rhodesia'. In *African Women and the Law: Historical Perspectives*, ed. M. J. Hay and M. Wright. Boston: Boston University, Papers on Africa VII

Cliffe, L. 1978. 'Labour Migration and Peasant Differentiation: Zambian Experiences'. *Journal of Peasant Studies*, 5, 3

Delius, P. 1980. 'Migrant Labour and the Pedi, 1840–80'. In *Economy and Society in Pre-Industrial South Africa*, ed. S. Marks and A. Atmore. London: Longman

Etherington, N. 1978. *Preachers, Peasants and Politics in Southeast Africa*. London: Royal Historical Society

Gaitskell, D. *et al.* 1984. 'Class, Race and Gender: Domestic Workers in South Africa'. *Review of African Political Economy*, 27/28

Guy, J. 1982. 'The Destruction and Reconstruction of Zulu Society'. In *Industrialisation and Social Change in South Africa*, ed. S. Marks and R. Rathbone. London: Longman

Guyer, J. 1981. 'Household and Community in African Studies'. *African Studies Review*, 24, 2–3

Harries, P. 1982. 'Kinship, Ideology and the Nature of Pre-Colonial Labour Migration'. In *Industrialisation and Social Change in South Africa*, ed. S. Marks and R. Rathbone. London: Longman

Hay, M. J. and Wright, M. (eds). 1982. *African Women and the Law: Historical Perspectives*. Boston: Boston University, Papers on Africa VII

Hindson, D. 1987. *Pass Controls and the Urban African Proletariat*. Johannesburg: Ravan Press

Hunter, M. 1979. *Reaction to Conquest*. Cape Town: David Philip

Kimble, J. 1982. 'Labour Migration in Basutoland, c.1870–1885'. In *Industrialisation and Social Change in South Africa*, ed. S. Marks and R. Rathbone. London: Longman

Kimble, J. 1983. '"Runaway Wives": Basotho Women, Chiefs and the Colonial State, c. 1890–1920'. Unpublished paper, School of Oriental and African Studies, London University

Legassick, M. 1975. 'South Africa: Forced Labour, Industrialisation and Racial Differentiation'. In *The Political Economy of Africa*, ed. R. Harris. New York: John Wiley

Marks, S. and Rathbone, R. (eds). 1982. *Industrialisation and Social Change in South Africa*. London: Longman

Marks, S. and Rathbone, R. 1983. 'The History of the Family in Africa: Introduction'. *Journal of African History*, 24

Murray, C. 1980. 'Migrant Labour and Changing Family Structure in the Rural Periphery of Southern Africa'. *Journal of Southern African Studies*, 6, 2

Murray, C. 1981. *Families Divided: The Impact of Migrant Labour in Lesotho*. Johannesburg: Ravan Press

Schapera, I. 1933. 'Premarital Pregnancy and Native Opinion: A Note on Social Change'. *Africa*, 6, 1

Schapera, I. 1937. 'Cultural Changes in Tribal Life'. In *The Bantu-speaking Tribes of South Africa*. London: George Routledge and Sons

Schapera, I. 1947. *Migrant Labour and Tribal Life: A Study of Conditions*. London: Oxford University Press

Shillington, K. 1982. 'The Impact of the Diamond Discoveries on the Kimberley Hinterland'. In *Industrialisation and Social Change in South Africa*, ed. S. Marks and R. Rathbone. London: Longman

Simons, H. J. 1968. *African Women: Their Legal Status in South Africa*. London:

C. Hurst and Co.

Slater, H. 1977. 'Peasantries and Primitive Accumulation in Southern Africa'. In *Southern African Research in Progress, Collected Papers 2*. Centre for Southern African Studies, York

Van Onselen, C. 1982. *Studies in the Social and Economic History of the Witwatersrand*, vol 1. Johannesburg: Ravan Press

Vaughan, M. 1983. 'Which Family? Problems in the Reconstruction of the History of the Family as an Economic and Cultural Unit'. *Journal of African History*, 24

Walker, C. 1982. *Women and Resistance in South Africa*. London: Onyx Press

Wells, J. 1982. 'Passes and Bypasses: Freedom of Movement for African Women under the Urban Areas Act of South Africa'. In *African Women and the Law: Historical Perspectives*, ed. M. J. Hay and M. Wright. Boston: Boston University, Papers on Africa VII

Wolpe, H. 1972. 'Capitalism and Cheap Labour-Power in South Africa: From Segregation to Apartheid'. *Economy and Society*, 1

Wright, M. 1982. 'Justice, Women and the Social Order in Abercorn, Northeastern Rhodesia, 1897–1903'. In *African Women and the Law: Historical Perspectives*, ed. M.J. Hay and M. Wright. Boston: Boston University, Papers on Africa VII

8 'A LIGHTHOUSE FOR AFRICAN WOMANHOOD': INANDA SEMINARY, 1869–1945

1. The first part of the title is drawn from a speech delivered by Mrs N. Tantsi at the Inanda Seminary 70th Anniversary Celebrations in 1939 (Inanda Seminary Papers (ISP), Killie Campbell Library, Durban). The vast bulk of the Seminary's papers in South Africa is housed in this library. They are referred to hereafter as ISP, for the sorted papers, and ISP (ap) for additional papers more recently acquired but unsorted at the time this chapter was written.

2. A brief explanation of terminology is appropriate: the areas set aside for Africans in colonial Natal were known as locations, and the areas within them set aside for mission work as reserves. In each reserve a glebe was demarcated for sole use by the missionaries and their converts, and on the glebe the mission station – church, school, homes of mission personnel – was situated.

3. For one of the very few composite histories of Adams College, as it was renamed in the 1930s, see Du Rand, 1987.

4. Booker T. Washington was himself an ex-slave, and Tuskegee, established in 1878, was a self-help industrial school for black students, the intention behind which was that they might acquire a practical skill and hold their own in Southern Society, thus bringing about a change of heart in whites and helping to eliminate racism.

5. Still the most comprehensive account of missionary work in Natal – one of the most heavily 'missionised' regions on the continent in the nineteenth century – is Etherington, 1978.

6. This organisation was the forerunner of the Natal African National Congress.

7. There is a large collection of American Board Papers (hereafter ABP) relating to Natal in the Natal Archives (NA), Pietermaritzburg.

8. Wood's book, written for the centenary of the school, is an 'insider's' history and an invaluable source.

9. Mount Holyoke, a female seminary, was established in the 1830s in Massachusetts by Mary Lyon, at the time of a religious revival in the United States. It trained a great number of women teachers and missionaries, aiming to attract those from less prosperous backgrounds who normally did not continue to higher education. Later, however, it became highly elitist. For more information see Sklar, 1979.

10. For the significance of sewing, see Gaitskell, 1986.

11. The Secretary for Native Affairs Papers (SNA) are lodged in the Natal Archives, Pietermaritzburg.

12. This was also a time when an increasing (although still relatively small) number of women were moving into Durban; Mary Edwards gave up her duties from 1895–8 to set up the first hostel for African women in Durban.

13 The term is adapted from Couzens (1985), which is an indispensable study of the culture of the African petty bourgeoisie in the 1930s and 1940s, traced through one of its leading literary figures, H. I. E. Dhlomo.

Primary sources

American Board Papers, Natal Archives, Pietermaritzburg

Colony of Natal. 1881. Evidence to the Native Affairs Commission

Colony of Transvaal. 1905. The South African Native Affairs Commission. (Lagden Commission), Minutes of Evidence from Natal

Secondary sources

Beall, J. D. 1982. 'Class, Race and Gender: The Political Economy of Women in Colonial Natal'. M.A. thesis, University of Natal, Durban

Berkin, C. R. and Norton, M. B.. 1979. 'Introduction'. In *Women of America: A History*. Boston: Houghton Mifflin

Bourne, G. 1984. *Change in the Village*. Harmondsworth: Penguin.

Christofersen, A. F. 1967. *Adventuring with God*. Durban

Couzens, T. 1985. *The New African: A Study of the Life and Work of H. I. E. Dhlomo*. Johannesburg: Ravan Press

Du Rand, S. 1987. '"Do I Belong?" Adams College: An Episode in Black Educational Struggle'. B.A. Honours dissertation, University of Natal, Durban

Etherington, N. 1978. *Preachers, Peasants and Politics in Southeast Africa, 1835–1880*. London: Royal Historical Society

Gaitskell, D. 1986. 'Girls' Education in South Africa: Domesticity or Domestic Service?' Paper presented to the Conference of the African Studies Association of the United Kingdom, Kent

Hughes, H. 1988. 'Promoting the Countryside: African Agricultural Shows in Natal in the 1920s and 1930s'. Paper presented to the Africa Seminar, University of Cape Town

Hunt Davis Jr., R. 1984. 'Charles T. Loram and the American Model for African Education'. In *Apartheid and African Education*, ed. P. Kallaway. Johannesburg: Ravan Press

Maharaj, S. R. 1979. 'Primary and Secondary Education'. In *South Africa's Indians: The Evolution of a Minority*. Washington: University Press of America

Marks, S. 1986. The *Ambiguities of Dependence in South Africa*. Johannesburg: Ravan Press

Marks, S. (ed). 1987. *Not Either an Experimental Doll. The Separate Worlds of Three South African Women*. Pietermaritzburg: University of Natal Press

Meintjes, S. 1985. 'The Ambiguities of Ideological Change: The Impact of Settler Hegemony on the Amakholwa in the 1880s and 1890s'. Paper presented to the Conference on Natal and Zululand, University of Natal, Durban

Morrow, S. 1986. '"No Girl Leaves the School Unmarried": Mabel Shaw and the education of girls at Mbereshi, Northern Rhodesia, 1915–1940'. *International Journal of African Historical Studies*, 19, 4

Sklar, K. K. 1979. 'The Founding of Mount Holyoke College'. In *Women of America: A History*, ed. C. R. Berkin and M. B. Norton. Boston: Houghton Mifflin

Slater, H. 1980. 'The Changing Pattern of Economic Relationships in Rural Natal, 1838–1914'. In *Economy and Society in Pre-Industrial South Africa*, ed. S. Marks and A. Atmore. London: Longman

Smith, E. 1949. *The Life and Times of Daniel Lindley*. London: Epworth Press

Tyler, M. 1872. *Life and Light for Women*. Boston: American Board

Vietzen, S. 1980. *A History of Education for European Girls in Natal 1837–1902*. Pietermaritzburg: University of Natal Press

Vilakazi, A. 1965. *Zulu Transformations*. Pietermaritzburg: University of Natal Press

Walbridge, C. K. (ed). 1978. *Thokozile. The letters of Margaret Walbridge*. Kansas: Mainline Printing

Webb, C. de B. and J. Wright (eds). 1976. *The James Stuart Archive*, Vol. 1. Pietermaritzburg: University of Natal Press

Welsh, D. 1971. *The Roots of Segregation. Native Policy in Colonial Natal 1845–1910*. Cape Town: Oxford University Press

Wood, A. 1972. *Shine Where You Are. A History of Inanda Seminary 1869–1969*. Lovedale: Lovedale Press

9 DESIRABLE OR UNDESIRABLE BASOTHO WOMEN? LIQUOR, PROSTITUTION AND THE MIGRATION OF BASOTHO WOMEN TO THE WITWATERSRAND, 1920–1945

1. The support of the Richard Ward Foundation of the University of the Witwatersrand, with whose assistance the research for this study was carried out, is gratefully acknowledged.

2. The following abbreviations are used for references in the text:

BMA	Benoni Municipal Archives
CAD	Central Archives Depot
DC	District Commissioner
DP	Director of Prisons
DNL	Director of Native Labour
GS	Government Secretary, Maseru
IA	Intermediate Archives
ISAS	Institute of Southern African Studies, National University of Lesotho

LA   Lesotho Archives
NAM   Non-European Affairs Manager
NC   Native Commissioner
NEAC   Non-European Affairs Committee
NEC   Native Economic Commission
SA   Union of South Africa
SAIRR   South African Institute of Race Relations
SAP   South African Police
SNA   Secretary for Native Affairs
UWL   University of the Witwatersrand Library

3. An exception to this pattern is Bradford, 1987. For a review of the literature see Rogerson and Hart, 1986.

4. Aside from the presence of Basotho women in Reef towns in the late 1920s, there is very little that allows us to date this movement. A useful fragment of information is, however, provided in a letter to *The Star* on 24 June 1935, from James Ntsala of Alexandra. Here he criticises J. D. Rheinallt-Jones's identification of Basotho women with skokiaan, saying that such beverages were 'in existence as far back as 1915 before the influx into Reef towns on the part of Basotho women'.

5. My thanks to Hilary Sapire for drawing my attention to this reference.

6. This issue touches on a vigorous debate opened up among social anthropologists by Max Gluckman in 1950. Among other things, Gluckman suggested a positive correlation between marriage stability and high bride-wealth payments (1950: 166–206). Murray (1982: 145) argues that much of that debate ignored the economic and social transformations being experienced by the societies under discussion, and that the impact of labour migrancy could explain why high marriage payments 'might co-exist with highly unstable patterns of conjugal association'. In transcending Gluckman's problematic, however, Murray succeeds in avoiding some of the key issues raised in Gluckman's argument, as does Kuper in his 1982 study of marriage in southern Africa. It seems possible to argue, as I attempt to do here, that unstable marriage (in all senses) in Basutoland in the 1940s and 1950s was at least partly a result of the combined effects of large-scale labour migrancy *and* high marriage payments.

Primary sources
Benoni Municipal Archives (BMA)
    Non-European Affairs Committee (NEAC) Minutes, meeting, 11 January
        1946 and 9 June 1952
Central Archives Depot (CAD)
    NTS 6671, File 87/332. Minutes of Evidence to the Vereeniging Riots
        Commission
    NTS 7032, File 31/322/6. Minutes of Evidence of the Native Affairs Com-
        mission appointed to Enquire into the Working of Provisions of the
        Natives (Urban Areas) Act Relating to the Use and Supply of Kaffir Beer
    NTS 7036, File 31/322/6 (aanhangsel). Third Interim Report to the Minis-
        try of Native Affairs, 10 Feb. 1941
    NTS 7715, File 53/331 (i)
    NTS 7725, File 166/333. DNL to SNA, 12 Sept. 1930, 20 Nov. 1930
    NTS 7725, File 166/333. Native Commissioner to Chief Native Commis-

sioner, Johannesburg, 13 Sept. 1937

NTS 7676, File 110/332

'The Financial and Economic Positon of Basutoland'. Cmnd 4907, H. P.

Institute of Southern African Studies (ISAS), National University of Lesotho. Interviews BWM 2 1983

Intermediate Archive (IA), Jhb. 'The Municipalisation of Kaffir Beer'. West Rand Administration Board Records, File 385/17

Lesotho Archives (LA)
  Major Bell, Tower Collection
    Box 39
    Box 57. File 1218. 'Matrimonial Disputes 1950–1960
    Box 65. File, Passes to Women and Influx Control
    Box 71. 41st session of Basutoland and National Council, 1945, item 44
  'Proceedings of the Basutoland National Council', 33rd Session, 1938; 48th Session, 13 September 1952

South African Institute of Race Relations (SAIRR)
  'Notes of a Discussion with Native Groups held by M. J. Merle Davis and J. D. Rheinallt-Jones, at Morija and Maseru, Basutoland, 30 and 31 August 1931'. University of the Witwatersrand Library, SAIRR Part 1, AD 843, B.18.3
  Paper read by E. W. Granger, Springs Mine, 18 May 1934. University of the Witwatersrand Library, Records of the South African Institute of Race Relations (B) AD 843 B67.3.1
  'The Urban Native', Memorandum. University of the Witwatersrand Library, Records of the South African Institute of Race Relations. Basement Archives Collection AD 1715 S.7

Union of South Africa (SA)
  Report of the Committee to Consider the Administration of Areas Which Are Becoming Urbanised But Which Are Not Under Local Government Control, 1938–9
  Report of the Native Farm Labour Committee, 1937–9. G.P.S. 5510–1939–250
  Report of the Native Affairs Commission appointed to Enquire into the Working of the Provisions of the Natives (Urban Areas) Act Relating to the Use and Supply of Kaffir Beer. Annexure 'A'. G.P.S. 4620–1942–3–1200
  Report of the Police Commission of Inquiry, 1937. UG50–1937
  Vereeniging Native Riots Commission of Enquiry, 1937

University of the Witwatersrand Library (UWL)
  'Evidence to the Native Economic Commission 1931'. Historical Papers, AD 1438, Box 3, File Kroonstad 17 Feb. 1931; File Rydal Mount, File Bloemfontein; Box 7, File Johannesburg
  Minutes of Evidence to the Native Laws Commission of Enquiry (Fagan Commission), 1946–7'. AD 1756

Interviews

A. B., Daveyton, 8 May 1985

M. F., near Roma, Lesotho, 24 June 1985

Maliehe Khoeli, Teyateyaneng, Lesotho, June 1986, May 1987

'Me L., Matsieng district, January 1987
'Me M., Teyateyaneng, Lesotho, 22 June 1985
'Me M. P., Matsieng district, November 1986
M. F., near Roma, 24 June 1985
'Me M. M., January 1987
'Me M. Ma., February 1987
'Me M. Me., October 1987
'Me M. Mo, Matsieng district, February 1987
'Me M. R., Daveyton, November 1986, 2 July 1987, 18 August 1987
S. Pelanyane, Daveyton, early June 1987
'Me R. O. T., January 1987
P. M. and C. Maguta, Roma, 9 April 1985
S. M. Majara, Roma, Lesotho, 26 April 1986
Nthodi, Maseru, 21 May 1987
L. Sefako, Daveyton, 18 December 1987

Secondary sources

Bradford, H. 1987. '"We Are Now the Men." Women's Beer Protests in the Natal Countryside'. In *Class, Community and Conflict*, ed. B. Bozzoli. Johannesburg: Ravan Press

Cohen, J. 1982. '"A Pledge for Better Times": The Local State and the Ghetto, Benoni, 1930–1938'. B.A. Honours dissertation, University of the Witwatersrand

Coplan, D. B. 1985. *In Township Tonight. Johannesburg: Ravan Press*

Edgar, B. 1987. *Prophets with Honour.* Johannesburg: Ravan Press

Gaitskell, D. L. 1981. 'Female Mission Initiatives: Black and White Women in the Witwatersrand Churches, 1903–1939'. Ph.D. thesis, University of London

Gaye, J. 1980. 'Basotho Women's Options: A Study of Marital Careers in Rural Lesotho'. Ph.D. thesis, University of Cambridge

Gaye, J. 1980a. 'Wage Employment of Rural Basotho Women: A Case Study'. *South African Labour Bulletin*, 6, 4

Gilfoyle, D. 1983. 'An Urban Crisis: The Town Council, Industry and the Black Working Class in Springs, 1948–1958'. B.A. Honours dissertation, University of the Witwatersrand

Gluckman, M. 1950. 'Kinship and Marriage among the Lozi of Northern Rhodesia and the Zulu of Natal'. In *African Systems of Kinship and Marriage*, ed. A. R. Radcliffe-Brown and D. Forde. London: Oxford University Press

Khaketla, N. M. 1976. *Peto ea Mouna*. Maseru

Kimble, J. 1983. '"Runaway Wives": Basotho Women, Chiefs and the Colonial State, c. 1890–1920'. Paper presented to the Women in Africa Seminar (17 June), School of Oriental and African Studies, University of London

Koch, E. 1983. 'Doornfontein and Its African Working Class, 1914–1935: A Study of Popular Culture in Johannesburg'. M.A. thesis, University of the Witwatersrand

Kuper, A. 1982. *Wives for Cattle: Bridewealth and Marriage in Southern Africa*. London: Routledge and Kegan Paul

Ladlau, L. K. 1975. 'The Cato Manor Riots, 1959–60'. M.A. thesis, University of Natal, Durban

Little, K. 1980. *The Sociology of Urban Women's Image in African Literature.*

London: Macmillan

Longmore, L. 1959. *The Dispossessed*. London: Jonathan Cape.

Majara, S. N. 1965. *'Makotulo*. Mazenod: The Catholic Centre

Majara, S. N. 1972. *Liakhela*. Mazenod: The Catholic Centre

Matlosa, S. 1946. *Molahleli*. Morija: Sesotho Book Depot

Minkley, G. 1985. '"To Keep in Your Hearts." The ICU, Class Formation and Popular Struggle, 1922–1932'. B.A. Honours dissertation, University of Cape Town

Mokwena, A. D. 1936. 'Boits'oaro ba Basutho Gaudeng'. *Leselinyana la Basutho*, 8 July 1936

Murray, C. 1982. *Families Divided*. Cambridge: Cambridge University Press

Petrose Masiea, S. 1962. *Lisebo*. Mazenod: The Catholic Centre

Phoofolo, P. 1980. 'Kea Nylala! Husbands and Wives in Nineteenth Century Lesotho'. Paper presented to the Mohlomi Seminar, National University of Lesotho

Poulter, S. 1976. *Family Law and Litigation in Basotho Society*. Oxford Clarendon Press

Ramohapi Lehloo Moketeli, A. 1940. 'Boits'oara ba sa' okang bas 'a sechaba sa Morena Moshoeshoe'. *Leselinyana la Basutho*, 20 February 1940

Rheinallt-Jones, J. D. 1938. 'Race Relations in 1937'. *Race Relations*, 5

Rogerson, C. M. and Hart, D. M. 1986. 'The Survival of the "Informal Sector": The Shebeens of Black Johannesburg'. *Geo Journal*, 12 December 1986

Sanders, P. 1975. *Moshoeshoe, Chief of the Sotho*. London: Heinemann

Sansom, B. 1974. 'Traditional Economic Systems'. In *The Bantu-speaking Peoples of Southern Africa*, ed. W. D. Hammond-Tooke. London: Routledge and Kegan Paul

Sapire, H. J. 1987. 'African Urbanisation and Struggles against Municipal Control in Brakpan, 1920–1958'. M.A. dissertation, University of the Witwatersrand

Thompson, L. 1975. *Survival in Two Worlds: Moshoeshoe of Lesotho 1786–1870*. Oxford: Oxford University Press

Tjokosela, J. F. I. 1956. *Mohale o tsoa maroleng*. Morija: Sesotho Book Depot

Wells, J. C. 1982. 'The History of Black Women's Struggle Against Pass Laws in South Africa, 1900–1960'. Ph.D. thesis, Columbia University

Wilson, M. 1981. 'Xhosa Marriage in Historical Perspective'. In *Essays in African Marriage in Southern Africa*, ed. E. J. Krige and J. L. Comaroff. Cape Town: Juta

Yawitch, J. 1978. 'Natal 1959 – The Women's Protests'. Paper presented at the Conference on the History of Opposition in Southern Africa, University of the Witwatersrand

10 DEVOUT DOMESTICITY? A CENTURY OF AFRICAN WOMEN'S CHRISTIANITY IN SOUTH AFRICA

1. I gratefully acknowledge financial support for my research from the universities of Cape Town and London, and the International Federation of

University Women.

Primary sources

ABC   Archives of American Board of Commissioners for Foreign Missions, Houghton Library, Harvard University, Cambridge, Mass.
AP   Allcock Papers, in possession of Miss Ruth Allcock, daughter of former Transvaal Methodist President
MMS   Methodist Missionary Society Archive, School of Oriental and African Studies, London
MU   Mothers' Union Overseas Records, London. No. V Africa:
           – 'Grahamstown Diocese. South Africa'. May 1910? (ts.)
           – Sixth Annual Report of the Mothers' Union in the Diocese of Grahamstown, South Africa. 1911
           – St John's Diocese [Transkei], Mothers' Union Assistant Organiser's Report 1962 [by Mrs Juliet Xaba]
Union of South Africa. 1942. Sixth Census of the Population of the Union of South Africa, Enumerated 5th May, 1936. Vol. IX Natives (Bantu) and Other Non-European Races. Pretoria: Government Printer
Union of South Africa. 1960. *Union Statistics for 50 years, 1910–1960*. Pretoria: Bureau of Census and Statistics
USPG   Archives of the United Society for the Propagation of the Gospel, Rhodes House, Oxford:
           – Series E: Original missionary reports
           – WW: Women's Work

Periodicals

Cape to the Zambezi (Transvaal and Southern Rhodesia Missionary Association, London)
Foreign Field (Methodist Society, London)
SWM [Society of Women Missionaries] Journal (Church of the Province of South Africa)
The Watchman (Diocese of Johannesburg)
TSR (Transvaal and Southern Rhodesia Missionary Association, London)
Transvaal Methodist (Methodist Church Transvaal District)

Secondary sources

Beall, J. *et al.* 1987. 'African Women in the Durban Struggle, 1985–1986: Towards a Transformation of Roles?' In *South African Review 4*, ed. G. Moss and I. Obery. Johannesburg: Ravan Press
Bean, L. and Van Heyningen, E. (eds). 1983. *The Letters of Jane Elizabeth Waterston 1866–1905*. Cape Town: Van Riebeeck Society
Beinart, W. 1987. '*Amafelandawonye* (The Die-hards): Popular Protest and Women's Movements in Herschel District in the 1920s'. In W. Beinart and C. Bundy, *Hidden Struggles in Rural South Africa: Politics and Popular Movements in the Transkei and Eastern Cape 1890–1930*. London: James Currey
Bozzoli, B. 1983. 'Marxism, Feminism and South African Studies'. *Journal of Southern African Studies*, 9, 2.
Brandel, M. 1955. 'The Needs of African Women'. Typescript
Brandel-Syrier, M. 1962. *Black Woman in Search of God*. London: Lutterworth Press
Christofersen, A. F. 1967. *Adventuring with God: The Story of the American Board*

Mission in Africa. Durban

Cott, N. F. 1977. *The Bonds of Womanhood. 'Woman's Sphere' in New England 1780–1835*. New Haven: Yale University Press

Davidoff, L. and Hall, C. 1987. *Family Fortunes. Men and Women of the English Middle Class 1780–1850*. London: Hutchinson

De Gruchy, J. 1979. *The Church Struggle in South Africa*. Cape Town: David Philip

Etherington, N. 1978. *Preachers, Peasants and Politics in Southeast Africa, 1835–1880. African Christian Communities in Natal, Pondoland and Zululand*. London: Royal Historical Society

Finnegan, R. 1970. *Oral Literature in Africa*. Oxford: Clarendon Press

Gaitskell, D. 1979. '"Christian Compounds for Girls": Church Hostels for African Women in Johannesburg, 1907–1970'. *Journal of Southern African Studies*, 6, 1

Gaitskell, D. 1981. 'Female Mission Initiatives: Black and White Women in Three Witwatersrand Churches, 1903–1939'. Ph.D. thesis, University of London

Gaitskell, D. 1982. '"Wailing for Purity": Prayer Unions, African Mothers and Adolescent Daughters, 1912–1940'. In *Industrialisation and Social Change in South Africa*, ed. S. Marks and R. Rathbone. London: Longman

Gaitskell, D. 1983. 'Housewives, Maids or Mothers? Some Contradictions of Domesticity for Christian Women in Johannesburg, 1903–1939'. *Journal of African History*, 24

Gaitskell, D. and Unterhalter, E. 1989. 'Mothers of the Nation: A Comparative Analysis of Nation, Race and Motherhood in Afrikaner Nationalism and the African National Congress'. In *Woman-Nation-State*, ed. N. Yuval-Davis and F. Anthias. Basingstoke: Macmillan

Gunner, E. 1979. 'Songs of Innocence and Experience: Women as Composers and Performers of *Izibongo*, Zulu Praise Poetry'. *Research in African Literatures*, 10, 2

Hastings, A. 1979. *A History of African Christianity 1950–1975*. Cambridge: Cambridge University Press

Hellmann, E. 1948. *Rooiyard: A Sociological Survey of an Urban Native Slum Yard*. Cape Town: Oxford University Press

Hewson, L. A. 1950. *An Introduction to South African Methodists*. Cape Town: The Standard Press

Hodgson, J. 1987. *Princess Emma*. Johannesburg: Ad Donker

Jabavu, D. D. T. 1932. 'The Fruits of Christianity among the Bantu'. In *Report of Proceedings of Eighth General Missionary Conference of South Africa*. Lovedale: Lovedale Press

Joseph, H. 1963. *If This Be Treason*. London: Hutchinson

Lehmann, D. 1963. 'Women in the Independent African Churches'. In *African Independent Church Movements*, ed. E. W. Hayward. London: Edinburgh House Press

Livingstone, W. P. 1918. *Christina Forsyth of Fingoland: The Story of the Loneliest Woman in Africa*. London: Hodder and Stoughton

Manyano-Kopano Jubilee Celebrations. 1959. Methodist Church of South Africa, Transvaal and Swaziland District: African Women's Prayer and Service Union

Mbili, T. F. (comp.). 1962. *Umlandu Wesililo Samabandla 1912–1962* ('A History of the Isililo of the Churches'). Pamphlet

Mills, W. G. 1975. 'The Role of African Clergy in the Reorientation of Xhosa Society to the Plural Society in the Cape Colony, 1850–1915'. Ph.D. thesis, University of California, Los Angeles

Moroney, S. 1982. 'Mine Married Quarters: The Differential Stabilisation of the Witwatersrand Workforce 1900–1920'. In *Industrialisation and Social Change in South Africa*, ed. S. Marks and R. Rathbone. London: Longman

Muzorewa, F. D. 1975. 'Through Prayer to Action: The Rukwadzano Women of Rhodesia'. In *Themes in the Christian History of Central Africa*, ed. T. Ranger and J. Weller. London: Heinemann

New Dimensions. The Report of the Bishop of Willesden's Commission on the Objects and Policy of the Mothers' Union. 1972. London: SPCK

Ngubane, H. 1977. *Body and Mind in Zulu Medicine*. London: Academic Press

Pauw, B. A. 1974. 'The Influence of Christianity'. In *The Bantu-speaking Peoples of Southern Africa*, ed. W. D. Hammond-Tooke. London: Routledge and Kegan Paul

Pauw, B. A. 1975. *Christianity and Xhosa Tradition*. Cape Town: Oxford University Press

Phillips, R. E. 1930. *The Bantu Are Coming*. Lovedale: Lovedale Press

'Pilot Letters' Describing the Work of Women Missionaries of S.P.G. 1915. London

S. Cuthbert's Mission in the Diocese of S. John's, Kaffraria. 1916. *Report for 1916*

Scheub, H. 1975. *The Xhosa Ntsomi*. Oxford: Clarendon Press

Shorter, A. 1975. *Prayer in the Religious Traditions of Africa*. Nairobi and London: Oxford University Press

Wells, J. 1980. 'Women's Resistance to Passes in Bloemfontein during the Inter-war Period'. *Africa Perspective*, 15

Wells, J. 1983. '"The Day the Town Stood Still": Women in Resistance in Potchefstroom 1912–1930'. In *Town and Countryside in the Transvaal: Capitalist Penetration and Popular Response*, ed. B. Bozzoli. Johannesburg: Ravan Press

Williams, D. 1959. 'The Missionaries on the Eastern Frontier of the Cape Colony, 1799–1853'. Ph.D. thesis, University of the Witwatersrand

11   MAN-MADE WOMEN: GENDER, CLASS AND THE IDEOLOGY OF THE VOLKSMOEDER

1. It would seem that a similar development took place in Nazi Germany. See Stephenson (1981) and Mason (1976 and 1976b).

2. Although Hobhouse was unable to visit the concentration camps established for blacks, she did bring the matter to the attention of the Aborigines Protection Society (Warwick, 1980: 181–2).

3. The book was translated in 1924 by N. J. van der Merwe under the title *Die Smarte van die Oorlog en Wie Dit Gely Het*. A second edition of this Afrikaans translation, published in 1941 by Nasionale Pers, Bloemfontein, is used as a reference in this chapter.

4. The Helpmekaar movement originated after the 1914 Rebellion to pay the fines of and assist imprisoned rebels. It demonstrated the united economic

strength of rich and poor Afrikaners and helped mobilise Afrikaners to conquer the business world (O'Meara, 1984: 97).

5. The Afrikaans title is ambiguous because *vrou* could be read as referring either to 'wife' or 'woman'. The former is perhaps the more likely translation.

Secondary sources

Anderson, B. 1983. *Imagined Communities: Reflections on the Origins and Spread of Nationalism*. London: Verso

Beyers, C. J. (ed). 1972. *Suid-Afrikaanse Biografiese Woordeboek*, Vol. II. Pretoria: Raad vir Geesteswetenskaplike Navorsing

Bird, J. 1965. *Annals of Natal, 1495–1845*, Vol. I. Cape Town: C. Struik

Bozzoli, B. 1983. 'Marxism, Feminism and South African Studies'. *Journal of Southern African Studies*, 9, 2

Brink, E. 1984. 'Plays, Poetry and Production: The Literature of the Garment Workers'. *South African Labour Bulletin*, 9, 8

Brink, E. 1986. 'The Afrikaner Women of the Garment Workers' Union, 1918–1939'. M.A. thesis, University of the Witwatersrand

Cachet, F. L. 1898. *De Worstelstrijd der Transvalers aan het Volk van Nederland Verhaald*. Amsterdam: Höveher en Wormse

Carnegie Commission. 1932. *The Poor White Problem of South Africa*, Vol. V. Stellenbosch: Pro Ecclesia

Davin, A. 1978. 'Imperialism and Motherhood'. *History Workshop Journal*, 5

Du Plessis, C. N. J. 1898. *Uit de Geschiedenis van de Zuid-Afrikaansche Republiek en van de Afrikaanders*. Amsterdam: J. H. de Bussy

Du Toit, M. 1921. *Vrou en Feminist: Of Iets oor die Vroue-Vraagstuk*. Bloemfontein: Nasionale Pers

Eisenberg, B. 1987. 'Gender, Class and Afrikaner Nationalism: The Suid-Afrikaanse Vroue Federasie'. B.A. Hons. dissertation, University of the Witwatersrand

Green, M. 1985. 'Redefining the Maternal: Women's Relationships in the Fiction of Marie-Claire Blais'. In *Traditionalism, Nationalism and Feminism: The Women Writers of Quebec*, ed. J. Lewis. London: Greenwood Press

Hall, C. 'The Early Formation of Victorian Domestic Ideology'. In *Fit Work for Women*, ed S. Burman. New York: St. Martin's Press

Herlan, J. 1985. 'Le Survenant as Ideological Messenger: A Study of Germaine Guevremont's Radio Serial'. In *Traditionalism, Nationalism and Feminism: The Women Writers of Quebec*, ed. J. Lewis. London: Greenwood Press

Hexham, I. 1980. 'Afrikaner Nationalism, 1902–1914'. In *The South African War: The Boer War, 1899–1902*, ed. P. Warwick and S. B. Spies. London: Longman

Hobhouse, E. 1902. *Die Smarte van Die Oorlog en Wie Dit Gelei Het*, translated by N. J. van der Merwe, 1941. Cape Town: Nasionale Pers

Hobhouse, E. 1924. *War Without Glamour: Women's War Experiences Written by Themselves, 1899–1902*. Bloemfontein: Nasionale Pers

Klok, J. 1901. *De Boeren Republieken in Zuid-Afrika: Hun Ontstaan, Geschiedenis en Vrijheidsoorlogen*. Utrecht: J. de Liefde

Lerner, G. 1986. *The Creation of Patriarchy*. New York: Oxford University Press

Lewis, J. (ed). 1985. *Traditionalism, Nationalism and Feminism: The Women Writers of Quebec*. London: Greenwood Press

McMillan, J. 1981. *Housewife or Harlot: The Place of Women in France, 1870–1940*.

Sussex: The Harvester Press

Mason, T. 1976. 'Women in Germany 1925–1940'. *History Workshop Journal,* 1

Mason, T. 1976b. 'Women in Germany 1925–1940'. *History Workshop Journal,* 2

Moodie, T. D. 1975. *The Rise of Afrikanerdom: Power, Apartheid and the Afrikaner Civil Religion.* Berkeley: University of California Press

Mostert, D. (comp.). 1940. *Gedenkboek van die Ossewaens op die Pad van Suid-Afrika.* Cape Town: Nasionale Pers.

Noble, J. *South Africa, Past and Present.* Cape Town: Juta

O'Meara, D. 1984. *Volkskapitalisme: Class, Capital and Ideology in the Development of Afrikaner Nationalism, 1934–1948.* Johannesburg: Ravan Press

Pakenham, T. 1979. *The Boer War.* Johannesburg: Jonathan Ball

Pollak, H. 1931. 'An Analysis of the Contributions to Family Support of Women Industrial Workers on the Witwatersrand'. *South African Journal of Science,* 27

Pollak, H. 1932. 'Women in Witwatersrand Industries'. M.A. thesis, University of the Witwatersrand

Pollak, H. 1933. 'Women Workers in Witwatersrand Industries'. *South African Journal of Economics,* 1

Postma, W. 1918. *Die Boervrouw, Moeder van Haar Volk.* Bloemfontein: Nasionale Pers

Reitz, F. W. 1899. *A Century of Wrong.* London: Review of Reviews

Roberts, E. 1984. *A Woman's Place: An Oral History of Working Class Women, 1890–1940.* Oxford: Basil Blackwell

Roodt-Coetzee, K. 1961. 'Susanna Smit, Skryfster van die Trek'. *Hertzog Annale van die Suid-Afrikaanse Akademie vir Wetenskap en Kuns,* 8

Rovers, J. J. 1896. *De Transvalers en Hunne Heldhaftige Vrouwen.* Amsterdam: J. H. de Bussy

Ryan, M. 1981. *Cradle of the Middle Class: The Family in Oneida County, 1790–1865.* Cambridge: Cambridge University Press

Schreiner, O. 1911. *Women and Labour.* London: Fisher and Unwin

Stephenson, J. 1981. *The Nazi Organisation of Women.* London: Croom Helm

Stockenström, E. 1921. *Die Vrou in die Geskiedenis van die Hollands-Afrikaanse Volk.* Stellenbosch: Pro Ecclesia

Theal, G. M. 1892. *History of South Africa since 1795,* Vol. VI. London: Allen and Unwin

Theron, E. 1943. *Fabriekwerksters in Kaapstad.* Stellenbosch: Pro Ecclesia

Thompson, E. P. 1978. *The Making of the English Working Class.* Harmondsworth: Penguin

Thompson, P. 1981. 'Life Histories and the Analysis of Social Change'. In *The Life History Approach in the Social Sciences,* ed. D. Bertaux. London: Sage Publications

Van der Loo, C. J. 1896. *De Geschiedenis der Zuid-Afrikaansche Republiek.* Zwolle: Van der Vegt and Mehler

Van der Loo, C. J. 1901. *Om Leven en Vrijheid: Geschiedenis der Oud-Hollandsche Republieken in Zuid-Afrika.* Arnhem: E. and M. Cohen

Van Jaarsveld, F. A. 1974. *Geskiedkundige Verkenninge.* Pretoria: J. L. van Schaik

Van Reenen, R. (ed). 1984. *Emily Hobhouse: Boer War Letters.* Cape Town: Human and Rousseau

Warwick, P. and Spies, B. (ed). 1980. *The South African War: The Anglo-Boer War, 1899–1902*. London: Longman

Weilbach, J. D. and Du Plessis, C. N. J. 1882. *Geschiedenis van de Emigranten-Boeren*. Cape Town: Saul Solomon

Wilmot, A. and Chase, J. 1869. *History of the Colony of the Cape of Good Hope*. Cape Town: Juta

12   GENDER AND DEVIANCE IN SOUTH AFRICA'S INDUSTRIAL SCHOOLS AND REFORMATORIES FOR GIRLS, 1911–1934

1. The following abbreviations are used for primary sources in the text:

CAS   Children's Aid Society
UED   Union Education Department

In the case of the latter, the relevant file is indicated in the text by the letters a–j, the full reference being given in the bibliography.

2. The history of industrial schools in South Africa begins in the mid-nineteenth century, with subjugated Africans and impoverished whites. The content of industrial education for both groups was instruction in trades and agriculture. In neither case was it associated with social deviance but was a class-defined form of schooling which was 'never seriously applied to the well-to-do' (Malherbe, 1977: vol. 2, 165). In 1908 the Transvaal Indigency Commission first proposed industrial schools as a remedy for indigent white children displaying 'immoral' and 'criminal habits'. It was particularly concerned with children in Johannesburg where an economic slump in the mining industry and the aftermath of the Anglo-Boer War had given rise to considerable social and economic distress.

3. At this stage most social workers were unpaid women volunteers; as a man and South Africa's first employed probation officer, Norman was an exception.

4. Stephen Clingman, writing about the 'madness' represented in colonial writing, argues that like 'madness' deviance was crucially linked to the framing of limits: 'The only way, it seems, in which white women could transgress the limits set up to protect them was through abnormality and deviance…. Indeed, if sexuality is where desire is active and transgression controlled, it becomes a key symbolic marker for colonialism … because it represents also the limit and shape of a whole "order" of being' (1988: 14–15).

Primary sources

Children's Aid Society

Annual Reports 1909–1934. Children's Aid Society Archive, Johannesburg

1909. Historical Documents, Children's Aid Society Archive, Johannesburg

1913. *Children and the Law: The Case for Legislation*

1914. General Committee Minute Book, 19.5.1914–17.4.1917. Minutes of Meeting held on 19.5.1914. Children's Aid Society Archive, Johannesburg

'Instituut vir Meisies, Durbanville, Geskiedenis', Durbanville Institute for Girls Archive, Durbanville

Moll, J. M. 1923. 'The Classification of Delinquents and the Establishment of Psycho-pathic Clinics in Connection with the Courts'. South African

Prisoners' Aid Association, *Minutes of Third Triennial Congress*. National Institute for Crime Prevention and Rehabilitation of Offenders (NICRO) Archive, Cape Archives Depot, Cape Town

Prisons Department
  File no. 1/691/30. Part 1. Transfer of Industrial Schools to Reformatories. Transfer of Reformatory Inmates to Industrial Schools. Correspondence to 1932.
  Annual Reports, 1911–1937

Roos, J. de Villiers. 1911. Address to South African Prisoners' Aid Association. Minutes of Meetings 1911, National Institute for Crime Prevention and Rehabilitation of Offenders (NICRO) Archive, Cape Archives Depot, Cape Town

Roos, J. de Villiers. 1914. 'Prison Aid Work Past and Present'. Roos Collection, Transvaal Archives Depot

Roos, J. de Villiers. 1920. 'Juvenile Delinquency and Mental Defect'. Roos Collection, Transvaal Archives Depot

Roos, J. de Villiers. n.d. 'Modern Penology'. Roos Collection, Transvaal Archives Depot

Union Education Department (UED). Transvaal Archives Depot
  a. UED 1983: e208, vol. 1
  b. UED 1971: e202/1/4, vol. 1. Monthly Reports
  c. UED 2000: e219, vol. 2. Minutes of Board of Visitors for Eshowe Female Reformatory
  d. UED 114: e6/63
  e. UED 2003: e221/6
  f. UED 1429: e55/2/1, vol. 1. Inspection Reports
  g. UED 101: e6/1, vol. 1
  h. UED 1974: e203/2
  i. UED 1926: e35/8, vol. 1. Board Minutes
  j. UED 953: e37/2/2, vol. 1
  Annual Reports, 1934–1937

Union of South Africa
  Annual Report for Department of Justice, 1917. UG36–1918
  Annual Reports of the Auditor-General

Interviews
Mrs Mpanza, September 1986, Eshowe
Eleanor Shipley, March 1986, Johannesburg

Secondary sources
Albertyn, C. F. 1935. *Jeugmisdaad*. Cape Town: Nasionale Pers
Bailey, V. 1987. *Delinquency and Citizenship: Reclaiming the Young Offender*. Oxford: Clarendon Press
Brenzel, B. 1975. 'Lancaster Industrial School for Girls: A Social Portrait of a Nineteenth Century Reform School for Girls'. *Feminist Studies*, 3
Brenzel, B. 1980. 'Domestication as Reform: A Study of the Socialization of Wayward Girls, 1856–1905'. *Harvard Education Review*, 50
Brenzel, B. 1983. *Daughters of the State*. Cambridge: The MIT Press
Chisholm, L. 1987. 'Class and Colour in South African Youth Policy: The Witwatersrand, 1886–1910'. *History of Education Quarterly*, 27, 1

Chisholm, L. 1988. 'Crime, Class and Nationalism: The Criminology of Jacob de Villiers Roos'. *Social Dynamics*, 13, 2

Clingman, S. 1988. 'Beyond the Limit: The Social Relations of Madness in Southern African Fiction'. University of the Witwatersrand, African Studies Institute Seminar Paper no. 244

Cock, J. 1980. *Maids and Madams: A Study in the Politics of Exploitation*. Johannesburg: Ravan Press

Cross, M. 1986. 'A Historical Review of Education in South Africa'. *Comparative Education*, 22, 3

Davies, R. 1979. *Capital, State and White Labour in South Africa: An Historical Materialist Analysis of Class Formation and Class Relations*. Brighton: Harvester Press

Dews, P. 1984. 'Power and Subjectivity in Foucault'. *New Left Review*, 144

Dubow, A. 1987. 'Race, Civilisation and Culture: The Elaboration of Segregationist Discourse in the Inter-War Years'. In *The Politics of Race, Class and Nationalism in Twentieth Century South Africa*, ed. S. Marks and S. Trapido. London: Longman

Foucault, M. 1977. *Discipline and Punish: Birth of the Prison*. New York: Allen Lane

Gaitskell, D. 1979. '"Christian Compounds for Girls": Church Hostels for African Women in Johannesburg, 1907–1976'. *Journal of Southern African Studies*, 6, 1

Gaitskell, D. 1983. 'Housewives, Maids and Mothers: Some Contradictions of Domesticity for Christian Women in Johannesburg 1903–39'. *Journal of African History*, 24

Gilman, S. L. 1985. *Difference and Pathology: Stereotypes of Sexuality, Race and Madness*. Ithaca: Cornell University Press

Goffman, E. 1961. *Asylums: Essays on the Social Situation of Mental Patients and Other Inmates*. Chicago: Anchor Books

Gould, S. J. 1981. *The Mismeasure of Man*. New York and London: W. W. Norton

Grobler, J. A. 1938. 'Juvenile Delinquency in South Africa'. Ph.D. thesis, University of Cape Town

Hahn Rafter, N. 1983. 'Chastizing the Unchaste: Social Control Functions in a Women's Reformatory, 1894–1931'. In *Social Control and the State: Historical and Comparative Essays*, ed. S. Cohen and A. Scull. Oxford: Basil Blackwell

Haug, F. 1987. 'Day Dreaming'. *New Left Review*, 162

Humphries, S. 1981. *Hooligans or Rebels? An Oral History of Working-Class Childhood and Youth 1889–1939*. Oxford: Basil Blackwell

Jones, G. S. 1977. 'Class Expression verus Social Control'. *History Workshop*, 4

Krut, R. 1983. 'Maria Botha and Her Sons. The Making of a White South African Family in the 20th c.' Unpublished conference paper, Dalhousie

Loram, C. T. 1917, 1927. *The Education of the South African Native*. London: Longmans

Malherbe, E. G. 1925. *Education in South Africa*, Vol. 1. Johannesburg: Juta

Marks, S. 1987. *Not Either an Experimental Doll*. Pietermaritzburg: University of Natal Press

Marks, S. and Trapido, S. (ed). 1987. *The Politics of Race, Class and Nationalism in Twentieth Century South Africa*. London: Longman

O'Brien, P. 1982. *The Promise of Punishment: Prisons in 19th Century France.* Princeton: Princeton University Press

Perrot, M. 1978. 'Delinquency and the Penitentiary System in 19th Century France.' In *Deviants and the Abandoned in French Society: Selections from the Annales*, Vol. 4, ed. R. Forster and O. St. Ranum. Baltimore and London: Johns Hopkins University Press

Schlossman, S. 1977. *Love and the American Delinquent: The Theory and Practice of Professional Juvenile Justice 1825–1920.* Chicago: University of Chicago Press

Van Krieken, R. 1986. 'Social Theory and Child Welfare: Beyond Social Control'. *Theory and Society*, 15, 3

Van Onselen, C. 1982. *Studies in the Social and Economic History of the Witwatersrand 1886–1914.* Part 1: *New Babylon.* Johannesburg: Ravan Press

Williams, D. 1982. 'The Role of Prisons in Tanzania: An Historical Perspective'. *Crime and Social Justice*, Summer

Wimshurst, K. 1984. 'Control and Resistance: Reformatory School Girls in Late 19th Century South Australia'. *Journal of Social History*, Winter

13 THE WOMEN'S SUFFRAGE MOVEMENT: THE POLITICS OF GENDER, RACE AND CLASS

1. This chapter draws heavily on material first presented in my B.A. Honours dissertation, *The Woman's Suffrage Movement in South Africa* (subsequently published by the Centre for African Studies, University of Cape Town). That book contains a more extensive bibliography on women's suffrage in South Africa.

2. For a discussion on the status of women within the ANC, see my *Women and Resistance in South Africa*.

3. See Wells (1982) and Walker (1982) for descriptions of this campaign.

4. See Vietzen (1980) for a discussion of female education in Natal at this time.

5. This was achieved by the Matrimonial Affairs Act of 1953. See Solomon (1968) for the history of this legislation.

Primary sources
Colony of the Cape of Good Hope
   Cape House of Assembly Debates. 1892, 1907, 1909
   Census of the Colony of the Cape of Good Hope, 1904. G19–1905
Debates of the House of Assembly of the Union of South Africa as reported in the Cape Times. 1916–1923. Pretoria: State Library
South African National Convention. 1911. Minutes of Proceedings with annexures (selected)
Union of South Africa
   House of Assembly Debates. 1910–1915; 1924–1930
   Report of the Select Committee on Women's Enfranchisement Bill. SC12–24
   Report of the Select Committee on the Enfranchisement of Women. SC12–26

Secondary sources

Beall, J. 1982. 'Class, Race and Gender: The Political Economy of Women in Colonial Natal'. M.A. thesis, University of Natal, Durban

Cock, J. 1980. *Maids and Madams*. Johannesburg: Ravan Press

Cross, I. K. 1913. 'The Women's Movement in South Africa – and Elsewhere.' In *Women of South Africa*, comp. T. H. Lewis. Cape Town: Le Quesne and Horton-Smith

Du Toit, M. 1921. *Vrou en Feminist: Of Iets oor die Vroue-Vraagstuk*. Bloemfontein: Nasionale Pers

Empire Group of South Africa, Cape Area Branch. 1931. *Franchise Rights and Wrongs*

Gollock, G. A. 1932. *Daughters of Africa*. London: Longmans

Hackett, A. 1976. 'Feminism and Liberalism in Wilhelmine Germany, 1890–1918'. In *Liberating Women's History: Theoretical and Critical Essays*, ed. B. A. Carroll. Urbana: University of Illinois Press

Jacoby, R. M. 1976. 'Feminism and Class Consciousness in the British and American Women's Trade Union Leagues, 1890–1925. In *Liberating Women's History; Theoretical and Critical Essays*, ed. B.A. Carroll. Urbana: University of Illinois Press

Karis, T. and Carter, G. (eds). 1972. *From Protest to Challenge: Documents of African Politics in South Africa,1882–1964*, Vol. 1. Stanford: Stanford University Press

Langenhoven, C. J. 1909. 'The Female Franchise and the Native Franchise'. *The State*, II, 7

Lewis, H. M. 1949. 'The Woman Movement and the Negro Movement'. M.A. thesis, University of Virginia

Lewis, T. H. (comp.). 1913. *Women of South Africa. A Historical, Educational and Industrial Encyclopaedia and Social Directory of the Women of the Sub-continent*. Cape Town: Le Quesne and Horton-Smith

Lloyd, T. 1971. *Suffragettes International: The World-wide Campaign for Women's Rights*. London: BPC Unit 75

Molteno, D. B. 1959. *The Betrayal of Natives' Representation*. Johannesburg: South African Institute of Race Relations

Rover, C. 1973. *Women's Suffrage and Party Politics in Britain*. London: Routledge and Kegan Paul

Rowbotham, S. 1973. *Hidden from History*. London: Pluto Press

Schreiner, O. 1883. *The Story of an African Farm*. London: Chapman and Hall

Schreiner, O. 1911. *Woman and Labour*. London: T. Fisher Unwin

Simmons, A. 1976. 'Education and Ideology in Nineteenth-Century America: The Response of Educational Institutions to the Changing Role of Women'. In *Liberating Women's History; Theoretical and Critical Essays*, ed. B.A. Carroll. Urbana: University of Illinois Press

Solomon, B. 1968. *Time Remembered*. Cape Town: Timmins

Spies, S. B. 1980. 'Women and the War'. In *The South African War: The Anglo-Boer War, 1899–1902*, ed. P. B. Warwick and S. B. Spies. London: Longman

The South African Woman's Who's Who. 1938. Johannesburg

Stapleton, F. 1939. *A History of the Women's Christian Temperance Union*. Cape Town: The Union

Staudt, K. 1986. 'Stratification: Implications for Women's Politics'. In *Women and Class in Africa*, ed. C. Robertson and I. Berger. New York: Africana Publishing Company

Stockenström, E. 1944. 'Geskiedenis van die Vrouebeweging en die Vroue-stemreg in Suid-Afrika tot 1930'. Ph.D. thesis, University of Stellenbosch

United Nations Department of Economic and Social Affairs (UNESCO). 1964. *Civil and Political Education of Women*. New York: United Nations

Van Heerden, P. 1965. *Die Sestiende Koppie*. Cape Town: Tafelberg

Van Rensburg, A. P. 1966. *Moeders van Ons Volk*. Johannesburg: Afrikaanse Pers-Boekhandel

Vietzen, S. 1980. *A History of Education for European Girls in Natal 1837–1902*. Pietermaritzburg: University of Natal Press

Walker, C. 1979. *The Woman's Suffrage Movement in South Africa*. Communications no. 2, Centre for African Studies, University of Cape Town

Walker, C. 1982. *Women and Resistance in South Africa*. London: Onyx Press

Walker, E. A. 1929. *The South African College and the University of Cape Town 1829–1929*. Cape Town: University of Cape Town

Walton, E. H. 1912. *The Inner History of the National Convention of South Africa*. Cape Town: Maskew Miller

Wells, Julia. 1982. 'Passes and Bypasses: Freedom of Movement for African Women under the Urban Areas Act of South Africa'. In *African Women and the Law: Historical Perspectives*, ed. M. J. Hay and M. Wright. Boston: Boston University, Papers on Africa VII

Index

Abdurahman, Dr A., 337

accumulation in precapitalist society, 7, 37–8, 40, 42–4 *passim*

Acts of parliament: Children's Protection Act (1913), 304, 306; Land Act (1913), 176; Liquor Law Amendment Act (1934), 223; Native Administration Act (1927), 185; Native Labour Regulation Act (1911), 176; Prisons and Reformatories Act (1911), 304; Urban Areas Act (1923), 176, 186, 222, 233, 242–3 *passim*, 246–7; Women's Enfranchisement Act (1930), 336; *see also* colonial legislation

Adams, Newton, 200, 202, 219

Adams College, 199, 213

adultery, 49–50, 64, 184, 239

African National Congress, 215, 241, 342; and women's franchise, 314–15

African People's Organisation, 241, 242, 315, 337

Afrikaanse Christelike Vroue Vereniging, 284, 285

age, 9; in precapitalist society, 41–2

Allan Quartermain, 102

Allison, James, 127, 129, 133–4

Allison, Mrs 133

amalaita, 232

Amanzimtoti Institute, 199

American Board Mission, 139, 197, 200, 206, 257, 259, 260, 263

Anderson, B., 274

Association for the Advancement of the Sciences, 328

authority and control: male, 8, 10, 31, 41, 55, 98, 160, 241, 249, 316; *see also* chiefs; gender relations; manhood; patriarchy

Ayliff, Rev. John, 92

Bantu Women's League, 329

Barker, Lady, 126, 144

Barkly, Fanny, 51–2

beer-brewing: and Basotho migrants, 227–34 *passim*; Cato Manor, 227; and Christianity, 256–7; conflicts over, 224–6, 227, 232, 315; and crime, 231–2, 245; Mozambican migrants, 227–8; municipal monopolisation, 222, 223–4 *passim*; Paynesville, 225–6; *see also* liquor trade

Beinart, W., 178, 270

Bell, Charles, 84

Bengu, Susiwe, 210–11

bigamy, 68

Blencowe, Mrs, 138

bohali: *see* bridewealth

Bokwe, Frieda, 92

Booth, James, 88

Botha, Annie, 286

Bozzoli, B., 1, 47, 178–9, 180, 195, 272

bridewealth, 7, 9, 36, 55, 58–60, 68, 70–2 *passim*, 141, 182, 254; explanations of, 36–8, 41, 44; and migrancy, 18, 236; missions and, 86, 141–2, 203; practice, 184, 235–6

Broca, Paul, 101

domestic service, 11, 14, 20, 76–96; coercion into, 77, 190; and employer relations, 80–4; as escape, 96; on the Reef, 256; in Victorian Britain, 104–5; *see also* education; labour

domestic sphere, 11, 27–8, 47, 125, 254, 317

Doveton, Ella, 104

dress, 143–4, 260–1

Dube, Dalida, 201

Dube, James, 201

Dube, John Langalibalele, 201, 215, 220

Du Plessis, C. N. J., 275–6

Du Toit, J. D. (Totius), 279

Du Toit, Marie, 281, 291

Du Toit, P., 284

Edendale mission, 13, 125–45, 263; differentiation and disunity, 130–2; and the family, 125–45 *passim*; origins and development of, 126–32; production, 134–7; schooling, 137–40; *see also* households

education: for domesticity, 13–16, 92, 132–4 *passim*, 138, 144, 202–3, 216–18, 255, 307; gender differentiation in, 138; industrial, 15, 90, 132, 137, 139, 214, 216–18 *passim*; mission, 13, 14, 71, 87–96, 125–6, 132–3, 137–40, 197–220 *passim*; Natal, 198–200; for women, 139, 322; *see also* under names of individual institutions

Edwards, Mary, 205, 206, 207, 208, 209, 211, 213

Eiselen, W., 246

Eloff, Elsie, 280

elopement, 57–8, 235–7 *passim*

Empire League, 327

employment, 11, 20, 92, 190, 217, 227, 242, 256, 282, 283, 285, 291, 303, 319, 322, 328, 331–2; *see also* domestic service; labour; wages

Etherington, N., 254

family: breakdown of, 329; Christian, 132–4, 251, 254, 262, 337; and colonial state, 164; concepts of, 169; defence of, 20, 227, 272; female-centred, 55–6, 195; heads, 55–6; Indian, 17, 149, 167; indigenous forms, 4; as a metaphor for development, 100–

2; new forms of, 20, 132, 193, 195, 323; precolonial, 9, 19, 191; size, 137; *see also* family life; family of man; homesteads; households; marriage

'family life', 17, 259, 272

family of man, 12, 98, 101–2, 103, 106–13

Farm Labour Committee (1939), 233

Federation for the Abolition of State Regulation of Vice, 328

feminists and feminism, 24, 25, 285, 291, 319, 326, 338

fertility, female, 5, 12, 14, 28, 34, 39, 41–3 *passim*, 47; control over, 4, 7, 34, 42; and infertility, 41, 253

Flashlight, 335, 336–7

Foucault, M., 298

franchise, 128–9, 313; Cape, 314, 324, 326, 334, 335; *see also* women's enfranchisement; women's suffrage

Fraser, Mrs Donald, 84

Froude, J.A., 106

Funamalugelo, 201

Galton, Francis, 101

Gandhi, M. K., 164

Garment Workers' Union, 22, 285, 288–9, 291

gender, 3, 4, 9, 13, 16, 27, 31–2, 88, 100, 272; *see also* gender ideology; gender relations; sex–gender system

gender ideology: African elite, 15; Boer, 317–18; British, 318–19; colonial, 11, 12, 126, 180; convergence between coloniser and colonised, 180–6 *passim*, 196; European, 92, 192; Indian, 149–50, 159–60; mission, 20, 84–7; settler, 10, 19, 20, 88, 159, 317–21; shifts in, 316; Victorian, 5, 11, 12, 87–9, 126, 274, 317, 319; *see also* domesticity; *volksmoeder*

gender relations, 3, 4, 7, 17, 18, 27, 46–7, 97–8, 149, 179, 193, 337

Gilbert, Sandra, 104–5, 121

Gilman, S., 99, 301

Gilpin, Deaconess, Julia., 259

Gluckman, M., 37

Goba, Evelyn, 213

Gobhozi, Mrs, 265

Gool, Cissy, 337

Gould, S. J., 102

Whiteside, J., 87, 91

widows: under customary law, 66–7; Hindu, 150; and migration; 234, 237; *see also* levirate

Williams, D., 86, 94, 298

Wilson, Monica, 72, 76, 83, 95, 236

witchcraft accusations, 15, 237, 253

Wolpe, H., 169–70, 171

'woman': meaning of, 7, 26

womanhood, 6, 15, 273, 275, 280, 281, 283–4

'woman-ness', 6

Woman's Outlook, 327, 328

women: acquiescence, 29–32; Afrikaner, 21, 275–92; and Anglo–Boer War, 275, 276, 277–9, 291; Basotho, 9, 19, 48–75, 169, 221–50; and Christianity, 4, 9, 13–16 *passim*, 86–7, 94–5, 191–2, 203, 251–72 *passim*; cleavages dividing, 26; Coloured, 5; control of, 36, 55, 168, 179–80, 181, 186; deconstruction of, 41; Indian, 16, 146–67; middle-class, 3, 24, 25, 241–2 *passim*, 274, 285, 290, 291, 315, 327, 329, 341, 342–3; migrants, 222, 228–34; as mothers, 31, 251, 252, 254–5 *passim*, 256, 267, 271–2, 274, 321, 339; position of, 2, 4, 7, 40; in South African historiography, 275–7, 281–2; and the state, 8, 9, 18, 22, 42, 164–6, 180, 185–6, 209, 241–7, 250, 272; in trade unions, 289–90; and welfare work, 286, 297; as wives, 254–5, 257, 271, 321; working-class, 24–5, 274, 287–92 *passim*, 319–20, 343; Xhosa, 76–96; *see also* beer-brewing; employment; labour; *manyanos*; migration; production; urbanisation; women's prayer unions; women's productive capacity

women's autonomy, 8, 13, 18, 19, 20, 29, 46, 95, 142, 191, 196, 247–8, 250; *see also* women's resistance

Women's Board of Missions, 205, 206, 212

Women's Christian Temperance Union (WCTU), 324, 327, 336

women's conservatism, 30, 47, 339

women's emancipation, 8, 9, 10; *see also* women's legal status; women's rights; women's suffrage

women's enfranchisement, 24, 313, 340; internationally, 318, 331, 344; and white supremacy, 313–14, 337, 340; *see also* women's suffrage

Women's Enfranchisement Association of the Union (WEAU), 313–15 *passim*, 323, 326, 342; campaign (1924–30), 334–7; establishment and direction, 326–31; non-racial policy, 335; post-war, 331; war effort, 330–1

Women's Enfranchisement League (WEL), 325

women's exploitation, 8, 27, 34, 44–6 *passim*, 156–7, *see also* women's oppression; women's subordination

Women's Help Society, 259

women's legal status, 142, 185, 209; in Basutoland, 48–75

Women's National Party, 333

women's oppression, 3, 27; consciousness of, 24–5; in the family, 17; participation in, 46, 47; in precolonial society, 7–8, 28, 33–47 *passim*; *see also* women's exploitation; women's subordination

women's prayer unions, 16, 251–72 *passim*; aims and origins, 255–6; fundraising in, 251, 268; membership, 267, 269; on the Reef, 252, 256–60; 266; southern Transvaal, 257; *see also* churches, *manyanos*; *Isililo*; Mothers' Union

women's productive capacity, 7, 29, 39–42 *passim*, 146, 196

women's resistance, 9, 16, 17, 19, 22, 29–31, 45–6, 157, 250, 273, 315, 328–9; *see also* pass laws

women's rights, 69, 71, 74, 315, 317–18; *see also* women's legal status; women's suffrage

women's solidarity, 24, 143, 145, 251, 256, 262, 272, 312, 316, 329; *see also* sociability

women's studies, 3–7

women's subordination, 18, 25, 27, 30, 31, 45, 46, 196; *see also* women's exploitation; women's oppression

women's suffrage, 24, 30; in black politics, 314–15; and gender, 316; in the industrial world, 319–20, 343–4; origins of, 321–4; and race, 11, 316, 324–6 *passim*, 329, 334–7 *passim*, 341–2, 344; and Union, 325; in white political organisations, 325–6, 330, 333–4; *see also* names of individual women's organisations; suffragettes; women's enfranchisement
Woods, Agnes, 216
Woods, Edith, 328
work: *see* employment; labour
work ethic, 89; *see also* idleness
Wragg Commission (1885–7), 153
Wright, J., 45
Wright, M., 182, 187
Wyndham, H. A., 330, 333
Young Ladies' Collegiate Institution, 197
Zonnebloem College, 139
Zuid-Afrikaansche Vrouwen Federatie, 304